365

WAYS TO STOP SABOTAGING YOUR LIFE

JAMES EGAN

ISBN: 978-1-956373-38-7 (sc)
ISBN: 978-1-956373-39-4 (hc)
ISBN: 978-1-956373-40-0 (e)

Because of the dynamic nature of the Internet, any web
addresses or links contained in this book may have changed
since publication and may no longer be valid. The views
expressed in this work are solely those of the author and do
not necessarily reflect the views of the publisher, and the
publisher hereby disclaims any responsibility for them.

THANKS TO

My family, especially my Da, for all of their support,
encouragement, advice, and love.

My wife, Julie, for being there for me when I was at my
worst and for bringing out the best in me.

CONTENTS

INTRODUCTION

A few years ago, I lost my father to pancreatic cancer. He put up a huge fight and lasted far longer than any doctor expected him to. After eight months, he passed away. It was very difficult, but I had the love of my friends and family and my fiancée, Julie, to keep me strong. As long as I had her, I knew I would bounce back from anything.

But less than a year after that, my better half got diagnosed with cancer. She went to the doctor because of an upset stomach. She was expecting to receive tablets and instead, they told her she needed emergency surgery the following week. She knew that she would lose her hair and would endure chemotherapy and radiotherapy.

Worst of all, four weeks after her seven-month treatment was expected to finish, we were to get married.

She didn't need the pressure of the big day when she was trying to recover. She would probably be too weak for the ceremony. Everyone would understand if she canceled. Any normal person would have delayed or called off the wedding.

But Julie isn't normal. She doesn't quit.

Instead, she used the wedding as a driving force. Her mentality was, "I need to be better by that day. No matter how tired I feel or how much pain I endure, I need to push through it to be well for my wedding day."

We did get married on the day we'd planned, and all of the suffering my wife endured made the day more special because it proved how strong she is.

But not everyone knows how to find that kind of strength. Everyone has it, but they may not know how to use it.

Julie could have wallowed in self-pity, but what would that have achieved? Nevertheless, we can fall into the trap of not helping ourselves during difficult times. We indirectly sabotage our lives so often and yet, we don't know how to stop it. Julie and many other people have given me the inspiration to write about all the ways we sabotage ourselves and what we can do to stop it.

I was worried that I wasn't entitled to write a self-help book because I am not a counselor or a therapist.

But one thing I do have is a passion, and I will not let this passion go to waste. In some ways, not being a therapist can be better for a person who needs help.

I had friends while I was growing up that had a lot of problems, and they had nobody to talk to. I always advised them to talk to a counselor or a therapist. My friends refused, saying they couldn't talk to someone who couldn't relate to them. They wanted to talk to a person who was on their level.

This mentality was another inspiration for writing this book. I'm not a psychoanalyst; I am just an average Joe, writing for the average Joe.

There may be chapters you feel like you don't have to read because they don't concern you. That's fine. Why read about smoking if you don't smoke? Or maybe you can read those chapters just to reaffirm why you are the way you are, or you can take some advice from it to use for someone who has that problem. You might not have a drinking problem, but you might know someone who does. Maybe you can find some advice in this book to use to help that person.

But there are other chapters you may feel like you don't have to read because you have already made up your mind about the topic.

There may be chapter topics about which you get defensive.

Perhaps these are the chapters you should read the most. I was afraid of reading books or listening to people that spoke about the opposite of what I believed. I wasn't scared because I thought they were stupid. It was because I was afraid I would be proven wrong.

If you choose to dismiss those chapters, that's absolutely fine. That's okay, so long as you gave them a chance.

Whatever comes of this book, I did enjoy writing it. It reaffirmed why I have every reason to be happy. Hopefully, it will have the same effect on you.

But enough with the intro. On with the book.

1. ACTION

We must overact our part in some measure, in order to produce any effect at all.
- William Hazlitt

There is a concept called the chaos theory, which states the smallest actions can have the greatest reactions.

Nowadays it is known as the "butterfly effect," using the metaphor of a butterfly flapping its wings to create a tornado on the other side of the planet.

What you may not realize about this theory is that everything causes a butterfly effect. Writing about it creates a butterfly effect. Reading this sentence causes a butterfly effect. Not doing anything can have a butterfly effect! If you were asked to go on a trip to Djibouti, and you rejected it, that decision is still an action because you are reacting to something.

Opportunity may present itself, but it is not exactly what we expected. So we may wait until the time is right and hope that another opportunity comes.

It may never come, and you might write it off as bad luck. But if you lie around and do nothing, then you decided that is how you are going to react to the world.

The question is, what's stopping you? A colossal event, a significant person, and a momentous invitation are not the only things that should force you to get up and do something with your life. You can react to your own thoughts. Don't act out of necessity but out of want. If you have a stray thought that says, "I remember when I was in a better place in my mind," or "I had a better job or a closer connection with a loved one," you can make that happen again.

You can become more by simply not settling for second best. A rail fence builder decided to go into politics and became President Lincoln. A choir singer pursued social activism and became the Civil Rights activist, Martin Luther King Jr. John Arden's son was expected to follow his father's work as a bailiff, but he fell in love with grammar and became the playwright William Shakespeare.

When things are good, we hope they stay good. When they get bad, some people just accept that's the way they are and refuse to change them. It's like being ill. You can wait it out, or you can do what you have to do to get better.

Most people only go for what they want when they see it head-on. Your quest in life is not a straight line. You need to take a lot of wrong roads, twists, turns, and dark corners to get to where you need to go.

Some people act without thinking. What's even worse is thinking without acting. Can you imagine how many different lives you could have led if you acted more or less in all the events of your life? A child. A family. A home. All of these are potential roads in life. You just need to start moving toward them.

We encounter the call unanswered; for it is possible
to turn the ear to other interests.
- Joseph Campbell

2. ADAPTION

Water is formless and flows. But if you put it in a cup, its shape becomes
the cup. If you put it in a teapot, it becomes the teapot. Be like water.
- Bruce Lee

There are fifteen billion brain cells in the human body. You are made up of one hundred trillion cells, 206 bones, and 656 muscles. Every one of those cells can heal, rejuvenate, and adapt to its surroundings to survive if need be.

Human beings are able to adapt mentally or physically, consciously or unconsciously.

But how? How have we been able to keep going as a species for over two million years? Evolution? All animals evolve, although some become extinct. So what makes us different?

Because we are the most adaptable. Did you know that every cell in your body lasts nine years at the longest? This means every cell will be gone and replaced in nine years. Your optic cells don't last more than three days, so in a few days, you will be using cells that don't even exist yet. This sounds inconceivable, but you don't have to understand the machinery of a miracle in order for it to still be a miracle.

If that is true, then it must also be true for your mental self. You can think things you never thought before. You can believe in ideals you never knew existed or you might have even disagreed with up until a few years ago. You may do things now that your past self would never consider. The reason why we are so changeable is because the mind is constantly adapting. It dumps bad thoughts that serve no good in order to make room for new thoughts, new ideas, new goals, and new dreams. It's always developing and improving to ensure its survival.

Technology keeps adapting to our every whim for our own convenience, but we can't use this as an excuse to be lazy.

There are times when a great change is upon us, forcing us to embrace it, whether we like to or not. We can get kicked out of our flat or house. How do we react? Do we sleep in hostels, on friends' couches, or on the street? Or do we prioritize to ensure we get back on our feet?

The second choice is not just a reaction; it's adaption. Adaption is a positive reaction. During difficult times, we can always act badly.

But there is potential to any circumstance, no matter how bad it seems. There could be a million bad reactions to something tragic, but there is bound to at least one good way to react.

Adapt yourself to the things among which your lot has been cast and love
sincerely the fellow creatures with whom destiny has ordained you shall live.
- Marcus Aurelius

3. ADDICTION

I admire anyone who rids himself of an addiction.
- Gene Tierney

A need is something we must have. A want is something we would like to have. An addiction is something we want, but we feel like it's something we need.

We know for a fact that booze, drugs, eating rubbish, living fast, and smoking will kill us. But we still do it.

Now, some people don't think they fall under this bracket because they are oblivious to their vice. Have you ever looked at someone with a severe addiction and say to yourself, "It's a good thing I'm not like that!"

If you think like this, don't get cocky. You're not out of the woods yet. Do you use your SmartPhone every day? How many hours a day are you on your laptop? How would you react if these things were suddenly taken away from you? In this day and age, many people would respond with withdrawal symptoms, just like a drug addict, proving that not all drugs are snorted or injected.

The scary thing is that any addiction has the potential to cause harm. Television is a good way to pass the time, but watching tv constantly causes laziness and a lack of fitness. You can't look down on a person for being addicted to something if you're addicted to something else. Your addiction may not seem as severe, but it's still an addiction, and addiction is always wrong. As soon as you become aware of this, you can overcome it.

We always need to feed what we have, even if it's bad, like addiction for junk food, depressing music, or even pain. We think that if we fulfill this addiction, it will go away. You shouldn't give your body or mind more than it needs. You can't fill a cup that's already full.

At times, addiction is seen as a disease. This is completely illogical, not only because it's inaccurate but because it makes the addict believe that he or she cannot fix their problem by themselves and so, must need outside help, whether it is medical, technological, spiritual, or cosmological. The number one rule of addiction is this: behavior is voluntary, an activity of choice. Addiction is a choice. You can choose to start. You can choose to continue. You can choose to quit.

Addiction is corrected, not just with prayer but with willpower. Self-belief is good, but you can't just have faith in someone watching over you from above. You need faith in yourself.

Smokers usually say, "This is the last time I smoke." The first time should have been the last time, not the hundredth or thousandth time. Kick the habit before you kick the bucket. Find what you like, enjoy it, and don't fall into obsession.

Every form of addiction is bad, whether it be alcohol or morphine or idealism.
- Carl Jung

4. ADVICE

Wise men don't need advice. Fools won't take it.
- Benjamin Franklin

Advice is not just about finding the right words but how to say them. Telling someone what not to do doesn't work as much as we hope to think. It's more effective to show what happens to someone who does the wrong thing than if they do the right thing. Telling someone not to do drugs is nowhere near as effective as a former junkie showing that person the life they might have if they goes down that path.

The problem with giving advice is that no matter what you tell a person, no matter how important or relevant it is, only that person can decide whether or not to take it onboard and help himself. Giving advice is as important as taking it.

When we give advice, we need to make sure it is for the benefit of the one seeking help, not ourselves. This is called the missionary impulse—to make others believe what you believe. It is not a wise tactic to use when a person is desperately seeking help.

I have heard some advice that changed me, not just by what was said but when it was said. A specific set of words at a delicate time can reshape you. Usually, the sooner it happens, the bigger the change, as it has more time to rewire you. If you impart wisdom and it looks like your words were ineffective, remember that change takes time.

It can be hard to take advice because you may feel reliant and weak. But you will look even weaker if you are too stubborn to admit you need help. One quote I love is, "A genius doesn't take the advice of an idiot, because he's a genius, and an idiot doesn't take the advice of a genius, because he's an idiot."

Good advice can come from the wrong person. A person that you would deem your enemy can make a relevant point that you may dismiss. But if a stranger said it, you might accept it. Hatred can blind us just as much as love.

I'll give you an example. My friend, Brett had arguments with his partner all the time. He told me stupid things she would say to annoy him. He started to read books about positivity and found it opened his mind. But what Brett "discovered" in these books was similar to the advice that his partner gave him, even though it was this same advice that caused them to argue.

It works both ways. A friend's advice may be wrong, but friendship can blind us.

Usually, we don't want help because we don't want to be told what we need to do; we want to be told what we want to hear. But the next time you seek advice, just ask yourself: would you rather be told something positive or helpful?

The only thing to do with good advice is to pass
it on. It is never of any use to oneself.
- Oscar Wilde

5. AFFAIRS

Affairs are easier of entrance than of exit; and it is but common
prudence to see our way out before we venture in.
- Aesop

Relationships are a big sign of commitment, which is why an affair is considered to be the ultimate type of betrayal. Nevertheless, those who sleep around will justify with the laziest hypothecates, showing no signs of remorse. "I didn't choose to be attracted to her!" is not a good excuse because you can choose to sleep with someone.

The one being cheated on rarely accepts excuses like "It's biology" or "It just happened!" Would you take it seriously? Is there an excuse your partner could use to justify betrayal? If there isn't, why does that excuse you?

There is an unwritten code that if other people know of an affair, they can't tell the person being cheated on because it's "snitching." There is a difference between snitching and allowing a friend to fall into the ultimate form of false security. If you have a friend in this situation, they have a right to know.

Some people can be so hurt by an affair, they can blame the whole gender. If a man cheats on a woman, she can be quick to judge any man as pigs. But one unfaithful man does not condemn all men as sexist pigs, nor does it nullify all unfaithful women. (Obviously, this same argument can be made if a man feels wronged by womankind if their girlfriend cheated on him.)

One of my neighbors, Ross, was astonished when his girlfriend of six years dumped him. It just wasn't working. He had a temper problem, which he took out on her a lot. After she dumped him, he acted like she was selfish. He would get angry, thinking about how she ruined his life.

The problem is that my friend had cheated on her with over twenty women. She never knew. But it was easier to judge her as if she had betrayed him because she didn't know of all the times he had violated her trust.

Affairs can be fun and exciting because they're naughty and there's a fear of getting caught. The affair, however, can turn into a relationship, and the original relationship with the person, lover, fiancée, or wife can get hurt or discarded.

Let's create a scenario: Gordon is cheating on his wife, Carol, with Sharon. After a year, Gordon realizes that Sharon is more than a bit of fun and decides to leave Carol for Sharon.

I don't have to point out the damage this can do to Carol. I can go into the whole "Gordon may simply be happier, more connected, or more attracted to Carol" argument. But if he is the kind of person to leave one for another, he could do the same again. Rarely do adulterers commit the act once. They are repeat offenders, like most people doing what they shouldn't be doing.

The one who loves the least, controls the relationship.
- Robert Anthony

6. AGE

It is better to be seventy years young than forty years old.
- Oliver Wendell Holmes Jr.

"When boys are boys, they want to be men. And when boys are men, they want to be boys again." My father used to say that. I didn't believe it. You never do when you're a kid.

But that's the scary thing. You could never picture yourself when you are older. The most unexpected thing to happen is also the most common—getting old. When you're six, you have no idea how you will be, what you will believe, how much you will change, how you will think, or how you will perceive the world when you are, say, sixteen.

Looking back, how different or naive do you think you were at six or sixteen or whatever age? In ways, you may seem more naive at sixteen because you think you know it all. I suppose the problem is, we just can't simply wrap our heads around it, and we have no control of what part of us stays constant. We may be stubborn or force parts of us to not change, but we forget that the world we live in shapes our future. Factors in our lives could change how we view life.

It seems impossible to imagine that one day, you will be old, just like it is hard to comprehend when you are old that once you used to run around, playing games, and tossing a ball around. As you get older, it's therapeutic to watch those younger and observe yourself from the other side of the spectrum, saying, "Wow! That used to be me." It feels like it will never happen, but time compromises everything. Observing such things allows you to have a grander comprehension of life, viewing it from all sides, at all ages. You may not have the same zest, realizing that those golden years are not recurrent, but you can look at the same thing from different angles and see something new.

We may get into a bad place in our minds as we age. But if we cast our minds back to our former selves, to a happier time, we can remind ourselves of how we use to think, how we use to live.

We always feel like our best years are behind us. We want to be thirty at forty, and we want to be forty at fifty. No one ever wants to be the age they are. But your life isn't worth less because of what you have left. It's worth more because of the years you've lived.

When you're a kid, you're innocent to the world. When you're a youth, you are old enough to appreciate life. As you get older, you bring life to the world and finally watch your children be a part of life.

Life is an amazing journey. There are no "best parts," just key moments in an emotional adventure. To be old and wise, you must first be young and stupid.

A comfortable old age is the reward of a well-spent youth.
- Maurice Chevalier

7. ALLERGY

....

I have been dairy free for several years, and I started because I felt it was going to reduce my allergies, which it did, and help me lose weight, which it did.

- Fran Drescher

I know what you're thinking. There's no point in reading this chapter if you don't have allergies or food intolerances. Well, that's the problem. Almost everyone has them, but over 90 percent of people have no idea what they are allergic to. They may not even consider that they have an allergy of any kind (although it would explain a lot), because they have been misinformed.

When I was a kid, I tended to get blisters on my lips, tongue, jaws, and gums. I assumed I was just "that kind of kid." My parents worried that it was because I wasn't getting enough vitamin C, and they demanded I eat more fruit. Yet the blisters persisted. I couldn't escape them, no matter what I did.

One day, my friend suggested I have an allergy test. She discovered that she was allergic to wheat (one of the most common allergies, alongside milk), which always made her tired, but she assumed she was just a drowsy person.

I reluctantly went for a test, assuming it would be a waste of time and money. I already knew, from an allergy test I'd had as a child, that I had a hypersensitivity to dust, which affected my asthma.

But I was under the impression that allergy tests (as well as any medical test) had not become more advanced. So although this new test reconfirmed my aversion for dust, it also picked up on other allergies I didn't know I had, including the main culprit—citric acid! This acid is in almost all fruit. This meant that I was triggering my allergic reaction because I was trying to be healthy!

You may not know you have an allergy, because you only have had a reaction to it recently. Allergies can be created during a violent illness or overexposure. My friend Bo has broken many bones and has been under an X-ray so often, he built up an allergy to X-ray light, forcing him to be careful in the sun.

You may only discover your allergy in unusual circumstances. My wife thought she had no allergies until she needed surgery. That's when she discovered she was allergic to penicillin, morphine, and other anesthetics. Luckily, there were no serious consequences, but some are not so lucky.

Even Bruce Lee, the supposed fittest man alive, died from an allergic reaction to aspirin because he was oblivious to his intolerance to the drug.

Even if you feel like you don't have any allergies, what's the harm in getting checked out? You could save yourself a lot of money, effort, explanation, suspicion, and agony.

Why is it that people assume that just because they are not allergic to something, they assume they never will be?

- Gregory House
(House MD)

8. ALONE

Alone we can do so little; together we can do so much.
- Helen Keller

The brain craves stimulation. Even if you stood still for five minutes, you would be compelled to shift, scratch, or mess with your hair.

When you are alone, you're compelled to evaluate your day, unwind, and plan for the future. Some people like to do this more than others. Others are not so inclined to engage. They are usually called loners.

Everyone needs their "me time," but too much of anything can be bad, especially when the mind is involved. Choosing to isolate yourself is a self-defense mechanism caused by a lack of trust. You are protecting yourself from others, but you are not protected from yourself. If you were let down by a friend, it may inspire you to enclose yourself from others to avoid a similar incident. You may do this to escape tragedy but scar yourself in the process.

Too much time by ourselves will force our minds to improvise to counter boredom. Over time, this can turn into eccentric, disturbing, or damaging habits, ideas, and addictions. We can't push away the world. We are a part of the world, and we need to find our place in it. That involves allowing other people to help us.

A loner may believe that needing someone else is a sign of weakness. It's not. It's human nature. We need others so that we can grow. Giving in isn't giving up. You can't lie to yourself by pretending the impulse to talk to others is not there. You may not choose to do so, but you will find yourself giving it a thought. We are social animals, after all.

But don't just be afraid to allow others to be a part of your life. You can go out of your way to be a part of theirs.

Chances are, you already do. You may be more important in someone else's life than you might realize. In your hometown, there are background players in your life, keeping your set alive with noise, bodies, smells, traffic, and laughter.

If, one day, one of the regulars simply wasn't there, would you notice? Now, if you were a background player in someone's life and one day, you disappeared, do you think that person would notice?

I worked in a shop a few years ago. A woman who had been working there for a decade quit because she felt she was stuck in a dead-end job where nobody appreciated her. When she left, customers would ask for her. They really missed her and said her delightful manner always made their day. She had no idea that she was affecting people's lives so much.

Don't let your private life become your life. Your private life is there to shed any façade or mask. It's not there to escape from life. You can't. You're in it.

Hell is other people.
- Jean Paul Sarte

9. ANGER

We have to experience the polarity of things in order to define where we need to live. Having lived as an imploder for years and then becoming an exploder, I had the means of what I needed to do in order to express my anger appropriately.
- Mike Fisher

Anger is a biological necessity to empower us. It's intended to make us come across as intimidating during a supposed threat in order to survive.

But you can't rely on it. When you close your fists, you close your mind. You need to pick your battles because there are times where aggression doesn't help.

I have seen quarrels where both people are simply trying to outshout each other. Sometimes you need to lower your voice to strengthen your argument. Or as Gandhi said, "You cannot shake hands with a clenched fist."

Although anger is meant to maintain a sense of control, to give into it admits you are losing control. When arguments get heated, no matter how tempting it is to go berserk, staying calm will make you seem more in control.

Anger comes in many forms. You may not even be aware of your anger, but we all have it.

Or maybe you have the opposite problem; you are always angry. You might feel angry for no apparent reason; you are "just like that."

All behavior is learned, even when it feels instinctive and out of control. So if you feel like you are "just angry," there is a deeper reason.

The best way to understand this concept is to be aware of one simple fact: anger is never the original emotion. You can be angry because you are depressed that your friends are getting what they want but you're not.

You can be angry because you are afraid you are going to lose your job, but you know your coworkers are lazy.

Anger is not the catalyst but the reaction. It's a defense disguised as an offense. If you trace where the anger comes from, you can learn to control it better.

Notice that I said "control anger." I'm not suggesting you "get rid of anger." Anger is needed. It can be an incredible asset because it can be converted into assertion or a practical driving force.

But you have to be careful not to convert it the wrong way. Justifying it can be dangerous. An overbearing father can be aggressive to his children, saying, "If I didn't care, I wouldn't be angry with you." You can be angry to feel powerful and become addicted to it. You can scare people to get what you want.

It's okay to use anger but not at the expense of diminishing others. It may cause momentary relief, but you must remember that anger has consequences.

People who fly into a rage always make a bad landing.
- Will Rogers

10. APPRECIATION

Men deal with life, as children with their play
Who first misuse, then cast their toys away.
- William Cowper

Nowadays, pretty much everything seems accessible: news, food, entertainment, etc. But because we have so much, it's tough not to take everything for granted. We naturally like anything precious or desired, but if passed around too freely, it loses its value as well as its takers.

We complain that life is unfair, that it would be fine if it were not for that one 'thing' we're missing. It could be money, a lover, career, or power. So we strive for 'it.' Our life revolves around 'it.' We are driven solely to achieve that goal, and when we finally get what we always wanted, what do we do? Complain about something else.

How many people are begging to get a job or a partner and when they get it, they take for it granted?

Whatever happened to appreciating nature? No video game console or CGI can ever be as endlessly entertaining as the beauty of nature or the wonders of people's thinking.

Some will think you're odd or old-fashioned because you are so easily entertained. It is better to be easily entertained than to have a thousand songs, five hundred movies, three consoles, enough money to spend all your wages on booze, and yet, still feeling unhappy.

Don't ever let people take you for granted. Don't let them see you as the familiar and rely on your helping, rather than hoping you will. If you help them out when they genuinely need help, rather than saying yes to everything, they will appreciate you more.

Most importantly, don't just appreciate "stuff" and people; appreciate life in general. Although your parents might annoy you, appreciate that they brought you into the world. Although your children might drive you up the wall, remember that they are still learning and you should appreciate them. Your partner or friend might be so good at looking after you, you can become desensitized to it and forget to show your thanks.

Even if you're having a really crummy day, try to appreciate your family, try to appreciate your friends, and most importantly, try and appreciate yourself.

Appreciation is wonderful:
It makes what is excellent in others belong to us.
- Voltaire

11. APPROVAL

A truly strong person does not need the approval of others
any more than a lion needs the approval of sheep.
- Vernon Howard

Which is better? Cats or dogs? For me, it's cats. What I have always admired about cats is that they do not necessarily have to show the loyalty of a dog to receive affection. A dog should be shown affection whether or not it does a trick, rolls over, or catches a stick.

But it doesn't know that. It will do what it can and be your loyal friend to seek approval.

When was the last time you saw a cat do a trick? Cats roll around and stroke you when they desire food or wish to go outside. That's all they have to do to get what they want. No fancy tricks. They don't need to seek approval, because they know they will get what they want.

You need to work hard to get what you want in life. But you shouldn't perform a task specifically for validation. To desire or need confirmation proves that your confidence is called into question.

"How do I look? Is it all right? Are you sure? Anything else I can do?' Do you need me to help?' Needing constant validation like this can make one come across as desperate. It can be perceived as overcompensating, fake, or pathetic, depending on the circumstances.

How many successful people have you heard say they never wanted to be famous? Obviously, there are exceptions but more often than not, a lot of iconic celebs became famous because they were following their passion rather than seeking approval.

It's people like this who don't try to make the world fall in love with them. Often, that is their charm.

If you keep your head down, look for opportunities, work hard, and don't jump up, expecting a treat, it's more likely to work out for you than if you were running around, begging for some validation. Lucky breaks are not doled out that much and when they are, it's rarely when you expect them. They can come at any time.

But if you look for them, then you don't look like someone who's confident. You look like someone waiting to be recognized. That should never be your incentive.

A man cannot be comfortable without his own approval.
- Mark Twain

12. ARGUMENT

Anger is never without an argument, but seldom with a good one.
- Indira Gandhi

I heard of a case in the United States years ago in which a man got away with murder because his lawyer found a loophole in the law.

But when the lawyer opposing him used the same trick two years later, he had some random condescending law memorized to prove it wrong.

This paradoxical situation made me realize something - Depending on which side of the argument you're on, you'll ignore things that go against you and emphasize whatever works in your favor.

But can arguments be good? Of course. I had a great debate for over two hours last night with some old school pals. None of my friends attempted to force their opinions on anyone. We didn't want an answer to our questions. We were just exploring issues without confrontation.

We need ambiguity to debate and to grow, especially for indefinite concepts. Disagreement does not mean argument.

Sadly, it is all too common for a debate to lead to anger. Arguments are usually out of reflex. The biggest problem is that many people don't argue to see who's right but to prove they themselves are right. Many continue to make their points, obviously not believing in it anymore but grasping on to that last strand of false ideals for the sake of their own egos.

The main reason that arguments get out of control is because people get defensive. It is difficult to be impartial and respect others' views, especially if they discredit something we feel passionate about. But reacting with emotion is reacting without logic. When that happens, the defensive one is usually the one who's wrong. Even if he or she is not, they will probably come across like they are.

Some have the opposite problem; instead of getting defensive, they become offensive. They shout and won't let the person they are quarreling with get a word in edgewise.

Putting words in other people's mouths and using vulgarity signify a lack of facts. Cheap tactics in arguments don't prove points. They're novelty gimmicks to make you appear right.

Usually, the truth of an argument is not absolute but, lies somewhere in the middle. After all, quarrels wouldn't last long if the fault was only on one side.

You can't dismiss an argument without hearing it, even if it's wrong. It doesn't matter how wrong a person may seem; they're entitled to defend themselves.

Behind every argument is someone's ignorance.
- Robert Benchley

13. ART

We all know that Art is not truth. Art is a lie that makes us realize truth.
- Pablo Picasso

A certain composer, born in Germany in 1770, had a remarkable life. Before he was thirty years old, he suffered almost total deafness. He avoided socializing, as he could only hear a constant ringing in his ears. He played songs to fine-tune himself to ensure his deafness wouldn't consume him, which inevitably, it did.

He suffered with suicidal tendencies, bipolar schizophrenia, syphilis, lead poisoning, typhus, insomnia, a disabled immune system, chronic paroxysms of pain that would make him spasm with agony, and lesions that covered his body.

His family was less lucky (as hard as that is to believe). Of his three siblings, one was born blind, another blind and deaf, and the last died very young of tuberculosis.

When the composer died at fifty-two, tens of thousands lined the streets by his home to commemorate his life. Do you know why? Because that man was Beethoven. The song he played that I mentioned earlier was "Ode to Joy," one of the most beautiful songs ever written. He wrote it simply to see if his hearing was getting any worse. Yet it became one of the most celebrated songs of all time. Beethoven became a musical legend and a historic genius.

Art can come from anywhere. When you saw this chapter's title, you may have thought I meant painting or drawing. But no. Art is universal truth. Paintings are not just pictures. That is like saying a violin is just wood and string. Art is utilizing a skill to create something that makes us wonder. Art nowadays, sadly, is misunderstood, dismissed, or misinterpreted. It will always be a coeval force that deserves to be celebrated. Too often in these modern times, art is washed away with logic. Some things aren't meant to be broken down and dissected.

Thinking outside the box is a lot more unpredictable and crazy, but it's where we get a lot more ideas.

But we can't just think it. We have to get it out with a pen, a brush, a song, or with drumsticks. We have to physically express our art to truly make it exist. If people happen to have a congenial feel for your art or you for theirs, all the better.

I used Beethoven as an example because you may not have known that he had such a miserable life. It is easy to assume his life was perfect, but most artists are in pain.

But instead of wallowing, they utilize their pain. It proves that even horrific circumstances can be transformed to create something beautiful. It would have been easy for Beethoven to feel sorry for himself, but instead, he used his passion to turn his music into a legacy. Let out the artist in you, and see what it creates.

Since reality is incomplete, art must not be
too much afraid of incompleteness.
- Iris Murdoch

14. ASSERTION

With confidence, you have won before you have started.
- Marcus Garvey

You can probably think of a time where you saw someone do something or say something so utterly reprehensible, every impulse in your body is telling you to act.

But in situations like this, we sometimes do nothing. We then try and justify our lack of action with thoughts like 'I don't want to be a bother,' or 'It doesn't concern me.'

Those thoughts come from a lack of assertiveness. Have you ever seen that cool guy in movies who stays unrealistically casual while everyone else is panicking? To assert oneself is to assert the situation. To feel assertive means you have an understanding and control of a situation. You don't need to shout or make fancy gestures to be self-assured.

Imagine a group of twenty—okay, scrap that—six hundred people in a room! You need their attention now! You need to make a few notes, points, or changes to whatever, but you need to be heard. What do you do?

I can't necessarily say you do A, B, and C. It's more of a reflective problem. Telling you to be more casual may not be as effective in practice.

But look at it from one of the six hundred people's point of view. What would someone have to do to get your attention?

We need to put who we are in every word we speak when we need to carry our points home to the listeners. But this isn't just in words but in movements, with actions, and with ideas. We must eliminate ambiguity and conformity. If you have something to say, say it.

In some situations, you only get one chance to say what you want. You may only have one moment to do what needs to be done. It's kind of stupid because a lot of times, before a massive decision, there will be questions like:

- "Do you agree?"
- "Anything to add?"
- "Care to say anything else?"

We can just smile, nod, and keep our mouths shut, or we can be brave and say what we believe needs to be said.

I am not sure if it is true that there is no such thing as a stupid question. But how can we know if it is stupid until we ask it? Better to ask twice than forget once.

Too much agreement kills a chat.
- Eldridge Cleaver

15. ASSOCIATION

A man only learns in two ways, one by reading, and the
other by association with smarter people.
- Will Rogers

The most famous example of association is the Rorschach Test, more commonly known as the Ink Blot Test.

Hermann Rorschach believed that when we see a seemingly vague blob-like image, our mind automatically tries to find an image. The image can then give an accurate idea of how the person's mind works. Or so the theory goes.

The Rorschach Test is considered pseudoscience nowadays, but it is still worth referencing because human beings associate all the time out of instinct. The seemingly most insignificant object can become powerful and cathartic if you tie it with an important person or event in your life. Unfortunately, we can associate even when we don't want to.

Geoff Thompson has a great allegory about association in his book, *The Elephant and the Twig*. To train elephants in certain countries, these mammals are tied to trees when they are young. They will try to break away, but will give up when they realise they are not strong enough. Each time the elephant is tied to the tree, it will put up less and less of a fight until it stops entirely. When it is fully grown, it can be tied to a twig, and it will not try to escape, because it assumes that it can't move when it it's tied down. Because of this, the poor elephant associates the tree with the inability to escape.

The depressing thing is that we can associate just like this elephant with things that should have no power over us. We only think they do. But we can stop if we just associate positively.

My wife lost her hair during her chemotherapy. She hated looking at our wedding picture because she had to wear a wig on the big day. At first, she felt the image was tarnished, knowing that her hair wasn't real.

But over time, she simply associated the image with positivity instead of negativity. When she looks at that picture now, she thinks about how strong she was to get through the wedding straight after her treatment.

We can turn all negative associations into good ones simply by understanding why we connect them to something bad. Only after doing that can we associate these things with something good.

Association with human beings lures one into self-observation.
- Franz Kafka

16. ATHEISM

The believer is happy, the doubter is wise.
- Hungarian proverb

In America, 2.3 percent of people describe themselves as atheists. Look at how that sentence is phrased. I didn't say 2.3 percent *are* atheists. I said that 2.3 percent describe themselves as such. Some people have a lack of belief but choose not identity as such because of prejudice.

Even nowadays, people are ostracized, bullied, and even killed for not believing in a god. Atheism can even impair you legally. You cannot hold public office in several states in the United States if you are an atheist.

Some religious people say that if we were all atheists, the world would tear itself apart with violence, lust, and murder.

Logically, most scientists, doctors, or people in the medical field are atheists because their career relies on seeing things analytically and drawing conclusions with facts, not hunches.

But what's the point of atheism? There are people who cure diseases, show kindness, and gives money to charity even though they believe there is no afterlife. They believe their actions will not warrant a reward in Heaven and yet, they still live a moral life.

Does that sound evil? Does that not sound better than a person who does everything right because she expects to be rewarded? Is it arguably more altruistic to do good without believing in God than to do good solely because you believe in God? People think if there is no God, life is pointless. However, atheism can help one appreciate life. If you believe this is the only life you will ever have, it can compel you to enjoy and appreciate it.

I'm not suggesting having faith impairs one's life but we must be careful how we implement it. My friend, Ava suffered from anxiety. One of my neighbors, Sy, had the same problem. If they get nervous or scared, they black out. Ava had anxiety attacks for six months. Sy has had them for ten years. Ava realized she had a problem, so she went to a psychiatrist and was hypnotized and hasn't had a paic attack since.

However, Sy didn't even know that what he was experiencing were panic attacks because he felt like God punishing him. Although his anxiety was eventually resolved with treatment, it took much longer since he tried to resolve his issues with faith alone for years.

Religious ambiguity is not as effective as understanding and dealing with a problem. Atheists aren't evil. Like many believers, they are just trying to live their lives.

A man said he didn't like what I had to say
about religion so I said, "Forgive me."
- Bill Hicks

17. ATTENTION-SEEKING

Not even the sun shines at all times throughout the day.
- Anon

Attention-seeking can be done by the most shy and quiet or the most cocky and arrogant. It can be big and loud or a mild plea, over-posturing, through words or acts, or subtle gossip.

People seek attention to reconfirm self-worth. You may feel like a paradigm of confidence, but looking for validation and confirmation is the antithesis of confidence.

Attention-seeking includes talking about yourself, denying others' achievements, emphasizing your own accomplishments, or fishing for compliments, all to hide an insecurity.

Let's look at how people fish for compliments. So many people have told me they look awful. People like this want a compliment to boost their ego, which is completely fine. But to depend on this sort of behavior isn't ideal. To have attention is nice, but to need it is desperate.

Although many people crave attention, having too much isn't worth it. If you are always the center of attention, that means your failings are just as visible as your achievements. If you like declaring yourself to the world, be prepared for the whole world to have a window into every flaw and insecurity that you have.

But we do all fall into this trap. It is fine from time to time. If you tried your absolute best in a football match and lost, you would be devastated. You want a friend to tell you that you couldn't have played better. When you hear that, it can be a weight off your shoulders.

But how many people need to say it? One? Ten? Everyone? Anyone? It would be nice if someone went up to you and paid you a compliment, but you shouldn't need to seek it out. Receiving attention is appealing but it should never be a requirement.

Are our accomplishments really any better when they are shouted from the rooftops? Sometimes, we don't need fanfare. We can enjoy our happiness all by ourselves.

I'm terribly attention seeking. It's very different once you get all this attention, though. Because then you want to control it. And you can't exactly.
- David Walliams

18. ATTITUDE

> Attitude is a little thing that makes a big difference.
> - Winston Churchill

A positive mental attitude has six characteristics:

1. Inner motivation — The voice inside of you that drives you to achieve your goals.
2. The value of higher standards — The morals that you hold true to your heart and why they drive you;
3. Breaking down goals — Every big obstacle is easier if you break it down into smaller parts;
4. Combining present and future time frames — Where you are now and where you have to be to consider yourself a success;
5. Personal involvement — How much you give to everything you do; how reliant on yourself you are; if you will pass the buck at the first sign of weakness;
6. Self-to-self comparisons — Comparing yourself to when you felt better or worse.

We all have principles that we hold to be true, and we need to channel these ideals in our everyday lives in a positive way to ensure we stay content and realize all of our aspirations. We must be prepared, anticipate obstacles to our aims, and deal with them by incorporating the six characteristics of a positive mental attitude.

I don't want to sound like I am assigning you homework with the information above, but it may help to write out your own thoughts.

When I was a kid, there was a snide shopkeeper who would tear me apart with insults. When I asked my father why he was like that, he replied, "He's got attitude"— as if to say he was born that way, and there was nothing he could do about it.

I have a card in my wallet at all times. On one side of the card, I have written my goals for the rest of the year.

On the other side of this card is my attitude to achieve these goals. This list reads things like, "Seize the day." "You only live once." "Be the best at what I do." "Say yes to every opportunity."

I update this list every year. Not only do I give myself new goals every year, I give myself new attitudes to strive for those goals. Your own ambitions may seem difficult or even impossible but with the right attitude, you will be able to obtain them.

> My attitude is that if you push me towards something that you think is a weakness, then I will turn that perceived weakness into a strength.
> - Michael Jordan

19. ATTRACTION

I suspect the secret of personal attraction is locked
up in our unique imperfections, flaws and frailties.
- Hugh Mackay

You may have asked yourself, "Why is someone I like not attracted to me at all, even though I'm nice, and we have so much in common?"

Or you might look at it from the other person's point of view: "Why am I attracted to people who I know are bad for me but I am not attracted to people who are stable, beautiful, and supportive. Why would any logical person be attracted to someone who is unsympathetic, uncaring, selfish, or immoral. How can this be a turn-on?" Is it simply because opposites attract?

Actually, it's because of biology. Philippa Gregory's Red Queen hypothesis breaks down biology on an evolutionary level and details why we are attracted to certain people, even if they seem bad for us. According to Gregory, biology states that we are attracted to certain aspects of a person based on what we believe is best for the future of our species.

This is not a human trait. This is a survival-of-the-fittest gene built into every single living creature.

Because of this, bad qualities like arrogance and aggression can be viewed as attractive because they showcase strength and power.

This sounds so animalistic, but we are animals, and Mother Nature can be just as cruel. Cats and birds do not mate with the "nice" one, if such a thing exists in the animal kingdom. They go for the strongest, the most commanding, and the most desired.

It's a horrible feeling when you're attracted to a person you don't want to have feelings for to, but attraction doesn't always work on a conscious level.

It doesn't help that society tries to convince us what a perfect man or woman is meant to look like and what we are expected to find attractive. This is ridiculous because what is considered "hot" or "sexy" changes all the time. Nevertheless, society still tries to fit beauty in a box as if it is an unchangeable thing that we must be attracted to. You need to push by what society regards as beauty and follow what you are attracted to.

But if you are attracted to something superficial or damaging, you need to reevaluate your life. That's the first step to finding the right person.

Most of us attract by default. We just think that we
don't have any control over it. Our feelings are on autopilot
and so everything is brought to us by default.
- Bob Doyle

20. AUTOPILOT

> Human progress is neither automatic nor inevitable...
> Every step toward the goal of justice requires sacrifice.
> - Martin Luther King, Jr.

It takes some time before you get the knack of tying your shoelaces. Looking back, it's funny how frustrated you got, trying to retain that little children's rhyme to memorize where the knot goes or where the loop is. Now it's second nature.

Just like riding a bike, taking your first step, or driving a car. How unnatural it must have seemed at first. You may have even said, "I'm never going to get the hang of this!" Now, you don't even think about it. You just do it. Wake up. Get dressed. Eat breakfast. Brush your teeth. Leave the house.

That is the routine of the day. We've done it thousands of times, to the point where our brains are working on the most basic level. It's not thinking, "Put left arm in left sleeve," or "Brush the back of my molars." We can't monitor every part of the day, especially if we have done it constantly. Luckily, we have evolved to rely on muscular memory in the mid-brain. It stores instinctive behavior patterns, so we don't have to be consciously aware of every individual motion.

While we are doing these things, we will process what lies ahead of us, what happened to us yesterday, and what we have to prepare for.

You can be in this autopilot mode for a while. You may only come out of it out of necessity—a random encounter, your phone ringing, or to pay for something. When this happens, you are not living in the now. You may not be aware of the steps you're taking, the streets you walk, or the surroundings you pass, because you're not paying attention.

It is overwhelming to process every detail, so you will miss a lot each day. But you shouldn't switch on only when you have to. If you do, you only get the minimum of experience life has to offer otherwise.

Don't talk out of need but out of curiosity or discovery. Don't exercise out of routine but with a clear goal in sight. Don't read out of boredom but out of exploration.

To be an automaton makes you what it sounds like—a robot, a cog, a machine. Doing only what you have to do, going through the motions, and never giving yourself a second to look around is a shallow life. You cannot enjoy life with that mentality. Autopiloting is done out of laziness and fear. That is not living. That is existing.

The majority of animals are on autopilot. The decisions that dictate their lives are based on impulse and necessity, not logic and reason. We were given the gift of awareness. We need to take full advantage of it.

> Just because it's automatic doesn't mean it works.
> - Daniel J. Bernstein

21. BAGGAGE

We humans have millions of years of evolutionary baggage
that makes us regard competition in a deadly light.
- Vernor Vinge

Everyone has baggage, some more than others. We may carry this weight around with us all of the time, composed of our apprehension, failure, and pessimism. This baggage can stem from an early tragedy, a family burden, or a sudden death.

It's taxing to stop this baggage from spilling over in other aspects of who we are. Your family problems may impede your social life. A spiteful partner may cause you to lash out to others. A drunken parent may create a violent streak within you.

We all have problems that come and go—you're low on money, got your jacet ruined, been told off at work, had a fight with a partner, and so forth. This will probably affect you for a few days, and people may notice you are in a bit of a mood, and that is acceptable. Problems like this will probably work themselves out with time.

But baggage is not like that. It sticks. To allow your baggage to influence you persistently can impede your life. It sounds unfair but you need to find a way to juggle your baggage with the rest of your life. Of course, you are allowed to blow off some steam. But if you allow it to overwhelm you, it will become you.

My friend, Aoife has a lot of baggage in her family, especially with her mother. She is always stressed and freaking out about how every single thing is sullying her life.

Another friend, Joy, also has a lot of baggage with her alcoholic mother, and from what I have heard, she seems to deal with a lot more than Aoife.

But Joy never uses her problems as an excuse nor does she let it consume her life. When she wakes up in the morning, she will deal with her mother. As soon as she leaves the house, she gets on with the rest of her day. When she gets back home, she will deal with her mother as best as she can.

Even if the baggage you lift isn't yours, it can still weigh you down. If the baggage is not your own, you don't have to carry it.

You also have to be careful how you talk about your baggage. Although having a shoulder to cry on is perfectly fine, people will tire of it if you keep bringing up your baggage, even if they revolve around serious problems. Your friends will stop listening once they have heard the same sad story for the millionth time.

Your baggage is a part of you. You cannot wish it away. Deal with it as best you can.

Kids- in a really good way - can talk about their differences
without the baggage that adults have.
- Jim McKay

22. BALANCE

Perhaps there could be no joy on this planet without an equal
weight of pain to balance it out on some unknown scale.
- Stephanie Meyer
(The Host)

As I started to write this book, I focused or leaned toward certain matters because of the life I lived, as we all do. I know a lot of people who are alcoholics, and I don't drink, so it's difficult for me to be fair when I talk about alcohol. When I talk about drinking, I point out why it's bad and how it can sabotage your life. But I have to explain that there are some benefits. It can help us relax and unwind, and it is a great way to bond.

But it's important for us to find the balance. To show this point, let's look at a tightrope walker, a person who literally needs balance to do his job! Imagine a tightrope walker holding a pole to maintain his composure. If the pole is not perfectly level, that doesn't mean he's necessarily going to fall. But the longer it stays that way, or if he doesn't see it as a problem, then he can stumble. Unless he regains his balance, that stumble can become a fall. Some falls we don't recover from, and even if we do, it can take a long time to get back on our feet.

You may feel balanced in yourself, but the people around you can affect you too. I had an alcoholic housemate, and the fact that I didn't drink didn't stop his alcoholism from affecting me. But if someone affects your balance, realign it based on what the other person is missing. When I realised this, I spoke to my old housemate about why he felt like he needed to drink. And as he spoke to me, he tried to understand why I didn't have the impulse to drink. Over time, he didn't see alcohol as a crutch and got a lot better. Although he still drank, he had a much better control over his vice, allowing him to bring balance to his life.

We may think that some people are better or worse than us, but we all balance in some way. None of us were born with less capability to change our lives than anyone else. We just need to see what we were given and make the most of what we have. We can take out anything we don't like about ourselves, and put in more of what we do like.

We may think we are balanced because we excel in certain aspects of our lives. But if you focus too much on aspect of your life, even a good one, you can neglect other aspects. You may be a successful businessman, which causes you to neglect your family. You might be the most desired and liked person, but you don't like yourself.

Finding a balance in one aspect in our lives is hard. In all aspects, it appears unfeasible. But that's not going to stop us from trying.

Almost every wise saying has an opposite one, no less wise, to balance it.
- George Santayana

23. BELLS AND WHISTLES

A peacock taunted a crane with the dullness of her plumage.
"Look at my brilliant colors" cackled the peacock.
Replied the crane, "But when it comes to flying,
I can soar whereas you are confined to the earth."
- Aesop

'Bells and whistles' is a term often used to refer to non-essential features added to an object. Although many updated products for computers and SmartPhones promise brand-new, life-changing features, the changes are usually only surface-level. Basically, bells and whistles refer to something that is added, but not needed.

Although this phrase normally references products, especially technology, it's also applicable to human beings.

There is a technique called peacocking where a person dresses in distinctive clothing, unusual garments, and dazzling trinkets to help them stand out.

Now, if you are the type of person who feels like dressing outlandishly is the best way to show the world who you are, then go for it.

However, if you feel like you are dressing in this garb because you are hiding who you are instead of revealing yourself, that's a totally different matter.

This sort of issue is not limited to clothes or appearance. We can stick on the bells and whistles to how we speak and what we talk about.

To find your own life interesting is good, if you have to talk about yourself 24/7, you come across as insecure. Are you the funny guy because that's who you naturally are or are you compensating because you feel like you have nothing to contribute?

There's no point trying to hide who you are because you are only going to fool people for so long.

You should know if you are presenting yourself accurately, based on other people's reactions. They can be your mirror to help you see what you may be doing wrong.

You know when you feel like some people don't get you? Maybe it's something you are doing wrong with how you present yourself. You should just look like you. Just be you. You can dress up, but you shouldn't cover up. Who we are on the outside is important but who we are on the inside is crucial.

A groom spent long hours combing and clipping the horse he
charged but daily stole a portion of his oats to sell for profit.
The horse got into a bad condition and at last cried,
"If you want me to look sleek and well,
you must comb me less and feed me more."
- Aesop

24. BEST

I believe that a simple and unassuming manner of life is
best for everyone, best both for the body and the mind.
- Albert Einstein

We all want to be the best. However, it can be a curse. We've all have that experience where we were led to believe we were the greatest at something, only to see someone better take that title away from you. You're only the best until you're beaten.

If you try a new skill, and you aren't good from the start, it can be frustrating. But it can feel just as bad as feeling like the best and then being proven otherwise. We have to get out of this mentality that we have to be the best. Being unsurpassed is not an eternal glory.

We are under the impression that we have to be at the top at everything—have the newest phone, the coolest clothes, and the flashiest car.

But when you brag about your new glorified trinkets, remember that for the first few weeks, it's the new Mercedes. After that, it's just your car. For the first month, your friends will be jealous of your SmartPhone. After that, it's just a phone.

Famous entertainers, Penn and Teller once performed a tv special about society's obsession with being the best. They hired a fancy restaurant for the night and asked a couple if they would like the richest, finest, most pure dish on the menu for free. The couple naturally agreed. When they tasted it, they said it was divine.

What they didn't realize was that the food had come from cans, cost about $3, and was popped into the microwave for a few minutes.

They were asked to look at the water section of the menu as well. Some of the water was from the most graceful waterfalls or from an ancient fountain in the Far East. In reality, all the water came from the tap.

My point is that people will want what is desirable because it is meant to be the best. That doesn't mean it is. We are all individuals. What's best to us can be drastically different to someone else.

You don't need to be the best. You shouldn't be in competition with anyone but your past self. What limits and goals are suited for you? How far do you want to go? If being the manager of a corporation is what you consider to be the best, then that's fine.

Or maybe you can be just as happy owning a small shop or raising a family. Let no one tell you what's best for you. You should already know.

It is no use saying, 'We are doing our best.' You
have got to succeed in doing what is necessary.
- Winston Churchill

25. BETRAYAL

Is it possible to succeed without any act of betrayal?
- Jean Renoir

Never has betrayal enraptured us as much, be it in myth or history, as the tale of Judas Iscariot betraying Jesus Christ. When Judas realised his actions would lead to Christ's demise, he took his own life. This story shows the impact and consequence of betrayal.

Many acts can be considered equally treacherous—telling a friend's secret; breaking a promise; going against your friend's actions, your family's teachings, your country's ways, or your religion's beliefs.

Betrayal seems obvious in stories, but we can fall into this role ourselves by simply being a victim of circumstance.

Here is a simple example: imagine you have two friends who hate each other. I have been in this situation countless times. Any time I spent time with one, the other saw me as twisting the blade in his back.

I didn't feel like I had to justify who I was friends with, and I didn't need my friend's permission. So, when I went to see my friends without telling them, it was like I was doing it secretly, which just made it worse.

If you feel like you have been betrayed, don't overreact. There needs to be a reasonable leniency, a sign of mercy. Before we condemn those who we feel betrayed us, we need to have all of the facts.

We can commit acts that can be easily misinterpreted as betrayal. We might not consider that our actions can be perceived in such a way until we put them into context or see ourselves with a wider perspective.

Lashing out at a friend for betraying your trust can cost a friendship. But you should make that friend understand why you consider it a betrayal or, at the very least, demand an explanation. After all, wouldn't you deserve exactly the same if the roles were reversed?

You may have to make a choice of what to do, where to go, who to see, and what to say. You may have to choose between people, an idea, or a course of action. We can be caught in a bind, where people get hurt, and there might have to be sacrifices.

But we can also decide if we have to double-cross someone. At the end of Christ's life, Jesus was going to be arrested one way or another. But Judas didn't have to give up his soul to speed up the process.

A man who does not trust himself will never really trust anybody.
- Jean-Francois Paul de Gondi, Cardinal de Retz
(Memoires)

26. BIOLOGY

Attraction is beyond our will or ideas sometimes.
- Juliette Binoche

In the fable, "The Scorpion and the Frog,' a scorpion asks a frog if it can climb on the amphibian's back to get to the other side of a river.

The frog is not keen on the idea, certain the scorpion will sting him. The scorpion argues that if he stings the frog, the frog would sink and drown the scorpion. The frog agrees to the scorpion's terms.

But halfway across the river, the scorpion stings the frog, dooming them both. Just before they both die, the frog asks why the scorpion stung him, knowing the scorpion would perish as a consequence. The scorpion said, "Because it's in my nature."

This tale highlights that all animals, including humans can be slaves to their biology. We can say we will do certain things or stop ourselves from doing stupid things. We think that logic and willpower will combat biology. That is commendable and, in some cases, possible.

But that doesn't mean you will enjoy it. You may go too far and turn willpower into repression and denial. I know over a dozen people who have combated depression and suicidal tendencies because they were in denial about their sexuality. As soon as they stopped fighting who they were and embraced themselves, many of their insecurities dissolved.

Others have the opposite problem; they use biology to justify their stupidity, laziness, or prejudice. They say things like:

- "Of course I cheated on her! What did you expect? I'm a guy!"
- "She won't be able to lift it. She's a girl."
- "Women aren't hardwired to drive."
- "All men act that way. They can't help it."

But here's the point we need to take away from The Scorpion and the Frog story – animals may be creatures of instinct, but human beings are creatures of intelligence.

Obviously, people have instincts as well, and we have desires that can seem too hard to control. But we can't use that mentality as an excuse to act out our primal instincts all the time. We can't deny that certain impulses are there, but we can choose whether to act on them. If someone rubs you the wrong way, your biology can kick in, compelling you to pick a fight. But you don't have to give into your base instincts, especially when you know it will cause more harm than good.

Although there are times where we can't deny our biology, that doesn't mean we can't understand it better.

Subdue your appetites, my dears, and you've conquered human nature.
- Charles Dickens

27. BITTERNESS

> Bitter experience has taught us how fundamental our
> values are and how great the mission they represent.
> - Jan Peter Balkenende

A few years ago, Laura Jackson wanted to be a cheerleader more than anything. During the tryouts, she fell over and broke her neck, crippling her for life. This story was seen as an absolute tragedy since this girl had her whole life in front of her.

And she still does. Although her original dream is gone, she is not bitter about it. What happened to her is the worst-case scenario, but she knows that it was a freak accident. She understands that it was so unlikely, she has said that any girl who wants to be a cheerleader should not be put off due to her experience and follow their passion.

I couldn't believe a girl who is still a teenager could have that level of maturity. She has every right to hate the world. She could sue everyone or try and take down that school or the cheerleading squad. But she didn't. She just moved on.

Where she pulled out that inner power, I have no idea. I believe that you can't let the past get in your way, and you have to be strong in dark times, but even I can't comprehend where inner strength like this comes from. I'm not sure if I could have that willpower if I was put in the same circumstance.

I believe I may not be that strong because I became so bitter when I had to repeat a year in college. I was enraged and hated the school, my friends, my old class, my new class, teachers, and the whole industry.

What happened to that cheerleader helped me put my life in perspective. My life just needed some adjustment, nothing more.

Phrases like, "It's not the end of the world" and "Better to have loved and lost" and other ineffective phrases during bad times are trite nowadays. But you only realize how right and relevant they are when the real "end of the world" happens.

Although I was devastated when I was forced to repeat a year in college, I overreacted. What good would it do to focus all that energy into hate?

Energy can change its form. So don't turn the original positive energy you had into a negative. And whatever negative energy you have, you can turn that into positive energy.

Hating the world is a way of hating yourself. We don't choose what tragedy happens to us, but we can choose to be petty about it. You are responsible for what happens next.

> But O, how bitter a thing it is to look into
> happiness through another man's eyes.
> - William Shakespeare

28. BLAME

A man can fail many times, but he isn't a failure
until he begins to blame somebody else.
- John Burroughs

One of the hardest sentences to say in the English language is, "I was wrong."
You can blame a lot of things before you blame yourself. People make up rules,
so they feel less guilty. Some people blame all their failures on those who failed them.

Blame is like responsibility, except it's always bad. That's why we often fix the
blame before the problem. If we accept blame, we will suffer the consequences.

So why would we ever accept it? Well, if you don't, someone else might who
shouldn't deserve it.

There's a difference between accepting the blame and tormenting yourself with
it. It can affect you on a deeper level. A lack of accepting blame can easily lead to
guilt.

We also need to accept blame to have a margin of error accounted for. To not
accept blame means you're not accepting the ramifications of your actions. Avoiding
responsibility can create more and more difficulties, which snowballs the problem
to cataclysmic proportions. Why add to a problem? Accepting the blame quickly
will diminish the consequences.

We can turn blame into a game. Couples do it all the time.

"You are always drinking!"

"Because I can't deal with you shouting at me!"

"I shout because you drink and take it out on the kids!"

"What kind of mother are you to the kids?"

"Me? You are never home!"

It just goes back and forth like a game, trapped in automatic responses, with no
deviation or end in sight. Usually in cases like this, both parties did wrong on some
level, but that doesn't make anyone any less to blame. Pointing fingers is the easiest
thing in the world, but rarely is the easy thing the right thing to do.

But what about when we avoid blame? Get away with it scot-free? Well, it is up
to you if you're man or woman enough to face the music.

To apologize to someone takes guts, but to do it when you have no chance of
being caught is an act of courage.

It's up to you, and it depends on the consequences of accepting blame, but to do
so would be a brave act indeed, especially if there is no reward.

But sometimes, there is no redemption when it comes to accepting blame.
Occasionally, you have to face what's coming, even if it's punishment.

If you reveal your secrets to the wind, you should
blame the wind for revealing them to the trees.
- Khalil Gibran

29. BLASPHEMY

Is it not blasphemy to call the New Testament revealed religion,
when we see in it such contradictions and absurdities.

- Thomas Paine

Is it so bad to be misunderstood? Pythagoras was misunderstood. So was Copernicus, Socrates, Luther, Galileo, and Newton and every pure and wise spirit that ever took flesh. To be great is to be misunderstood. So is it so bad?

Yes. In fact, it can be dangerous, even lethal. Any radical idea will be defied, and any savored truth will be protected. Any time there is a new idea that could actually change the world, society is swift at getting out the fire sticks and pitchforks. All great truths start as blasphemies.

Before you get offended, I know that blasphemy tends to have religious connotations. But any lie that contradicts a great truth can be regarded as blasphemous. It doesn't have to do with religion. It can be anything.

My friend, Ricardo is a mathematician. He travels the world doing lectures, declaring potential new mathematical theorems. This may not sound like the most exciting job in the world, but he is making mathematics simpler and therefore, less boring!

If he showed me a document consisting of a hundred pages composed of his theories (some of which contradict the way mathematics has been taught for decades), 90–95 percent will be marked in red by his mentor. Anything that was marked in red connotates that it's sloppy, ill conceived, or flat-out wrong. Because Ricardo's theories were regarded as non-sensical and blasphemous, he could've given up. But over the years, more and more of Ricardo's notes were taken seriously, until his theories were being taught in lectures worldwide.

If you have a great idea, follow it. It may only exist as an idea in the beginning and may not have a place yet within the boundaries of reality. But you won't know until you've tried.

We should feel obligated to uncover the truth. Our ancestors were just as radical and inquisitive in their time as we are now, and the consequences of their radical thinking were far less forgiving. Humiliation, banishment, rejection, beatings, torture, burning, hangings, and being guillotined, racked, and drawn and quartered was a real possibility for anyone questioning the status quo.

That doesn't happen as much anymore, (although it still exists.) But nowadays, we are more likely to listen after learning from the wrongs of the past. We learn from mistakes, and we learn from change.

So whatever you have to say, say it. Whatever you have to do, do it. Whatever has to be corrected, correct it. Whatever has to be changed, change it.

One man's blasphemy doesn't override other people's free-speech rights,
their freedom to publish, freedom of thought.

- Dan Savage

30. BLINDNESS

Haste is blind.
- Titus Livius

The most blind are not the ones who don't see but the ones who choose not to. Blindness is comparable to ignorance. Ignorance is more within the lines of oversimplification and dismissal.

But blindness is absolute ignorance; a blindfold that covers everything. You don't stand a chance of glimpsing what's really going on. It is a terrifying concept to imagine the thousands of things in the world to which we are helplessly oblivious to.

There are wars, conflicts, nations, concepts, beliefs, cultures, customs, and histories that we don't even know about. It's not just because they are in a different country, continent, or hemisphere. At times, we just don't see everything.

You could pass people on the street and have no idea that they are drug dealers or celebrities. You may walk by a building every day for years, unaware that it is a famous landmark. You may not notice the pain in your father's eyes, the scars on your lover's arm, or the drunken, glazed look in a friend's face. How do we miss things like this? We just can't catch it all.

Now and then, the blindness comes and goes. It's impermanent, but that doesn't change the fact that it is wrong or dangerous.

Revenge and emotion are excellent blindfolds. Revenge can make us blind to reason, understanding, or law. Emotion can make us blind to … well … everything. Emotion can be the catalyst to performing the most wonderful acts or the most stupid or the most lethal.

You can be so passionately hateful to foreigners who take over all the jobs in the country, that you are utterly blind to your own racism. You might be so hateful of chauvinistic piggish men, that you cannot see your own sexism. You can hate life so much that you don't realize you are just scared you may not have a place in it.

We live in a world today where we can finally cure true blindness. We are in the process where this can become a regular treatment.

But we have always been blessed to have the ability to remove personal blindness from ourselves. A moment of clarity can expel years of retained blindness on matters, whether it's politics, emotion, or religious beliefs.

From time to time, you are only blind because you are too scared of the world, so you close your eyes. You need to open them, no matter how scary it can be, or you will miss so much the world has to offer. No matter how much you squint and strain, you cannot see through a blindfold. You just need to figure out how to take it off.

You are blind in your ears and mind, as well as your eyes.
- Sophocles

31. BLOCKS

Ambition leads me not only farther than any other man has
been before me, but as far as I think it possible for man to go.
– James Cook

During a marathon run, the average runner will reach a point where they cannot keep running through pure willpower alone. Some believe that if they keep running and have faith in themselves, they can make it. But they can't keep going because of "the wall." When your body has exhausted all it can, it hits a wall, and your body refuses to go another step.

The wall mentality is similar to a common problem—psychological blocks. This is when we put up a wall, a limitation, or boundary on a part of our mind.

The four core emotions are fear, anger, sadness, and joy. You are easily connected to at least one of these emotions.

If you are late for a meeting—social, work, or otherwise—what is the first emotion to get to you? Are you angry that you're late?

Are you scared of the consequences of your bad timing?

Are you sad because you feel like you can't do anything right?

Or maybe you find the funny side of it and just laugh it off.

So which emotion is the last one you would try to access? We all have favorites, even in emotions. Then you have to ask yourself why you won't access certain emotions.

None of us wants to feel terror, despair, or fury, but we are only human. Some people think certain negative emotions will go away if we simply don't act on them.

But they won't. Instead, we will get used to not using certain emotions, but we will still feel the same impact of them.

Usually, the emotion we think we're not using is actually the most powerful and even the most damaging. If you don't express anger or sadness, it can only go inward. Internalizing emotion can be just as bad as externalizing it.

Expressing trepidation or sadness may seem like showing weakness by giving into it. But look at it this way: if you scream or cry or shout, imagine that emotion is a physical thing hurtling out of your body. No matter how livid we get, we eventually burn out. No matter how sad we get, our tears inevitably run dry.

But if we keep it in, it keeps affecting us because it sticks to us. It festers. We need to shatter these blocks and allow ourselves to emote because inevitably, it will come out.

But if you let it come out, it can be controlled. If you don't let it, it will come out anyway but more horrifically. It's your choice.

Nothing in life is to be feared, it is only to be understood.
– Marie Curie

32. BOASTING

He who displays himself does not shine.
He who stands on his toes does not stand well.
– Old Chinese Proverb

Boasting is not the same as egotism. Ego is self-assurance and self-belief, which is practical. It's only when the ego and self-belief goes higher than the actual accomplishments of oneself that we get into boastful territory.

We boast so others will think we have achieved something, but we usually brag because we feel the opposite.

The only thing people should brag about is happiness, but that will never occur, because bragging stems from a lack of contentment.

Am I suggesting that we can never relish the few times in life where we get precisely what we want?

Well, we don't have to revel in the moment, just acknowledge that we have succeeded in our ambition. How is making others feel worse by raising oneself on a pedestal a sign of happiness? Immodesty shows a lack of control, diversion, misdirection, and absence of real power.

The less power someone has, the more they blow their own trumpet about it. The more you have achieved, the less you have to prove.

So when is a good time to fly your own kite? Honestly, never. It's not a good sign of humanity. Bragging implies that you have accomplished all you can.

The most influential people throughout history were those who kept pushing themselves for the good of mankind but were never truly satisfied because they always believed they could do more.

Florence Nightingale never forgave herself, because she believed she could have saved far more patients. This mentality motivated her to dedicate more time to the hospitals she worked at.

Writer of the Declaration of Independence and former US president Thomas Jefferson always wore casual clothes because he didn't want to come across as if he was above anyone else.

Playwright George Bernard Shaw rejected knighthood and only accepted his Nobel prize after his wife insisted. He, however, gave all prize money to charity. He didn't believe his work should be glamorized with money and award ceremonies.

I believe the only good thing boasting truly accomplishes is that it may push others to accomplish their goals in order to surpass the braggart. But a person who boasts tends to only gain one thing: enemies.

He who vaunts himself does not find his merit acknowledged.
– Old Chinese Proverb

33. BODYBUILDING

It is not by muscle, speed or physical dexterity that great things are achieved, but by reflection, force of character, and judgment.
- Marcus Tullius Cicero

There is more emphasis on physical health than mental health nowadays. If you see any magazines highlighting what health is, you will usually see a bodybuilder with muscles bulging out of his arms, veins popping everywhere, with a rock-hard six-pack or even an eight-pack! It's telling you, "This is what you need to look like to be considered healthy. This is the pinnacle of fitness everyone should strive for."

Being muscle-bound puts strain on your body—your lungs, liver, and heart. It's because your body is always healing itself from intense workouts and damaged muscle tissue. Intense workouts create tension, which will take a toll on your body in every way, especially the most important body parts, such as the spine, the upper jawbone, and the tip of the neck.

There is no point in having loads of muscles when you're older and you can barely move. How many stocky bodybuilders do you see in their later years? Almost none. That's because their muscles shrink or because their bodies give out. Bodybuilders tend not to achieve longevity because they push their bodies to the max. It's more important to have exercise, like jogging, skipping, swimming, football, yoga, or whatever you prefer.

If you commit to more cardiovascular exercise, you may not seem as physically impressive as an enormous bodybuilder, but you will be healthier, less tense, and overall, more relaxed. Bodybuilders are in constant pain from their muscles healing constantly. The more you work out, the more likely you will suffer an injury, which can take months or even years to recover from.

If working out is an important part of your life, I can understand if you wish to dismiss this chapter. My good friend, Leon is a professional bodybuilder. He commits to this lifestyle 100 percent, so it's easy for him to dismiss the negative side of bodybuilding.

But he doesn't. He knows the dangers. He takes precautions to ensure he is in the best health because he believes you need to know what you are doing before commit to something so intense. Don't just drink protein shakes and lift as many weighs as possible. Educate yourself. Use your head before you use your body.

Physical health is important as long as you don't push yourself to the extreme, and you are going about it the right way. Stay in control. Know when enough is enough. If you start obsessing about your physical health, you will start to neglect your mental health.

Still using all the muscles except that one that matters?
- Agent Smith
(The Matrix Reloaded)

34. BODY READING

Accuracy of observation is the equivalent of accuracy of thinking.
- Wallace Stevens

Eighty-five percent of human communication is not verbal but physical. We pick up more physical cues than we think we do. Signals, shifting weight, momentary changes in pitch and intonation, altering posture, broken voice—these signals mean more than what is said. A person can lie with words far more than with their body.

If you have difficulty reading body language, it can cause problems. You may see pride as cockiness, seduction as charm, or depression as attention-seeking.

You can have a simplified understanding of body reading. The clichéd example is if you saw a guy crossing his arms, you may assume he has a defensive personality.

That can be true, but that doesn't mean everyone that does that is defensive. It could mean he's cold; he may be more comfortable; or he may be the type of person that holds himself that way.

When I talk to people now, I take notice of how they use their hands. Gesticulating rapidly is a sign of relinquished control. I see if they use props to hold up a barrier (drink, phone, cigarette, etc.).

I will check if they mirror some of my physical patterns. Or am I the one doing the mimicking?

When they lean back, I lean in and then reverse, to see if they do the same.

I check to see how much their bodies are tuned into mine. The more they are tuned in, the more comfortable they feel. Understanding body mechanics can help connect with people on a completely different level.

There is a technique called *kino*, which is a gradual increase in touching in quantity and pressure. You're probably touchy-feely with your mates, but if you acted this way when first meeting someone, you would come across as weird.

But kino has a system of building up physical contact. It may start with a handshake, a cheeky nudge, a high-five, or even reading someone's palm.

It's a step-by-step way of allowing people to be vulnerable with you because allowing physical contact shows comfort and trust. Talking and agreeing on the same matters is all well and good, but to connect physically is great because they will not even realize that you are also connecting on a subconscious level.

If you know how to read other people's bodies and how to present your own to make others feel comfortable, then you will connect on a stronger level much faster than normal.

If you make listening and observation your occupation
you will gain much more than you can by talk.
- Robert Baden-Powell

35. BOREDOM

Every hero becomes a bore at last.
– Ralph Emerson

You know those big boring chapters in books that go on and on, and nothing's happening, everything is filler, and it just won't end, and you don't even care anymore? (I hope this chapter isn't like that!) That's what you can do with your life—fill it in instead of doing something that propels you to the end. There are certain times of your life that can be pinpointed, usually from a huge event, either in the world or something much more at home.

But another important event is when wisdom is given. When I was twelve, I was in school and distinctly remember my teacher Mrs. MacNamara ask the class, "What is boredom?" The common answer (for those who were listening) was, "When we have nothing to do," but she wasn't satisfied with that answer and asked us to keep going and think more outside the box.

Eventually a girl called Lynn simply said, "It's the opposite."

"And what do you mean by that?" said my teacher.

Lynn replied, "When you have so much to do that you end up doing nothing."

This was the answer the teacher was looking for. We could not be more spoiled, yet we complain that we have nothing to do.

The more we have, the more bored we become, the less time we seem to have to do practical things, and the less we give to commit to the necessary.

Don't challenge yourself just to alleviate boredom. Do something that fulfills you. Having "nothing to do" does not mean sitting there and literally not doing anything. You can be bored watching television or even doing a seemingly exciting activity because you are so bored with what you are not doing.

You could be out clubbing, but you are bored because you want to have a real job. You are on holiday, but you are distracted because you need to do something with your life.

Being bored is being tired of a repetition in your life—bored of your life, of yourself, of the charade, of your family and friends, or of the rut you are in.

The cycle of boredom can feel endless because you are not stepping in to stop it. Cycles keep going until you decide to make a difference. It won't stop by itself. If you have that feeling, get out of that rut, and make a move in life.

Simply by sailing in a new direction you could enlarge the world.
– Allen Curnow
(Landfall in Unknown Seas)

36. BOTTLING UP

An exploder drops his bombshell and then ten minutes later is
OK, - but what about the person on the receiving end? It can take hours,
days, weeks, months or even years for them to recover from the blast.
- Mike Fisher

Anger experts believe that a passive-aggressive person is more dangerous than a person who is openly aggressive. If you are not prone to being angry openly, you can be picked on for coming across as an easy target.

Sadly, anger can work like a coiled spring. Being pushed down all of the time presses you more and more until you snap back. This may feel good because you are standing up for yourself, but doing this rarely makes you come across as unpredictable and scary.

I am not advocating a lack of control, but inevitably, it happens. Giving in to anger is more acceptable than society thinks, as long as it is controlled. Even letting it out for ten seconds to yourself can save you from having a nervous breakdown in the future.

Am I suggesting getting angry or "venting" is okay? Not necessarily. But if you feel genuinely enraged, it is not healthy keeping it in since it will build up.

Have you ever known someone who has a tendency to get aggressive all of the time? You get used to it surprisingly quickly, don't you?

Then there's the other guy, the guy who never gets angry, no matter what. Mocked. Bullied. Dumped. Fired. Nothing.

But then this person might get skipped in a queue, and he snaps and becomes consumed with uncontrollable rage. People will freak out because this person always came across as so together.

A lot of people forget that just because we choose not to act on anger does not nullify its existence. The common angry guy may not be the most stable person but anger is better than rage, which tends to derive from passive aggression.

People will put up with a regularly angry person before a passive-aggressive person lets out his anger because human beings don't like change. We learn to tolerate aspects of our lives that are constant. Any difference can be perceived as a potential threat, so we become cynical and wary of it.

If you don't want to let out your anger because you are afraid that people will judge you, you're missing the point. It will come out eventually, one way or another. When it does, people will judge you more harshly than you ever imagined. Instead of them seeing you with an anger problem, they will see you with a psychological problem. You won't be perceived as angry but terrifying.

Always write angry letters to your enemies.
Never mail them.
- James Fallows

37. BRAINWASHING

Destiny can justify a tyrant's authority for crime or a fool's excuse for failure.
- Ambrose Bierce

Brainwashing isn't just for the paranoid to worry about, nor does it only happen in alleged conspiracy stories. Brainwashing is very real.

It isn't as big as it seems in television, with secret societies, but it is there, creeping in, little by little, through any number of mediums—advertisements, billboards, magazines, politicians, celebrities, indoctrination, propaganda, family, bullies, work, and so forth. Visuals are the most effective medium but not the most truthful.

Brainwashing can warp our perception of reality; force us to lead a life we do not want to lead; prevent us from obtaining any of our goals, and see wants as sins, dreams as illogical, and the possible as the impossible.

Brainwashing is not just a trap for the stupid and ignorant and immature to fall into. It can happen to anyone.

The sad thing is that brainwashing can start almost from birth. We can be taught from an early age to hate a certain type of person, belief, or race. As a child, it can be difficult to believe any other version of what we are told, especially if we have only heard one side of it for so long. In a way, we don't stand a chance, because we accept teachings like gospel in our eagerness for knowledge.

We may not even notice warped teachings are seeping into our mind. It can happen to you as an individual, a group, or even an entire nation. In times of war, it is easy to paint the enemy as evil, and hatred stems from a warped patriotism and love for one's country. During the McCarthy era, Americans who disagreed with the need for war were accused of being Communists. So, people would give into this hatred because of fear, not of Communists but of their own government.

Brainwashing at its most basic is a series of precisely placed subliminal prompts, positioned inside the subconscious, prohibiting the subject from accessing anything other than the desired command. If you have been told something long enough, anything new that comes along won't matter, even if it is backed up by history, experience, and facts.

There are so many parts of the mind; we choose what we find convenient, and as life develops and changes around us, we listen to some parts more and some parts less. We shut out clutter no longer needed and may start using other parts of our mind for the first time.

But thoughts are never created from scratch. All that potential just lies dormant. So if you think you are set in your ways, remember that you always have the ability to change.

All propaganda has to be popular and has to accommodate itself to the comprehension of the least intelligent of those whom it seeks to reach.
- Adolf Hitler

38. BRIBERY

In the last few years, the very idea of telling the truth, the whole truth, and nothing but the truth is dredged up only as a final resort when the alternative options of deception, threat and bribery have all been exhausted.
- Michael Musto

You use bribery all the time, even if you are not aware of it. You may not realize it, because you may not bribe with physical means, like money or a gift. You can bribe with a simple favor.

You might pay for your family's dinner, so your mother won't tell the rest of the family that she caught you smoking.

A friend may buy you a pint because he knows you found those texts on his phone, talking about you behind your back.

You pay for the cinema because it's the least you can do when your partner finds out you broke the window.

Flowers, money, and presents have been used many times to bury the hatchet in arguments with friends, family, and partners, but there's no point unless you are truly sorry. Everyone bribes, just not necessarily with the same tools.

When we make a seemingly kind gesture to end a conflict, are we doing it to apologize, or is it to end feeling guilty? Have we learned from the experience and are we actually going to change for the better?

But what about when we are on the other side of bribery? What's it like being the one who is bribed?

If someone is bribing you, they are using you. A favor is a bribe you can't see. You need to decide if it's worth it. You may get a quick fix—a favor or money—but you need to make sure it's worth the price.

The bribe may pass itself off as a favor, nothing more. But some are more devious than that. My housemate, Dominic would act like the nicest guy in the world when he wanted something. Once he started playing nice, I always knew what he was up to, and I would just have to wait when he finally needed to call in a big favor. He could keep this up for weeks, so that when he asked for a favor, I would seem rude to refuse him. All of the nice little favors he did for me all added up to one big bribe, and he would guilt-trip me if I refused because I owed him. But I owed him on his terms without my even being aware of it! He was only being nice because he wanted something. None of his "good deeds" stemmed from a genuine impulse. He was just using me.

You may give your friend a gift after an argument. That's not to make him forget why he is angry, but because you are genuinely sorry. If you know what the gift truly stands for, then it is an act of apology and nothing more. But that's the point. Know what your actions stand for. Don't make them just fit your end.

It is less shameful for a king to be overcome by force of arms than by bribery.
- Sallust

39. BULLIES

You have a choice - you either joined or formed a gang or you let others bully you.
- Jack Bowman

Bullies pick on others for a reaction. If you don't give in to them, they've got nothing. This is timeless—from kids to adults, most bullies antagonize out of boredom, so if you don't alleviate their boredom by not reacting to their tactics, they'll give up.

My friend, Michael never got bullied, simply by not reacting to bullies trying to intimidate him. They would scream at him, throw stuff at him, and even get desperate and pin him down.

Quiet, shy kids can be easy victims, but when bullies attempted to scare Michael, he always looked completely calm. They could see that he had no fear in him.

Once the bullies could see that they had no power over him, they left him alone. I asked him how he didn't get scared, and his answer was, "They're kids. They don't have any real power." I have had a similar mentality ever since, and I was never bullied in primary school or secondary school.

You need to be aware of the causes of bullying. It obviously originates from insecurity. There could be more going on than can be imagined, so we just need to focus on their drive—insecurity. It's amazing how less intimidating a bully becomes when you realize how truly insecure he or she is. Even pointing this out usually catches prevents bullies from establishing dominance over a group.

I know two people who got horribly bullied in school for years. One of them turned into the most wonderful, sweetest, caring, kindest, unrealistically nice person I ever met.

The other turned into one of the most hateful, negative, manipulative people I have ever known. And he became a bully himself. I knew him in college, and he said he bullied the new students because if he got bullied in school, it was only fair, and he needed to do it to balance it out.

Sadly, this mentality is surprisingly common. I tend to notice that the bullies in college are the ones who got picked on the most as a kid. They finally had that kind of power, and they wanted to use it.

I understand that mentality, but it's not a justified excuse. Some bullies redeem themselves. But they have to work hard to do that. It's hard to change, especially as a kid. Kids don't know any better. But if you are an adult and choose to act like this, what excuse can you possibly use?

You can discover what your enemy fears most by
observing the means he uses to frighten you.
- Eric Hoffer

40. BUSY

A man has always to be busy with his thoughts if anything is to be accomplished.
- Antonie van Leeuwenhoek

My wife complains that she never has time to relax. Once, she said she wanted to have a weekend where we just watched television. That weekend, she built a barbecue, a wardrobe, and a bed.

She said that performing these activities made her look forward to the following weekend of relaxation even more. But when the time came, she bought an outside bench and spent hours building it. After she built it, she dismantled it because she thought she could do it better and so, built it again. However, she thought it still wasn't perfect so she dismantled it again and rebuilt it for a third time!

She said she couldn't wait until the next weekend of just lazing about the house. But instead, she repainted the kitchen and bedroom.

Now don't get me wrong; my wife is the most practical and organized person I know. No one can accuse her of being lazy.

She has an extremely busy job, and she has adapted this into her daily life to always find practical jobs to do with her time.

But you don't have to force yourself to be piled up with things to do. Multitasking is a resourceful skill, but you can't do everything you want at the same time. As James Maxton once said, "No one can ride two horses at once."

You need to pace yourself. It's good that you want to get things done, but if you are in the middle of a task and then start another, every extra task will slow down the completion of any task. Collectively, you will never be finished.

Being busy can be addictive. It's great to be doing lots of practical jobs, and it beats being lazy and procrastinating, but you need to give yourself some time to unwind and relax, or you won't be able to perform to the best of your ability when it counts.

Usually, when we're busy, we complain, but we are in better form because we are active and look forward to getting some free time when, ironically, we are not so busy! We don't have to kill ourselves with Sisyphean tasks and endless impractical labors, but that's not an excuse to be lazy.

Find a reasonable balance between the two. When you have some free time, you can relax and watch television, but give time to do a practical task, even a simple one—meet up with an old friend, start spring cleaning early, go for a run, clear out the garage, or go shopping. Choose what to do and spend your time wisely.

A bee is never as busy as it seems; it's just that it can't buzz any slower.
- Kin Hubbard

41. CALORIES

It can't be something that you're doing to lose weight, and then once you do, you're done. I do it every day of my life.
- LeAnn Rimes

Surprisingly, a lot of people don't actually know what a calorie is. A calorie is energy needed to increase the temperature of 1 gram of water by 1 degree Celsius.

In the last twenty-five years, walking has decreased by 20 percent. Cycling in that same time has decreased by 10 percent. Driving in that same time has increased by over 70 percent, showing that we aren't burning as many calories as we used to.

So what can we do? We see calories as scary because losing calories equates to exercise and that does not equate to fun.

But you can burn off calories more ways than you know. Do you know you burn off a calorie by just standing still every two minutes? That's thirty calories an hour just by standing!

Don't be under the impression that you only burn off calories when you exercise. You burn off about sixty-six calories with an hour of steady cycling, forty minutes of tennis, or thirty minutes of swimming.

Now sixty-six calories doesn't sound like much. On top of that, you may find it tedious or boring.

But there are some jobs that are fun or even necessary, and when you become aware of how much energy you burn off, it will force you to embrace practical tasks, as well as urge you to stay fit! You can burn at least 250 calories an hour by walking a dog, over 300 at an increasd pace, or 500 in a hilly area. That's a quarter of all the calories you need to burn in a day!

Ninety minutes of light housework burns nearly 300 calories. Washing windows for fifteen minutes burns sixty calories. That's almost as much as an hour of cycling! Even wearing fewer clothes causes your body to generate more heat, which sheds calories. With this mentality, you will start cleaning your house when would usually make excuses to avoid it.

There are so many things you can do that seem basic, but they all add up to a lot of calories burned off. Walk down escalators. Get off the bus one stop early. If waiting for anybody or any transport to arrive, walk up and down where you are.

Even if you're quite a busy person, you can burn calories sitting down! When sitting, occasionally lift your feet from the floor and hold the position. You will feel your muscles at work. Even fidgeting can burn as much as 350 calories daily!

If you want to know more, check out *365 Ways to Get Fit* by Andrew Shields. You will find many more ways to stay fit that should surprise you.

You get fat if you take in more calories than you burn. That's simple science. Everyone knows this. It doesn't sneak up on you. It's a fact.
- Ricky Gervais

42. CARBOHYDRATES

For me, it's all about moderation. I don't kick things out of my diet, like carbs.
- Bobby Flay

Modern society considers carbohydrates to be the ultimate enemy of our bodies. However, we need more carbs in our bodies than any other food group by a considerable margin. Women need 230 grams of carbs a day, and men need 300 grams. To compare, you need approximately 45g of protein, 70g of fat, 80g of sugar, 25g of saturates, 24g of fiber, and 6g of salt.

So why does it get such negativity? One word: accessibility. Each food group has its purpose and carbs are needed to give us energy. Our ancestors would try desperately to get some carbs into their bodies. Our bodies naturally crave them, so we will pursue food that has carbs as a means to stay alive. Usually, when we are starving, we don't crave protein, because our first priority is having energy. Nowadays, we don't have to fight for our lives.

But evolution is a gradual process, so the craving for them is still there. What's even worse is that carbs are in abundance. Although carbs are the food group we need to eat the most, it is also the one we overeat.

Unfortunately, any food group that is eaten in excess automatically is held as fat reserves.

The reason you should eat over 230–300g of carbs a day is because that's how many grams of carbs the human body breaks down daily. If you exercise intensely, you will burn carbs much faster, and once you have used up all of your carbs, your body starts burning fat. If you don't burn off all of your carbs, it will be stored as fat. This is the reason why carbs have such a bad reputation.

But here's the dilemma: your body needs carbs. You can't cheat and cut them out. It may prove to be a temporary solution, but no one can maintain a healthy lifestyle carb-free. You will suddenly have cravings you can't control, and you will eat nothing but carbs, and you will regain all of the weight you lost.

One trap a lot of new bodybuilders tend to fall into is limiting their carbs so they can lose more fat. But if your body has no carbs to burn, it may start burning protein! Your body has evolved and adapted to break down carbs. Cutting them out will just cause damage. You can't trick evolution or shortcut your own body.

You need energy to function. Without carbs, you have no energy. If you eat a healthy amount of carbs without overdoing it, and you exercise moderately, you will lose weight, and more important, you will lose fat. You may not lose as much as if you cut carbohydrates out entirely, but what weight you do lose, you won't pile back on.

*Any kind of advice that I've been given to cut out carbs forever, don't do it.
It just doesn't work. You do okay for a while and then you just overcarb.*
- Erica Durance

43. CAUTION

A careful driver is one who honks his horn when he goes through a red light.
- Henry Morgan

We have become safer throughout history. The more we are aware of diseases, dangers, and potential hazards, the more we arm ourselves with sprays, equipment, medicines, and knowledge.

If there is a crisis, steps are always taken to minimize it happening again. But it is so easy to look at a problem in hindsight. After September 11 happened, people actually bought parachutes and brought them to work in case they needed to jump out of their building in case their complex was terrorized.

There is such an emphasis on safety nowadays that it can make people go into a paranoid frenzy. Unfortunately, there are scammers who will prey on people like this. One charlatan made a fortune selling radiation blockers on mobile phones, even though he is clearly aware that the radiation it spreads is too faint to cause harm.

People can get scared and become too cautionary. They then waste money, resources, time, and energy and thus, become fearful for nothing. They shield themselves from a nonexistent threat, like an animal living in terror for its life in an environment without predators.

In some situations, it doesn't matter what precautions you take, disaster is always possible, no matter how unlikely. Every lock in the world will not make it impossible for a safe to be broken into; it only makes it harder.

Although I have never fired a gun in my life—nor handled one—I do believe that they are not good or evil, godly or demonic, helpful or detrimental to the human collective. A gun is a tool, and the intention and skill with which that tool is used will determine its value.

There are times where people do not take enough precautions. Imagine if a person in your neighborhood had a big dog. One day, this dog gets out of its house, runs around the neighborhood and bites a child.

As a result, the dog's owner ties his pet to a chain to ensure it doesn't happen again. But the dog is so big; it breaks out of the chain and attacks another kid.

Then the owner takes further precautions by locking it in a crate inside the house. But one day, it gets out and bites another kid.

At one point does the owner just... get rid of the dog?

Precaution isn't enough. Sometimes, you have to simply dispose of the problem itself.

After all, disaster is always a moment's carelessness away.
Don't play with fire, but get close enough so you can get warm.
- Anon

44. CHANGE

Because things are the way they are, things will not stay the way they are.
- Bertolt Brecht

Change means new. Change creates bewilderment and bad preparation, and that runs the risk of being hurt. We nitpick how things could be enhanced if we had this and that, but the source of one of our biggest complaints is our inability to adjust to change.

People are so obstinate; they actually refuse to change, not realizing that it's not viable in an ever-changing world. A lot of people don't fix their problems, and they don't stop sabotaging themselves because they're use to it, and the alternative requires effort.

People change when situations change, even if they try not to. Change requires a lot of work, but all progress has resulted from people taking unwanted positions in life throughout history. Real changes can take lifetimes, like abolishing slavery and decreasing racism and chauvinism.

This can be understood better by talking about a concept called the hedonic treadmill. It means that no matter how good our lives are, we will get used to it and take it for granted. This sounds depressing, but what's even worse is that it works for the negative parts of our lives too. If our lives are horrible, we may eventually get used to it and take no steps to get out of it.

It's like putting a frog in boiling water. If a frog jumps into water that's too hot, it will jump out. But if the frog is in cold water, and the water is gradually heated, even when the water is boiling, the frog will stay until it dies. But just because our life has been a certain way doesn't mean that's the way it has to stay.

If you are surrounded by negative influences, you might try and change. But some people may not like this change in you. Family and friends may stand against you when you start being different, even if this change seems to be for the better. Oprah Winfrey lost friends when she lost weight because she was no longer the fat girl of the group whom they could chastise and use to make themselves feel better.

If you do make the change, remember to not change back. Just because something has changed doesn't mean it can't change again.

People look at their state of affairs and say "This is who I am." That's not who you are. That's who you were. If you don't have enough money in your bank account, that's not who you are, that's the residual outcome of your past thoughts and actions. If you define yourself into your current affairs, you doom yourself to nothing more but the same in the future.
- James Ray

45. CHANGING THE WORLD

An era can be said to end when its basic illusions are exhausted.
– Arthur Miller

When Jesus talked about a better world, he was called the Savior. But when honest people nowadays make a tremendous effort to fulfill this yearning, we think they have an ulterior motive.

When you try to make the world a better place on any scale, you will be mocked, bullied, and threatened. But only you can decide how much this antagonism affects and limits you.

We can make drastic changes to the world through physical acts or wisdom and ideas. We can make the world a better place as an individual or as a group. We can help our planet through politics, discoveries, peace, inventions, or humanitarianism.

But how? How does one create such an impact on a whole planet? Most people who have made major influences on a global scale weren't trying to. They were simply protecting, defending, or fighting for something they were passionate about.

Also, how do we know if our actions are healing the world or hurting it?

Countless juvenile kids are pushed into the army to get away from their family. Their mentality is, "I want to do something with my life. I could die, but at least I'll die defending my country."

They are not angry with their family or even with themselves but with life itself, and they get themselves killed just to defy it.

They could channel that energy to do something practical, like helping people or donating to charity.

Others walk out of where they are studying or where they are working because it's not helping society.

That's a good start, but don't walk out to sit on the sidelines. March out to make a difference, and make sure you are on the right team. It's not about making a difference; it's about making the right difference.

People traipse across the globe as if it were disposable, gorging on every whim, every fantasy, and every single indulgence with little care for the planet.

We keep talking of the world of tomorrow, doing little to change the world that is. If we don't change the world soon, eventually there won't be a world left to change.

To change the world, you have to change yourself. Nobody can make a greater mistake than those who do nothing because they could only do a little.

We have it in our power to begin the world again.
- Thomas Paine

46. CHARISMA

*If you are truly confident with who you are rather than
how you look, you can get through anything.*

- Anon

One profession that requires great presence and showmanship is a magician. Harry Houdini was the most famous magician of all time and one of the greatest escape artists in history.

Houdini was so talented, other magicians were worried they were going to lose their jobs. They had to overcompensate with beautiful assistants to distract the audience, and the most basic tricks became far more elaborate.

Houdini would do tricks in a couple of seconds, but inferior magicians would drag them out for ten minutes.

But for Houdini, it was all about the trick. No pyrotechnics, no gimmicks, no showmanship. To him, it wasn't just entertainment. It was art.

But there was a reason why Houdini didn't dress up his magic any more than he needed. Although he was legendary for being one of the greatest entertainers of all time, Houdini was said to possess no presence or charisma!

He originally wanted to be an actor. This was the early twentieth century, and he wanted to be one of the first movie stars. But his films were considered dreadful, and he was often told his performance was wooden. Even when he was on stage performing magic, he would simply do one trick and then move immediately on to the next one. He didn't jazz it up or milk it.

Some people simply exude a natural charisma that makes them feel powerful and attractive. Some people have such presence that they can walk into a room and affect everybody immediately.

But there is a problem with too much charisma. You might have so much natural presence that you may have nothing to back it up with. It's great to have charm, humor, and be naturally entertaining, and this will open many doors and offer lots of opportunities in your life, which can benefit your career and broaden your social circle.

But it only gets you so far. What do you actually have to offer?

Houdini was said to possess no dynamic magnetism, but that didn't stop him being the best at what he did. How many other magicians can you name in his era?

I suppose the lesson is to possess natural confidence instead of some sort of false machismo. Houdini didn't jazz up his tricks because he didn't need to. Charisma is a great tool, but you should never become reliant on it. You can't force charisma, or it will come across as arrogant instead of confident.

It's not about charisma and personality, it's about results.

- Steve Jobs

47. CHARLATANS

If one doesn't know what they want, any opportunity is the right opportunity.
- Anon

Have you ever heard the saying, "A bargain is something you don't need at a price you can't resist?"

Whatever your profession is and no matter what your selling point is, you are trained to make potential buyers, not only want your product, but make them believe that they need it.

But you, as a consumer, have to be aware that there are charlatans out there who are just want your money. And they also have many ways of getting to you. We have seen grifters on the street telling us a terrible story or a wonderful tale, or we have received a life-changing e-mail, or a website says you won a competition you didn't even enter, or someone thinks you have the right look or the right walk to take you up in their books, and they will be in contact with you really soon. And such encounters all end with two things: money and bank details.

Dozens of my friends were worried about their voices after being cast in a musical. As a result, a few of them got extra lessons from a charlatan who literally taught them nothing and ran off with their money.

A man in my hometown posed as Santa Claus during Christmas for a children's hospital charity for weeks and then fled with the cash.

We can't believe something just because we really want to. Harry Houdini was absolutely crushed when his mother died. He was so desperate that he went to many who claimed to be clairvoyant. Houdini wanted to believe he could communicate his mother so badly, but because of his profession, he knew about suggestibility, persuasion, and distraction, and he concluded that every supposed soothsayer he saw was a fraud.

I admire Houdini because he only wanted one thing in life. He just wanted to talk to his mother one more time. Many people would have fallen under the persuasion of these grifters. Even though Houdini would've been at peace if he embraced the lie, he refused to compromise.

If a stranger makes you an offer that sounds too good to be true, it probably is. There is the odd chance that it could be a real opportunity. You don't have to say yes straight away to any offer. Do the research, and see if it's legit. Scammers will always bully and pester you and force you to make a decision now. We never think straight under intense time restraints. Real offers will not put you under the same pressure.

If a man with experience meets a man with money, the experienced
man gets the money and the formally rich man gets an experience.
- Anon

48. CHAUVINISM

The fact remains; chauvinism is prevailing.
- Emma Bonino

When I was a kid, I saw a list of the two hundred most important discoveries of all time, and noticed that only two of the people mentioned were women. I was young at the time, so I assumed men were simply better inventors, scholars, and scientists.

However, my mentality completely changed when I heard of a woman called Rosalind Franklin. Rosalind was an X-ray crystallographer who discovered DNA. Her partners, James Watson and Francis Crick, pooled her data. Combined, they uncovered the double helix structure that is the building block of all life. Watson and Crick won the Nobel prize in 1962.

Tragically, Rosalind Franklin died from radiation poisoning from overexposure during her research. She won nothing. Her name wasn't mentioned at the ceremony.

These men's names are associated with the dawn of genetic structure, and Ms. Franklin is a footnote in their story. She literally died for her discovery and was awarded nothing, not even a legacy after death.

We can't pretend chauvinism is no longer an issue when the majority of pilots, ship captains, mechanics, landowners, religious figures, politicians, and world leaders are male.

We have to stop looking at the world with rose-tinted glasses and see the problems of the world for what they are. Just because some problems aren't desperate doesn't mean they are resolved.

The Bechdel Test was devised to determine how limited female characters develop in stories. More specifically, it determines if two women in a story talk about anything except a man. Most of the biggest novels and most successful movie franchises fail at the Bechdel Test.

There are few examples of when the law favors women, but when they do, wow, do men put up a fight! When matters involving divorce, child support, or sexual harassment favor women, men are outraged, but it gives them a little taste of what some women have to go through on a daily basis.

Ladies of civil rights, like Irene Morgan, Lizzie Jennings, Sarah Louise Keys, Claudette Colvin, and of course, Rosa Parks, had to remind the world that women had to work twice as hard to be taken half as seriously.

And they shouldn't have to. Women are different from men, but they deserve to be equal.

Our material eye cannot see that a stupid chauvinism is driving
us from one noisy, destructive, futile agitation to another.
- Anne Sullivan Macy

49. CHOICE

Every choice you make has an end result.
- Zig Ziglar

We always have a choice. Every choice we make branches out from possibility to reality. Every choice recreates the world.

We have a choice how to act and a choice how to react. Too often we fall into Hobson's Choice, the term used for apparent free choice with only one option offered. This scenario stems from blackmail, bribery, peer pressure, and desperation.

To choose whether or not to make a mistake is better and more human than being forced to always do the right thing and never live a day of your own.

You can choose to be a thug, a president, a curer of ailments, a paragon for the next generation, or simply a better you.

What is as important as allowing yourself to have a choice is to give others the same opportunity.

I have too often had the chance, as we all do, to interrupt a chain of events in a relationship, an argument, a fight, or to create or prevent an irrevocable change in a person's life.

You can choose to involve yourself, but you cannot force your hand. You can never force your choice on another. You can reason, enlighten, and befriend, but you cannot compromise someone else's choice within reason.

My former housemate, Brian wanted to move to England and leave Ireland forever. I knew he'd been in a lot of trouble with the law, and he was running away from his problems. He was making a choice, but it was the wrong one. He had to take responsibility for his actions, not run away from them. But he looked at it from the point of view that he was starting anew. Sadly, he made the same mistakes in England and came back two months later.

I knew Brian wouldn't last abroad but I couldn't push how I felt. Most people have to gain knowledge from their mistakes. A mistake should not just make us stop doing the wrong thing. It should make us question if we are doing the right thing in the first place.

These are the questions we don't want to ask, but the most important questions usually are. We have to ask questions like, is the choice we make the right one or the most exciting one?

We are not animals. We are not a product of what has happened to us in our past. We have the power of choice.
- Stephen Covey

50. CLIQUES

> The most important thing to a lot of people, is to belong to something that's
> hip or whatever. To be a part of something that's not society, just a clique.
> - Ric Ocasek

A clique is the set people in a group of friends. If a new person tries to introduce himself or herself to the group, and the group frowns upon it because "their group is already set," then it becomes a clique.

How many close friends do you have? Now how many people do you know? If there are a hundred people in your area and you are close friends with three of them, the other ninety-seven people are "the people you know." You will give them a nod, say good night after a long day, or talk to them because they are the only person in the lunchroom or because you were put together for a project.

And then what? Do you continue to talk to them?

Once we have established our clique, it's hard to open it to new people. Every time a new student became a part of my class, my classmates would flip out, saying that it would imbalance the order of things. They assumed a new component in the mix would make it worse, but who's to say something new might not make it better? That new person might be what the group is lacking.

But when we go out and socialize, that person in your school or work who you always see but never talk to might strike up a conversation with you. The two of you have a chat and realize that you both have something to offer each other.

Then the next time you see each other at work or school, what happens? Now that you know each other on another level, do you open up, or are you still in the awkward stage and save the conversations for only when you go out?

This mentality limits with whom we interact. It is true we let down psychological walls when we go out to socialize, but now that we know how to climb those walls, we can reach that person. We can even knock down that wall and meet that person eye to eye.

We don't need to categorize people as jocks, nerds, drama queens, drinkers, stoners, Goths, and gossipers. A clique does the complete opposite of what we hope to do. A clique draws a small group of people together and closes them off from the rest of the world.

Have you ever been to a party, and you can see four groups divided into the four corners of the room? It's like they are all having their own mini-party. Then there's this big space in the middle. A gap. A hole. Parties are more vibrant when they are filled with people. Gaps imply closing off.

So get out of it. If you see someone interesting, talk to him or her. Everybody has something to offer. But you will never find out what it is until you break away.

> Try to have as diverse group of friends as possible
> and don't get into the clique scenario.
> - Andrew Shue

51. CLOSURE

> Do not brood over your past mistakes and failures as this will only fill your mind with grief, regret and depression. Do not repeat them in the future.
> - Sivananda

When tragedy strikes, we feel regret, remorse, and dread. Yet we don't feel something else that is more important: closure. I was thrilled when I broke up with my first girlfriend. I felt free. I rode that buzz for about two weeks.

Then I suddenly started to crumble, lashing out at the wrong person, and experiencing pangs of rage and fear.

I didn't know what was happening to me. Then it hit me: I needed closure. All the things I wanted to say were sticking to my mind like a poison that prevented me from having my closure. I met up with my ex-girlfriend, and the negativity within me dissipated over time.

So that's the solution. Now here's the problem. Most of the time, we can't always feel closure or even know where to begin to find it.

My friend, J. J. had been beaten by his father, and he said when he got older, he would beat his father so bad, he would never lay a hand on him again. When J. J. was sixteen, he got kicked out of his house.

He came back at twenty-one to discover that his father had died. He was never contacted, because he'd lived off the grid and only came home to a broken family. He said to himself that he would never get closure, because the only man that could give it to him was gone.

But all he had to do to get closure was be a better man than his dad ever was. A parent that walks out on us may warp us to not care about anyone. An early death in our life can prove that life is cruel. Our judgment on certain matters may be clouded with grief, love, or happiness and our unresolved issues with that emotion.

One of my friends called Luther must deal with closure a lot since he is a journalist who is tasked with committing 'death knocks.' This is when a reporter meets a family who have lost someone recently, and he tries to get enough details about the deceased to write an article. Luther will try to write about the deceased in the best possible light. Some families see this meeting as the only possible closure they can have. If someone they loved passed away, they can make sure that their deceased son or daughter or brother or father will be viewed in a light that can perhaps ease their grief.

Some get defensive, as if Luther is taking advantage, praying on their emotions just so he can make a name for himself in the paper. But that is their decision. You can choose to have closure.

> Begin thus from the first act, and proceed; and, in conclusion, at the ill which thou hast done, be troubled, and rejoice for the good.
> - Pythagoras

52. CLOTHES

Fashion is a form of ugliness so intolerable, we have to update it every six months.
- Oscar Wilde

Fashion makes a statement but not always as intended. How we dress can be the polar opposite of how we feel. People may wear makeup, not to show off their looks, but to hide their natural appearance.

You may wear a tight dress because you won't be able to fit in it soon.

You might feel like a suit empowers you, but that's only because you feel powerless without one.

Perhaps you style your hair because you found a few grays, or you get a trendy hat because you're afraid your hair is falling out.

Your image does not necessarily define who you are but who you are trying to be. It seems silly, looking back at what "cool" was in primary school or as a teenager. We acted like those clothes in secondary school, college, work, or social networks encapsulated us. Whether you wear one thing or the other, you are still the same person underneath.

I am not against modern fashion. I am just pointing out the traps it can have. You shouldn't try to look cool; just have a look that you believe represents you accurately.

What do you feel comfortable in? How do you want to be perceived? If someone sees you wearing what you wear, do you think he or she gets a good idea of who you are as a person? Or does the person perceive you in a way you want them to? Or maybe you just dress outrageously for shock value and attention.

Don't just copy someone else's style. It can be embarrassing. There was a certain coat that one guy wore to my class at college and within a month, almost everyone had the same one. Then a new jacket came out, and everyone bought into this "blink and you'll miss it" fad.

Pickup artist, Adam Lyons, who gives lectures about dating, confidence, socializing, and dress sense said that style is more important than fashion.

Let's look at an example. Posh Beckham is a fashion icon. What she wears looks great but within three months, it's dated and in six months, it's ancient history, and she moves onto a new product.

Then there's James Bond. He represents style. What he wears was cool in the '60s and now, little has changed. He is wearing the same type of clothes, and they don't look dated. They look cool. Style wins every time because it's universal; timeless and above all, cheaper.

We think getting a new wardrobe is the start of a new change, and it is, in a way, but it doesn't mean you will change. It means you have changed already and now, you are going to embrace it.

Fashion is more usually a gentle progression of revisited ideas.
- Bruce Old

53. COMMERCIALISM

Cults are not just chanting and rituals; there are urban cults, fad cults.
- Anon

I was walking with my wife in a busy street when she suddenly darted across into a shop. I couldn't imagine what could have possibly gotten her attention. I went into this shop, and then I saw it—a sale ... for clothes. My wife insisted that we had to get as much as we could because the sale would be over tomorrow, and we could save a ton of money.

I don't have to point out the fact the shops regularly sales like this to make their customers go into a spending frenzy.

But I will say this: my wife and I had never walked into that shop before. Nor did we ever set foot in it again. Neither of us even knew what it was called. All she saw were the words: "Sale Finishes Today!" Words like that make buyers feel like they are missing out if they don't buy now.

Sadly, commercialism is very good at manipulating us at buying things that we don't really need.

Do you want the seventy-two-inch TV? Do you need an iPad? Will you feel incomplete without the latest version of a phone, even though they are updated more times than we can count?

My first mobile phone worked fine for five years. I have had so much trouble with the next five phones. Now I just stick with a straightforward one. Simple products create simple problems.

Complex, well-marketed products guarantee you get sucked into contracts you can't work your way out of and cost far more than what we were guaranteed.

This type of commercialism isn't going to go away. It's a part of life—consumerism —and what we like and buy.

You should never buy something because your favorite celebrity tells you to. Don't sign a subscription just because the presenter is pretty or charismatic.

Just buy what you want to buy. That's harder to do than you think because it's hard to remove all the years of being told what we want.

You are not your job. You are not how much money you
have in the bank. You are not the car you drive. You are not
the contents of your wallet. You are not your khakis.
– Tyler Durden
(Fight Club)

54. COMMITMENT

The truest form of love is how you behave toward someone.
Not how you feel about them.
– Steve Hall

It's horrible when someone you love lies to you. It's a lie so bad that it actually makes you trust everyone a little less. This lack of trust can make you a little more unpredictable and a little bit angrier, depressed, and scared—all because of one lie. That's how powerful lies are. That's how dangerous they are.

You fight with a loved one more than with your friends because you take the love for granted. You assume that it will be strong enough to keep you together, and that's what can break it up in the end.

When your friends screw you over, you can come to blows and still walk away the tightest of friends, time and time again.

But with your partner, the one that you cherish, you can argue over who spilled a drink or whose turn is it to take out the trash. We get annoyed by the minor things because of the pressure of a committed relationship. You friends are meant to be screw-ups. You want your partner to be perfect. So when you realize your partner isn't, you tend to take it out on him or her.

Some people only want to get married to be trapped. Being trapped means safety and refuge because you can't go anywhere once you're tied to that leash.

If you lash out or fool around, a relationship can end. But when you're married, you feel like you need to exonerate your other half because of your sacred vows. However, your partner can use that to his or her advantage. People like this will dishonor marriage for their own gain, to satisfy their own self-seeking wants. Marriage is precious, not a "Get Out of Jail Free" card.

John Gray's *Men Are from Mars, Women Are from Venus* is the most famous book about relationships. It stresses the fact that we expect our other half to be similar to us in terms of what we want and how we feel. This is the biggest mistake couples make, and it tends to be a recurring issue throughout a relationship.

You can't just ask what our partner wants. You need to understand why they want it. They might want the same thing as you but they want to go about it a different way.

When we reach that level, we can meet eye to eye and have discussions (not arguments) about the bigger issues, like "Where is the relationship going?" or "Do you see us together in five years?"

Don't settle with someone you can live with.
Settle with someone you can't live without.
- Anon

55. COMMON SENSE

Common sense is the realized sense of proportion.
- Mahatma Gandhi

We complain about little things, make daily blunders, agonize over that which we cannot change, squabble over trivialities, fight repeatedly, behave immaturely in serious situations, and do incredibly stupid things. We don't need a 365-page book to tell us what we should do. You don't need to eat a whole egg to know it's rotten.

Common sense is latent in us all. It is a human condition, utilized as rarely as possible. The urge to see reason and sense is compromised by impulse, obsessions, lust, curiosity, greed, craving, and temptation. After all, common sense is simply instinct while using your brain.

But just because you can discern what you should do doesn't mean you are going to do it.

If all it took to stop making silly mistakes was to hear some decent advice, human beings would be flawless. But we're not. When we commit the unjustifiably stupid, we have that moment where we realize that bad consequences will outweigh the advantages. You take a joy ride, get drunk the day before a big exam, or pick a fight. There is a moment where we can listen to that voice that says, "Don't do it."

But we don't listen. We commit acts of stupidity. Looking back, it is clear how moronic our childish exploits were.

Although we acted this way when we were young, that excuse doesn't work once you reach a certain age. At a certain point, you have the maturity to have a greater grasp of the consequences of your actions.

And yet, we do dangerous stunts that will cost us more than a detention or being sent to our room. We get into situations with sex, drugs, and violence that we know we should avoid. When we are in bad situations, we need to get out while we still can.

Are you in a situation in your life that you can get out of? Forget wanting more success, money, or whatever your dreams are. Are you doing something you know you shouldn't be doing? Can you choose to walk away from it? If so, what's stopping you? If yes, then ask yourself why you haven't gotten out of this bad situation already.

Common sense is more important than you think. You have a built-in advisor. Listen to it.

Common sense is the most fairly distributed thing in the world,
for each one thinks he is so well-endowed with it that even
those who are hardest to satisfy in all other matters are not in
the habit of desiring more of it than they already have.
- Rene Descartes

56. COMPETENCE

Whether you think you can or think you can't, either way, you're right.
- Henry Ford

Abraham Maslow famously put forward the four stages of learning theory. It breaks down our competence in skill, potential, and achievements into four stages, from when we start a new skill up to mastering it. It is as follows:

1. Unconscious incompetence—not only can you not perform to your potential, but you are not even aware of the problem.
2. Conscious incompetence—you are aware of your lack of potential.
3. Conscious competence—you are finally starting to perform to the best of your capability and are aware of it.
4. Unconscious competence—you perform to the best of your ability, and you don't even have to recognize it; you perform so effortlessly.

Here is a standard example with these stages:

1. Unconscious incompetence - When you ride a bike for the first time, you will fall over. And when you get the hang of it, you probably think you're an expert, even though you are still wobbly, and making jerky movements. This is called the Dunning-Kruger Effect, which basically means "unskilled and unaware."
2. Conscious incompetence – This is the worst stage because you acknowledge how bad you are at something. When you ride a bike for the first time, there's a point where you get so frustrated by how bad you are, you genuinely think you'll never get the hang of it.
3. Conscious competence - Now you're getting the hang of it. You are consciously aware that you can easily ride a bike.
4. Unconscious competence - Last week, I cycled for the first time in six years. I didn't realize it had been that long until ten minutes after I was cycling, because it was second nature.

Obviously, people should strive to reach Stage 4 of any task. But even if you reach Stage 4, that doesn't mean you'll stay there. You can get knocked so badly, you can be sent back to Stage 1 or 2, meaning you have to go through all that uncertainty again.

My friend, Giles went through this situation after she was in a car crash. Although she was an excellent driver, she became rattled after her car collided into another. Even though driving was second nature to her, she was left so shaken, she made the simplest mistakes on the road without even realizing it. Although it took a while, she did eventually regain her confidence in driving.

Giles taught me a very valuable lesson. Just because you're good at something doesn't mean you always will be. But just because you lose the knack to perform a task or hobby doesn't mean you can't get it back.

What this power is I cannot say. All I know is that it exists.
- Alexander Graham Bell

57. COMPLACENCY

I hate complacency. I play every gig as if it could
be my last, then I enjoy it more.
- Nigel Kennedy

Complacency is a scary thing, especially if you have a stressful job. In my acting school in Dublin, the first year class consisted of approximately forty-eight people. There were some students who were certain they would become Hollywood stars and Oscar winners. One of them had his Oscar speech ready. (He quit acting a year later).

By second year, there were only forty students left. By third year, there were just twelve. And in fourth year, there were merely six. Of the final six, two quit acting within two years.

Many of those actors saw themselves as predestined celebrities. When they received compliments for their work, they would get complacent and not push themselves, which is what led to many of them being removed from the course.

One of the most tempting traps that even the most flourishing and experienced people can fall into is taking their foot off the gas and just riding cruise control for a while. But it only works for so long, and then they lose control. By the time they have found control again, they are way off course, and it's going to take a long time to find it again.

On the other hand, you can decide how to react to it. My friend, Boland had the lead in a play, and the pressure was tremendous. He never complained, while everyone else was stressing because of their lines and scenes. He performed in the show, and he was absolutely spectacular. He had every opportunity to allow the praise to go to his head and rub his success into people's faces.

But Boland he decided that he had to strive to that standard and beyond from then on because if he could hit the mark once, he could hit it again and again.

And he did hit it—again and again. Because he didn't let complacency set in. He had every chance to listen to that little voice saying, "You've worked a lot. Now take a breather." But no matter how much praise he received, he always said, 'I could be better,' which pushed him to strive for more.

It we don't push ourselves, we can become our own greatest enemy. Don't become complacent. We are at our most destructive when we think we are indestructible.

Whom the gods wish to destroy, they first call promising.
– Cyril Connolly
(Enemies of Promise)

58. COMPLIMENTS

Compliments cost nothing, yet many pay dear for them.
- Thomas Fuller

Human beings are sensitive creatures. When we receive a negative remark, it can really impact us, not just physically but mentally. If you are led to believe you are unworthy or unattractive, you will restrict your body. This will make you feel tenser and affect your muscles, health, posture, and even your breathing.

Good feelings will have the opposite effect—release. Release and connection means opening yourself and feeling positive.

When we give someone a compliment or receive one, we feel good. Making a positive comment is so easy and yet, so effective. However, insults are just as easy and far more effective, so we must be careful. Compliments wear off, but insults stick to us like glue.

It takes more than a simple compliment to eradicate the effects sustained from a heartless comment. Action is reaction, but sometimes one is more effective than the other, so it requires more than equal force to revert back.

Complimenting strangers is a great tool. It may seem insignificant but like giving money to one in need, we feel good when we help others without any intention of a reward. It allows us to hold on to our self-worth.

I compliment strangers almost daily—on the bus, waiting in queues, at shops and banks, and so on, and some of these encounters have created friendships that last to this day. You can never tell when an innocent question or innocuous observation may turn into a full-blown conversation or a lasting friendship or even more.

Complimenting like this can set off a chain reaction that can go much further than you think. If a stranger or anyone you know is having a bad day, a compliment can pick them back up. It may be exactly what they needed to get through the day. They might pass on that positive energy to someone else, who will do the same, creating a positive cycle.

Obviously, if the cycle began with a negative comment, the cycle could still continue, just in a more negative direction. So, when we compliment, we affect more people than we know or intend.

Wouldn't you feel good if a random passerby gave you a genuine compliment? It can make your day sometimes, can't it? So that is your objective. Make someone else's day.

People ask you for criticism, but they only want praise.
- W. Somerset Maugham

59. COMPROMISE

You get what you want in life, but not your second choice too.
- Alison Lurie

We all have to compromise at some point. We can compromise over our ideas and wants, but we should never compromise ourselves. We can't conform our lives away. We compromise because we think that we are being stubborn or our opinion is stupid.

That way of thinking is suppressing what we really want, what we need to say, and what we want to do.

Visions cannot be compromised. The greatest achievements are always actualized because they were created by people who refused to say no. We all have dreams, but they can dwindle over time or pressure. But there are some accomplishments that were dreamed by great people who, when they awoke, kept that dream alive.

It's hard to draw the line between passionate and stubborn, following your dream or fulfilling your ego, so I suppose I would draw the line myself with how much compromise benefits.

If you are in a group of ten, and you suggest something that is dismissed by another, ask yourself, "Will my idea benefit me more than the group?"

Then ask, "Perhaps they are dismissing my idea for their own. Does their idea benefit the group or just them? Does it benefit the group more than mine would?"

Ego can blind you from what's what and can mesh your priorities with everyone else's. But when I say you can't let anyone compromise you, that includes you. Do what's best for you and for everyone.

Just because your idea or vision or theories are considered silly, idiotic, or laughable, that doesn't mean it's true.

After all, there are many ideas that may sound amazing but can prove to be flawed, so why can't it work both ways?

You will never know if your ideas and dreams are worth following unless you give them a shot. Pursue it as far as you can without letting anyone else alter it. Dream your dream without interference.

Men are much better than their ordinary life allows them to be.
- J. B. Priestley

60. CONSEQUENCES

A positive attitude causes a chain reaction of positive thoughts, events and outcomes. It is a catalyst and it sparks extraordinary results.
- Wade Boggs

Colonel Claus von Stauffenberg led Operation Valkyrie, the mission to kill Hitler in 1944. Two bombs were to be placed in a briefcase near the Fuhrer.

At the last minute, they decided one would be enough to kill the mad dictator, and it would avoid any collateral damage.

The briefcase was noticed just before it was meant to detonate and so was moved. When it exploded, Hitler escaped with only minor injuries.

If there were two bombs, as originally planned, Adolf Hitler would have died then and there. Can you imagine how many lives could have been saved if he had died then and not the following year?

A year may not sound like a long time, but when you're dealing with a murderer with a death toll to the seventh digit, it makes you wonder how different everything could have been if not for a last-minute change.

This may seem like a drastic example but it highlights the effect of consequences. Anything you do knocks stacks of dominoes and yet, we rarely think of the long-term effects of our actions.

A friend of mine beat up someone who insulted his girlfriend, which caued him to he got arrested. He thought he was doing the right thing because he was protecting his girlfriend's honor. Unfortunately, he didn't take into account the consequences of the law. He took in the consequences of one thing but not the other.

Even the tiniest action can result in the most devastating consequences. When I was in high school, a student called Ger jokingly tried to fling a rubber band at his friend but accidentally hit the class bully, Oisin. Oisin naturally assumed the student directly behind him, George hit him with the rubber band and so, broke his nose, which caused Oisin to get expelled. Shortly after, Oisin found himself on the street selling drugs. I'm not suggesting Oisin became a drug dealer purely because he got expelled but it is possible. If that's the case, it's demonstrates that the simple act of firing a rubber band across a classroom can have major consequences.

Although I wasn't involved in this altercation, I still feel somewhat guilty. Although Ger could've stopped George from having his nose broken by admitting he was the one who fired the rubber band, I could've done the same. So could have any student in the classroom that day. But we didn't. This incident taught me that my actions (or lack of) can have results far beyond my wildest dreams for better or for worse.

No phenomenon can be isolated, but has
repercussions through all of our lives.
- Arthur Erickson

61. CONSPIRACY

The simplest explanation is probably the correct one.
- Sir Arthur Conan Doyle

One of my favorite movies is *Cube*. It is about a group of people locked in a cube-shaped prison. Every room has doors that lead to identical rooms. Only one of countless rooms leads to the way out. Most rooms are lethally booby trapped. Naturally, viewers assume the characters are imprisoned because of some conspiracy. But what kind? Aliens? The Us government? A crazy, rich psychopath's mind game?

Then you find out the truth. The cube was built by… nobody. Or everybody, depending on how you look at it. Part of every person's paycheck went into the cube's construction. Someone designed the bolts of the door. Someone else designed the blueprints for the structure but didn't know for what because he did it on the phone. Never met his employer.

But who is this employer?

Doesn't matter. The cube was made for one thing. Now it's for something else. Just got bought by another company.

Oh, that company went bankrupt. Someone else owns the cube now and wants to do something different with it. But who? Why?

When I saw this "twist," I thought, *No! There is definitely more to it than that! What an anticlimax! I was expecting something epic!*

Over time, I realized that the anticlimax was intentional. We all love a good conspiracy. But that movie taught me that the bigger our expectations, the bigger the letdown. A lot of people who follow conspiracies don't truly believe it, they just want to because it's more fascinating.

I have heard of conspiracies about the Bermuda Triangle, the pyramids, Bible codes, the Merovingian bloodline, the Philadelphia Experiment, the Voynich manuscript, cryptozoology, the grassy knoll, and the Easter Island heads.

Myths like crop circles, the Loch Ness monster, and the mummy's curse have all been disproven, and the people behind them admitted they were hoaxes.

Yet people still believe them because human beings are always more fascinated by what they don't know. Or what they don't want to know.

You might look at one of the above and think, *I believe that.* And maybe you're right. There may be some truth to it. There may be a lot of truth to it.

But if you ask a thousand conspiracy theorists what really happened on the day of JFK's assassination, what they really know about crop circles, or how much the government are hiding about aliens, no two opinions will be the same. If they can't agree on such delicate concepts that nobody has all the facts about, then maybe they should reconsider their evidence. Or lack thereof.

Better the rudest work that tells a story, than the richest without meaning.
– John Ruskin

62. CONTEXT

*Having been an educator for so many years I know that all a
good teacher can do is set a context and raise questions.*
- Godfrey Reggio

When you go through a good time, you can never truly know if it was good or not until it's in context.

But one day, you may remember that period for the first time since you had it because it connects with your precise given circumstances. You can't change some things, but you can change how you want to perceive them. The right perspective can be more real than reality itself.

Movies are always forcing us to see a scene, a character, a life, an object, a line, or the movie in a context. If your life were a movie, would it be a comedy? Or a romance? A tragedy, maybe? You can't tell because you haven't lived it fully yet.

Is what you are going through right now the funny part to a tragic tale or the sad part before everything turns out for the best? Do you ever think that you are going through the best time of your life, but when you look back on it, does it feel forgettable and pointless? Are the times where you complained the most seem the easiest now by comparison? Can you even tell? Can you put these situations in context accurately?

If you had ten key scenes in your life lasting a few seconds or half an hour that would represent you perfectly, like in a movie, what would they be and why? Did you ever think in a million years the scenes you chose would be even significant? You may not have thought of them in a long time or ever considered them important until now.

If any of these queries have hit home, then maybe you can get a better idea of how your life has turned out by gazing at it from a third point of view. And you can see how you or your life has been perceived by an outside source, and maybe you can also have a better idea of what will happen to you in the future.

As Nelson Mandela said, "True reconciliation does not consist in merely forgetting the past."

Maybe you can see patterns in your life. You see good patterns which you can continue to follow and bad patterns that you can finally break. Maybe you can see recurring themes, which helps you focus on the good and avoid the bad. Maybe you can see the same people letting you down, time and time again. Perhaps you should close the door to a few of them. And maybe the same people who keep being there for you should play a bigger part in your life.

For me context is the key - from that comes the understanding of everything.
- Kenneth Noland

63. CONTINGENCY

It seems to me that everything that happens to us is
a disconcerting mix of choice and contingency.
- Penelope Lively

What do you hope to do in life? What do you really want to do more than anything? Now, how close are you to accomplishing those wants? How much of your time, effort, and money are you giving yourself to realize those ambitions? If you want to making a living as a musician, how far are you from achieving that? On a scale of one to five:

1. You work in a local shop with nothing more than a pipe dream.
2. You can play the guitar.
3. You can play the guitar well.
4. You have a gig next week.
5. You have a sold-out show tonight.

Now the next question is, "How seriously do you take this dream?" Is it just a dream or a foreseeable future? Is it probable? Or is it possible? Is it more of a hobby, and you hope you may get lucky? Or do you see it as something to do to stir the fire within you, but you have no intention of pursuing it seriously?

Or maybe you will never stop until you succeed. Although that is an admirable mentality, it's not always practical.

You will have to ask a lot of questions when you talk about dreams and failure. These questions lead to bigger questions like how far do you have to go before you throw in the towel on your goal? And if you do quit, what's your Plan B? Do you have a Plan B?

If you don't have a back-up plan, how much will it affect you if your goal falls apart? I need to stress the urgency of a plan or the consequences of a lack of one. We should not expect failure, but we should prepare for it.

Not only does a contingency make you more ready if your dreams don't come through, it also cushions the fall. You can move to America to make it as a movie star, as most of my friends tried to do, with an "I will get what I want because I believe I will" mentality.

But months later, they found themselves with no money and heavily in debt, forcing them to come home. If you fail without a back-up plan, you can find yourself miles away from where you began, having no idea how to get back to where you started or how to continue.

Then what? The best of us can fall. It can happen to anyone. Just make sure you can get up by yourself afterwards.

If one does not know to which port one is sailing, no wind is favorable.
- Lucius Annaeus Seneca

64. CONTROL

The components to power are those who-
Want it, Give it, Control it.
- Anon

We strive for control for most of our lives. When we are given the chance to establish control, we may become control freaks. It's quite difficult to maintain the balance between control and controlling.

You can become a control freak because you're overcompensating, have obtained power again after not having any for a long time, or because you have suddenly been given a position of power and want to prove yourself.

But when being in control turns into a desire to control everything, you can easily fall into a power trip.

Even when you are in charge of everything, you still need to accept ideas and input from other colleagues, friends, or workers. They listen to you since you're the leader.

You may feel like you have less reason to listen to them because they are not as important, but you are all on the same team. You have different positions, but you are after the same goal. It's like a football player never passing the ball to "less important" players. Rudyard Kipling said, "The strength of the pack is the wolf, and strength of the wolf is the pack."

You can look at this from other angles. We need to maintain control over ourselves, of others as rivals, as friends, of goals, wants, needs, and obstacles. Order and authority are important in our own lives, but they cannot rule us. Controlling our lives and maintaining equilibrium is necessary but hard to regulate. Having too much control is just as damaging as not having enough.

In life, you seem to be the main character. No one seems more important in your life than you. No one should be more in control of your life than you. Your parents, friends, and lovers will guide you and hold your hand in the blackest days, but you, ultimately, decide what to do.

Whatever problems you have in your life, grab the bull by the horns and take charge. But you don't need to take charge of everything. Sometimes it's nice to take a backseat. You should play a hand in most things, but when you take a backseat once in a while, it's therapeutic and can lead to valuable reflection. You should try to juggle being in charge, team playing, and having a break. Learn to control the control.

The world is an oyster, but you don't crack it open on a mattress.
- Arthur Miller

65. CONVERSATION

The opposite of talking should be listening, not waiting.
- Anon

I have certain friends with whom I habitually intend to meet up in a pub for an hour of catching up. By the end of our chat, it's five hours later, the bar is closed, and my jaw is stiff from talking too long.

Everyone has friends with whom they click with so well, you finish each other's sentences. You can talk forever, and you seem to get each other.

Then there are some people you cannot access. They seem to just lock you out. It might be frustrating and bothersome, since they seem to get on with everyone else. Why not you? You didn't do anything to them. So what's the problem? Is it you? Is it them? Is it something else?

I always assumed that certain people just don't click. It's not necessarily that you have an aversion to each other or that you have nothing in common. We all have friends with whom we don't have much in common, or we know people with whom we seem to have a lot in common, and yet we may not be friends.

So what's the deal? My supposition that you can't get on with everybody dissolved when I met one of the most influential people I ever knew.

My friend Ben could simply befriend everybody effortlessly. I had to always keep my hometown friends separate from my acting friends because they were from two different worlds, but Ben could talk to them all with no problem. He could walk into any party, not knowing who anyone was, and he'd be the life and soul of the place by the end of the night. He could smoothly walk up to a stranger in a cafe, bus stop, or train station without making them feel uncomfortable or awkward. He knew the secret—he genuinely cared what they had to say.

I realized that we get on with certain people because we have the same interests or there is some similarity, so we know what makes the other person tick, but we can only knock down the walls people have up if we come with open arms and a warm smile.

When you're locked in conversation, don't fall into the trap of knowing what you are going to say after the other person stops talking. Genuinely feed off what the person says, and you will have a better chat. Having a lot of wacky stories prepared makes you come across as fascinating, but they run out, and people become wary that it's all shtick when you start repeating the same old tales.

The secret lies in everything—your posture, your eyes, looking engaged, and listening. Do you look like you want to leave or butt in with your "interesting stories," or does the other person have your undivided attention? He or she won't want to listen to you if you just want to talk. We all need to have a say.

It is the province of knowledge to speak and
it is the privilege of wisdom to listen.
- Oliver Wendell Holmes

66. COOKING

The discovery of a new dish does more for human
happiness than the discovery of a star.
- Anthelme Brillat-Savarin
(The Physiology of Taste)

"Tell me what you eat, and I will tell you what you are." That is the original version of, "You are what you eat."

You may think it's unnecessary to have a chapter about cuisine in a self-book surrounded by chapters on depression and rage.

But food is a need, one of a few we have. Since it's vital to have food to survive, we should partake in the design of our nourishment.

Cooking is therapeutic since you get to create the energy that you will absorb into your body. If you are having take-aways, dirty kebabs, fast food for breakfast, greasy chips, and ready-made meals, do not be surprised if you are prone to nausea, sickness, and feeling run down.

Cooking is a characteristic that your friends, family, partner, and housemates will be thankful for because it's healthy, practical, and creative. Like a sport or painting, there is an art to cooking because you can make whatever you like. It's like you are your own boss. There is an inner delight in making anything for someone else who appreciates it or just for yourself.

But you might ask, what can I make? Nowadays, it is so easy to access what was once inaccessible. Cookbooks are a good start for novices. Cooking programs show you how it's done, so that's handy.

Even magazines have articles on how to make simple and cheap but quite tasty dishes. They help you experiment with new foods, sauces, spices, salts, aromas, vegetables, and meats. You will find new foods to enjoy.

I tend to make meals for friends and teach them how to cook by watching me. In return, they teach me their own signature dish, so that's one new dish introduced into my routine and another dish introduced into theirs.

I set myself a challenge to make a new dish at least once a week. Some of my dishes work, and some don't. But what works is now a part of my diet. You can save a lot of money eating at home, compared to dining at expensive restaurants, so the question is, what's stopping you? You appreciate food so much more when you know it is made by your hand.

Cooking is the most ancient of the arts, for Adam was born hungry.
- Anthelme Brillat-Savarin
(The Physiology of Taste)

67. COOL

> All books are divisible into two classes, the books
> of the hour, and the books of all time.
> - John Ruskin

One guy I knew in college got a tattoo that was the Tibetan word for "wind." The first thing I said when he told me this was, "Nobody is going to understand it!" He retorted, "But it looks cool."

Sadly, this mentality for engraving your own body is quite common. But some people but a lot more thought into tattoos. I saw a documentary about a guy who wanted to be a writer. When he was diagnosed with diabetes, he quit his job and pursued writing. He got a tattoo of an insulin needle that looked like a pen. This tattoo showed how the worst thing that ever happened to him inspired him to follow his passion.

That mentality is a wonderful reason to get a tattoo. You should have a better reason to permanently change your appearance than "it looks cool." Doing anything for the sake of being cool automatically makes it *not* cool!

Those who get suckered into being cool get caught in the trap of fads. "Coolness" has to keep up with the times, meaning you must constantly change with new music, clothes, lingo, and gossip.

What is considered cool and trendy changes so quickly that looking back, you may look ridiculous by present standards.

When I look back at old photographs from high school, I see whole classes with the same folded arms, bleached hair, and gelled fringes. When I look back at my father's high school pictures, every person's hair reached their shoulders. Looking back at these pictures makes me realize how fickle and exhausting it must be to try and stay cool.

The Emperor's New Clothes is a great story at showing how desperate people are at fitting in. It's the story of an emperor who wants the greatest robe in the world, and a charlatan pretends to give him a robe that is invisible to buffoons and can only be seen by the intelligent. Too afraid to point out that he can't see the robe himself, the emperor marches around the streets naked in his "new garment."

At first, no one spoke out about the emperor's nudity, afraid they would be labeled as foolish. Eventually, a child pointed out the emperor's nakedness. Only then did the rest of the rabble pipe up and mock the emperor.

This cautionary tale shows that we are afraid of disagreeing with what is trendy. However, trends are just another word for fads. It is common to get caught in the age and become part of the zeitgeist, but you should never follow the crowd for the sake of it.

> Nothing gives one person so much advantage over another as to
> remain always cool and unruffled under all circumstances.
> - Thomas Jefferson

68. COSMETICS

Celebrities who have plastic surgery don't look younger or more attractive. They just look like people who had plastic surgery.
- Kate Winslet

One of my classmates in college was a girl called Sandra. One day, she came into class without any makeup. For a couple of minutes, nobody knew who she was because we had never seen her without her makeup. She wore so much lipstick, hair extensions, dyed hair, eyeliner, and other cosmetics that I didn't know what she actually looked like.

Not all cosmetics are for "looking beautiful." Some people just want to take care of their skin or be healthy. That's fine, but make sure you know what you are doing and what you are using.

But cosmetics can be addictive, even dangerous. Nowadays, surgery is so accessible, it's scary. Adolescents nowadays are obsessed with it and are getting surgery at younger ages for pettier reasons. Instead of dealing with physical irregularities, surgery may look like the only option to bullying or insecurities.

I saw a documentary about a woman who has had more plastic surgery than anyone in the world. Most women's role model is Marilyn Monroe in terms of natural beauty (even though plastic surgery is the opposite of natural). This woman aimed a bit higher and got surgery to look like a Barbie doll. She even married a guy called Ken (and he got surgery too, to look the part).

Not only has she had every kind of surgery you could imagine, she had makeup tattooed on to her face so she never has to put it on. (I didn't even know you could do that.)

I don't like my eyes. But they are my eyes. I would never consider surgery because I wouldn't look like me. I would hate to look in the mirror and not recognize myself.

But if you go too far with cosmetics, you will stop using them to dress yourself up and instead, use them to hide yourself. It goes without saying that too much can be damaging to your hair and skin, which then makes you rely more on cosmetics. This can cause you to get trapped in a spiraling cycle that makes you look worse and feel worse, and it financially cripples you.

I have never gone out with a person who wore makeup. I never saw the lure or desirability. That doesn't mean I'm against it. There's no shame in flourishing your best features.

But I would like to see a person's finest features rather than having makeup, eyeliner, and mascara sitting on top of them.

Beauty is a short-lived tyranny.
- Socrates

69. CRAVINGS

When you gradually add in nutrient-dense, fiber-rich foods, you simply stop feeling cravings. Instead of craving, you feel full, fulfilled, and content.
- Kathy Freston

When you are eating well and exercising moderately, you should feel good. You might feel like you will lose your belly if you keep doing this for a few weeks.

But then something happens. In the evening, you are suddenly dying for a chocolate. It's a craving. You assume it will go away but it doesn't. Every hour that passes, the feeling grows stronger. It is so hard to resist but you think you can beat it with willpower. If you get through the night, you will be fine.

The next morning comes, and the craving is gone. You wake up refreshed and proud that you beat it—until that evening when the craving returns. And the next evening. And the next evening. Eventually, you crack and wolf down lots of fatty foods and regain all the weight you have lost.

Why was the urge too strong to fight? Why does it tend to happen at night?

The answer is ghrelin.

Ghrelin is an amino acid peptide and hormone that stimulates hunger. If you're wondering why we have it, the answer is evolution. Our ancestors had little shelter and few means to stay warm. When we are cold, we naturally use up our fat reserves. If our ancestors didn't stay warm during the night, they could become ill or die. Ghrelin combats this by forcing us to seek fatty foods before nightfall and even more so when it is cold.

Fat has many uses, but one of its purposes is that it works as a padding on our bodies. The more we have, the more resistant we are to cold. But when we are burning fat, we naturally crave more.

Your body temperature is 37 degrees Celsius (98.6 degrees Fahrenheit). If this temperature drops by even half a degree, you can become ill. So not only is your body constantly regulating your temperature, it's a top priority. If your body's heat is threatened, it will all it can to stay warm. Even when we are not cold in the evening, the ghrelin recognizes the night as the time to activate the craving as a preemptive step.

Unfortunately, we can't switch off how our DNA is wired. But cravings will only happen if we neglect the food we need. Your body needs fats and carbs just as much as it needs protein and vitamins. Many professional bodybuilders have "cheat foods" or "cheat days" where they eat what they want because they know when to eat it to get the best results. If you have a reasonable amount of each food group throughout the day, you will not give into the craving later. Having a little snack in the day will save you from having a huge snack at night.

I don't need the fillers and additives to taint
the natural goodness of real food.
- Mark Hyman

70. CREDIT

Credit goes to the man who convinces the world,
not the man whom the idea first occurs.
- Franic Darwin

The world is split between those who achieve and those who get the credit. One name tends to stand out for any accomplishment. Even if ten, a thousand, a million, or an entire country helped a goal become a reality, one person usually reaps most of the benefit, fame, and glory.

Why? Well, somebody has to. And it may not necessarily be the one who triggered the original action.

It is difficult to say who gets the credit and who should because it can be down to a matter of opinion. But if you were worried about getting credit for any achievement, nothing would get done.

If you had a great idea, what would spur you on? Would it be that your vision could see the light of day? To make the world a better place? Fame?

Of course, we all want to play some part in making the world greater than it is and we would appreciate some level of recognition for it. It doesn't seem like much to ask. It is a marvel to witness something you created in your mind becoming a part of the world.

But how much credit do we need? It is always welcome and at times necessary. After all, recognition of our work forces society on small or big scales to treat our future works with more faith and belief.

So it is good and, at times, practical to be recognized. But my point is, it should not be sought but accepted when or if it comes. It's like accepting a thank-you. You don't necessarily wait for gratitude, but we are content when we are appreciated.

Even if you get the credit for something, don't be too quick to accept you deserve all the glory. Performers, athletes, and politicians always stress team effort that molded the world into what it is today.

No matter how many great things I have done in my life, someone played a part in every single one of them, be it with a helping hand, guidance, or inspiration. They should get as much credit as anyone else. Or, in the words of Harry Truman, "It's amazing what you can accomplish if you don't care who gets the credit."

To be nameless in worthy deeds exceeds an infamous history.
- Sir Thomas Browne

71. CRITICISM

A critic is a bundle of biases held loosely together by a sense of taste.
- Whitney Balliett

Imagine cooking a meal for someone and watching your friends and family eating it. You then asked the dreaded question - What do you think? More often that not, we just want a compliment and are not looking for an honest answer.

Even though we tend to dread criticism, it's not always bad. Even though constructive criticism can be helpful, some still take offence because it feels like disparagement.

This sort of criticism is like an injection—everyone hates it because it hurts, but it is completely helpful—but only if you allow it to happen. If you are told nothing but good things about your work, it feels good, but you never learn as much as when you do wrong, because then you have something to strive for.

Dustin Hoffman said one of the biggest lessons he ever learned was during the making of the movie *Ishtar*. Upon its release, *Ishtar* was regarded as one of the most unsuccessful movies ever. As heartbreaking as this can be for any performer, Hoffman said he learned a greater lesson from *Ishtar*—he can't always do good work. He needed to figure out why the film went wrong to make sure it never happened again.

If you do nothing but good, that is something to maintain. But a goal to strive for always provides more drive than to maintain something. There is always that sense of, "I'll prove you wrong," or "I'll show them what I can really do." That thought process forces you to push yourself.

I used to do stand-up comedy, and when it went badly, I felt awful because I couldn't blame anyone else. Any fault was completely my own.

But I had no choice but to be better. My friends were proud of me when the gigs went well, and I would feel a million times better. It was the most empowering feeling in the world. But I wouldn't have pushed myself without that niggling criticism in the back of my head.

It might sound counter-intuitive but you should let criticism affect you. Don't deny the criticism, but don't take it personally. If you want people's opinions, be ready to take them. If someone criticizes you about something you didn't expect, don't be too eager to dismiss it. I might help you. After all, if you don't know what your faults are, how can you improve?

You should never be so afraid of criticism that you never try to push yourself. Everyone gets criticism, no matter the level of skill. The only way to avoid criticism is to say nothing, do nothing, and be nothing.

Critics, like eunuchs know how it works but
they can't do it themselves.
- Anon

72. CRUELTY

> Cruelty, like every other vice, requires no motive
> outside of itself; it only requires opportunity.
> - George Eliot

After the Second World War, Nazi soldiers attempted to justify their heinous actions with excuses such as, "We were only following orders." Interestingly, this ridiculous excuse inspired a very interesting test.

Yale psychologist, Stanley Milgram devised a trial to see how willing people are to obey orders, even if those orders conflict with the person's conscience.

In these tests, an authority figure told volunteers to press a button, which sent an electric charge to test subjects in the other room. The shock that the subjects received would stun them, but it was not lethal. The volunteers nearly always accepted this fact, as long as it was in the name of science and every precaution was taken.

But during the experiment, Milgram gradually increased the voltage but explained it was safe because it would take 350 volts to kill a person.

As Milgram increased the voltage, it eventually reached 350 volts, but he assured the volunteers that all was secure, and they should continue.

Do you know what that means? After being told that 350 volts *will* kill the subjects, the doctor asked the volunteers to shock them anyway.

How many do you think pressed the button? Surveys thought it would be 3 percent. It was actually sixty-five percent. Sixty-five percent of volunteers accepted the doctor's order willingly, understanding that it would kill another human being. All it took was a little coaxing and persuasion.

It goes without that this trial was a fake. No person was being electrocuted. It was just a test to see if people would follow orders to commit the most unspeakable acts, simply because they were in a reassuring environment.

As disturbing as this trial was, it was very insightful since it proved that more people harbor the potential to be cruel than we ever imagined.

Even though we want to be good, darkness can creep into any of us. I have a friend whose boyfriend use to beat her all the time. Even thought it's easy to see him as an evil man, he used to be a lovely guy.

But a torn family, violence, losses, tragedies, and deaths took a toll, and it twisted his mind to where he felt beating his girlfriend was the only way he could show he was still in control.

Don't pretend you have no inner demons. Being aware of them is half the battle.

> Cruelty would be delicious if one could only find
> some sort of cruelty that didn't really hurt.
> - George Bernard Shaw

73. CRYING

Are all men in disguise except those crying?
- Dannie Abse

We have always been told to hold back when we are crying, which is practically impossible at a young age, since it is the first thing we do as we enter the world. When we cry for the first few years of our lives, parents will do what they can to comfort us.

But when we are toddlers, our parents' patience wears thin. We have all fallen over and banged into something or scraped our knees and started bawling, only to be told to "be quiet" or "shut up." However, holding back tears isn't a good idea since you are holding back a natural response.

If a parent dismisses a crying child, it can desensitize them, which is one of the reasons why children cry less and less as they get older. We grow up believing that crying doesn't work anymore.

But we do need to cry. Just because we hold our true feelings behind an impenetrable wall doesn't change the fact that our feelings are there.

I use to hate crying. I felt like such a child, even when I was. I couldn't wait to be an adult, because I thought adults never cried since they were big and strong.

But I was wrong. When an adult is deeply hurt, either physically or mentally, they tend to just bottle it up. A lot of adults try not to cry even when they feel the impulse because they want to stay strong. To me, this mentality feels like a big building with crummy rooms inside. They'll crack open more and more until the whole thing collapses.

But because I saw crying as a weakness, I refused to give in for years, even when it was completely justified. I thought it was because I was strong. But it was the opposite. It was because I was too much of a coward to be seen as weak.

I used to hold back all potential negativity, never allowing myself to register it or even feel it. But you can't hold it all back forever. Energy can't be created or destroyed; it only changes its form. So if you're not going to deal with these problems, they will stay.

Let a good cry out. At times, it's exactly what you need. To cry is to still care about something. If your body is starting to well up, the first thing you will probably do is tense up to stop it.

You don't have to. It's so painless to let it flow out of you. Tears want to come out because they have to come out. A good cry here and there is better than a nervous breakdown in a lifetime.

The first voice which I uttered was crying, as all others do.
- Solomon Ibn Gabirol

74. CULTS

A good metaphor can make any idea look good.
- Scott Adams

A religion is a set of beliefs determined by faith, but there are religions that are seen as bankable exploits. In situations like this, the religion can be perceived as a cult.

Cults are scary because they revolve around manipulations and preying on the weak and emotionally frail. When people go through a terrible loss, they might be tempted to believe or give up anything to get closure. Cult members know this and will prey on these sorts of people by using charisma to lure them into their faith.

The gullible believe cult leaders because they know what their followers want to hear. Just by using the right words, one is capable of coloring any perception.

Many cult leaders make promises, and all they ask for in return is faith.

But eventually, they will eventually ask their devoted followers for a staggering amount of money. I have seen it happen firsthand to those close to me, and it is not a pretty sight to watch someone's beliefs become warped and compromised.

A friend of mine, Reece lost his father suddenly. He said he would do anything to speak to him again. Reece spoke to a medium called Pamela that was a member of a "new religion." She promised him that if he joined her cause, he would speak to his deceased father.

But it came for a price. Pamela expected an astronomical amount of money from Reece. However, Reece was so desperate, he gave almost all of father's inheritance to this medium. Unsurprisingly, this charlatan fled to America with Reece's money.

Reece has since spent years warning people and getting the message out about cults after he was twisted himself by this duplicitous "religion." People thought he was a nut and a hypocrite because he was in a cult himself. But that's why his voice needed to be heard more. He has firsthand experience. He knows what they do.

The garden is beautiful without filling it with fairies.
- William Occam
(Occam's Razor)

75. CULTURE

It is not part of true culture to tame tigers,
any more than it is to make sheep ferocious.
- Henry David Thoreau

When I was in Israel, I found it interesting how many women had authoritative jobs, like cops and armed security guards.

In South Korea, I was perplexed by how many people were asleep on the pavement during the daytime. I remember walking around two men asleep on the sidewalk and asking my brother, "Aren't they going to get mugged or attacked?"

"No," my sibling answered. "It's so safe here that you can go to sleep anywhere, and no one will touch you."

I was shocked. I couldn't believe I was in a country where people wouldn't take advantage when a person was so vulnerable. However, this sort of behavior is completely normal in South Korea.

We do not see how ridiculous some aspects of our culture can be because we were born in it. Other cultures may seem wrong, even if they have nothing but positive qualities. Half the world can't understand the pleasures of the other half.

It says a lot about how human beings perceive different cultures with cynicism and skepticism. Any difference can be seen as out of place, illogical, stupid, or flat-out wrong.

People think if something bad happens abroad, it's because it's a bad place. Because my friend, Sean was robbed when he was in Florida, he always warns people about how dangerous it is in America.

But Sean has been robbed many times in his hometown. It's farfetched to encapsulate a nation's danger level in a single bad incident. One robbery in America does not speak for the entire nation.

Being abroad, you will be affected by their politics, their history, and their religion. Their customs may seem alien, even offensive. However, the people there may find your customs wrong, and some of their reasons may have some relevance.

You don't have to accept everything every culture has to offer but you try to understand their customs. It would be a pity to take part in another culture and walk away from it without allowing it to affect you. Experiencing multiple interpretations of the world will allow you to grow.

Who are we as individuals and as a national collective to know if we were born into the best culture? Perhaps one culture agrees with one person and not another. So we shouldn't condemn cultures for being different. Instead, we should try and understand them.

A people without the knowledge of their past history,
origin and culture is like a tree without roots.
- Marcus Garvey

76. CYBER-BULLYING

Cyber-bullies can hide behind a mask of anonymity online and do not
need direct physical access to their victims to do unimaginable harm
- Anna Maria Chavez

A few years ago, my niece, Lilly-Mae made a video on YouTube, which went viral, garnering millions of views. As she was showered by hundreds of positive comments on a daily basis, her self-confidence skyrocketed exponentially.

Although this was a wonderful experience for my niece, it made me acknowledge a growing concern in the world – cyber-bullies. Every once in a while, an internet troll would leave a comment about Lilly-Mae's video that was mean, inappropriate, or racist. Sometimes, the comment had nothing to do with the video in question and it was clear the troll was just baiting.

Thankfully, YouTube filtered out hateful comments like this so Lilly-Mae never saw them. However, it did make me realize that cyber-bullying is a very real and very damaging problem in the world.

Because most schools and businesses across the world have a zero-tolerance policy for violence, this should stop people from being bullied. However, policies like this has made bullies find more creative methods to pick on others. If you learned a bully took the effort and time to make a gif, meme, or webpage solely to upset you, that can be more hurtful than a physical altercation.

Although anyone can fall victim to trolling, it mostly affects children, since social media is such a universal part of their lives. This is disturbing since human beings, especially kids, were never designed to process hundreds or thousands of negative comments.

It's hard to believe but there are people who genuinely like trolling. For them, cyber-bullying is a hobby. They like winding people up online because they get a reaction, which makes them feel powerful.

If you have ever been a victim of cyber-bullying, remember this inspirational story - When Stefani Germanotta talked about becoming a singer in university, her classmates set up a Facebook page dedicated to her called "Stefani Germanotta, you will never be famous." Although Stefani was devastated when she learned about this, she didn't quit. In fact, she went on to become Lady Gaga - the first woman ever to win an Oscar, Grammy, BAFTA, and Golden Globe. Lady Gaga fulfilled her legacy because she refused to let the trolls win. You need to do the same.

If someone online is annoying you, have them muted, blocked, or reported. They don't know you so you shouldn't allow their unhelpful comments to live rent-free in your mind.

Unless and until our society recognizes cyber-bullying for what
it is, the suffering of thousands of silent victims will continue.
- Anna Maria Chavez

77. CYCLES

Worry is a cycle of inefficient thoughts whirling around a center of fear.
- Corrie Ten Boom

There are so many dangerous cycles in life that we can fall into. You worry about your weight, so you starve yourself and then have cravings, so you eat junk food, and then you're back to square one.

But there are also good cycles. Wealthy parents can provide for their children, who grow up to be doctors or lawyers, who use their professions to protect and save those who need help, which gives them inspiration that spreads to their friends and children, and so on.

Then there are cycles in generations. A kid is picked on for being poor, and he becomes resentful. He grows up to become a neglectful father and deserts his daughter because he doesn't want to have a burden. That girl feels unloved and puts pressure on her mother. The mother stresses and turns to drink, taking out her frustration on the daughter with abuse.

But what if you are stuck in a bad cycle? A cycle does not have to continue. Or maybe it can, but it can change its direction. If you don't make a snap decision to break away from bad cycles, they tend to get worse before they get better. You can interject at any point, and divert a bad cycle, transforming it into a good cycle.

A friend of mine called Olivia had a violent boyfriend. She broke up with him for a drug dealer and then dumped that boyfriend for a gangster.

This happened time after time, until she reflected on her vicious cycle and just tried to meet Mr. Right.

Over time, she met a guy called Eli. He wasn't her type, but her types were never good to her, so she thought of trying something different. They moved in together within six months, and after all these years, they are still together.

She was with her bad boys because of what happened in her life. That bad-boy cycle was just a part of a bigger cycle. It's like a small cog in a big machine. But cogs can stop and be fixed or replaced.

Sometimes, you can find a positive cycle in a tragedy if you look at it with the right mentality. My friend, Ward had an aunt that died. At her funeral, Ward's uncle stood at the church podium and told the audience that he had only been informed that day that his wife had saved three children due to her death because she was an organ donor. Ward told me that the applause that followed was absolutely deafening. Even though death is usually seen as a tragic end, Ward saw his aunt's passing as part of a cycle. Her death saved three lives.

So, if you find yourself trapped in a cycle of misery or bad luck, change its direction. Make it go in a direction you want to go.

Without forgiveness life is governed by... a
n endless cycle of resentment and retaliation.
- Roberto Assagioli

78. DAMNATION

It is better to risk saving a guilty man than
to condemn an innocent one.
- Voltaire

True change is often violently resisted. In 1840, Dr. Ignaz Semmelweis was in a hospital delivering babies when he noticed something peculiar. The mothers he was treating tended to die from puerperal fever five days after giving birth. Although Semmelweis knew complications occur when delivering the baby, the autopsies of these mothers showed the deaths weren't caused by childbirth.

One day, a doctor who worked with Semmelweis cut his finger during one of these autopsies. Five days later, he died from puerperal fever.

Semmelweis concluded that the doctors were indirectly spreading the illness by performing an autopsy and then immediately going back up to the delivery room to deliver another baby, therefore infecting the mother.

It was a cycle that could easily be fixed with a simple change—the doctors needed to wash their hands after an autopsy. For this claim, Semmelweis was fired, ridiculed, and spent his last days in an insane asylum. He died humiliated, terrified, and alone simply because he did his job.

Rubin "Hurricane" Carter was a professional boxer before he was falsely accused of triple homicide. It took eighteen years for him to be exonerated, despite the fact that several witnesses of the grisly murders insisted that he was not the killer.

Alan Gell, Kirk Bloodsworth, Randall Dale Adams, and many others were on Death Row; some of them were mere hours from the lethal injection or the electric chair when they were exonerated.

Even though these people suffered, they were the lucky ones. Derek Bentley, Timothy Evans, and Mahmood Hussein Mattan were exonerated of their crimes *after* their death sentence was carried out, meaning they were executed for nothing.

Sometimes, society is so desperate for blood, they condemn those who have done no wrong. They can be so eager to damn someone for a tragedy, they put any face on a crime, regardless of evidence or facts. We are too ready to point fingers and condemn. We often forget that the accused always deserve the benefit of a doubt.

Condemn none: if you can stretch out a helping hand, do so.
If you cannot, fold your hands, bless your brothers,
and let them go their own way.
- Swami Vivekananda

79. DEATH

Dying is nothing. So start by living. It's less fun and it lasts longer.
- Romeo et Jeanette

You have no idea how you are going to react to death until it happens. You may be surprised how you react. When I lost my father, I assumed I would react through anger and depression. Death is such a big thing that it will affect all of our emotions.

When my Dad passed away, I reacted every way possible. I laughed to lessen its impact. I tried to repress the tragedy by distracting myself with trivial tasks. I vomited from stress. I noticed that my mind would latch onto bad stuff, and my attempt at killing negative thoughts made them stronger. I said to myself that this was simply a phase of grief, and I would, over time, have closure.

But death is not like losing anything else. It's a permanent, irrevocable loss. There *is* no absolute closure. We will never be the same after a death, but we try to become stronger when it occurs.

We can use death to change our perspective of life. Maybe it's the ultimate way for us to rethink our life, to remind us to appreciate everything, and stop doing stupid things.

There are others who go the other way and see themselves as being cheated by death. After someone they love has been taken away from them, they might lash out at the world. Although this behavior isn't irregular, it's pointless. The dead always stay dead, but their deaths can have a meaning. The only way we should go on with our lives after losing a person close to us is to honor their name. We shouldn't use them as an excuse to become miserable and hateful.

We try to make peace with the dead but to do so tends to reopen the wounds of sadness. Grief can define us if we let it. That's why we need to find a practical and helpful way to mourn.

If you feel like crying about it, there is no shame in reacting like a human being. We are celebrating all of the great times we had, knowing we can't have them again, but people can dwell on such feelings. That can control us if we allow it.

You can become bitter, wondering what's the point in living and growing attached to others if we are going to lose everyone anyway.

But life is not about losing a lot. It's about losing as little as possible and living it with what you can before it disappears.

The end of man is an action and not a thought,
though it were the noblest.
- Thomas Carlyle

80. DENIAL

A likely impossibility is always preferable
to an unconvincing possibility.
- Aristotle

If everyone says you have a problem, they may be wrong. It is completely possible. But which is more likely—that you are wrong and everybody is right, or vice versa? If an overwhelming number of people are against you in a matter of opinion or action, you have to at least consider you may be wrong, rather than blindly following it out of bravado or because you have "a feeling" that it is the right thing to do.

When you fall victim to denial, you might say to yourself, "I know I'm right, and nothing will ever change my mind."

But what about facts? What about an overwhelming amount of evidence that outweighs your opinion? You can't just believe something because you want to. If the facts aren't in your favor, it's time to rethink where you stand on certain matters.

Denial works like hiding a rubber ball under a bunch of cups, and you have to guess where it is. Every time you get it wrong, it makes it more likely you will succeed next time.

But what if you take away the rubber ball? Every time we look somewhere, and it is not there, it seems less likely that it exists. It's like there are a million cups, and every one of them is empty. You are convinced the ball is in there somewhere, and you're latching onto that last shred of hope that you can find it.

Conspiracy theories usually have a serious problem with denial since they refuse to admit that they can be wrong. One very common tactic they use is Moving the Goalposts. This is when a person keeps changing the rules of an argument, so their point of view is permanently valid. Although this method sounds astoundingly childish, it's disturbingly common.

Most people only listen when we say what they want to hear. You have their attention when it suits them, but your words of wisdom fall on deaf ears once there is some criticism thrown in. People tend to never believe more than what's convenient. Or what's beyond them.

There are times where you don't even need proof to confirm someone's denial. Just because the necessity of proof is beyond us doesn't mean we don't know what is true.

There is no point evaluating dead ends. There is no safety in blindness; there's only blindness.

There is no worse lie than a truth misunderstood by those who hear it.
- William James

81. DEPENDENCY

Dependency is death to initiative, to risk-taking and opportunity. It's time to stop the spread of dependency and fight it like the poison it is.
- Mitt Romney

My favorite fairytale about independence is "The Farmer and His Magic Ring." A struggling farmer goes into town and sees a beggar on the street. Although the farmer is making just enough money to get by, he gives the beggar some change. The beggar says that the farmer was the first person to give him any money all day.

To show the farmer his appreciation, the beggar gave him a ring, which he claims is magic. This ring is said to make any wish come true but can only be used once. The farmer wondered why the beggar didn't use it himself, to which the beggar replied, "You may not get what you wish for."

The farmer was so happy that all his struggling were over, he invited a few friends over for dinner to talk about his sudden good fortune.

But one of his friends was jealous and stole the ring and replaced it with a normal ring. He skipped town and made used the ring to wish that he was rich beyond his wildest dreams. The beggar's warning of "You may not always get what you wish for" was right since the man was crushed to death by a million gold coins.

The farmer didn't realize his ring had been switched, so he and his wife were eager to make a wish. She wanted more cows to make more milk. He wanted a bigger farm.

But the farmer reminded his wife that the ring could only grant one wish. He thought that a bigger farm and more cows were not impossible dreams, so he convinced his wife that they could accomplish these tasks themselves, and they should only use the ring if in dire need.

So they worked twice as hard over many years, until their milk output was far greater and the farm was twice as big.

The wife thought they deserved a reward and said they should wish for a bigger house. The farmer believed that if they kept working, they would eventually be able to afford an extension. This kept happening for many years, until they were in their old age, and they realized they had accomplished all of their dreams without relying on the ring they thought was magic.

This story teaches us that we don't have to rely on luxury. The more we have, the more we tend to rely on it. We forget that we are independent individuals. If we think we need something, we will act like nothing without it.

We have broken the cycle of dependency. People
have found out they're better off working.
- John Engler

82. DEPRESSION

One is never as unhappy as one thinks, nor as happy as one hopes.
- Dud de la Rochefoucauld

Depression is a clinical disorder that makes a person feel pangs of intense fear, sadness, or anger. Although depression is usually caused after suffering a tragedy, it can develop at any time, seemingly for no reason. Depression is genetic, meaning it's likely you will suffer from it if one or both of your parents have it. It's so unbearable that many depressed people say the illness is the worst thing about their lives.

Now, I am not going to suggest that you can magically fix depression with advice. It needs medication and treatment.

But there are people who know they suffer from depression but don't take steps to treat it. They might refuse medication because they see it as a sign of weakness or they're worried about side effects.

I am speaking from experience because I suffered manic depression for six years. During this period, I would experience a pang of numbing dread 31 times a day. It made my life a daily struggle.

Desperate for a cure, I tried everything – Listening to music, exercise, mediation, venting, punching a pillow, walking, joking about it, hypnotism, counselling. And yet, nothing seemed to work. Feeling defeated, I decided to take antidepressants.

Do you know how long it took for my depression to disappear? One day. I have been taking my medication for years now and have never felt depressed since nor have I suffered side effects. For years, I absolutely believed depression was an inescapable burde that would weigh me down for the rest of my life. Thanks to my tablets, I can close that chapter of my life forever.

I am absolutely not suggesting that medication is the answer. Different things work for different people. But you won't know what works for you unless you try potential remedies.

If you don't know where to start, talk to your friends and family. I expected some of them to be dismissive, saying comments like, 'Suck it up,' and 'You can beat depression just with willpower.' Thankfully, everyone I spoke to was incredibly understanding and pushed me to seek help.

It might be frustrating to seek out the remedy that works for you trying to find all sorts of things to take the edge off your depression but it's better than doing nothing. Remember – complaining about depression has never cured depression. You need to do something about it.

Depression is frozen anger.
- Sigmund Freud

83. DESENSITIZATION

That's the great paradox of living on this earth, that in the midst of great pain you can have great joy as well. If we didn't have those things, we'd just be numb.
- Kathy Matthea

How many times in a movie have you seen a hero being blown up in an explosion, only to pick himself up straight away, even if he was smashed against a wall?

The majority of people don't realize that proximity to an explosion can be lethal, and if you're knocked into the air, it is usually fatal because your lungs can't take the force.

We see people getting shot in movies so often nowadays that we don't take in the fact that a chunk of metal tears through muscle tissue, rips arteries, cracks bones, and shreds organs.

Even when we watch violence like this on the news, it can look so simple and anticlimactic, we can't grasp the pain behind it, the inner battle the body must go through to stand a chance to survive.

What I'm trying to say is that we can become deadened. The first time we have a glimpse of death or tragedy, we are bound to become fearful. Like anything else, good or bad, it's not as traumatic the second time. Or the time after that.

We become desensitized by some things but not to others. It's curious to see someone's heart melt when they see a puppy but don't bat an eyelid at a penniless beggar. A baby is the most adorable thing in the world, but jokes about Middle Eastern war and poverty are not uncommon. It's not hypocritical. It's self-preservation. If you weren't desensitized to all the world's hardships, you would be a nervous wreck.

But we can also become deadened to personal issues. We can be desensitized to bullying, to punishment, and to not being listened to or cared about.

At times, we divorce our minds from who a person is and what he or she does. We can be nasty to cops because "they are all pigs," but we expect them to help us when a crime has been committed against us. We jeer at actors for "not having a real job" and then go home and watch a movie. We mock the rich for "not giving a damn about the poor people," but we all want to be rich.

It's easy to switch off the emotional side of us, but sometimes, we just need to feel human. The only thing worse than your heart breaking is your heart hardening.

People become desensitized to many things going on around them. It is because always see it on the tv, hear it on the radio, read or watch it on the internet, hear about it at work, etc. Then immortal acts are turned to a deaf ear. Then no one wants to take action or speak up for what's right.
- Amaka Imani Nkosazana

84. DESIGNATION

What's in a name?
- Juliet
(Romeo and Juliet)

If someone asked who you were and didn't mean your name, how would you answer?

What external link would you answer with? If a Northern London mechanic described himself as a Northern London mechanic, he has designated himself with where he is from and what his job is. But is that who he is? Maybe those two things are the most important parts of his life. Or maybe it's something much deeper.

How hard is it to identify yourself without mentioning your kin, skills, experience, history, heritage, language, ethnicity, marriage, children, parents, partners, home, achievements, failures, thoughts, occupations, deeds, mistakes? Can it be done? Can we even express who we truly are when we are limited to words? Or are actions needed? Or can it be done at all?

Maybe you are identified by all of these things. Surely if you are designated by one or another of these things mentioned, that must be a pretty accurate portrayal of who you really are. It's not just about with what you designate yourself but why.

People might see you as chilled-out, but the real you is waiting to be let out. You just may not know how to express yourself.

It's important to understand where your motivations come from, not just knowing that you have them. Learning of their origins helps you understand yourself. Exploring them makes them more noticeable, and you will discern that a lot of your wants start to tie together and formulate a whole.

You will designate your whole life. You do it yourself, and people will do it for you. It will change over time or certain situations. You will be designated as the foreigner, the kid, the idiot, the father, the enemy, or the friend, and you will become these labels if you start to believe them. Hearing something enough times can make it become so. You can challenge or disqualify these labels if you choose to.

You are in charge of your own life, and you can decide who you are by understanding what you are. Don't get caught up in what the whole world thinks of you. We usually don't understand ourselves, so how likely is it that the rest of the world will understand? Decide who you are. Decide what is important for you.

One man that has a mind and knows it can
always beat ten men who haven't and don't.
- George Bernard Shaw

85. DESTINY

As far as we can discern, the sole purpose of human existence is
to kindle a light of meaning in the darkness of mere being.
- C.G. Jung
(Memories, Dreams, Reflection)

To talk about destiny is difficult without spouting fortune-cookie wisdom. Not that fortune cookies are wrong (on the contrary, I wouldn't be surprised if some quotes in this book are hidden inside them.) But destiny is one of the most sought-out notions for us to understand, while ironically the most indistinguishable.

We are under the impression that we cannot control our own destinies, but we were created to create ourselves.

If you believe in your own destiny, if you believe that there are forces out there that will set you to do great things, then that is okay.

But it doesn't give you the right to sit back and wait for that day. You have to go for it yourself. No one fulfills his lot while sitting on his backside, and if he does, I don't see how it would make that person feel fulfilled. Don't act like you need cosmic permission to do basic actions. You need to seize the day.

Don't act like you can settle for second best. Nobody's vocation was meant to come second. We only do that because we quit trying. Our rewards fall short of what we believe we deserve.

Destiny is not even a concept spoken about anymore with real conviction. It's more to do with fairy tales, comics, and mythology. Providence lies in myth, and we see it as stories, forgetting that we can also defeat incredible obstacles.

But what's the aim of seeking a seemingly unobtainable, even invisible, or perhaps nonexistent goal?

We are never going to get all of the answers we want in life, but we can find some of them. Hypothetically, if we knew everything at the beginning of our lives, then it might feel like we cheated ourselves. If we found the answers to all of life's questions, life would no longer have purpose, so we reject the prize in favor of the quest.

So what is your destiny? Or what sort of destiny should you have? There are obvious goals, like power or wealth, but surely it's more fun and adventurous to go down a path that doesn't exist yet, so you can create a brand new destiny. Don't go down the same road everybody else does. Make your own. Make one only you wish to venture on.

Free will and destiny are two different paths that will hopefully meet each other at the end of a long road.

Coincidence is the word we use when we can't see the levers and pulleys.
- Emma Bull

86. DIAGNOSIS

Most cancer-related deaths can be prevented through simple
and painless preventive measures. A late diagnosis can
result in more serious, long-term consequences.
- Olympia Snowe

Did you know that malaria was thought to be a virus caused by "bad air?" Only in the 1930s was this disease associated with the mosquito. It's scary that we assumed the most common death in humankind was left to chance, rather than something that could be inoculated against, corrected, and understood. It makes you wonder if there are other disorders with an external source, outside the parameters of bad luck? Let me give you an example.

My friend Dolly's husband, Michael, started to feel ill. He went to doctors numerous times, and they said his debilitating health was caused by stress or a virus. Michael was afraid of coming across as a hypochondriac or that he was simply falling victim to psychosomatic symptoms so he soldiered on.

But he started to lose a lot of weight. He felt weaker, less energetic, and more prone to sickness. After being turned away by his regular doctor too many times, he sought a clinic that dealt with more obscure disorders.

About explaining his symptoms, he later said, "It was the first time in over a year where doctors were listening to my problems without looking at me as if I was crazy." They knew what it was. A parasite piggybacked into his immune system when he was abroad in Africa. It took over a year to develop, so Michael never associated his deteriorating health with his travels long past.

Michael is doing much better. He is still weak and will have a damaged immune system because he left it too long before treating the problem.

Some disorders can be tricky to diagnose, and we don't have the time or the money, but it can prevent us from suffering a lot of hardship. My friend, Henry has dyspraxia. People with this disorder tend to get diagnosed before they are twelve years old. But Henry didn't know about his condition until he was twenty-five. He hated making excuses, so when his dyspraxia kicked in, he would blame it on stress, fatigue, or laziness. He didn't want to blame it on a disorder, because he thought he would be making excuses. If he didn't acknowledge it, he would naturally work twice as hard. When he eventually gave in and discusses his condition to his specialist, she said it was a commendable mentality but nevertheless damaging because he had a disorder that hadn't been dealt with professionally for twenty years.

We may fall to psychosomatic tendencies at times, but we know when something is wrong. We know when it is not just "in our heads." If you have a problem, and it is simply not going away, listen to your gut.

The power of intuitive understanding will protect you from harm.
- Lao Tzu

87. DIALECT

I wonder if Americans aren't fooled by our accent into
detecting brilliance that may not really be there.
- Stephen Fry

If you've been living in the same place for most of your life, you may not realize how your accent sounds. You may not be able to hear it or differentiate it from others.

Your voice develops separately to your accent. With your voice, you will have many mild speech variations (I don't mean lisps or stutters but slightly different ways of saying certain sounds or letters.)

Your accent develops from decades, centuries, and millennia of voice patterns changing over and over. Your accent can tell who you are as a person.

If you think that is absolutely untrue, you will still be judged by it.

I shouldn't complain. I am blessed with an Irish accent that comes across as friendly, funny, and warm. However, I find it annoying, repetitive, and unoriginal when I heard "I love your accent!" for the twentieth time when I moved to England … on the first day.

It could be much worse. One of my friends, Zuleika, has lived in England her entire life. Her father is English and her mother is Indian. But because of her Indian accent and dark complexion, she is often told to "go back to your own country" even though she's already there.

Some say, "I don't have an accent!" Three percent of people have what is known as RP, or received pronunciation. This is a perfectly clear dialect that gives no sense of the original accent or where that person is originally from.

Depending on your accent, you may be regarded as a simpleton, an aggressor, or a braggart. Because of this, you may feel like you want to hide your accent. My accent used to be so thick that I was told I would never get work outside of Ireland.

So, I tried to get rid my accent. Although I managed to tone down my dialect after performing vocal exercises for years, I suffered intense pains in my jaw from tension because I was trying to speak in an unnatural way.

I didn't realize that although there can be bad connotations with an accent, there may also be good ones. An accent may come across perhaps as romantic or friendly. If you know the good qualities your accent possesses, play them up! If you were born with an accent that naturally sounds friendly, why wouldn't you use it to your advantage? You don't have to work on it! It's there when you entered this world. An instruction manual is not necessary. Become conscious of your accent's traits and then use them to your advantage.

I learned to change my accent. In England, your accent identifies you
very strongly with a class, and I did not want to be held back.
- Sting

88. DISCOVERY

A man's errors are his portals of discovery.
- James Joyce

Numerous times, we think we have cracked the mystery that is life, but then we realize there is so much more. It's like finishing a massive jigsaw puzzle and then finding another piece. We want to make discoveries—about life, about ourselves, those close to us, the way we live—and it is tempting to go to the other side of the planet to make these discoveries, while everyone on that side of the globe is coming over here to find the answers.

That's not innovation. That's escapism. Just because something is a challenge doesn't mean we should go for it.

Just because a path isn't well lit does not mean it cannot be walked on.

Just because the answer is right in front of us doesn't mean we have to go around it. A breakthrough about ourselves can come anywhere—in a vision, guidance from a friend, or just from a long, uninterrupted thought.

Two things that motivate people to achieve success: inspiration and desperation. We shouldn't wait until we get desperate. We must be ready to perform the seemingly impossible now. The greater the difficulty of a task, the greater the glory will be by surmounting it. We must rise to the top of whatever heap we are thrown to. We can't be everywhere at once, so we should be somewhere that counts so we can make a difference.

But we must not be rash about discoveries. You may discover you are not as strong as you thought you were when you crumble unexpectedly, but you must turn this on its head and look at it—look at everything positively and productively.

I went from feeling unstoppable to being utterly helpless in less than a year because I didn't ask myself the big questions in life. I dodged them for years and refused to deal with a lot of problems I had. I was afraid of being weak, but adapting to temporary conveniences isn't a permanent solution. Even in a well-tended garden, weeds will grow.

We don't need to be strong to *be* strong. There are times where we need to fall apart to put ourselves back together.

When you go on a journey of self-discovery, expect the unexpected. Expect to find things that you assumed you didn't have or problems you thought were dealt with a long time ago. Light must exist with dark. The knotted, ugly, twisted roots of a tree are just as important as the green leaves soaking up the sun. Don't expect the answer to life to be a simple philosophy that counters all odds. You can have all the facts and be wrong. We need to make time to nurture ourselves and ask what we really want.

Discovery consists of seeing what everybody has
seen and thinking what nobody has thought.
- Albert von Szent-Gyorgyi

89. DISMISSAL

Mediocre minds usually dismiss anything which
reaches beyond their own understanding.
- Francois de La Rochefoucauld

Some scientists or experts in their fields thought they have found everything that there is in the universe, and every other possibility is just science-fiction drivel. In 1900, it was said that everything that could be invented and discovered had been.

But science fiction still has science in it. Just because we invented and learned so much since then doesn't mean we're finished creating and learning.

Cynics will only believe things when they see them and probably not even then. People like this usually say, "Don't believe everything you hear," but I say, "Don't dismiss everything you hear."

Society has a common hatred for new ideas, not because they believe the ideas themselves are wrong but because of the likely probability that they themselves are wrong.

There are times when people act like they don't want there to be more than there is. That's why they challenge and question everything there could be. They become so accustomed to the way things are, even when things are bad, that they reject new ideas and possibilities, even if those ideas can make lives better.

Our own biology does this. Imagine you need a heart transplant desperately, or you will die. After you receive a new heart, do you think your life will be back to normal?

No. Even though your heart is keeping you alive, your antibodies will attack it for the rest of your life because they perceive it as an alien threat because it's not your original heart. They attack it to protect the body, even though it's the only thing keeping the body alive. We reject the new, even if it is helpful, convenient, practical, and necessary.

Everything is impossible because it seems so, but impossible things have happened before. Steve Jobs was fired when he first talked about a one-inch-thin portable television that would let you see and speak to anyone in the world, which also held information on every subject imaginable. This concept became the iPad.

That idea stayed in his head for thirty years before it became a reality because he didn't give up on his supposed fantastical invention. Imagine what impossible invention he had in his head at the time of his death that he was hoping to make thirty years in the future. We can't even imagine what the next impossibility for humanity to achieve will be.

If people have split views about your work, I think it's flattering.
I'd rather have them feel something about it than dismiss it.
- Stephen Sondheim

90. DISORDERS

Concealing an illness is like keeping a beach ball under water.
- Karen Duffy

There are so many disorders that are misunderstood. They can range from something frustrating, like dyslexia, to a problem as scary as bipolar, as disheartening as dementia, or as hazardous as schizophrenia. What is even scarier than having one of these problems is not knowing you have it, not comprehending when another person has it, or not knowing how the disorder truly works.

Years ago, I volunteered for a charity organization called Halow that looked out for young people with disabilities. During that time, I was introduced to dozens of people with disorders I had never heard of. It was intimidating, and I felt out of my depth, and I realized that there is so much more to learn about what can affect people.

It's easy to categorize someone with a disorder as "crazy." But, with a little education, we can understand the condition. If you have a disorder, you may feel like it is something that you have to put up with. But this isn't always the case.

My classmate, Tanya was dyslexic and was told it was incurable. She wanted to be an actress but refused to read scripts and demanded that other people read them for her.

But my friend, Lorelei, who had Irlen syndrome dyslexia, had a different way of dealing with her problem. After getting corrective glasses and understanding her disorder, she was able to read much better. She will always struggle, but she can manage better now because she realized what the problem was, acknowledged she needed help, and then sought it out. Although Tanya made an excuse out of her dyslexia, Lorelei found a way around it.

Even if you have treated your disorder, that doesn't mean it's gone for good. My friend, Jackie suffers from arrhythmia, meaning she has an irregular heartbeat. Her heart beats too fast when she is stressed, which induces panic attacks. Because she knows how to deal with it, she has not suffered from anxiety in years.

However, she still checks to see if she feels okay, psychologically and physically, so she is prepared if her anxiety come back. She acknowledges that her panic attacks may return. That's not paranoia. That's preparation. Maybe she will never suffer from anxiety again. But if she does, she will be ready.

When it's your body, your mind, your sanity, or your life; you need to do more than live with it. You can't reject, dismiss, and deny. You need to accept it, experiment, inquire, understand, control, and hopefully expunge.

The secret of learning to be sick is this: Illness doesn't
make you less of what you were. You are still you.
- Tony Snow

91. DISTRACTION

Acclaim is a distraction.
- James Broughton

We are often distracted by curiosities in life. You may have goals you wish to achieve within the next few hours, days, weeks, months, or years. You may have started prioritizing aspects of your life to ensure that these attainable goals will become a reality. You may be aware of difficulties, obstacles, and the improbability of obtaining more extreme goals.

The journey to your goals can be elongated unnecessarily, however, by distraction. Diversions can turn hours into days, days into months, months into years, and years into a lifetime. A distraction can turn a simple goal into something you can "do later" or a big goal into something that's "too hard to do."

Let's say you have five things to do. They can be a few basic tasks: exercise, pick up shopping, cook, and meet a friend.

You've worked it out in your head how long it will take to do these things, but you are not taking into consideration simple distractions such as your SmartPhone, an unexpected phone call, a sudden thunderstorm, or a visitor. If one thing is delayed, it can set off a chain reaction.

When I was a teenager, we played a game in school. I wrapped my index finger and thumb together to form a circle and held it below my waist, and I would have to make someone look at it. If they did, they would get a punch.

I am not advertising this game, but it fascinated me because the other person would be compelled to look even though they knew the consequences of doing so.

It's human nature to be wooed by something that catches our attention, causing us to follow it on impulsive and childish curiosity.We are naturally intrigued by what we don't know, enticed by the unknown, and blinded by mystery. Distractions usually look captivating or harmless, but they can be anything but that.

Distractions can be good or bad. If I have a bad day at work, I want to go home and watch television to relax

A good distraction is fine as long as it doesn't turn into procrastination. A good distraction gives you time to unwind and process what's happened in your day.

You can also use distractions as an excuse to be lazy. You will always find a distraction if you are looking for one. It's your choice. Go to the door that's open, not the one that's closed.

Art is the fatal net which catches these strange moments
on the wing like mysterious butterflies, fleeing the
innocence and distraction of common men.
- Giorgio de Chirico

92. DOGMA

The cosmos is a gigantic flywheel, making 10,000 revolutions a minute.
Man is a sick fly taking a dizzy ride on it. Religion is the theory that
the wheel was designed and set spinning to give him the ride.
- H. L. Mencken

When I was in primary school, my classmate, Mullins asked my religion teacher, "Why was Mary in a stable when Jesus was born? I thought Joseph was a carpenter." He was sent home, and his parents were brought in to discuss Mullins's disrespect of religion. He was six years old. He was a boy who was punished for asking a simple question. That was my first taste of dogma as a child.

While the Council of Nicaea wrote the Bible in AD 325, they decided what went in and what was left out. Three hundred thousand documents that didn't make it into the final cut are stored in the Vatican vault. Who knows what else nearly made it into the Holy Book? Who knows what else society could have believed or been forced to believe through scare tactics or indoctrination? Their documentations were written by people, not God.

I am not an antitheist, but I am against abusing power in the name of anything: God, power, revenge, love, or family. Even with good intentions, abuse is still abuse. Religion stops being about belief when it starts relying on control.

It's great to believe in God but it can be dangerous to push your beliefs. Seeing a problem as God's will prevents us from solving it. When the Black Death swept through Europe, many people saw it as the wrath of God.. Doctors thought the plague originated from a virus, and so, took steps to cure humanity from its effects. How much damage would the bubonic plague have caused if humanity just accepted their doom?

You can't be adamant in your beliefs unless you know what those beliefs are based on. If you claim to be devout to your faith, you mut be knowledgeable of your sources. Some claim the Bible is the Word of God, yet they've never read it.

Don't just accept your religion because you were born into it. You would have a different religion if you were born on any other continent. It's good to keep this in mind when people condemn a religious belief but defend their own.

I am not suggesting we do away with religion, but we need to stand for what religion originally stood for, which is love and acceptance and peace.

Unfortunately, it's human nature to get defensive over that which we hold dear, which then twists religion into fear-mongering. This is what gives religion a bad name, but it's not religion itself that's the problem; it's the insecurities that lie in every human being. If we don't let these flaws get in the way, we will never fall into the trap of dogma.

A casual stroll through the lunatic asylums
shows that faith does not prove anything.
- Friedrich William Nietzsche

93. DOUBLE-STANDARDS

It is forbidden to kill; therefore all murderers are punished unless they kill in large numbers and to the sound of trumpets.
- Voltaire

Most of the pet peeves we have are things we believe we don't do. If you regularly complain about bad drivers, it's a safe assumption you think you are a great driver.

But when someone accuses you of doing the very thing that you complain about, you try to justify your actions.

You can make jokes about people going through hard times and claim that these are justified because the joke is just a way to release tension, and you don't mean any harm. But jokes about you and your insecurities are insulting and over the line because that's "different."

You might say people shouldn't judge you for your appearance, but you would never date a person who's overweight.

These are all common double standards, but the most popular one is that everyone has double standards except you. This was tested in Stanford University and became known as the "bias blind spot." In this exam, people were asked how often they would be affected by different biases compare to normal people.

Nearly everyone said they were among the few who never gave into their biases. But this can't be possible, because the majority can't all think they are in the minority!

Even when this fact was established to the participant, they firmly believed that everyone else must have overestimated themselves, but they themselves didn't.

Double standards are a psychological trick to keep us feeling significant. The test suggested that we are more inclined than ever to give into double standards, thanks to every television show, movie, book, novel, and story that forces us to heavily identify with characters that are misunderstood, underestimated, and underused.

We are all prone to this trait at one point or another. Admitting to your own self-hypocrisy can help you deal with excuses, limitations, and insecurities. If you have a serious problem with a person, group, or topic, is it because that person genuinely offends you, or is it because you see a part of yourself in that person? Do you hate someone because that person reminds you that you hate yourself? Figure out the source of your problems. The source can be you.

Every man carries two bags about with him, one in front and one behind, and both are packed full of faults. The bag in front contains his neighbors faults, the one behind his own. Hence it is that men do not see their own faults, but never fail to see those of others.
- Aesop

94. DRAMA

Gossip is called gossip because it's not always the truth.
- Justin Timberlake

We all get caught up in our own microcosm of life. We want to get on with our lives, but we can only do that if we accept and deal with our insecurities. This is a lot of hard work, so the easiest way to make an excuse out of our problems is to overdramatize them.

We act like a broken fingernail is petrifying. Being unable to find specific shoes means that we cannot go out tonight. Forgetting where we put our phone is the end of the world.

If you think about all of the things you complain and worry about in a week—exams, work, money, bills, and all of the other stuff like gossip and other trivial things—how much of it do you truthfully believe is worth worrying about?

Drama is rarely worth fretting about since there may be no truth to it at all. The zebra analogy is a good example of this. When a patient had mild symptoms, he shouldn't be diagnosed with an exotic illness. As the old saying goes, "When you hear hooves, don't expect a zebra." If you see a two people chatting, they are probably not flirting, kissing, dating, or cheating on their partners. They are probably having a chat. There's no need to overdress it.

Drama can be dangerous because if you are constantly obsessed with dramatizing the little things, you might find it difficult to deal with a real problem. If you freak out because you miss a bus and have to wait ten more minutes, imagine how you would react if your bank account was frozen or if you were suddenly fired.

My father's business friend had a terrible financial loss, losing all his money. Some could see this, at best, as the beginning of depression and, at worse, the road to suicide.

But he saw it as nothing more than a minor setback. He got back on his feet and restarted his business.

There is no need to act like any small problem is the end of the world. It is only the end of a small chapter of your life. It's best to wait until the epilogue before you get dramatic.

As big as all the drama in your life seems to be, it's just the prologue. You will have plenty of time for real drama later in life.

Serenity isn't boredom. Drama addiction is.
- Anon

95. DREAMS

Our last thoughts before we sleep follow us into our slumber.
Make the most of your last thoughts.
- Lisa Nichols

In *The Matrix*, Morpheus is the resistance leader who is tasked with finding the chosen one, Neo. In the first half of the movie, Morpheus communicates to Neo through our world, which he calls the dream world.

This character is based on the Greek god of dreams, who is also called Morpheus. The Greeks believed that the people you meet in your dreams—family, lovers, friends, enemies—were all the same person: Morpheus. They believed this deity morphed into different guises to help people connect with themselves while giving them advice.

Mythology can explain things better than reality sometimes. Even though the concept of Morpheus sounds like pure fiction, there is some truth to it. Each character that we interact with in our dreams is the same person. It's not an ancient god; it's our subconscious. Our subconscious is trying to communicate a message of import. But what is it?

Our body needs to sleep. Not just because it is physically exhausted and drained but because it has to mentally recharge and psychologically unwind. We take in more data than we think we do every waking moment of every day.

Even when our physical body is at its most inactive, our mind is going a million miles a second, bombarding us with so many images that we only remember the bare bones.

You may not remember your dream, but you know you had a dream. You know it was important or funny or poetic, but you may not have a clue what happened. It's because it is all in the subconscious part of the brain. When we are conscious, all the dreams start to filter out because it's a different section of the mind.

But that's the funny thing. We think that we don't always use the subconscious part of our brains. The truth is we cannot turn it off. The conscious part of our mind will take a break after fourteen hours or so, but the subconscious has to calculate and comprehend every single detail of life.

It's a common phrase to "follow your dreams," but that is more literal than you might imagine. Elias Howe's first vision of a sewing machine was in a dream. The same thing happened to Dmitri Mendeleev when he concocted the periodic table. Imagine how different life would be if those ideas never went beyond the dream.

Keep a journal of your dreams if you have an idea, or if they bother you, or you are simply curious.

There is a place where dreams survive.
- Stan Bush

96. DRINK

Always do sober what you said you would do drunk. That will teach ya.
- Ernest Hemingway

I have seen my fair share of alcoholics and lived with several. People drink for many reasons—relieve stress, to reward themselves, to loosen up, to forget their troubles, or to forget they are alcoholics.

Even though I have been a teetotaler since 2004, I am not suggesting you should renounce drinking. If you take pleasure in having a beer or wine, go for it! I'm not even going to scare you with false information by claiming alcohol kills brain cells. This is not a Stop Drinking book, but I still need to remind you of the dangers of alcohol.

We drink to drown our sorrows, but sorrows swim. Drinking your problems away is like using an anesthetic on a wound. It numbs the pain, but you still need to treat the problem.

Alcohol is usually used as an excuse. We cannot be blameless in our drunken actions, because we chose to put the alcohol in our bodies. We can't use excuses to justify what is done and what is said while intoxicated. What is said while drunk has been thought beforehand.

There are some people who are thought to perceive alcoholism as a disease. This mentality prevents an alcoholic from ever getting over his problem. It's tolerated instead of dealt with. Alcoholism should never be considered a disease since you can't catch it. You choose to drink, so you can choose to stop.

Some people seem to change into a different person when they drink, and they feel like this gives them free license to get away scot-free with any stupid action. But you are what you drink. We like to think that who we become when we're drunk is not us.

But different types of alcohol bring out different aspects of you. Alcohol can bring out the paranoid you, or the lustful you, or the depressed you. But they are all still you at the end of the day.

All these feelings of anger, resentment, or fear you may have while intoxicated do not sprout from nowhere. They have always been in us, but a drink too many may make them come out.

You may not know these feelings are there until you drink more than you can handle and then have a violent outburst or a meltdown. If you become aware of this, you can use it to your advantage. You can ask, "Why do I only feel depressed now? Now that I know this is a problem, what can I do to correct it?"

You don't need to stop drinking entirely like I did, but asking questions like this can help you enjoy it more and avoid doing silly or dangerous things while under the influence.

Never trust a brilliant idea until it survives the hangover.
- Ernest Hemingway

97. DRONE

Without the element of uncertainty, the bringing off of even the greatest triumph would be dull, routine and eminently unsatisfying.
- J. Paul Getty

Drone bees accumulate honey for the hive. Their life is performing this mundane but compulsory activity until the day they die. Although this behavior is expected from bees, humans can easily fall into such a lifestyle by obeying orders at work or being trapped in a world of routine.

Life can wear you down. Hardly any person is born with a bleak outlook of the world. Life batters that mentality into you. No one wants to be despondent.

Then life tells you to shut up, be quiet, and do this and that. We are hammered by rules, limits, and regulations, which can outweigh aspirations, desires, and needs. That situation is easy to fall into because so much of the beginning of our lives involves being forced to obey and doing what others want us to do, like taking orders from our parents or teachers.

When we hit puberty, some people become rebellious and defiant, but this period usually doesn't' last long since we have to get jobs to survive. So now we have to become drones, performing menial tasks, not just to avoid punishment but for self-preservation.

Although we all feel like an automaton at some point, we actually have more freedom than ever before. There are more choices and fewer limits than ever before. Nowadays, many of us can work from home and live a more comfortable life than we could've ever imagined.

And yet, we still find ourselves stuck in repetitive patterns, causing us to go through the motions of the day without even thinking about it.

You can become a drone without even noticing. You can find yourself trapped in a monotonous routine because you don't stand up for yourself. Or maybe you go along with everyone else to social activities even though you have no impulse to do so. Or maybe you find yourself complaining about the same stuff every day.

You may not get out of your job because you have certain responsibilities, and you can't let the team down. Thoughts like this will ensure that you will never do what you really want, and you will never be fully satisfied.

You don't have to be just a small cog in a big machine. Not all of the parts have to be there for something to work. Break the chain before it breaks you.

As long as habit and routine dictate the pattern of living,
new dimensions of the soul will not emerge.
- Henry Van Dyke

98. DRUGS

Drugs are a bet with your mind.
- Jim Morrison

A drug is any substance that alters normal bodily functions when absorbed into the body. The most simple and common drug is caffeine. This psychoactive drug stimulates the body with a sudden burst of energy, which allows the individual to stay active and energetic.

Dependency on caffeinated drinks will create addiction and side effects, like headaches, crankiness, and lethargy. That is a drug side effect at its most tame. Now let's look at the more extreme effects.

There are so many types of drugs—recreational, chemical, administrative—and they can be used for spiritual, medical, or personal reasons.

I used to be uncompromising in my opinion on drugs. I thought they were all bad, but I realized that they can be necessary for medication, and there are legal drugs that can be beneficial within reason and control.

A drug, by definition, changes the way your body and mind works. Remember that the next time you want to have some "fun."

Drugs are supposedly escapism and freedom in pill form. Ironically, they make you feel more imprisoned as you depend on them more. We always try to find the answer to our problems. If one thing doesn't have the answer, we try somewhere else.

The last resort is in a pill or needle, and the mind works in a way so you have this psychedelic experience, where you believe the answer is right behind this door, but you don't have the right key to open it. You have to keep going back to it, but every time you reach that same door, the lock has changed. It's a never-ending journey. The door never opens. Chances are, you already found the answer at some random moment in your life. You just didn't notice because it wasn't as epic or awe-inspiring as you had hoped. You don't need an external source, especially a volatile stimulant, to decide what to do in life.

Some people use the weakest arguments to justify the usage of drugs, such as, "They don't kill as often as they say. Fatty foods, smoking and drink kill way more."

It's true that drugs don't kill people as much as smoking or a bad diet. But I have never heard of anyone take one smoke, one beer, one burger, and dying of it that same day.

Also, death isn't the only the consequence of drugs. Other results include ruining your health, home, mind, friends, partner, body, family, job, mind, or life. The truth is, you start doing drugs when you can't sink any lower … and then you do.

If you are happy, you don't need drugs.
If you're not, then they are not helping.
- Anon

99. EGO

The man who is always talking about being a gentleman never is one.
- R.S. Surtees

Although ego means self-assurance and self-esteem, its definition is often linked to arrogance. When we have an ego boost, we want to maintain it. Nobody wants to feel insignificant, so we can become addicted to putting people down to make ourselves feel powerful.

People are most egotistic when they are moving up the ladder of success, not because they are going to make it, but because they won't. If you only had one chance to rub it in people's faces, would you take it?

Ego is to show people what we have, but it does the opposite. Talking about oneself is a means of concealing one's insecurities.

If you were genuinely content in an aspect in your life, would you need to declare it to the world? A lot of people boast about their partners, yet these same people's relationships never last long and tend to end horrifically. People like this brag because they won't have a chance to boast when it falls apart. We only brag about what we know won't last.

It's tempting to have a big ego. It makes us feel powerful and important. There are times when people will admire you for your looks, your efficiency at work, your inner strength during hard times, or your recent achievements. This can give you a boost in self-belief, but we have to be careful that we don't believe our own hype, or our confidence will overweigh our accomplishments and ability.

We can't rely on people feeding our ego. A fool always finds a greater fool who admires him, and flatterers live at the expense of the listeners.

Becoming an egomaniac doesn't just stem from achievement but a lack of achievement. We get frustrated that we are not recognized for our success, while other people are recognized for theirs. I've seen many actors in minor roles get frustrated when the main actor doesn't know his lines or is not performing to the best of his or her ability. They acted resentful, claiming they could perform the part much better.

But when we make claims like this, we don't take into account the extra responsibility that comes with extra work. It's easy to sound confident when you are not in the spotlight. Anyone can hold the helm when the sea is calm.

Goals must never be from your ego, but problems that cry for a solution.
- Robert H. Schuller

100. EMOTION

When dealing with people, remember you are not
dealing with creatures of logic, but creatures of emotion.
- Dale Carnegie

Emotion can feel like a straightjacket. When we are taken by an emotion momentarily, our reasoning, logic, and control are suspended. We don't want to lose control. That is why we hold emotions back. You might think you are strong because you haven't cried in years, but your brain is still firing out more emotion than you can imagine.

Compartmentalization is a concept of dividing good and bad thoughts, memories, and energies. The notion was originally a regulation for fire protection, structuring subdivisions to limit the spreading of fire. This concept made its way into the psychological world, as the concept is the same—sealing off a danger to prevent damage.

Ironically, blocking off fire doesn't stop it. Instead, compartmentalization forces the flames to build and eventually explode, causing more damage than anyone could've anticipated. Unfortunately, if we try to block our emotions, we will have a similar outcome.

Men may not be as outwardly emotional as women, but that doesn't mean they feel less or hurt less. Men may not express emotion as much, but it's still there, internally.

We all fall victim to emotion, either by letting it consume us or not using it enough. It's out of control when we are kids, and we show it less and less as we age, but it always stays as strong.

Women are more connected to their outward emotions, so they suffer the opposite problem—over-expressing. It's great to connect to a natural reaction, but like everything else, overindulgence is unhelpful.

It's ironic how whether you show too much emotion or not enough, you can end up as a nervous wreck. But because our emotions are a key part of who we are, we need to understand them.

We're always going to have emotion, and it is silly to divorce ourselves from it because it lets us understand where we are coming from, what makes us tick, and who we really are.

Emotion, like all fragile things, must be handled with care.

A disembodied emotion is a non-existent one.
- Theodule Ribot

101. EMPATHY

> When you start to develop your powers of empathy and
> imagination, the whole world opens up to you.
> - Susan Sarandon

The Beta Paradox is a concept that suggests the worst thing you can endure is not an obvious tragedy like the loss of a family member. Instead, the worst thing to befall you is a period where you experience no support or empathy. If one of your parents died, it is likely you will get overwhelming support that will cushion the impact.

The Beta Paradox occurs when you are devastated by an incident that isn't as obvious or apparent. You may go through a bad break-up, and you might find your friends laughing at you because you are so hung up on your ex, and they keep telling you to "get over it."

Then your friends move on with their lives, so they don't notice that you're still in shock about the break-up, months or even years later. It's the last thing on their minds because they assumed that you made peace with it in your own way a long time ago. The lack of empathy can be worse than the break-up itself.

When people don't acknowledge the difficulties you've had to endure, it makes you feel betrayed, invisible, and alone. There are no rules to reacting to tragedy. You might react better than you expected, or it might hit you worse than you could've ever imagined.

When we are in need, there are times when we refuse help because we believe others cannot understand our pain. Or perhaps we do not listen to those in need because we can't empathize with how they feel.

Empathy is better than advice. If people are devastated by an incident that we believe wouldn't affect us, we can't just act like they are overreacting and that they should brush it off. We can react to the same tragedy different ways.

When people are upset, they need a friend to talk to. They don't want others to solve their problems; they just need somebody to listen. In some ways, having empathy is the easiest thing to do. Listening means so much and requires so little energy.

We have the power to feel for others, so we might as well use it as a tool. It is how all great causes start. It is incredible that we were blessed with the ability to share each other's joys and carry each other's tragedies.

> Suffering is only intolerable when nobody cares.
> - Cicely Saunders

102. ENDOWMENT

> If we don't empower ourselves with knowledge,
> then we're gonna be led down a garden path.
> - Fran Drescher

The Super Bowl is the top prize in American football. The Heavyweight Championship belt is the most coveted honor in boxing. An Academy Award is the most desired trophy for an actor.

But why? It's not just because the prize is big and shiny. It's because we endow it with that power. The World Cup is not simply a big cup. It's the World Cup because we say it is. People train hard, not to win a cup but to win what the cup represents.

There's nothing wrong with this kind of endowment. People do it all the time. You mightn't even realize it. That's when you can get into trouble.

My friend, Ted was obsessed with his laptop. He was also terrified that a virus would infect his laptop one day and wipe his entire hard drive.

However, he stopped being so paranoid when I told him he could back up the contents on his computer on an external hard drive. He didn't even know such a device existed. When he backed up his files, he stopped being so protective of his laptop.

Ted endowed his computer with the idea that if it broke, his life would end. That endowment changed when he realised there was no danger.

But people endow things dangerously all of the time. We can endow ideas. We can endow a new town with the image of a dangerous, scary neighborhood. We can endow the future with an uncertain downward spiral.

We project so much negativity on our jobs and relationships, yet we recover and survive when the worst happens. You give yourself so much stress over many things that may never even happen.

All of that energy could be used for something practical—like endowing good things. Instead of seeing a new job as a hassle, see it as an opportunity.

A new place doesn't have to be scary. Endow it with the chance to have an adventure.

Even if a situation is clearly bad, choose the lesser of two evils. Is a broken bone the opportunity to procrastinate and wallow in self-pity, or is it merely a mild setback that will eventually heal?

Is a break-up the end of the world or an experience you can learn? You choose.

> If people keep throwing stuff at you, build something with it.
> - Anon

103. ENDURANCE

There is no cure for birth and death save to enjoy the interval.
- George Santayana

Many animals have to toil and suffer on a daily basis to get enough food to sustain themselves. We rarely have to experience such endurance. We can go two months without food. Yet most people eat 120 meals in that time.

There are animals that go to their hunger threshold quite often in their lives. When they finally find something to eat, the wait starts again. They travel thousands of miles to seek out prey and flee from predators, while losing teammates, putting up with harsh areas, bad weather, and no level ground to sleep on.

Tortoises live for over 150 years. That's twice as long as a human being, and we have television, friends, drink, and drugs to fill up the time, and we complain that our lives are worthless. Let's put things in perspective.

That's just animals. If you take our history into account, it's incredible what people have endured. A few hundred years ago, it was not uncommon to die of a cut or the flu. When you look at all the plagues, famine, pestilence throughout the ages, you can see our ancestors put up with agonizing hardship.

In certain parts of the world, people live in poverty, with almost no water, and they must travel miles to get some—and that's probably unclean anyway. They must put up with more war and death than we will ever see.

Today, we live more in luxury. So, what do we have to endure? Expectations. Failure. Depression. They are not as bad, but they are a part of our society. It's important to see what others have to endure. It helps us know where we stand. So many people have been put through worse.

Nevertheless, there are still a lot of things the average person must endure. We must endure the pressure of success, not disappointing our family, or not disappointing ourselves. Sometimes, it feels like our life is never going to get easier.

But it's never meant to be easy. Life gets harder because the benefits you reap will be worth more.

We are not supposed to avoid life's hardships. We are supposed to endure them and, instead of falling apart, allow ourselves to become stronger.

The genie is a metaphor that you have the power to wish anything into
being because you believe you can. The universe is at your command.
- James Ray

104. ENERGY

It takes as much energy to wish as it does to plan.
- Eleanor Roosevelt

One of the most mind-blowing concepts is the cosmic fine-tuning idea. It's the hypothesis that there were seven dials that made up the laws of the universe. These dials were turned in a specific way for the universe to be the way it is.

If any one of those dials was turned differently, one way or another to the minutest degree, the entire universe could not exist.

This is merely hypothetical, but the reality is even more fascinating. There are not seven variables of the universe; there are countless variables.

Human beings have the power to change their current situation, their lives, the lives of others, or the future by turning a dial in their own lives, changing some aspect of themselves, or diverging to a new path.

Orson Welles once said that when you are talking to someone in a room that has five or six people in it, and one or two leave or another comes in, it changes the energy. How you talk, how you hold yourself, what you say, and how you hold your attention or gaze is channeled through your surroundings. We feed off other people and feed those around us.

Our energy is always changing. We all have a high energy or low energy. If you want to look at it a different way, we have good energy and bad energy. I am aware of the actual scientific categories of energy, such as chemical or kinetic, but I am looking at it as a concept. If a person has high energy (hyper, chatty, social) and another person else has lower energy (shy, reserved, quiet), it is unlikely that they will act the same way after an extended period of time. The hyper person will lower his or her energy to a more tolerable level, and the low-energy person will heighten his or hers to be "more fun."

This is why we are so shy when we first meet people. We are not sure what we want to give away, because the other person may not have the "right energy," and we don't want to freak out that person. If we don't give anything away, the other person will have nothing to feed off—and neither will we—so we need to share a little bit of our organic energy.

Energy is the life force of the universe and has been broken down continuously in science, but it still works as a concept.

Our awareness of energy is an irrevocable force within us and within all things. It's there, waiting for us to connect to it, and to use it to pursue dreams, love, and goals.

The eternal mystery of the world is its comprehensibility...
the fact that it is comprehensible is a miracle.
- Albert Einstein

105. ENVIRONMENT

Punctuated Equilibrium
– We are not guaranteed Earth. We must earn this world.
- Stephen Jay Gould

It's a great thing to appreciate nature. The environment is one of the only things that, no matter how often you look at it, it always seems beautiful. We get used to almost everything else, no matter how amazing it is the first time we see it.

But it's nice to see something so simple and fall in love with it. This thought process makes you want to look after the world.

However, the world is becoming more technologically based, industrial, and commercial. Even philosophies and religions with nature at their core are beginning to dwindle.

The words "epidemic" and "pandemic" are thrown around a lot with problems like the recession, obesity, and the environment, to the point that people just tune out. That doesn't change the fact that these problems need to be addressed.

When we make problems that jeopardize the world itself, the threat can be too massive to comprehend, so we don't let it register.

Maybe if we allowed ourselves to look at the problem on a human level—something we can grasp and absorb, it would register with us more deeply.

Let me give you a personal example. My hometown is called Portarlington. Every trashcan is labelled with the mantra, "Be a Sport. Clean up Port."

Teenagers find this label cheesy and an incentive to trash even more. What they don't realize is that the trash problem became so large that more people had to be hired to fix it, which means the government had to spend more on the problem. And guess what? That money comes from the taxes from each of the inhabitants' paychecks. These litterers don't understand their actions are shooting themselves in the foot because they can't see the bigger picture.

Littering is the most primitive form of pollution and, as you can see, we will literally pay for it. Pollution has always diminished nature's beauty. People let these things happen because they think all resources are renewable.

But we're running out. Coal. Oil. Clean air. We need to be aware of the problem, or we will have consequences.

We can't keep acting like pollution can go away while we create more problems. It doesn't make any sense. One day, we just may push the planet's luck too far. We only have one Earth, after all.

Neither by nature, then, nor contrary to nature do the virtues
arise in us; nature gives us the capacity to receive
them, and this capacity is brought to maturity by habit.
- Aristotle

106. EPIPHANY

Imagination is the preview for life's coming attractions.
- Albert Einstein

You don't only get ideas from epiphanies, or life-changing moments, or life-or-death situations. They come from anywhere—mistakes, misunderstandings, drunken stupors, fights, break-ups, divorce, death, and dreams.

In films, epiphanies are an everyday occurrence, accompanied by jazzy camera angles, cheesy slow motion, and sappy music. In real life, most people don't realize when they're told the most important thing in the world. They prefer to take what they want to hear, rather than what they need to hear.

Every cathartic moment in your life, every epiphany you have experienced, and every illusion-shattering wake-up call you've had makes you feel like you have a much more solid foundation in the world.

However, we must realize that every breakthrough we have seems microscopic in the grand scheme of things. To someone else, it might seem insignificant, stupid, wrong, or unnoticeable.

Occasionally, we will be wrong. At times, we will be convinced we are making the right choice, but we end up with a lot of bruises, both inside and outside, with damaged egos or empty wallets. So we need to be wary of the likelihood of our "epiphanies" actually panning out the way we hope.

I am not disregarding epiphanies. They are the catalyst for great ideas, and our next action can set us on a great path. What success can we obtain from life without an epiphany?

If you have a great idea or sudden realization, think about it thoroughly before you go for it. If it makes sense, pursue it. I think it's wise to write down the epiphanies of your life. I can think of about ten in my life. They were all very different. Some of them I didn't appreciate until years later. Some were said to me, or it was something I overheard, read, wrote, saw on television, or witnessed.

As I said, they can stem from anything. It's just a question of picking up on the underlying message and how you act upon it.

Think of the times you could have gone down a different path, but you didn't. Was what you did the right choice? Did you go down the right road? Or were you cowardly? Naive? Immature?

Or maybe you don't know. Or maybe it doesn't matter, because what you chose has worked out for the best, but it's nice to question your actions. It's nice to know from where your inspiration is drawn. Maybe pondering such matters will awaken another epiphany.

No great improvements in the lot of mankind are possible,
until a great change takes place in the fundamental
constitution of their modes of thought.
– John Stuart Mill

107. ESCAPE

All human beings should try to learn before they die
what they are running from and to and why.
- James Thurber

When we try to escape from our mistakes, we tend to run towards them. Offers sound so appealing if they involve running away. How we react should be a sense of expression and a communicative form of our perception and passion, not a means of escape. If you enjoy going out for a few pints, do it, but don't do it just to forget your problems. We all need a bit of escapism, but sometimes we're just running away.

Most people move away to move on, be on their own, to change, or to be independent—or so they say. Some are just running from something.

To run away or to get out of the country to start afresh, a life anew is thoughtless. Running away implies that the problem will stay put. Whatever happened to cause such problems that required running away means the problem has not been dealt with or even acknowledged.

Therefore, it is destined to happen again and again. I've seen it happen many times. No one I know ran away from their responsibility without making the same mistakes.

You think you can just skim over the surface, barely ever making contact. Then you realize that where you're running is nowhere, and everything you want is under the surface. It'll hurt digging through it, but it will be worth it.

You might think you can buy your way out of your problems or cover yourself up with lavish luxuries. Shiny trinkets don't burn off years of mistakes.

My friend burned way too many bridges in his life to recover—or so he thought. The truth was, he just didn't want to make the effort.

So he suddenly decided to go to America before he got into any more trouble. I didn't take it too seriously, even though he seemed so absolute about moving and changing his life, and his bad boy days were behind him.

The day before he left, he told me that he had no intention of ever coming home. I gave him two months before he'd be back, but I was wrong. It was six weeks. He got into trouble over there, which he never fully explained, but now he's back at home.

He just went back to his old job, still talking about the same stories, making enemies with the same mistakes, and getting into fights with the same people. Years later, he is still at the same job.

It's like the same clown in a different circus. In the end, the joke's on him. After all, the same sun and moon shine on us no matter where we are in the world. Don't go somewhere that's got no answers.

You cannot escape the responsibility of tomorrow by evading it today.
- Abraham Lincoln

108. EVALUATION

Take a step back, evaluate what is important, and enjoy life.
- Teri Garr

If you are worried about who you are, how you present yourself, or what people think about you, that is human nature. One universal trait we all have is that we are not universal. We are all different in our own special way, but the way we evaluate ourselves is often the same. Here are examples; tell me how familiar they sound:

- Your relationship with your parent or parents is somewhat withdrawn. You wish to remain fond of them but recent issues are causing frustration, from your side far more than theirs.
- You always had a set group of friends, but it seems to have changed recently, and you are not sure why. You are dividing yourself to a degree. You say it's because you are busy, or have to work, but the fact is you are not having as much as fun as you used to.
- You're a bit disorganized. Anything put away is crammed and thrown into closets and cupboards with no order—out-of-date items and medicines, broken items not fixed, useless stuff lying around that you have been meaning to get rid of, and notes you wrote months ago. You said you would do something ages ago and now, nothing is drastically in the way, but a lot remains undone. The reason is that you lack motivation.
- You worry that you can be self-absorbed, but it's only because you worry that people are misinterpreting your actions, so you tend to show a jazzed-up "better" version of you. Others see this as fake, and then you wonder why people don't "get" you.

If you are surprised by how accurate the above statements are, I'm afraid that it's a trick called cold reading. This is when you can psychoanalyze a stranger accurately but you are actually being intentionally vague so your psychoanalysis applies to almost anybody. Saying things like, "You worry about the future and your looks" sound specific but they apply to almost everyone.

I use this tactic to show you that people share your frustration and insecurities. Don't feel like it doesn't make you special. It just means that you are not alone in your insecurities.

The examples above are typical daily evaluations we make of ourselves, but a lot of people over-evaluate. They read too much into people and situations, and act like they are the only people who have these observations and revelations.

We are all different, but we are not as different as we seem. We feel like our problems are one of a kind, but if we open up about them to others, we may be surprised by how much others can empathize.

To enter into your own mind you need to be armed to the teeth.
- Paul Valery

109. EVIL

As soon as men decide that all means are permitted to fight an evil,
then their good becomes indistinguishable from
the evil that they set out to destroy.
- Christopher Dawson

An old Cherokee told his grandson, "There is a battle between two wolves inside us all. One is Evil. It is anger, jealousy, greed, resentment, inferiority, lies, and ego. The other is Good. It is joy, peace, love, hope, humility, kindness, empathy, and truth."

The boy thought about it and asked, "Grandfather, which wolf wins?"

The old man quietly replied, "The one you feed."

Every time you tap into your dark side, it costs you a piece of your soul. Evil is usually not as obvious as you think. It's subtle, almost unnoticeable, which makes it more evil. The most disturbing part of evil is how secretly and silently it creeps in.

A belief in a supernatural source of evil is not necessary; mankind alone is quite capable of every wickedness imaginable. As Duc de la Rochefoucauld said, "There is scarcely a single man sufficiently aware to know all the evil he does."

We live in a world where everyone can cause evil or become a victim of evil. People can be beaten, violated, tormented, or killed, and these people could be the next Martin Luther King Jr., Abraham Lincoln, or Norman Borlaug.

Most of the time, no one is to blame for even the most heinous crimes. Take war, for example. People go to war to protect their families. Politicians work to protect their country. Slaves or sweatshop workers who build the guns have no other way of making money.

In truth, out of the millions of people involved, directly or indirectly, voluntarily or involuntarily, only a handful here and there, with their own private agenda, are responsible. As Alan Moore said, "It is .0000001 percent of the people who make 99.9999 percent of the important decisions of the world."

If we ever lose our way, we can always find our way back. Remember, there are no necessary evils, only weak compromises. It's only evil if you make a conscious decision.

The story of Pandora's box is that when the box was opened by Pandora, it released all of the evils in the world. Many people forget one element of the story— that at the very bottom of the box was a sliver of hope. It can make all the difference.

Man is neither good or bad; he is born with instinct and abilities.
- Honore de Balzac

110. EXAGGERATION

An exaggeration is a truth that has lost its temper.
- Kahil Gibran

Some people claim they never lie. I find that hard to believe, especially since exaggeration is lying.

I am talking about exaggerating as understatement as well. If you were asked if you or your partner does the cleaning up, and you said your partner *never* does the cleaning up, that's exaggerating. Saying "never" is just as much of an exaggeration as "always" in that context because you are protecting your ego.

We emphasize our achievements, jazz up our job, and heighten our accomplishments, while simultaneously ignoring our disappointments, understating our failures, and shying away from all of our let-downs.

There are times when we don't do that. We can be open about where we went wrong, but we might go too far. We can exaggerate our failures to justify them. We might act like it is the end of the world.

If you keep hearing something long enough, you eventually believe it. Exaggerating can begin as an ego boost, but it can eventually become a flat-out lie and after a while, you will see it as the truth. Your friends may hear you and think an exaggerated story you told is factual.

If you act like you have done more than you have, accomplished more than the bare average, or that you are on the road to great things, you might be farther away from your goals than you realize.

If your friends believe you are a stud who can get any woman, you may feel like you have nothing to prove because they already believe it. So that can stop you from meeting others and from having a partner.

Sometimes, we use hyperbole while telling a story to make it more entertaining. But if our exaggerated stories are taken completely seriously, people can get the wrong idea or think you're a liar. Most stories get twisted and warped anyway, so be careful how you tell an entertaining anecdote.

If you want to tell a funny story or sell yourself, the main thing to do is to cut the flab out of a story and only say what needs to be said.

When you're talking about yourself, emphasize what's important, but try not to overdo it. Otherwise, it'll come across like you're overcompensating.

Exaggeration is a blood relation to falsehood and nearly as blamable.
- Hosea Ballou

111. EXCEPTIONS

A good teacher must know the rules; a good pupil, the exceptions.
- Martin H. Fischer

We are told that we can only attain success through hard work. Yet we have heard stories of someone's winning the lottery on the first try with a single ticket. That person is an exception.

We have been brought up to treat other people as we would like to be treated. It's the right way to get through life. However, some people who have never worked a day in their lives have the world handed to them on a silver platter because of dumb luck. I know people who have never taken a drug, never lit a cigarette, never taken a sip of beer, yet they have had to battle cancer in their early twenties. How can they possibly be unhealthy, while everyone else swamps their body with these substances and not suffer the same outcome?

Super-models have had agents just walk up to them when they were young because the agent liked the way they looked and catalyzed their careers.

Hundreds of Hollywood movie stars have never taken acting classes.

But don't let these exceptions cloud your judgement. With billions of people populating the globe, there are bound to be exceptions to the smallest rule, the biggest gamble, or the most unlikely statistic.

But the problem with exceptions is they can make people become lazy.

A lot of my actor friends quit college, citing dozens of examples of actors who became famous despite having an education. Of the millions of actors in America, I'm sure many of them are not taking acting classes and far, far fewer have had any success, but arrogant, lazy actors will see the minority as proof that anyone can make it. Exceptions to the rule never constitute a valid central argument.

Bill Gates never went to college. That is probably the shortest argument you need to prove you don't need college.

But he is one man! It is a well-known fact that he didn't go to college because he is the exception. Do you know how many people quit college and ended up missing so many opportunities?

Do you know how many performers will end up working at 5:00 a.m. on a Wednesday to play a small part in a short movie that no one will see? (That may sound like an awfully specific example, but I know a couple of people who believed they were destined for Hollywood, who found that example was a regular part of their careers.)

Be careful when you say you can make it big because so-and-so became a success. Focus on yourself. Using laziness as an excuse is not a good way to justify your failings.

Nothing is absolute, with the debatable
exceptions of this statement and death.
- John Ralston Saul

112. EXCUSES

Several excuses are always less convincing than one.
- Aldous Huxley

Let's say there are two people. One of them is always busy, and the other lies about the house all day. If you told both to tidy the house, by the end of the day, which of them do you think is more likely to have done it?

The correct answer is the busy one. Why? Because busy people are so used to their hectic lifestyle, they usually find a way to cram every little job into their already full schedules.

Lazy people will see it as a task that can be done at any moment, which means they can do it later. This mentality usually means that they will keep pushing it farther in the future and it will never get done.

We have all seen it happen. The more time we have, the less we do. If you want something done, give it to someone who already has too much to do.

When we go through a big drama, it is easy to use the drama as an excuse. Anytime anything goes wrong, blame it on the Thing. No one can blame us or judge us.

When you make excuses, you seem immature, sloppy, and unreliable. Bad excuses are worse than no excuses.

We can make excuses to ourselves. My friend, Owalabi used to do crazy things, like cliff jumping and parachuting, and talked about living life to the fullest.

One day, he told me that he quit all of that to focus on becoming a novelist. I asked why, and he said he realized that he had "jumped the shark."

"Jumping the Shark" was the name of an episode of the TV show *Happy Days*. In this episode, Fonzie had to jump over a shark on his motorcycle. To "jump the shark" means that a story reaches the point where the plot spins off into absurd storylines that have nothing to do with what the show was originally about.

What Owalabi meant by this analogy was that he wanted to be a writer originally but got distracted by life or tried to fill a void with crazy and wacky adventures, but it just proved more and more that they were not his original objective. He was using his crazy persona as an excuse not to try writing because he didn't want to potentially fail.

If you can do better, why don't you? Don't wait to be better than you are because you have to but because you want to. If you are good at making excuses, you are rarely good at anything else.

Why accept the second rate version of yourself?
- David Mamet

113. EXPERTISE

An expert is someone who knows some of the worst mistakes that
can be made in his subject and who manages to avoid them.
- Werner Heisenberg

I had back problems in my teens, so I went to a few specialists, and after trial and error, I found that insoles that were designed for my skeleton were the most effective solution. The soles were shaped for my feet and my alignment so they allowed my spine to gradually realign. I couldn't believe such an easy and painless solution could eradicate my back pains with no side effects.

A few years later, I injured my back again, which caused me to develop nerve spasms. I was in Dublin at the time, so I couldn't visit the insole specialist and instead, settled for a physiotherapist. I was skeptical because the insole specialists claimed that physiotherapy was overrated, expensive, and potentially damaging.

But I was desperate, so I went. I found a physiotherapist called Duncan. I expected he would be underqualified, but he turned out to be overqualified. He fixed my back with one single session.

What was even more mind-blowing was that when I told him about the insoles, he dismissed them.

Over the following years, I have seen or have observed yogis, gurus, osteopaths, chiropractors, fitness instructors, masseuses, and acupuncturists, and all of them said their training was correct and the other techniques were "inferior."

But here's the thing – they're not all wrong… but they're not all right either. They saw their own training as the correct way because it has worked for them. But that doesn't mean other techniques are wrong

Personally, I found acupuncture completely ineffective, but I know people who swear it changed their lives for the better.

Remember, all of the physical experts I mentioned have their own aspect of expertise! What about experts in sports? Food? Movies? Politics? Geography? History? There is no ultimate expert; it is all about what works for us and who we listen to.

If you believe the doctors, nothing is wholesome;
if you believe the theologians, nothing is innocent; if
you believe the soldiers, nothing is safe.
- Lord Salisbury

114. EXTREMES

All empty souls tend toward extreme opinions.
- William Butler Yeats

Too much of anything is a bad thing, but so is too little. If you realized you were too loud, you might try and be quieter. However, you can run the risk of becoming too quiet.

If you're afraid you eat too much food, you might starve yourself. You party too often, so you become antisocial. You want to stand up for yourself, so you become confrontational and aggressive.

If one element of your life is considered too extreme, you have to be avoid falling into another extreme. If your friends complain you read too often, that doesn't mean you should stop reading. If you are an avid moviegoer, I can't argue with your passion.

Don't cut out what you are passionate about. If you do, it's like you're cutting out yourself. I see a lot of people do this. They go out all the time and drink and party, and one day, they stop doing it completely. They are trying to present themselves in a "mature" way, but it's unnatural. They are denying their basic wants.

That may sound great because they are limiting their vices. You don't need to eliminate every bad habit. You just need to be in charge of them. Everyone in the world has some bad in them—indolence, resentment, self-centeredness, and so on. You can get rid of these. You can completely get rid of some of them, but there will always be a little niggle or scruple left.

So don't ever feel like you must purge yourself of everything, especially if it is a large element of who you are. Just uphold a sense of balance. Going from one extreme to the other is more hectic than having that one extreme just by itself.

If you feel like you're not socializing anymore, you don't have to nuts. Instead, you can just meet up with an old friend. If you are a party animal, chill out at home every once in a while.

It's healthy to go out of your comfort zone from time to time. Leaving it too often or for too long, however, can make you forget where the real you used to be.

Extremes, though contrary, have the like effects. Extreme heat kills, and
so extreme cold: extreme love breeds satiety, and so extreme hatred;
and too violent rigor tempts chastity, as does too much license.
- George Chapman

115. FACTS

Logical consequences are the scarecrows of fools and the beacons of wise men.
- T.H. Huxley.

Fifty years ago, scientists believed we had found 99 percent of all that there is. But we have found so much over recent years—antineutrinos, tachyons, mesons, hadrons, leptons, gluons, baryons, positrons, quarks, antimatter, dark matter, dark energy, the Higgs-Boson, superstrings, etc. Chances are we have 99 percent left to find!

However, whatever we regard as truth, there's always a supposed expert who has alternative "facts." Usually, when you are in an argument, your opponent will say the infamous words: "Prove it."

I always respond, "Are you willing to accept the possibility that you can be wrong?" If you are not, there is no point in starting an argument. You must meet each other halfway. Everyone can be wrong. There are times when it's not even your fault.

We were taught many facts in school that are now considered untrue. Elisha Gray invented the telephone, not Alexander Graham Bell. Henry Woodward and Matthew Evans created the light bulb, not Thomas Edison. The earth was considered round almost two thousand years before Columbus landed in America. Human beings have at least eleven senses, not five. Benjamin Franklin never performed an experiment with a kite in a thunderstorm to discover electricity.

Facts can help us find the truth when surrounded by angry opinions. But there are times where facts don't matter to some, and a lack of facts matters even less. When a new idea comes along, the masses say, "You have to be wrong about this because it's not what we were told and believed."

Galileo was persecuted for his claim that Earth was not the center of the universe, even though he could verify his claim. Giordano Bruno was burned at the stake for saying the sun does not revolve around the earth.

It took hundreds of years to accept these claims as facts because society were too afraid to change. Think how different it would have been if these claims had been accepted without hesitation.

Just because a million people believe in a dumb idea, that doesn't change the fact that it's a dumb idea. Just because ideas are new and considered ridiculous and blasphemous doesn't change the fact they have substance, documented accounts, and above all, probability. If something doesn't make sense, don't force it, just because it's what the masses say.

The deepest sin against the human mind
is to believe things without evidence.
- T.H. Huxley

116. FAILURE

I have not failed;
I have just found 10,000 ways that don't work.
- Thomas Edison.

Many great people have had many failures in their lives. Great writers such as Virginia Woolf, Mark Twain, Beatrix Potter, D. H. Laurence, James Joyce, and Alexander Pope could not get their books published. But it didn't matter. They simply published their books themselves. The poet, William Blake made his own ink, hand printed his own pages, and got his wife to sew on the covers to ensure his work was published.

The book, *The Help*, which inspired the movie of the same name, got rejected over a hundred times. The self-help book, *Chicken Soup for the Soul*, got rejected over five hundred times! But the writers didn't quit. If you don't quit, you can't fail.

Even though failure is perceived as a terrible thing, it can help you succeed more than a success. A failed actor can know more and teach more than a successful one. A success can make us fall into a false sense of security. You need to learn to fall to learn to stand.

Failure was an expected part of life when I used to perform theatre. We had many slogans about failing because performers dealt with rejection more than almost any other profession. The slogan that stook with me most was Samuel Beckett's, "Fail, fail again, fail better."

This slogan can be explained better with what director Steven Soderbergh said: "Studios are okay with a movie failing the same way over and over. What's wrong with failing a new way? You haven't tried it before so at least failing isn't a guarantee!" Who knows? Maybe you'll find something that you expected to fail at but it works."

How you deal with your failure is more important than the failure itself. Good people fail every day. Great people keep going until they succeed. You are only as good as your losses. Don't see where you have failed but where you have succeeded.

Remember what Albert Einstein said: "We have not failed until we have exhausted every possibility." The greatest achievers in the world have their accomplishments built on a mountain of failure.

Obstacles are those frightful things you see
when you take your eyes off the goal.
- Henry Ford

117. FAME

Good fame is like fire; when you have kindled you may easily preserve
it; but if you extinguish it, you will not easily kindle it again.
- Francis Bacon

Celebrities are targets for a lot of unnecessary hate. Weirdly, a lot of celebs are
criticized when they do something practical and kind! Because we perceive
actors, athletes, and singers as a source of entertainment, its breaks the illusion when
they talk about bettering the world.

We listen to these people's music or watch them perform in movies to forget
about our troubles. Our illusion is broken once they start talking about the very
thing we are trying to forget about.

John Lennon was a legendary musician, but a lot of people thought he went mad
when he started to talk more about peace and love.

Sadly, regular people demonize the rich and famous because the media usually
focus on the negative side of it. I have heard countless people mock Keanu Reeves as
an actor, but they are oblivious that he donates more money to charity than almost
any celebrity in the world.

There are those who hate celebrities because they come across as arrogant and
aloof. We have all heard countless tales of a celeb lashing out at fans, going berserk
on a plane, or screaming because they received a speeding ticket.

But this is how human beings react. Fame doesn't exclude these people from
the most basic emotions. If they were just random people reacting the same way, we
wouldn't give it a second thought.

So why are we so harsh to those we claim we admire and aspire to? It might be
because it proves they are flawed, like us, and our idols become a bit of a let-down.

Famous people are just regular people in extreme circumstances. Next time you
think of skipping a queue or losing your temper for a second, think how it would look
if the media tweaked it for maximum shock value. (This is a lot easier to imagine
nowadays thanks to social media and videos going viral.)

Some people are not just famous but legendary. These people may not have been
nice, or they could have had a miserable life. We all have the potential for greatness,
and fame does not necessarily have to be a part of it. Those who cheer today may
hurl stones tomorrow. We're not actually engrossed in fame, just the novelty of it.

Indeed, wretched the man whose fame makes his misfortunes famous.
- Lucius Accius

118. FAMILY

85% of families are dysfunctional.
- Jack Canfield

The idea of a perfectly functional family is rare. Even if you have no brothers or sisters, you can be affected by more than just your immediate family. With all your cousins, uncles, nieces, sons, daughters, and grandchildren, it's asking a lot for your family to turn out just right.

I am lucky to have a great family. I have had problems like the next person but nothing catastrophic, but it's tempting to get complacent. We forget that although we cannot escape family, it does change.

The family you are born into is not the family you die in. When you think of family now, you may think of your parents and your siblings, and everything seems perfect. In the future, you may have kids you cannot control, and you may not be able to take the pressure of being a parent.

But some people grow up to be great parents because they had rough lives. They are giving their children the life they themselves could never have.

Your family affects you. You may disagree because some people remove themselves, and try not to associate with their family, and do not consider them a priority, but it is inexplicably inescapable.

My housemate, Jay hated his father because his father beat him and his mother. He left the house when he wasn't even eighteen. When Jay was twenty-one, he went to his father's house and pummeled him until his knuckles bled. Jay felt like he got closure because the beating proved his father didn't intimidate him anymore. But all it proved was that monsters create monsters. Jay was trying so hard not to become his father that he went down the exact path his father did where he thought he could solve all his problems with violence.

If you think your family isn't part of your life, that may be, but don't pretend they don't affect you. Jay thought his family didn't affect him when he left his house. Even though he couldn't see it, he was reacting directly because of his family's actions.

Even if you have the same people constantly in your life, that doesn't mean they are not going to change. You can be close with your parents or siblings, but you may have a falling out that alters the dynamic of the family. This can work both ways. You may always feel like your father is the bane of your existence or that you will never get on with your brother or sister. Anything can change for the better, but only if you take steps to improve the relationship with your family.

Whatever psychological baggage our family lays upon us, we have to deal with it because it's been building since the day we were born.

Happy families are all alike; every unhappy
family is unhappy in its own way.
- Leo Tolstoy

119. FANTASY

Getting rid of a delusion makes us wiser than getting hold of a truth.
- Ludwig Borne

There is a fable about a gnat that flew into a lion's face and bit him on the nose. As the gnat flew off, the lion swiped his nose, cutting his own face. The gnat laughed that he had humiliated the king of the jungle. Surely this meant he was the most ferocious creature in the kingdom.

But this did not come to be, for the gnat got caught in a web shortly after and was devoured by a spider. It was irrelevant that the gnat momentarily defeated the king of beasts since an insignificant arachnid killed him.

The moral of this story is that we may often be of more consequence in our own eyes than in the eyes of others.

People twist facts to make the stories sound fantastic and romantic. People love the tale of Pocahontas. Most people are familiar with the Disney version, where English colonists invade Virginia to plunder riches from the natives. One man, John Smith, falls for a native and stands against his own men to protect her.

But in real life, the colonists enslaved, kidnapped, tortured, and killed the natives. Pocahontas was only thirteen and her real name was Matoaka. Pocahontas was a nickname her tribe gave her, which meant "frisky." It was a derogatory term because she left her tribe to be with the settlers who killed her people.

Disney couldn't tell a story that plays with the idea of genocide so the cartoon was turned into a fairy tale. People argued that the Disney film was "just a movie," but it was like making a *Titanic* movie where nobody dies! It's misinforming and damaging. These ideas can force you to create fantasies that you believe are applicable to real life.

A girl I know called Dawn met a guy called Ali on the other side of the world and was convinced he was "the one." I thought she was simply being romantic. Then she found out her neighbor, Brock, who was her first partner, was still in love with her. More importantly, she still had feelings for Brock. I was relieved that she didn't have to complicate her life.

But I was wrong. She didn't pursue Brock because it was "too easy." She wanted a romance on the other side of the planet because it sounded like a fairy tale.

A few weeks later, she traveled thousands of miles to surprise Ali, but she surprised herself by meeting his wife. She went back home to Brock, hoping that she still had a chance, but Brock didn't want to be her "second best."

If you are creating a fantasy, that creation is to fill a void. If you are naturally content, you don't have to dress it up.

For me, it is far better to grasp the Universe as it really is than
to persist in delusion, however satisfying and reassuring.
- Carl Sagan

120. FATS

Foods high in bad fats, sugar and chemical are directly
linked to many negative emotions, whereas whole, natural
foods rich in nutrients - foods such as fruits, vegetables, grains
and legumes - contribute to greater energy and positive emotions.
- Marilu Henner

Fat is the most misunderstood food group. Fat can be one person's worst enemy, while another might see it as a necessary part of the daily diet.

Nowadays people are more familiar with good fats and bad fats, saturated and unsaturated, and so forth. This is good because people used to view fat in the worst possible way.

Nevertheless, many people are unclear of fat's purpose. Protein builds muscle, carbs give us energy, but what does fat actually do?

A little bit of everything, actually. Like carbohydrates, fat gives us energy (more than twice as much as carbs). Fat gives so much energy, it prevents your body from using up your protein instead. So a reasonable amount of fat per day doesn't hinder your putting on muscle; it helps you put it on. It also absorbs vitamins, forms structures in your cells and tissue, and supplies essential fatty acids.

But fat has one more use that gives it a bad reputation: padding.

Excess fat is deposited just under the skin and becomes subcutaneous fat. This is used to keep us warm. Although it has a practical use, it's there on your skin for the entire world to see. You may worry about food, but you need to remember: fat is not your enemy. What you are actually afraid of is subcutaneous fat. If you eat good fats, this will be avoided.

If you try to eliminate fat altogether, your cells, tissue, and muscles will suffer, and you will most certainly give in to cravings, eat more fatty foods, and have even more subcutaneous fat.

If your willpower is strong enough, you can avoid fatty foods entirely, but you don't have to torture yourself. Eat within reason.

How do you fix it? Simple. Eat fatty foods! When people say, "Fats are bad," what they really mean is that you need to avoid certain fats.

Good fats can be found in nuts, olives, fish oils, avocado, canola, and seeds.

The earlier in the day you introduce good fats into your body, the less likely you will have cravings for bad fats later.

It's simple; if it jiggles, it's fat.
- Arnold Schwarzenegger

121. FAVORS

Favors too plentiful will be lost, favors far and
between will always be remembered and treasured.
- Anon

My old housemate, Stephen, was one of the few guys who had a car while I was in college. The first time he offered his friends a lift, my schoolmates really appreciated it because they were late for work, had appointments, or didn't want to walk for ages.

But Stephen was a nice guy. Too nice. Eventually, they expected him to be kind and relied on his giving them a ride. If he couldn't give them a lift, my schoolmates acted like he'd let them down or deserted him when they needed him most.

Stephen was doing these people a favor. If you do someone a favor, they will feel like they owe you something.

Ironically, the more favors you do, the more people take advantage. Or maybe they're just taking advantage of a nice person. They don't see opportunity. They see expectancy.

I have had the good fortune to be on both sides of it. I have had friends too good for me, who would literally do anything for me. Too much. I felt like I owed them and tried to do something nice for them or give them a present. Just when I was about to do it, they would give me a gratuitous gift or take care of something I was stressed about. Because this was on top of their original favor that they did for me, I felt like I was playing catch-up. I felt like I had to choose between giving presents to return the favor or think about the contents of my wallet.

After a while, I realized that playing catch-up is too much effort. It was so much easier to accept good gifts and opportunities.

I can completely understand the selfish feeling of just taking advantage of generosity. I don't like it and never thought I would be on the self-centered side of it, but we are all busy and have our own lives to lead. We cannot repay every favor. What we can do is make favors count.

One well-thought-out favor every now and again is more effective and appreciated than ten presents lined up ready for you.

I was given three presents from three people: a good-bye letter from Jake, a poem from Clare, and a friendship bracelet from Elga. They were the only presents these people ever gave to me.

To this day, I still have those gifts. They are among the most important things I have, the type of things I would try to save in a fire. When there are fewer favors, it says more, and it means more.

I'm not one of those actors who asks for too many favors.
So when I do, people tend to listen.
- Ryan Kwanten

122. FEAR

The chief danger in life is that you take too many precautions.
- Alfred Adler

I love the idea of the boogeyman. There are many variations of this amorphous creature, but we tend to know him as a monster that lives in our closets and preys on our fears. Being scared of this monster makes him exist. As soon as we stop believing, he dies.

He represents the idea that we give fear power. If we don't, we can destroy it. It's easier said than done because it is hard to understand fear.

Our unconscious and subconscious develop tactics, usually without our knowledge, to protect us.

Subconscious protection can be anxiety, aggression, or phobias. Since we are usually only aware of the conscious mind, priorities to protect ourselves can jar us.

Mahatma Ashayana Deane said that logic develops like a frog in a fish bowl. As a tadpole, it could swim around in circles. It doesn't learn or develop, but it won't get hurt. As it grows, turning from tadpole to frog, it gets too big for the bowl so it has to adapt. In this case, it grows legs to get out of that glass coffin to explore the world.

It might get scared, looking through the glass. The world looks ugly and distorted, so it might decide to stay and keep swimming. But every day that passes, it has less and less space as it keeps growing, not realizing that it has adapted for a reason. Those legs didn't just appear through chance; they appeared to help the frog get out and explore the world.

When we are given the tools necessary to fulfill the greatest outcome of a situation, we cheat ourselves if we react any other way. Which are you? The explorer or the shallow swimmer?

Some fears are embedded into us, like phobias. Look at it this way: animals don't think as we do. They react to their circumstances, making them slaves to their biology. We are intelligent beings and should use reason and logic to understand that our fear may be irrational.

It's easy to fantasize about what might have been, secure in the knowledge that it will never be, making it a great excuse for not dealing with the risks and demands of reality.

The simplest unknowns instill fear. It's better to take a beating than spend your life anticipating one. Any person who gives into fear becomes a slave to himself.

It is said that when you are at a moment when you are in great fear, your life flashes before your eyes. Maybe it's not your life. Maybe it's the stuff you missed out on. Maybe it's stuff you want to do in life. You still can.

Courage is not the absence of fear but the
capacity for action despite our fears.
- Mark Twain

123. FEMINISM

I am trying to make art that relates to the deepest and
most mythic concerns of human kind and I believe
that, at this moment of history, feminism is humanism.
- Judy Chicago

In 1792, Mary Wollstonecraft protested against subordination of women. In 1848, the first US women's rights convention was held at Seneca Falls in New York. In 1869, J. S. Mills publicized *The Subjection of Women*.

In 1918, the Suffragettes launched a movement seeking to give women the right to vote. After a long and arduous path, the Suffragettes emerged victorious. This moment was seen as the true beginning for women's rights in the twentieth century.

So what's wrong with feminism? As an idea, women's rights was exactly what the world needed. In practice, it worked successfully and continues to do so. In itself, there is nothing wrong with equal rights for women, much like there is nothing wrong with equal rights for any creed, color, or sex.

The problem lies when someone goes too far. When a person is weak and finally has a chance to be in power, it is not uncommon for it to go to the person's head. It's what can turn the desire for equality into a need for superiority.

This world needs more power and control for women. They are gradually getting there, as women of today's world are getting more opportunities, politically and universally.

However, feminism can breed man-haters. We will all defend our own sex, but to claim superiority over the other is simplistic and illogical.

The Suffragettes movement could have succeeded sooner, but the women of the time got aggressive and violent during their campaigns. Sexist men used these examples as proof that women weren't reasonable enough to vote. This behavior turned many women off the idea that the Suffragettes were a good cause and encouraged them to stop.

It's good to be proud of who you are and what hardships you have come by as an individual and as a mass, as a creed, or as a gender.

Men and women may not be the same, but they are equal.
Feminism's agenda is basic: It asks that women not be forced to
choose between public justice and private happiness.
- Susan Faludi

124. FIFTEEN MINUTES

To appreciate heaven, it's good for a person to have some 15 minutes of hell.
- Will Carleton

An actor lived in my complex when I was in college. He was given $50,000 to do a bank advertisement. Naturally, he accepted the offer immediately.

In the advertisement, he was pale, skinny, clean-shaven, and had short spiky hair. But whe I saw him, he had shaggy hair down to his shoulders, and a beard that consumed his mouth. He had thick glasses, so the only part of his face that I could see was his nose.

But I knew he was the guy from the commercial because his face was plastered on posters everywhere. He told me that he looked the way he did because he hated being recognized. He thought he was living the dream when he got cast, but it all fell apart because he was offered a quick buck. Sadly, the money didn't last a year. He couldn't work because he had a two-year buyout. After that, he still struggled to get a job because he was too recognizable.

I am not suggesting that he should have turned down the money. I doubt I could have at the time. We might see an offer as a great opportunity, but only in the long run will we see the downside.

You only realize that something's amiss when you are at the point of no return. You just have to carry on and expect some pain and punishment.

But you're thinking that this is an impossible circumstance. No one would say no, but you're wrong.

My friend, Gabe was offered a two-year contract on one of the biggest television programs in Britain. He would have received two thousand pounds per week. After a lot of consideration, he rejected it because he didn't want to hit his acting prime before he was twenty-one and then spend the rest of his career as a Z-list celebrity, doing guest lists for failing shows.

He instead continued his acting training on his own and is now doing a lot of consistent work, with more on the horizon in plays and movies.

Some people want to be in the spotlight, to have any excuse to become more than just an irritating attention-seeker. They can have labels like "class clown," "local drunk," "daring stuntman," or "street thug," but at the end of the day, it may be just for attention. There are many ways to have fifteen minutes of fame, where you hog the show that is your life.

But eventually, the light dies down and shines on someone else. It rotates endlessly and only has so much time for you. It only stays on you if you really make an effort to stand out by doing something totally new. Do something truly great if you want to last longer than a mere fifteen minutes.

Everybody has their day and some days last longer than others.
- Winston Churchill

125. FINALIZATION

These things happened. They were glorious and they changed
the world... and then we screwed up the endgame.
- Charlie Wilson

My friend, Finbarr spent years writing a play. He wrote it and rewrote it many
times. It meant everything to him, but it never materialized into anything
beyond the piece of paper it was written on. It was not because it was poorly written—
he put blood, sweat, and tears into his work. I believe it had potential to be something
truly special.

When Finbarr finished the play, he got a little too excited. He saw the final draft
as the last stage and thought that was all he needed to make sure it become a reality.

He didn't know how to meet directors. He didn't have a clue how to organize
auditions. He wasn't covered financially to find a place to rehearse.

All these problems were not the end of the world. In fact, these issues are quite
common. A lot of people have found themselves in Finbarr's shoes, but he got
frustrated and gave up. He thought the last step was a lot closer than it was. In his
frustration, it made all his work and effort count for nothing.

I know people who trained to be actors for eight years and gave up in the acting
world in less than two.

I have a friend who was a comedian for seven years and quit because one of his
gigs went badly. He didn't have a string of bad luck. One single bad gig was enough
to make him quit his dream.

One of my friends wrote a book and got a bad review. Now, he refuses to write
anymore. Since then, he has gotten good reviews, but still refuses to right since the
first bad review rattled him.

You can't give up when you are so close to your goal. We usually start with small
objectives and then build up to greater triumphs. It seems logical that the final steps
to reaching our goals should be the hardest ones, yet this is when we tend to give
up on ourselves.

These hurdles will be the most satisfying once we cross them. We may drop the
ball or stumble, and that can be embarrassing, but you can choose to go back to the
start. Or you can continue to the end.

We can easily be thrown off, nearing the finish, because it may not be what we
were told it would be. It may not be as glamorous, and it may not come at us the way
we were expecting.

But if it is what we want, we should see it to the end. Rarely will anything come at
us the way we anticipated. If this was enough incentive to quit while we were ahead,
we would never accomplish anything.

Discussion is just a tool. You have to aim;
the final goal must be a decision.
- Harri Holkeri

126. FIRST STEP

It's easier to resist at the beginning than at the end.
- Leonardo da Vinci

Once you start some things, you can't put them back the way they were. To coin an old phrase, "Once the toothpaste is out of the tube, it's awfully hard to get it back in."

In the film Falling Down, Michael Douglas's character, D-Fens, talks about the point of no return. He says this is the point of a journey where it takes longer to go back to the start than to carry on.

This sounds like the midpoint. There are some things in life, however, where once you start, there's no going back—or at least you shouldn't. After all, why start something if you're not going to finish it?

But what is worse is never taking the first step. Some say they will move to America, become famous, quit their crummy job, and become an actor or singer because that is their true passion.

The only thing worse than never carrying out your passion is never trying. Even if we don't fulfill our dreams to their ultimate potential, we can still let the fire inside of us burn. You may want to be a world-class drummer.

That might never happen, but you should keep it up. You should get the drum kit out every once in a while, do a gig here and there, and keep that fire inside of you alive.

I know people who are in their thirties, in jobs that pay quite well, but they always wanted to be actors. However, they take no steps to pursue it. I encourage them to perform in a workshop or try out for one audition to keep the passion burning. Passion is hard to kill. Suppressing it forces it to fight more.

How many of your dreams you have fulfilled or tried to fulfill? We rarely have one dream, and even if we do, it can change.

You may have said years ago that you wanted to be successful at work, and now you are. You seem content, but your priorities can shift. Maybe you want something else.

We may not notice new desires because we are still caught in contentment from succeeding at our last goal.

Maybe you won't take the first step to your dream because it seems too unlikely, too crazy, too dangerous, or just too late.

But you won't ever know until you try. It's like removing a Band-Aid. The initial tear is painful, but the healing is so much faster after the first step. There must be a beginning of any great matter, but the continuing to the end—until it's thoroughly finished—yields the true glory.

Coming together is a beginning; keeping together
is progress; working together is success.
- Henry Ford

127. FLAWS

All creatures are flawed, but out of the flaw may come the universe.
- Marguerite Young

Hamartia is a person's central flaw. In stories, it tends to be the downfall of the character, be it the heel of Achilles or Iago's ego.

As you look back on your life, you may see one problem you always seem to have. It could be you're too timid, too confrontational, or too aggressive. Learning to identify your own hamartia will not only help you correct it but also help to use it to your advantage.

You don't necessarily have to get rid of your hamarthia. Human beings need to have flaws. Flaws have a way of balancing out so their asperity dampens.

If you are an angry person, then you can stand your ground. If you are shy, you won't cause trouble. If you're spoiled rotten, you're financially secure.

Now you can look at these traits the other way around. You may be able to fight your corner, but that's because you have anger issues. When I phrase it that way, it suddenly doesn't sound so glamorous. Being aware of your flaws is necessary because you can rid yourself of them or turn them on their heads. If you're an angry person, accepting it will help you control it and use it to your advantage. If you need to stand up for yourself or fight someone else's corner, you can activate that side of you. Only be angry when you need to be.

Your friends will rarely say something potentially hurtful and personal to your face because they don't want to hurt your feelings. If a friend points out a bad habit, don't get dismissive. Take it into consideration. Look at the flaw constructively because it is a part of you that you can work on.

Whatever flaws you have, you may have had them for years, oblivious to their impact and how they hold you back.

My friend, Holly said I had a dainty way of making physical gestures. She said it casually and didn't realize the impact it had on me. I realized that I needed to be firmer and stronger when I am making my point, taking command of a situation, or even shaking a person's hand. Dainty movements show weakness and a lack of control.

Everyone has a lot of little flaws here and there. These traits seem insignificant separately but are the foundation of your insecurities when added up.

There are parts about you that you may not like. You say to yourself every single day for years, "I am going to fix this!"

You can say this every day of your life, and it will never change a single thing until you are ready to change. You have flaws. They will only hold you back as long as you let them.

No man is wise at all times.
- Pliny the Elder

128. FORGIVENESS

It is easier to forgive an enemy than to forgive a friend.
- William Blake
(Jerusalem)

I used to have too much trust in people. When those close to me made mistakes, I assumed they would change for the better. However, they made the same mistakes over and over, seemingly never learning from their errors.

I started to lose patience and developed into a less tolerant person. It seems cruel, looking back on it, but I just couldn't risk being screwed over or taken advantage of. I shunned my friends' foolishness and stupidity. I thought if no one hurt me, I couldn't be hurt.

Unforgiveness prolongs past mistakes. Choosing not to forgive is choosing to stay angry. You will only lose people and gain nothing. If I could not forgive others, I would run out of friends quickly and stop being a friend to others.

We all do stupid things. I have wronged people many times and have asked for forgiveness. I have been a terrible friend, an unappreciative son, a jealous brother, a self-indulgent housemate, a self-serving boyfriend, an undependable classmate, an unprofessional worker, or just an idiot in general.

If we have no belief in our friends when they betray us, why should they forgive us when the circumstances reverse? Forgiveness is about a second chance.

If you feel like you are already a forgiving person, there is another trap you might fall into. You have to be careful that you are not too forgiving.

Some people will pick up on your virtue use it against you. They will act selfish and idiotic because they expect to be forgiven, which allows them to continue doing stupid things.

Almost everyone deserves to be forgiven, but only if they have truly learned and changed from the experience.

When we are bombarded by an incredibly simple philosophy like "forgive and forget," it deadens and lose the original impact. We forget that that idea has stood for so long because it is a human necessity. It needs to be integrated.

To say someone is beyond forgiveness is to suggest that person has no good in him.

We should not see some people as "bad people" but as good people with bad in them. Some have more or less "bad in them" than others, but there is always good. We need to tap into that.

We read that we ought to forgive our enemies; but we do
not read that we ought to forgive our friends.
- Cosimo de' medici

129. FRIENDS

A friend is a single soul dwelling in twin bodies.
- Aristotle

You like your friends based on how much time you spend around them, at what point in life you met, what you know about them, and what you don't know.

Seeing a person or living with that same person can determine how much you like or dislike them. You could hate someone until you live together and find out you have so much in common.

However, you could be best friends until you share a flat and finally see the person's true colors. It makes you wonder if you ever really knew or liked someone.

You can tell a lot about a person from the people around him. I used to be a quiet, shy kid, but when I got older, I hung out with a few bullies. It seemed a bit of them rubbed off on me. We feed off the energy that surrounds us.

If bad company surrounds you, get out of it. It sounds cruel, but you will learn there is no long-term advantage in staying with them out of loyalty. People like that sink and take whatever is near with them.

Alternatively, good company and reliable friends build a great atmosphere. I have seen miserable people change into the happiest, most positive of friends.

A bad atmosphere can destroy much good. Some people can be trouble incarnate but with the best intentions. Distance yourself from those prone to making bad choices. It's for your own good.

Having friends isn't just about learning about others but learning about you. To do that, you need a true friend, one who adds to your joys and diminishes your sorrows by sharing them.

To be alone is to be in bad company. Make sure you are not a friend for the sake of it, but go out of your way to befriend everyone.

Avoid taking advantage of your friends. Good friends are hard to find, harder to leave, and impossible to forget. One of the blessings of old friends is you can afford to be stupid with them.

Don't define yourself through your friends, but allow them to influence you positively. Don't let a friend take advantage of you, and vice versa. As Arnold Bennett put it, "It is well, when judging a friend, to remember that he is judging you with the same godlike and superior impartiality."

Sometimes, all you can do as a friend is *be* a friend. Nothing else is necessary.

We have fewer friends than we imagine, but more than we know.
- Hugo von Hofmannsthal

130. FUTURE

There is always one moment in childhood when
the door opens and lets the future in.
- Graham Greene

Worrying about the future is one of the most common fears. What's wrong with wondering what comes next? Is it scarier to know what's coming or to know what's not?

If you knew your future, it would hold no surprises, wonder, or suspense. It would shackle you to permanent triviality. It would trap you in a past that hasn't happened yet. It makes you a prisoner of your fate and a slave to your destiny.

You can't wish the future. It has to be paid for. We can say what we want to happen, but we need to work on it to make our future happen. We have to take steps so that the future we want becomes a reality.

We can't arrogantly believe our intended future is guaranteed. Everyone has an idea of what he or she wants with the future, but there is only room for one. How many futures can you hold on the head of a pin?

We can worry about what lies ahead, but we can also look at it positively. What you are going through in harsh times feels bad, but tomorrow becomes today, and today becomes yesterday.

Worries come and go. They come again, but you know that they will go again. The bad times can become the glory days.

We worry for the future, so we can prioritize, prepare, and adapt for the future. This is perfectly understandable in the short term, but people worry about issues that will not be a concern for years—or ever! Will they be married? Have a family? Pay the mortgage?

Deal with today's troubles first before moving onto potential problems in the future. The creator of the Alexander technique, F. Mathias Alexander, believed that people live in the past and future much more often than the present. It is not healthy to do so. If you lose focus on things that have already happened or have yet to ensue, you lose focus on what you are doing right now. If you lose focus on what you are doing in the present, this will impair your abilities in the future. It is now that matters most. It can be your very next action that makes all the difference.

Consider your destiny. We didn't choose life. All we have to do is live it, with all its changes, adjustments, challenges, obstacles, disappointments, joys, and successes. I am not sure what the future will bring, but I accept the future will come. I will rise to meet it. Everyone's a part of what happens next.

Do not worry about tomorrow for tomorrow will worry about itself.

Each day has enough trouble on its own.
- St. James Bible

131. GAMBLING

Bigger pay means longer play.
- Nevada Casino Sign

It's ironic how that quote above is used as an advertisement, not as a deterrent. Having a bit of fun with money can spice up a game, but it can consume your life.

Casinos actually have a design to make gambling more addictive. You probably know about how some casinos have no clocks. If gamblers can't see how late it is, then there is no concept of time. As a result, customers in the casino won't know it's getting late and won't realize that they just wasted three hours.

The flashing lights, buzzing, and coins clattering from a few dozen machines give the illusion that "everybody's a winner," but did you know that casinos tend to have low ceilings, which make the area look fuller, busier, and more exciting?

If you ever wondered why the carpet designs in casinos are ugly, it's deliberate. If you don't look down at it, you'll be looking straight ahead, meaning you will be focusing on the slots, the craps, and the roulette. It's a tactic to avoid distraction. There are many more examples, but let's look at the crux of the issue: the gambling itself.

I did online gambling once and won $800 in half an hour. I lost all of it the following week. I played again and won $600. Then I stopped, canceled my subscription, and uninstalled the program.

I was lucky that I didn't end up with a colossal loss, but some aren't so lucky. My friend Ben won $14,000 on online gambling in three weeks and lost all of it in three minutes. I asked him why he didn't stop after he won $10,000. He said he asked himself the same question when he won $100.

Gambling is an addiction that should be taken just as seriously as an addiction to drugs. The part of your brain that is stimulated when you are gambling is the same part that cocaine stimulates.

In other ways, gambling can be even more dangerous because it's not a chemical addiction, like smoking or drinking, but a psychological craving. You convince yourself that you can't lose—until you do.

Smoking and drinking can ruin your life after a few years, but gambling can financially cripple you in a single afternoon.

It's good to let go and be spontaneous in everyday life, but if money is involved, you need to remember that there is a difference between taking a chance and being financially stable. Nobody ever bets enough on the winner.

Gambling is a disease of barbarians superficially civilized.
- Dean Inge

132. GAMES

I've missed more than 9,000 shots in my career. I've lost
almost 300 games. 26 times, I've been trusted to take the
game winning shot and missed. I've failed over and over
and over again in my life. And that is why I succeed.
- Michael Jordan

Playing games stop for a lot of us when we reach a certain age. When you're in
college, have a job, a relationship, or a child, you may not have time for that
sort of leisure.

We are under the impression that adults don't need to play games. You might
think they aren't for you, but I believe there is a game for everyone. There are physical
games, mental games, card games, board games, video games, and everything in
between.

Even if you enjoy games, you may not play them because you think they're
impractical. But games are necessary for us to unwind. We can play games to
improve our team-playing abilities or strengthen our leadership skills. Or maybe
we just play physical games to stay healthy. Games are never brainless, because our
brain picks up on patterns whether we try to or not.

Games can also set us up in life because the world is itself a game. We can learn
from all the different type of players. Are they leeches? Team players? Cheaters?
Sheep? Shepherds? Leaders? Winners? Losers? Sore losers?

A game can tell a lot about someone as a person. Look at pool. It's not just about
potting balls with a cue. Do you try to pot the balls? Or do you try to pot them, so the
white ball is lined up for the next shot? What kind of personality would a person like
that have? Maybe it would be a person who lines up his goals so when he succeeds
with one, another one is ready.

Maybe you are sly player who tries to set up impossible shots for your opponent.
A player like that might have a personality that says, "I will do anything to win."

Maybe you blast the shots and hit the balls as hard as possible, hoping that one
might pot by chance. A person like that may think he is cocky, but it may come across
as desperate, using arrogance to hide a lack of technique or skill.

We turn life into a game without even realizing it, so it's best to know what kind
of player you are.

Play the game for more than you can afford to lose...
only then will you learn the game.
- Winston Churchill

133. GENERALIZATION

Every generalization is dangerous.
Even this one.
- Alexandre Dumas

Do you see ballet as extraordinarily skillful in physicality and durability, or is it too "girly"? Are you knowledgeable in politics because you need to know how the world works or because you believe there are conspiracies and ulterior motives behind every political decision? Is religion God's true plan or a means of controlling the gullible and an excuse to be prejudiced against other races?

You may feel that you don't generalize; that you are a person who only deals with solid facts. Unfortunately, it's human nature to generalize. We have a presupposed concoction of how things are, how they should be, and how they will be.

One of Aesop's fables perfectly demonstrates this notion. One day, a local village set up a tournament to see who could impersonate a pig's squeal the most accurately. One farmer claimed that he could do a perfect impression of a pig squeal. When he did it, everyone laughed because it was atrocious. Then another farmer jumped up and squealed like a pig. He was applauded for how real it sounded.

The first farmer was certain his pig impression was more convincing, so he rechallenged the other farmer the following day. The first farmer was stubborn and was determined not to lose this time, so he concealed a live pig under his coat.

When the two farmers were ready to compete, the farmer who won the day before squealed again. The audience applauded once more.

Then the disgruntled farmer tugged on his pig's ear, which caused it to let out a loud squeal. The audience thought it was an excellent impersonation, but they were adamant that the other farmer was more convincing.

Outraged, the farmer revealed the pig and challenged the audience, claiming that they didn't even know what a pig actually sounded like.

I had to study animal sounds and movement for classes in the past, and I discovered that not one animal moved or sounded the way I expected.

This observation is obviously not limited to animals. We can generalize so easily, we don't realize that we are doing it.

In the future, give yourself more time to look at all the facts, reconsider your thoughts, and give yourself a second to doubt yourself. Being wrong is better than living in a world of ignorance and oversimplification.

It is very difficult to generalize.
Everyone's adventure is original.
- Bernard Pivot

134. GENETICS

You have to work with what you are given and that's called genetics.
- Tamilee Webb

Tamilee Webb is a fitness guru famous for her '80s and '90s workout videos, *Buns of Steel* and *Abs of Steel*. Her videos became a sensation and made over $10 million. The purpose of these fitness videos was to have the same body as Tamilee. Even nowadays, many of her customers accept her exercises as genuine. After all, she has a master's degree in exercise science and is currently the CEO of Webb International.

What many people don't realize is that Tamilee looked the way she did in her videos *before* she did the exercises. She looked physically fit because of her genetics, not because she exercised. Promoters were looking for a woman that could do the exercises they had decided on for their promotion, and Tamilee fit the bill. She had a physique that women desired, which the promoters put on posters and covers, so people would believe they could have Tamilee's build if they exercised like her.

But for some people, you can't have a perfect body through willpower or endurance. You cannot change the structure of your body. Your muscles can grow, and it can shrink, but your body cannot transform its design.

Of course, the people who did these exercises became healthier and stronger, but the promoters shouldn't have offered something that they could not deliver.

Unfortunately, many aspects of ourselves that we desperately want to change or eradicate may be a part of us.

If you don't have the right genes, it's virtually impossible to look like Olympic athletes or bodybuilders without resorting to steroids. When people learn this, it can cause them to give on trying to be healthy. But just because you don't have the right genes doesn't mean you can't be fit. N

Understanding genetics can help us understand our problems, which is the beginning of finding a solution.

I recently saw an article about a girl who weighed 322 pounds. People around her said it was disgusting how the parents overfed her.

However, the girl's twin brother weighed 126 pounds. The brother and sister were always given the same lunches and ate together every day. She obviously had genes that made her fat, while her brother had the opposite.

Delve into your genes. Understanding your genetics can help you understand what you are good at and what you have difficulty doing.

Intellectuals today have a phobia of any
explanation of the mind that invokes genetics.
- Steven Pinker

135. GIVE AND TAKE

It is more agreeable to have the power to give than to receive.
- Winston Churchill

A give-and-take relationship is ideal but surprisingly difficult to maintain. Most of us do one more than the other. Using one or the other excessively leaves us feeling empty. If we give and give, and get nothing back, we feel weak and spineless, as if we're trying too hard.

If we take all the time, we will be seen as selfish and unappreciative.

Doing one or the other says a lot about you. If you give all the time, it shows a lack of self-worth because you act like you need people to like you.

If someone you barely know gave you a present for your birthday, you may be flattered, but most people would find it a little weird.

The giver will think that he or she was generous and will not understand if you react in any way except joyfully. People can be self-centered, and a lot of people will not appreciate generosity.

If you take all the time, you will eventually expect people to always give you what you want. These people see offers, presents, friendship, and affection as a one-way road, which they use to their advantage.

People like this expect to get what they want without working too hard to get it. Although it sounds wonderful and luxurious, it usually makes the individual feel empty.

People quickly learn if you are a taker and will become wary of you. If you have a reputation as a taker, and you act nice to someone, that person will assume you have an ulterior motive. It's like "The Boy Who Cried Wolf." Even when your intentions are good, people won't believe you.

Human beings try to maintain evenness. We have an automatic balancer in our minds. If someone shows kindness to us, we try to give some back to keep the equilibrium. We would expect the same from someone else if we gave something. It's a built-in leveling complex.

Going one way or the other too much isn't healthy because we are compassionate and empathetic beings. Personally, I look forward to and love seeing the expression on a person's face when receiving a gift, more than receiving a present myself. The give-and-take rule doesn't just pertain to gifts or rewards but to offers, invitations, promises, agreements, guarantees, and deliveries.

Giving's better than lending and costs around the same.
- Anon

136. GLORY

I am looking for a lot of men who have infinite
capacity to not know what can be done.
- Henry Ford

What is the greatest thing a person can do? Well, the worst thing a person can do is murder. So, the greatest thing a human being can do should be to save a life. Which begs the question, "Who has saved the most lives in history?" Cops can save hundreds of lives in a lifetime. Soldiers making snap decisions can decide whether thousands live or die. Presidents' decisions decide millions of lives.

But there is one man who trumps them. Norman Borlaug has saved approximately 1.15 billion, which is the world record.

Borlaug spent over half his life recreating and replicating wheat and grass. In laymen's terms, he clones food. He travelled to the Third World and shared his research, created crops from scratch, saved millions, and then moved on to another country. These countries are usually war-torn. He was in the thick of it but carried on with his life's work. His achievements have earned him a Nobel Peace Prize.

You may be asking, "Why have I never heard of him?" It's because some people do everything they can to undermine Borlaug's achievements. Some people consider his food to be an abomination, dubbing it "Frankenfood." They say it's poisonous (even though it's modified to be healthier than our processed food), and unsafe (even though every crop is scanned to detect deficiencies). They say the food will not grow properly in Third World countries because they suffer from winds, droughts, and storms (even though it's designed to grow eight times faster and be strong enough to survive bad weather.) It's the same food we eat but better.

Despite what the facts show, Borlaug had a lot of enemies. A few years ago, Borlaug travelled to Zambia to plant grain and corn, but disillusioned people demanded the Zambian government reject the crops because it was poisonous. Because of those lies, the Zambian government declined Borlaug's offer, and 450,000 people died of starvation who could have been saved. Seventy percent of them were children; 40 percent were under the age of five.

Borlaug sought no glory, to the point that people loathed him and wished to destroy everything he stood for. Is there a better example of a person wanting to do the right thing, not for glory but because it should be done?

What satisfaction is there in seeking goals solely for glory? This silent hero never tried to make a name for himself, and he accomplished more than anyone. To want to be a glory hound makes dogs of us all.

That's one small step for man, one giant leap for mankind.
- Neil Armstrong

137. GOALS

All that we are is a result of what we thought.
- Buddha

We all live by moral codes that we use to keep us strong when we feel weak and to counter obstacles and achieve goals. If we aren't strong enough, we will compromise our dreams.

Our feelings and actions are created and naturally adapt to achieve our desired ends. We don't just have certain abilities or attitudes, but we adopt certain skills and knowledge. We combine these traits to aim toward our final, desired goal and cast off any characteristics that may seem harmful to our ambitions.

If you win the lottery, you know the money is yours before it is in your hand. We have been in situations where we know something is ours before we touch it. You believe it is yours. That is the level of belief you should have to earn everything you want.

Everything deserves to be challenged so it can be bettered. Don't admire what has been done; see what has yet to be done. Experience is never limited or complete. We triumph without glory when we conquer without danger.

We should set our goals high to achieve as much as possible, but from time to time, we may see them as being overwhelming. Jack Canfield had an analogy regarding goals in the book The Secret: "Think of a car driving through the night. The headlights only go two hundred feet forward, and you can make it all the way to New York driving through the dark because all you have to see is the next two hundred feet. And that's how life tends to unfold before us. If we just trust the next two hundred feet, and we know that the next two hundred feet will follow after that, life will keep unfolding. And it will eventually get you to your destination or whatever it is you truly want because you want it."

A simpler metaphor is, "To take away a mountain, move it stone by stone."

A mountain represents overcoming. The higher you go up, the harder it gets, yet the more satisfying it feels. You are so close to the top, and when you finally get there, you relax and stay there for a while.

And why not? You reached the peak. You can't go any higher. Either you stay there, or you go back down. Some descend slowly, some tumble, some fall, but everyone goes down eventually.

You can always climb back up. Whatever your goals or dreams are, remember this: whatever you become, be good at it.

He turns all injuries into strengths, that which
cannot kill him makes him stronger – he is superman.
- Friedrich Wilhelm Nietzsche

138. GOD

God must love the common man, he made so many of them.
- Abraham Lincoln

Whether you're an atheist, an agnostic, or a believer, it's very easy to get your arguments for a higher being mixed up. Many religious people dismiss The Big Bang Theory while many believers see it as proof that God doesn't exist. However, few people realise that this hypothesis was devised… by a priest. In the early 20th century, a Belgian minister called Georges Lemaitre theorized that all of existence expanded from a single point. Scientists of his day mocked his theories, as they believed the universe was never-changing and always existed.

But Georges was right. The Vatican said it is one of the ultimate examples of a scientific discovery that strengthened religious belief, rather than diminished it.

If you believe in God, make sure you know what you believe unerringly. Don't follow your faith for the sake of it. Understand the history and challenge it to maintain and strengthen your belief. That's what Georges did. Not only was he a priest, but he was also a physicist, so he tried to scientifically back up his theories with scientific research, rather than blind faith. And he succeeded.

There is nothing wrong with believing in God, but overrelying on Him can cause trouble. Humanity's salvation lies with humanity, not outside it. The more we wait for him to save us from ourselves, the more we will remain unsaved.

God can be a social reflex. Saying bad things happen because it's part of God's plan gives people no solace or peace in times of need. Instead of waiting for Him to make sense of tragedy, we should take steps to ensure tragedies are not repeated.

Some people see God in everything. There are famous slices of cheese and Doritos that look like they have a face of Jesus or the Virgin Mary on them. These "priceless" objects have been witnessed in galleries by thousands, earning their owners a fortune.

You can argue that people will see what they want to see. A more accurate way to do this is to explain pareidolia. This phenomenon is when you see an ambiguous picture in a nonspecific image. It works the same way how a cloud can look like a cat to one person or a bus to another person. It's our mind's way of making sense of images. God and the Virgin Mary have more important things to do than appear in food.

But pareidolia isn't just about physical things; it's about seeing God in everything—justifying every good deed, every tragedy, and every judgment. We don't need to twist religion's teachings and warp quotations for our own sake.

God does not play dice.
- Albert Einstein

139. GOSSIP

'Did you gut the pillow with a knife?' What were the results?'
'Feathers,' she said. Feathers; everywhere, Father."
Now I want you to go back and gather up every last feather,'
'Well,' she said, 'it can't be done. The wind took them all over.'
'And that,' said Father O' Rourke, 'is gossip!'
- Father Brendan Flynn
(Doubt)

Bullying in school used to be name-calling or physical abuse. Now people just spread spiteful rumors. It's scary because when I finished primary school, I thought all the bullying was out of the way, and I could concentrate on my studies.

But in college, the bullying came back. But this time, the bullying was verbal, not physical, which made it more complicated. Instead of using fists, students used gossip as their weapon. Even though gossip sounds innocent, it can be used to destroy people's reputations, jobs, or their lives.

Gossip can get out of control through no fault of any one person. But there are those will intentionally stir half truths about whomever or whatever, just to see where it leads.

Most of the time, gossip is quickly to disprove, which should give us ample time to accept that speculation isn't a reliable source of information. But before people get a chance to acknowledge this, they have already moved onto the next piece of inaccurate gossip.

Gossip is scary because it can change people and turn friends into enemies. Things are more vivid in rumor than reality. People believe in conspiracies because they are more interesting than facts. But remember, whispering half-truths doesn't make you less guilty. If you gossip about others, don't be surprised when they gossip about you.

There can be more power in rumors than in truth. A fact can be disproven, but a rumor lingers forever. Gossip can begin as truth, but it can spiral out of control.

The mechanics of gossip can be beyond your control, and you might find yourself a part of it, even indirectly. You can overhear something, mumble it to someone else without a thought, and before you know it, the whole area has heard of it, except their version is ten times worse.

Never go to second-hand sources for good leads. It's a version of the truth, not the truth itself. Do not believe all you hear, and do not tell all you see. Remember, the only thing that gets thicker when spread is rumor.

Nothing is so firmly believed as that which we least know.
- Montaigne

140. GREED

One should eat to live, not live to eat.
- Moliere

In the film, *Wall Street,* Gordon Gekko has a famous monologue where he states that, "Greed is good. Greed works."

Despite the fact he's the bad guy in the story, this simple philosophy of "greed is good" took a lot of investors and stockbrokers by storm. They didn't pick up on Gekko's downfall which shows that greed doesn't work.

For millennia, our ancestors scavenged for food as desperately as most animals in the wild today. Our two main functions were to seek out food and to procreate. It can take generations before basic impulses change, not to mention diminish, so even though we have more food than ever, we still feel inclined to eat.

Gluttony has always been perceived with revulsion. The thought of overeating food is not only a moral issue an unhealthy one.

In China, it is custom for people to eat until they are 80 percent full. Whatever is left is left alone. You might wonder why don't the people there stop eating when they are not full? But a more important question is why do we eat when we are full? Why consume more than you need? Being full is your body's signal that anything else will be overindulgence.

But it's the same with any type of greed. You can eat more just as you can always have more. All your possessions could have better quality, be shinier, larger, brighter, louder, newer, but where do you draw the line?

We have all become lovers of luxury. We buy things that we have never opened, buy food and throw out most of it every week, and buy clothes we never wear. I know someone who bought three Porsche cars in six months.

Having more "stuff" doesn't equate to more contentment. I was briefly addicted to gambling. I didn't do it out of desperation but fun. I had money, so I wasn't aiming for a number, which meant I had no reason to stop. I just kept betting. It's scary when you don't know how much is enough. You may have passed "enough" long ago, but you're addicted to your own greed. Put an end to it before it consumes you.

The appetite grows by eating.
- Francois Rabelais

141. GRIEF

Grief for the dead is mad; it is an injury to the living, and the dead know it not.
- Xenophon

A death isn't like losing a job or getting a divorce. There is no "getting over it." You have to integrate it into your life and live with it. It isn't like stopping a bomb going off. It is the bomb going off, and you have to survive somehow.

When you go through trauma, it can actually help you push your dreams in ways you never would have because now you have the ultimate motivation. Your friends will be behind you more than ever to ensure you succeed.

But because death is the most horrible thing that can happen, we will have the deepest reaction. We need to decide what kind of reaction it will be.

Will it be consumed with depression, or can we convert all that energy into something useful? That same energy was created from love of the deceased, so why make it into anything ugly? Put it to good use.

My friend, Simon lost both his parents within six months of each other. I expected him to lose his way. Two years later, I got a call from him. He had a great job, a girlfriend, and a healthy lifestyle. I congratulated him for his positive attitude. What he said next was something I did not expect. Simon said, "I feel like the best thing that ever happened to me was my parents being taken away from me. If I still had them, I'd take advantage of them, steal from them, and hate them because I didn't know better. But their absence pushed me to embrace my life."

When you lose someone, desperation tends to override logic but not always. Erin Renyen was a mother whose daughter, Samantha was kidnapped. Her dead body was discovered twenty-four hours later. This tragedy occurred eleven days before her sixth birthday.

What was astounding was the mother's reaction. She did not live her life in fear and demand every parent should use scare tactics on their kids to make them aware of stranger danger. She was not overly protective of the rest of her family and friends, because she understood that she was part of that tragic minority—one chance in 350,000 that your child will be kidnapped. Sadly, she had to be that statistic.

Even though her daughter never had a chance to live, Erin didn't believe she should use that as an excuse to impair her other children enjoying their lives. It's incredible how that woman could be that rational under such tremendous emotional turmoil.

Some people seem to just shake off death, but you need to react to it. You can find a little happiness in losing someone. You are upset because you lost someone important to you. It would be so much worse if you weren't upset because it would mean you never loved anything worth losing.

Given a choice between grief and nothing, I'd choose grief.
- William Faulkner

142. GROWING UP

At the age of six I wanted to be a cook. At seven I wanted to be
Napoleon. And my ambition has been growing steadily ever since.
- Salvador Dali

It's hard growing up. When I say "growing up," I don't just mean physically. I mean growing up mentally. As you get older, you have to take in a lot more information, have less fun, do more work, prioritize more, and so on.

It's hard because sometimes, your friends just won't let you. Usually, when you go through a great change, your friends and family may not even notice for a while. Maybe they will never notice and will see you the way they want to see you. Your friends may have a set way of looking at you, and it can take time for any deviation to register. If you want to read more books, get up earlier, get a job, take an interest in politics, be healthy, have a stable relationship instead of flings, you would expect a bit of support.

Let's just say you want to be healthy. Some people may support you, but there will be others who will dissuade you with negativity.

"You'll give up after a week! You never exercise! You can't even do a pull-up! You've said that before, and you gave up!"

You want to do it to prove them wrong. You use it as a driving force. Week after week, you feel good. But then it starts all over.

"It hasn't made a difference! You look the same! Actually, you look like you put on weight!" That mentality can make you quit.

When you decide to grow up and start looking at things in the long term, you will probably be picked on and teased by your friends instead of supported.

Some of your friends won't like the idea of you changing because they don't recognize the person they befriended originally. They may feel like you are starting to outgrow them and may not like that you are growing up faster than they are.

You need to do what you feel you need to do. You are not doing it for your friends or your family or anyone but yourself.

A time may come when you outgrow your friends. They won't like that and will belittle you or try to drag you down.

If you don't want to go out and get wasted every night, then don't. If your friends don't want you to change, lay it out for them. Tell them how you feel. You may end up telling them to go to hell, or they might tell you the same, but it's sad doing the exact same thing with the same people, decades later, except without the enjoyment.

We cling to our own ideals and hope in the face of adversary,
we will be strong enough to stand by them.
- Anon

143. GUILT

I don't believe in guilt by association.
- Marion Jones

Guilt is one of the most important aspects of self-preservation. Without guilt, there would be no learning from past transgressions and therefore no way of avoiding repeating them.

Guilt forces us to keep to a moral code. It is actually fascinating that guilt can be so strong that a person will come forward, even if there is no other way the person could be discovered for their wrongdoings.

If you feel guilty, it usually has to do with something you have done wrong. You need to locate the source of the guilt and deal with it as soon as possible to reverse as much emotional damage as possible.

That's the easy part out of the way. Let's look at guilt from slightly less obvious angles. You can feel guilty because you are the only one who knows that someone else has committed misdeeds.

You may have ancestral guilt or family guilt—a bloodline passing on the guilt to their successors—and you bear that burden, even though the guilt does not lie with your own actions. The circumstances are out of your control, sometimes occurring even before your lifetime.

All of humanity is capable of error, regardless of race or belief. No one should carry the guilt of another person, especially outside of his or her lifetime or generation. We should not look for someone to blame or to feel guilty for any misdeed, especially if it is long past, buried, or forgotten.

Guilt is there to make you better than you are, to ensure you keep to what you believe is right. A lot of people fight against it for the sake of embarrassment, control, power, and ego.

But if you fight guilt, it will count against you. You cannot make it disappear by ignoring it. It can only stop eating at you once you have dealt with your inner demons.

Within time, guilt becomes shame, and that's a sickening feeling to sustain. Nip it in the bud. Do what you have to rectify yourself. The consequences are rarely as bad as you think.

If you don't accept these consequences, the guilt will stay within you. With no enemy within, no enemy can hurt you. No one has more power than you to create guilt and to eliminate it.

It is the confession, not the priest that gives us absolution.
- Oscar Wilde

144. GULLIBLE

Men are nearly always willing to believe what they wish.
- Julius Caesar

Have you ever wondered why the headline, "Psychic Wins Lottery" has never materialized? The idea of psychic powers stems from magic. History tells us that Dede, the earliest recorded magician, made his debut in ancient Egypt in 2700 BC.

He famously performed a trick whereby he removed and replaced the head of a bird.

Even though the polytheistic Egyptians' beliefs delved into cosmology and countless gods, they were still completely aware that Dede was an entertainer. They didn't believe he had magical power.

Nevertheless, magic is an incredible concept that shows how suggestible we can be and how human beings tend to believe what they want to believe.

For a split second during a magic trick, we do believe that the magician sawed someone in half or he knows your mother's maiden name—because we really want to believe!

But gullibility doesn't end with magic. You might believe things will get better, even though they never do. You might believe your unreliable friend will repay a loan from you, even though it's been six months and you still haven't seen a penny.

You are certain that new political power will change the world for the better, even though it's been promised time after time without materializing.

To believe something will happen just because you want it to is not having faith; it's gullibility. Gullibility can be found in paranoia, gossip, urban legends, religion, superstition, and flat-out lies.

Adolf Hitler said, "The bigger the lie, the more people will believe it." Granted, Hitler isn't exactly the greatest source of reliable information, but he did have a point.

Voltaire said, "Those that can make you believe in absurdities can make you commit atrocities."

What we hear in day-to-day life or on the news can easily be accepted as fact, but how do we know how accurate it is? I don't mean to question and challenge everything.

I am saying that we take in a lot of information every day; a lot of it is incomplete or opinion-based. It's hard to get all the facts and harder to draw an accurate understanding of them. It's too tempting to accept a watered-down simplified version.

Our suggestibility knows no limits.
- David Mamet

145. HABITS

It is easier to prevent bad habits than to break them.
- Benjamin Franklin

How long does it take before a bad habit becomes permanent? How long does it take to kill a bad habit? How long does it take to make a positive habit a part of your daily routine?

There is an answer to these questions: sixty-six days. In 2009, Phillippa Lally investigated the formation of habits and discovered that whether they were good or bad, habits took the same length of time to form.

If you try to start a practical hobby, like going to the gym, and it is interrupted by unforeseen circumstances, it is likely you will quit.

If you have successfully kept going to the gym for over ten weeks and then you fall prey to unforeseen circumstances, it's much more likely you will adapt to ensure you keep trying to be healthy. Even if it's impossible to maintain, you will be inclined to resume your practical routine once the circumstances are no longer an issue.

This is not to say you must stop if something affects your progress before you reach sixty-six days. You can keep it up if your willpower is good enough. But no matter how much you want to quit, just look at that sixty-sixth day as a goal.

My friend, Danny was the person who told me about this sixty-six day habit concept. When he learned about it, he decided to put it to the test by trying to get into shape. But after a few weeks of his fitness regime, his mother became terminally ill. At the same time, his family was trying to be healthy too but that went out the window because they couldn't handle the stress.

Danny, however, used it as a driving force. If he gave up his fitness regime, he would have sat in bed for hours, worrying about his mother, making him drowsy and prone to illness when he needed to be alert and focused.

Since he was taking care of himself physically, his attentiveness was entirely on his mother while others were getting ill from stress or falling into bad habits. It was tough to maintain his new lifestyle, but he thought, "If I can do this when things are hard, then I can do this when things are easy."

When you try to change for the better, inconvenience will inevitably get in your way, and using it as an excuse will be your first step to failure.

Gradually changing habits makes more
difference than changing them all at once.
- Ian K. Smith

146. HAPPINESS

Follow your bliss and the universe will open doors
for you where there were only walls.
- Joseph Campbell

All human problems tend to fall into three categories: health, wealth, or relationships. Each of these problems have an inner and outer component. These cannot be permanently fulfilled, though.

The reason why we evolved so we are never fully happy is so we can always better ourselves. It was so we would force ourselves to improve, to succeed, to create, to invent, to cure, and to influence. After all, if our ancestors were satisfied in the caves thousands of years ago, we would've died out before we got started.

Some people go on wild, crazy adventures to feel alive. It's nice to blow off steam, but avoid using it as an excuse to run away from yourself.

We spend our whole lives trying to be cool and popular but rarely spend time to be happy. Getting what you want never makes you happy, unless you are happy first.

It's hard to gauge our level of happiness. Regardless, studies and tests have been conducted to measure what makes us happy. The one I find most fascinating was in 1978, where researchers found a person who had suddenly won a vast sum of money and another person who was paralyzed in a car accident. You would think that the one who won the money would be the "happy one," and the paraplegic would be the "unhappy one." This was the case but only momentarily because their circumstances had just changed. Within a short time, they both leveled out and were in the same state mentally as they were in before their circumstances altered.

One trap we all fall into at times is "oneitis." It's that mentality where you believe you will be happy if you get that one thing—your other half, money, or a job. But when you get it, you're not satisfied. It's not about what you want but how you feel.

We have all met people who are in unfortunate circumstances yet seem naturally content. We all know others who have had life handed to them, and they don't appreciate how lucky they are.

Happiness doesn't begin or end with the amount of "stuff" we have. It's more to do with a positive mentality. If you feel like you need something, you will feel incomplete until you get it.

We have no more right to consume happiness without producing
it than to consume wealth without producing it.
- George Bernard Shaw

147. HARD WORK

Don't work harder, work smarter.
- Anon

We all like to hide behind hard work, but hard work doesn't guarantee results. It can register more frustration, strain, and disbelief than for someone who does less work. Letting this fact get to you will exacerbate your problems.

Anyone can do a ton of hard work, but not all of us do. It's not just because of laziness but aggravation. In any group, the most efficient workers are not necessarily the hardest workers. Or maybe they are, but they don't work in the same way. They may not go by the book, memorize things, or do a lot of paperwork. Anyone can do that.

But can everyone take huge risks, time and time again, and risk failure? If their dreams do shatter, will they be able to get back up and try again? Can everyone think outside of their comfort zone and work outside the box?

A lot of us will not try because we may believe that we are not that kind of person. If we work hard, we believe we will get our due.

But a lot of people work hard for years and feel like they're not getting a shred of gratitude. You may not have time for leisure or a partner. Your mates have the time of their lives, and you seem to get less recognition for your work.

If our hard work gets recognized, it might feel great. We might be given more money, qualifications, bonuses, and promotions.

But this also means we may be given more responsibility. It means that there are far bigger consequences to our actions and failings. So if we were stressed before, it's only going to get worse.

There are two kinds of speeches given—one written and memorized and the other from the heart and in the moment. If you have to say a speech on the spot for a wedding, a celebration, or an award ceremony, you may panic because you don't know what to say. In a way, it is actually less work. You don't have to write anything. You don't have to spend time memorizing words. You just say how you feel. It will sound more honest and more real than any rehearsed speech.

Why settle for more work with fewer results when you can take a chance and blow people away? You can't play safe forever.

During the Space Race, the Russians and the Americans realized that
pens didn't work in space because the gravity messed with the ink. The
Americans spent millions experimenting to create the perfect pen that could
be used in intense heats, freezing cold and even in the depths of space.
The Russians just used pencils.
- An old joke

148. HATE

Love, friendship, respect do not unite people as
much as common hatred for something.
- Anton Chekhov
(Notebooks)

There is little room for hate, not just because it's a negative feeling to bestow on someone else but also because it can be a sign of self-damage. It creates a cycle. Hatred is not like sadness or fear. When we are sad, we cry. After we cry, we feel better. We can feel fear, but eventually the feeling passes.

Unfortunately, hate doesn't work this way. Like anger, we don't burn out our hatred by overusing it. The more we hate, the more we feed it. Over time, this can twist us into a disturbed and dangerous individual.

Hatred should never be used as a solution. Even in times of anger or depression, where it is easy to focus on what we hate, focusing on what we love will always be a far more potent driving force. As Martin Luther King Jr. said, "Darkness cannot drive out darkness; only light can do that. Hate cannot drive out hate; only love can do that."

At times, we can't tell how similar we are to that which we claim to hate because of a minor difference, such as gender, age, or ethnicity.

It's like the clichéd circle of violence—the son of a violent father grows up and takes out all his hatred of his parent on his children. I think we are all aware that there is a part of us that hates others sometimes, when they remind us of ourselves or parts of us that we hate.

You can hate a person, a group, a race, or a concept, but the hatred will not start with them but with you.

Maybe there is a person in your life that you hate because he or she is a horrible person who stands against every moral fiber you have. Or perhaps that person reminds you of your moral hypocrisy. You might hate someone because he or she makes snide comments about you that aren't true—or because you are afraid that they are true.

We need to question our hatred. If we acknowledge our hatred, we can find its source and deal with it, rather than using another person as a mirror to our insecurities and projecting our own negative feelings on others.

Hatred has to come from somewhere. We don't just hate instinctively. As the late Nelson Mandela said, "No one is born hating. People must learn to hate."

If you hate a person, you hate something in him that is part
of yourself. What isn't part of ourselves doesn't disturb us.
- Hermann Hesse

149. HEAVEN

Is the pious loved by the gods because it is pious,
or is it pious because they love it?
- Plato

Everyone wants to believe in something beyond the here and now, a place where wrongs can be righted, questions answered, regrets dissolved, death destroyed, justice restored, and love is triumphant. Such a place has never been found.

Regardless, there are those who will give up all chance of bliss and contentment for a reward that can only be found in death. They will never know happiness in this life and will throw away every opportunity for joy because of the unquestionable belief that it will be balanced out a millionfold after death.

But will it?

There is no proof that such a realm exists. Should we commit so utterly to a vague, possibly nonexistent reward? Such a gambit seems extreme for a pay-off that may not be. You can be a wonderful, positive, happy person without giving up your life for "the greater good."

This is not an excuse to sin. That's just as overly simplistic as believing blindly in the afterlife.

There is a saying that goes, "Better to reign in hell than serve in heaven." Although that expression may be a bit severe, it isn't right to live a life caged in fear. You can easily live a gratifying, prosperous, and adventurous life while maintaining your belief in God.

My friend once said, "Even saints behave to get into heaven." That may not be true, but I do see his point. To serve such a pious regime just to go to heaven does not sound particularly humble. It's like when a kid behaves just to get a treat, not because they acknowledges it is the right thing to do.

One of the most maddening and insincere things a believer can do is condemn those who do not follow the Way and put himself on a pedestal as if they are the chosen one. We all have seen people like this. They do not look happy. They look crazy. They look, act, and talk the complete opposite way to how they think they are.

A genuinely good person usually doesn't see himself or herself as holier than thou. They get off their high horse and get on with their lives.

We can live in heaven now by just taking every day as it is, looking at it from the best possible angle, and making the most of it. I

f you think you're better than everyone else, you've already lost the battle. Don't be good for the sake of it. Just be good.

No morality can be founded on authority,
even if the authority were divine.
- A.J. Ayer

150. HELL

Hell is empty and all the devils are here.
- William Shakespeare

In several religions and cultures, it is believed that those who live a sinful life will be sent to hell for all time after they die. In this realm, the sinners will be tortured forever. When you phrase it like that, you can see why hell is such a terrifying concept.

But that doesn't mean it's a useful one. When children first hear of hell, the idea is usually so scary, it encourages them to be good.

But you shouldn't do good just to avoid hell. You should be a good person because it is the right thing to do. If you are only avoiding sin to avoid punishment, you're not being good for the right reasons.

There are few religions left in the world that have a hell in their belief system because it isn't practical. When I was a child, I was terrified I would burn in hell because I ate meat on Good Friday. Being tormented by demons and hellfire for all eternity is a fear no child should have to go through. And yet, overly religious people instill this fear into others.

Even if the fear of hell makes someone a decent human being, the sheer terror of the afterlife can leave them unhappy and anxious for the rest of their life.

Even though hell sounds like the worst fate imaginable, it's still not compelling enough to stop religious people from sinning. We all know religious people who have done so many wrongdoings, you wonder why they don't take the concept of hell more seriously.

On the other hand, I know atheists who don't believe in hell and yet, go out of their way to be kind and considerate.

Trying to scare people into a religious belief can never be good, even if it is for the right reasons. People need to find their own way to differentiate between right and wrong, without having to resort to scare tactics. Living in fear is living in hell.

We can learn from our transgressions, but there is no point torturing ourselves with our wrongdoings. To live that life doesn't prevent us from entering hell because we make ourselves go through it in this life. Hell exists, maybe not in a hellfire and brimstone way, but we live our own private hells.

If you have done something wrong, do all you can to redeem yourself rather than fearing for your soul. You will go through hell until you do.

The Gates of Hell are locked from the inside.
- C.S. Lewis.

151. HELP

He has a right to criticize, who has a heart to help.
- Abraham Lincoln

We are usually too nice to ask for help or too ashamed or too proud. Or we may be too selfish to give it.

If you ask your friend if they are okay, and they clearly are not, what is the most common response? "Fine." "Great." "Never better!" We try not to be a bother, and we don't need to be a burden, so we will act like we are fine when we are not.

Or if you are looking at this from the side of the helper, you probably won't push the issue, fearing you are being rude. Your friend clearly doesn't want to talk about what's bothering them, so you should leave them alone.

You don't want to press on because you are their friend. You feel like you should give them some space, but a true friend would lend a helping hand. People don't want to burden friends with their problems, but friends are there to help with problems.

We may be afraid that people will laugh at us when we seek aid, but we are usually more than grateful to be of some help to others.

Asking for help is the same as admitting we are wrong or apologizing. It's one of those things we hate to do because we will look weak. But people tend to respect us more for admitting that we can't do everything by ourselves.

Some people ask for help, but they see their helpers as disposable lackeys, not teammates, and use them as a means to an end. Anyone who helps should get credit, no matter how small his or her contribution.

Every inspirational person throughout history achieved greatness with the help of others. Even though Socrates encapsulates the field of ethics, he would be nothing without his teachers and students.

Recent advancement in computers is often credited to Steve Jobs despite the fact that thousands of engineers made his dreams possible.

We tend to think of Stephen Hawking when we talk about quantum theories but his work was built off the work of countless astronomers and astrophysicists.

All of these people had help; directly or indirectly. Help can come as direct assistance, faith, constructive criticism, or correction. Even enemies help because a rivalry can spur us on.

We can achieve a lot by ourselves but not everything. Things only get done in the long run with help.

We cannot teach people anything; we can
only help them discover it within themselves.
- Galileo Galilei

152. HISTORY

We are not makers of history. We are made by history.
- Martin Luther King, Jr.

I am fascinated by history as a concept—if our current affairs are so convoluted at times, how reliable are documents of history from ten years ago? Fifty years ago? Or two thousand years ago?

Who knows how our time will be perceived in the future? Will it be seen a time of vast medical advancement, the beginning of space travel, equality for women and all races, cloning, and the Internet? Or will it be seen as the century of overpopulation, misinformation, and pollution?

Who knows? As you can see, history can be subjective, and our account of it is not solid fact.

Many people we see as heroes in history had a dark side that we tend to overlook. Historic figures we paint as villains had their noble moments that we ignore. Historic movies don't necessarily help us glean a more accurate picture.

King Edward Longshanks is immortalized as a villain, thanks to the film *Braveheart*, but in reality, Scotland invited the king over to help their nation. He wrote dozens of laws and formed England's first constitution.

Antonio Salieri was considered the arch nemesis of master composer Mozart because of the play and movie *Amadeus*. Salieri is often perceived as a jealous hack but in fact, he and Mozart were good friends. Salieri was one of the most respected composers of his time.

The past can be corrupted. Some use the bloodier side of history to revitalize past hatreds and grudges with former oppressors.

As my own Irish heritage shows, 751 years of oppression was ended, thanks to the heroics of Michael Collins. However, the Irish Republic Army refused to accept this because England still owns the six counties of Northern Ireland. Michael Collins tolerated this because he didn't want any more Irish people to die. The IRA saw him as a hypocrite and refueled the rift between the Irish and the English.

I speak as an Irishman, saying that our history was brutal. The IRA fought because they believed they were being patriotic, but their actions do the complete opposite of what they hope to do. We are lucky to get back our home. Not all countries are lucky. Don't let mistakes made hundreds of years ago by faceless people ruin future generations.

Instead of using history to hate, we should use it to learn. We can see patterns in human nature by analyzing history. Maybe if we look hard enough, we can stop making the same mistakes and continue making the same advancements.

History is written by the victors.
- Winston Churchill

153. HUMOR

A dirty joke is a sort of mental rebellion.
- George Orwell

Years ago, I went to the airport after finished a tour of stand-up comedy gigs. As I waited, I was beside an American. We got chatting, and I told him that I was doing stand-up comedy. He was intrigued.

He told me that he'd just finished eighteen months in Iraq. He told me of all the horrible, traumatizing things he'd seen—destroyed cities, burning houses, explosions, and gunfire from all directions.

I felt like an idiot. Here I was, talking about comedy, while this silent hero had been in the thick of the world. When I mentioned my concerns to him, he gave me a wonderful reply. He told me he would find life so depressing if it wasn't for comedians making jokes about taboo subjects.

Because he spent a year and a half being completely serious in a foreign country, he wanted to come home to unwind and have a laugh. To him, humor wasn't fun, it was vital.

There are those who see performance jobs like acting, singing, comedy, and dancing as entertainment, rather than "real work." But when you have a bad day and want to blow off steam, what do you do? You watch something funny, listen to music, or watch a comedy.

Humor is needed. Making snide jokes about society may be considered offensive and disrespectful, but as long as we know where our boundaries stand, it can be good fun.

I have a Polish friend called Cubert who always makes jokes about World War II. Naturally, his friends find this weird. Cubert said that he thinks that period was so horrifying, he wants to make fun of it so it doesn't have any power over him.

I saw a documentary about a woman who had six months to live. She spent those last few months making jokes about her health and her inevitable death. Even though a lot of people were baffled by her behavior, she didn't see the problem. She said she can laugh about it because "I'm still going to die either way! At least I can decide how I go, and it will not be crying when I can actually still make the most of what time I have left."

Humor creates one of the greatest feelings; it's healthy, and it allows us to destroy negativity by converting it into something positive. What would life be like without the likes of Bill Hicks, Eddie Murphy, Billy Connolly, and Chris Rock looking at the hilarious side of all of life's tragedies? Laughter is the best medicine—and the cheapest.

Humor is the weapon of unarmed people: it helps people who
are oppressed to smile at the situation that pains them.
- Simon Wiesenthal

154. HYPE

Ice cream stores sell all kinds of flavors, most want vanilla or
chocolate. It's simply higher demand, there is always a preference but
once in a while, you'll get someone who just wants plain. No
sprinkles, flake, flavor, just ordinary. That's what works for me.
- Sue Dibney
(Identity Crisis)

The most hyped movie ever was *Star Wars: Episode I - The Phantom Menace*.
For many, it was also the most disappointing movie. Since die-hard fans had
been waiting to see another Star Wars film for 16 years, there was no way it could
never live up to the hype. (It also didn't help that The Phantom Menace was really,
really bad.)

Sadly, everyone falls for hype in one way or another. We hear how the winner
of *X Factor* or the finalists of *American Idol* are going to change everything, yet we
can't even remember who won last year.

A tech company claims their new gadget will alter how we interact, yet we barely
remember what it's called.

We think newly elected politicians will solve everything but are often met with
disappointment.

We spent years and saved tons of money to travel across the world but are
annoyed when our dream holiday doesn't exactly to plan.

If you go to a quaint little town for a holiday instead of Paris or New York, you
might enjoy it more because there is no hype. You might enjoy an obscure movie
instead of a classic since you had no expectations.

If you watched a great film like The Godfather, knowing that it has a reputation
as one of the best movies ever made, you will probably enjoy it. But you would most
certainly enjoy it more if you know nothing about it.

Unexpected joys are better than prepared joys because our reactions are
absolutely caught in the moment. We connect to them more because we don't think,
"I thought it would be better" or "Was that it?" or "Did it live up to my expectations?"

Give the unknown a try. It can't let you down if you don't know what to expect.

Men travel faster now, but I do not know if they go to better things.
- Willa Cather
(Death Comes for the Archbishop)

155. HYPOCHONDRIA

> Before getting meningitis, I was such a hypochondriac,
> worrying about the slightest ache. Ironically, I overlooked
> meningitis because the symptoms seemed like flu. I guess you
> don't realize how healthy you are until it is taken away from you.
> - Petra Ecclestone

Hypochondriacs are always afraid they might become sick. Any sign of sickness can be seen as a dangerous virus, a deadly infection, or a contagious disease.

Even though it's easy to belittle hypochondriacs, we all fall victim to it. If you sneeze while a cold is going around, it's easy for you to assume you have a virus. Even if you don't think that way, it's easy for other people to become overly cautious of you.

When you hear about epidemics and potential pandemics on the news, whispers on the bus about quarantines, and strangers on the street wearing protective masks, you can't help being paranoid. You might be overly concerned while talking to a friend who seems a bit under the weather.

Making yourself ill can work on a cellular level. Worrying about falling ill will make you have racing thoughts like, "I can't get sick. I don't want to be sick again. I can't lose any more time being sick."

Your mind just hears the words, "sick, get sick, sick, sick, sick," over and over. When this occurs, your body will prepare for an illness to come. Any cough or sneeze will be seen as a potential illness. When that happens, it's like you are giving your illness power.

If you think that's an exaggeration, here's an example. My father had a friend who was allergic to daffodils. He hated going to see his doctor because there was a vase of daffodils in the waiting room. No matter how far away he was from the flowers, he started sneezing the instant he arrived.

He got so frustrated by the daffodils, he eventually asked the doctor to remove the flowers. The doctor told him that he took away the daffodils weeks ago and replaced them with plastic ones. So, my father's friend was making himself sick for literally no reason.

If we have the power to make ourselves ill, then surely we have the power to make ourselves healthy. Even when we are genuinely ill, we can fight it by saying to ourselves, "No, I am not sick. I can keep going." It's not denial; it's a positive attitude, and it can combat almost anything.

> I'm always sick but my friends say its hypochondria.
> Yeah, I think I have that too.
> - Anon

156. HYPOCRISY

The "cognitive dissonance" hypothesis...would appear
to be based upon a culture-specific discomfort Americans
have with noticing themselves being inconsistent from one
occasion to another or possessing mutually inconsistent aims.
- N. Much

We see people lie to themselves, contradict their supposed ethics, and desecrate their beliefs. It's easy to judge people like this, but for all we know, we might be just as prone to such hypocrisy.

We mightn't notice because we may be using different props and tools.

If you're having a night out, primal urges and instincts override reason. Addiction can overrule willpower. Bribery can countermand hard work. A forgetful thought can cancel a promise. One drink too many can reverse a pledge to a friend. Hypocrisy can come at us from anywhere.

I know people who claim to be health freaks because they exercise and eat right, but they puff twenty cigarettes a day. I have plenty of friends who gossip constantly but hate when people invade their private lives.

It is difficult to be aware of your own hypocrisy unless you look at it from a third point of view. You may not even see how you could possibly be considered a hypocrite until someone points it out to you.

It's hard to acknowledge aspects of us that seem contradictory. No one wants to change routines, especially when they have to face them ourselves, but it's better than living in a world where ignorance reigns supreme.

We are afraid that if we admit to being hypocrites, we will be exposed as fakes and liars.

Quite the opposite. My alcoholic friend was already perceived as a hypocrite when he was a constantly drinking.

So when he admitted he had a problem, he was not met with disgust or disrespect but admiration, because he accepted his flaws. When he accepted he had a problem, that was the beginning of correcting his alcoholism. He is a changed man now.

Every now and again, we need to contradict our egos or reputations for the sake of friends and loved ones.

Hypocrisy is the outside of cynicism.
- Mason Cooley

157. IDEAS

> Once an idea has taken hold of the brain it's almost
> impossible to eradicate. An idea that is fully formed –
> fully understood – that sticks; right in there somewhere.
> - Domm Cobb
> (Inception)

When was the last time you thought an original thought? Most of the time, we just repeat what we hear or what we have been told.

I used to write plays and stories. I thought my ideas were clever when, in fact, I was just borrowing lots of ideas from other far superior storytellers.

I had a tutor who had a colossal scope of storytelling. He annihilated my old ways of looking at stories and characters. It made me realize how much harder it is to truly create an original idea.

It's good to dabble in the best thinkers in all mediums: Aristotle, Darwin, Socrates, and Shakespeare. You shouldn't copy them, but they should help you branch out your level of thought and your scale of knowledge.

Ask yourself questions about everything. What is your favorite painting? What is your favorite book, movie, person, political figure, or word? Now, ask yourself why is it your favorite?

What if you don't like reading plays or looking at paintings? You need to ask yourself why not? What about all the potential stories and ideas you will never read or hear or see because you didn't give them a chance?

There's no point in doing something that has been done a thousand times before. What's the point in using yesterday's ideas? How can we evolve imaginatively? Ideas don't have to be complex. Often the simpler an idea is, the better.

Usually, when a great book or movie comes out, no one sees it, and it is buried under some brainless blockbuster that came out at the same time.

Blade Runner was an astounding movie, but it was too original and ahead of its time. Now, it is hailed as one of the greatest science fiction movies of all time. *Moby Dick* was considered a totally forgettable story. *The Lord of the Rings* was panned as am indecipherable novel.

By today's standards, these stories are hailed as masterpieces. It takes time for a great idea to set, before it is appreciated. They can be misunderstood, but all the best pieces of art are misunderstood.

Ideas can be impersonated, but only once can they be given freely. Make an idea only you can make.

> Every now and then, a man's mind is stretched by a new idea or
> sensation, and never shrinks back to its former dimensions.
> - Oliver Wendell Holmes

158. IDENTITY

I am no bird and no net ensnares me. I am a
free human being with an independent will.
- Charlotte Bronte

How are you perceived? Do people see you as a jock. Are you considered a geek? Are you popular? Do you think you are best represented in your Facebook profile, your TikTok videos, your Instagram photos, or your Twitter page?

The truth is, there is no single thing that can encapsulate you. Because of this, you can be misunderstood or mislabeled. Some of your friends may think you are introverted, while others see you as an out-of-control alpha male. You have made yourself popular online because you have no idea how to be liked in real life.

There is so much in an identity that it is unfeasible to distribute it all at once. We are inclined to show different aspects of ourselves in different company, based on how those around us makes us feel.

The problem is that it works with good and bad identities. You can be seen as the confident jock back at home, but perhaps you are an unprofessional drone at work or an unintelligent dork at school. But if you can be the best version of you, why can't you keep it up in worse company?

It might be because you don't allow yourself to. We become used to whatever role we are given, and we have a propensity to accept it.

Of course, we want to be seen as well liked and admired. Why would we want to be seen as a failure? But if you hear something enough times, you start to believe it.

As soon as we see someone who thinks little of us, we may start worrying about what that person will say or do. That's when our defensive shields shoot up. People will pick up on that and feed off it.

But how do you combat this? Well, if narrow-minded people are so ready to put you in a role, then you can do the same. I don't mean that in a narrow-minded way. I mean you don't have to identify others as the bully or the one that makes you feel less than you are. Focus on the identities that are good for you—the hilarious one, the friend that listens, or the one who cares.

Which identity makes you see yourself in the most positive light? Keep it. Don't let insecure bullies take that away from you.

A strong sense of identity gives man an idea he can do
no wrong; too little accomplishes the same.
- Djuna Barnes

159. IGNORANCE

Point me out the happy man and I will point you out either
egotism, selfishness evil – or else absolute ignorance.
- Graham Greene

I went out with my friends a few weeks ago. We hadn't seen each other in a year, so we went to an exclusive restaurant where we could only get a table if we booked a reservation. I was going to book it, but I assumed one of the other guys did because they had a better knowledge of the restaurant and the area.

When we arrived, we couldn't get a table, because nobody made a reservation. The reason why nobody booked it is because everybody assumed somebody else did it!

This concept is called the "assumption of total knowledge." This is when nobody understands the circumstances of a situation, but everyone assumes someone else does.

Everyone's uninformed on different subjects. There are too many facets of the world, so it is impossible to be aware of them all.

One generation has been taught a certain way to look at matters. Let's look at Tourette syndrome for a moment. Tourette's movements and sounds were once believed to be signs of possession; it is now understood that it is a neuropsychiatric disorder.

Parents who have grown up hearing different facts will find it harder to change that idea. It's easy to perceive people in previous generations as naïve, but we can be just as ignorant now. We just don't know it yet.

You might not think ignorance is a problem for you, because you are educated. But being too focused can be a problem. If you focus so much energy on one thing in life, even if it is important, you may miss a lot of other important things. This concept is called the "invisible gorilla." Studies have been done in which a test audience is asked to do a simple observation, like watching a ball bounce. They are asked to determine how many times it bounces in a minute. While this is happening, a person in a gorilla costume walks into the room and slowly walks back out. Fifty percent of the test subjects were ignorant of the gorilla's presence because they were concentrating on the ball.

You may not feel like you are ignorant of what's going on in the world, but you can be blind to what's going in your personal life. You may dismiss your lack of progress at work, the constant pains in your chest, your partner's needs, your family's attempts to reconnect with you, or your own problems.

If you are going to focus, you need to focus on yourself first, or you will miss a lot. Don't be ignorant of your own ignorance.

How frightful is man's condition! There is not one of his joys
which does not come from some ignorance or other.
- Honore de Balzac

160. IMAGE

You are a human being, not a human doing.
- John Bradshaw

John Bradshaw is the author of *Healing the Shame That Binds You, Homecoming: Reclaiming and Championing Your Inner Child*, and *Creating Love*. In the first book, he talks about how you depict yourself. Who you see in the mirror might look different to how you picture yourself in your mind.

Do you remember that moment in *The Matrix* when Neo plugs his mind into a simulated world for the first time? His hairstyle changes, and he is wearing the clothes he likes to visualize himself wearing.

So the big question is, "What do you look like when you picture yourself? What are you wearing? Are your clothes worn, old, new, or baggy? Do your garments look good on you? Do you stand tall, or are you slumped? What do you think is on your mind in your image? Where are you, and what are you doing?

You can change your image into whatever you want. You can try to turn a bad image into a good image, but the residue of that bad memory will come back. Suppressing a bad sensation isn't healthy.

There are straightforward and effectual means to cancel out the bad image. If you're trying to visualize yourself looking good, why not envisage someone you know and respect, and that person is telling you how good you look. You can take any image, good or bad, and change your perspective of it.

I missed my plane by two minutes once, and I was infuriated because I had to fork out two hundred euro for a new ticket. I shouted and cursed and hit a wall so hard I cut my knuckle. Thinking about it made me furious. But if I was looking at it from different perspectives, I would be perceived in different ways. If someone who loved me saw me, they would be worried. Someone who hated me would find the situation amusing or scary. A stranger might be bewildered but would get on with her life.

Getting all these perspectives give a better collective image of how I looked. If I just focus on positive images and see the bad ones as constructive criticism, it can help.

If you find this idea interesting, try it yourself. Write how your day was. Write how you felt. Visualize what happened and write the feeling. If anything negative happened to you, find a way to rewrite it without necessarily denying what happened. Eventually, you will be able to do this unconsciously. That's when the real fun begins.

You are a human being, not a human performance.
- John Bradshaw

161. IMPOSSIBLE

Heavier than air flying machines are impossible. I have
not the smallest molecule of faith in aerial navigation.
- Lord Kelvin
(Said in 1895, eight years before the Wright Brothers first successful flight)

Zeus' demi-god son, Perseus was sent on a quest to obtain the head of Medusa, who could turn a man to stone with a single glare. This was an impossible task in itself but not with the right tools. He received a knapsack for Medusa's head, a sword from Zeus that could cut through anything, Hades' helm of darkness to help him turn invisible, winged sandals from Hermes to fly, and a mirror shield from Athena.

By himself, Perseus could not achieve his goal. But with help and preparation, he had a chance. And any chance is enough to make a difference.

It is staggering to look back on history, to reflect on all the impossible deeds we made possible. The harnessing of fire. Civilization. Laws. The Internet. Equality of race and gender. Space travel.

The greatest achievement in mankind is often considered to be placing a man on the moon. It wasn't a practical achievement. It was more about the gesture and the implication. The world wanted to know if could be done. In a way, you could argue that the entire space race was triggered by humanity's obsession with achieving insurmountable odds.

But in terms of practical progress, I would say the greatest achievement has to be splitting the atom. It allowed us to witness the fabric of creation and has opened the doorway to almost every fantastic technological wonder of the past century, either through invention or enhancing inventions—computers, laptops, robotics, laser surgery, the Large Hadron Collider, nanotechnology. And who knows what the future will bring?

There is a first for everything, even the impossible. You don't know it's impossible until you try it. Although so many goals worth seeking are unlikely, they can still be reached. If everyone gave up on his or her dreams, then everyone would be unfulfilled. We would have nobody to look up to because we all settled for second best.

If you have a ridiculous dream, it doesn't matter if it sounds impossible. You can accomplish anything. The last lotto winner had a 1 in 150 million chance of winning. The biggest factor of winning was not luck but in purchasing the ticket. They couldn't win unless they followed their dream. Somebody has to win. Somebody's dream has to come true, but that dream will never be more than a dream unless it is pursued.

We are all ill-equipped to comprehend the very small and very large.
- Richard Dawkins

162. IMPRESSIONS

> Above all, a query letter is a sales pitch and it is the single
> most important page an unpublished writer will ever write. It's
> the first impression and will either open the door or close it.
> - Nicholas Sparks

First impressions are important yet notoriously inaccurate. We can befriend someone because they made a good first impression, even though their personality doesn't suit us at all.

One place that is a hotbed for inaccurate first impressions is interviews. Imagine you are interviewing a woman for a position in your company. Even though her resume seems fine, you don't give her the job because she doesn't make a good impression. But she might be like that because she is shy. Maybe she was a little rattled because she got dumped the same day as the interview.

You may not see these circumstances, so you make an inaccurate observation about this person. You naturally remember and identify the first of many things in your life—first love, the first time you felt fear, and the first time someone lied to you. You naturally compare your first with every other experience after that.

Getting the wrong impression of someone can work against you. If a nice person makes a bad first impression, you may think they are playing fake when you see them acting kind. You might feel like you know their behavior is a front since you think you saw their real side.

Alternatively, a horrible person can make an excellent first impression, making it hard for you to acknowledge their true personality.

This brings me to the next dilemma. You may be too good at making an impression. You may oversell yourself, your abilities, and your accomplishments. This skill can count against you practically, especially at work. You may sell yourself because of your sharp wit and natural charm despite the fact you are lazy.

How many character traits can you count in yourself? How many of these traits come across when you are speaking to others? If you're a kind person, do people pick up on that when they talk to you? If it doesn't, why do you think that is?

Some personalities will clash, but if you have any doubts about somebody, give that person a chance. Maybe the first day you met him, he was simply impatient, which you mistook as rudeness.

On the other hand, maybe you should reexamine your friends. Is your best friend the same person you first met? Reevaluating your relationships with friends, partners, and family can make you realize who you're close with and why.

> Whenever two people meet, there are really six people,
> there is each man as he sees himself, each man as the
> other sees him, and each man as he really is.
> - William James

163. INDOCTRINATION

Can the devil speak true?
- Banquo
(Macbeth)

George Orwell's novel, *Nineteen Eighty-Four* revolves around a totalitarian government in the UK that feeds the inhabitants propaganda as a means of controlling them. The corrupt government, Big Brother, burn history books and revises it to suit their needs. Although the story is fictional, this sort of repression does happen.

When Emperor Qin reigned over China in the second century BC, he wanted his teachings to be mandatory. To prevent his people from learning alternative philosophies, he ordered the destruction of all philosophical literature.

For years, Qin's soldiers swept across China, burning every book they could find. One of the only documents that survived this era belonged to a teacher called Confucius. His teachings went on to influence, not just China, but all of Asia, and he is now regarded as one of the greatest philosophers to ever live.

But if his teachings were destroyed, we would've never of him and he would've had no influence on the world. Although it's reassuring that Confucius' work survived, it's a pity all the other philosophers work has been lost forever. We will never know how their work could've shaped the world due to Qin's obsession with indoctrinating his people. Qin's cruelty goes to show just how damaging dogma can be.

If you thought this level of indoctrination doesn't occur in the modern world, think again. I saw indoctrination firsthand when I was in North Korea. I witnessed thousands of people dancing and celebrating in the street over their country's monuments and statues with pride and honor.

Many of the inhabitants are oblivious to how the world works and the manipulation their own country has on its citizens. They truly believe their country is a proud nation, but that's because they are forced to believe it. There is penalty of death for having a belief in alternative ideas.

Sadly, many repressors try to justify their methods, saying it is for the greater good. If humanity was controlled the way it is in *Nineteen Eighty-Four*, it is true that crime would be suppressed and minimized. But do you know what else would be suppressed? The human spirit. Indoctrination can never ever be justified. To live in fear is to not live at all.

Propaganda does not deceive people;
it merely helps them to deceive themselves.
- Eric Hoffer

164. INFORMATION

People of quality know everything without
ever having been taught anything.
- Moliere

We are forced to cram in as much information as possible from an early age. It's like we are bred to believe that the more you know, the more intelligent you are, the happier you are, and the better you are as a person.

Filling yourself up with facts can prevent you from ever thinking for yourself. I have filled this book with quotes, but what's the point of knowing a bunch of quotations by a bunch of deceased historic figures if you are not going to think for yourself? It's easy to quote a philosopher. It's a bit trickier to come up with something on your own.

What's harder but more important is to act on it. I know a lot of actors that quote Stanislavski, Uta Hagen, Anton Chekhov, and Bertolt Brecht who can't get an audition.

You may be well informed in some matters but blind in others. You could be knowledgeable about politics, history, geography, and astrology but not about people, emotions, and feelings. You may be a brain box but have little experience in life.

It's not necessary to have all the information; but it's important to have the right kind of information. It's not just about what you know because you read it in a book or a teacher taught you. It's about what you know after taking risks, utterly failing, recovering from failure, and going out of your comfort zone. This may sound scary, but it's better than spouting the same anecdotes, telling the same stories, and blabbing the same gossip. Talking like that inevitably gets stale. But talking on another level allows the brain to mature, develop, and evolve.

I met some of my friends recently whom I hadn't seen in years. Some of them are still telling the same stories about the same people. There are some that I cannot recognize, not just physically but in the way they talk and what they talk about.

Information runs its course, but it's better to just talk about people, what we want, and where our future lies. Questions and answers like that keep changing. That's why they are always interesting.

As Nobel Prize-winning physicist Sir William Bragg said, "The important thing is not so much to obtain new facts as to discover new ways of thinking about them."

Much reading is an oppression of the mind,
and extinguishes the natural candle, which is the
reason of so many senseless scholars in the world.
- William Penn
(Fruits of a Father's Love)

165. INNER PEACE

What lies beyond us and what lies before us are tiny
matters when compared to what lies within us.
- Ralph Waldo Emerson

Some may believe that if your room is tidy, then you have a tidy mind. If you're good-looking and desired, then your friends consider you are confident and happy.

Unfortunately, no matter what you experience or accomplish, nobody can decide your happiness more than you.

You can go out, meet with friends, and have a great laugh. Everyone falls over you, and your friends envy all of your achievements.

But when the night is over and you head to your room, what is the first feeling that comes across you? What is the first thing your inner voice says to you? Do you like yourself? If you could see a version of yourself in the outside world, would you like that person? Or would you give that person a wide berth, and if you did, for what reasons?

If you are unhappy at certain parts of your life but content in other aspects, you need to integrate the positive aspects as much as possible.

You have probably seen this with friends and family. They may act depressed or angry at home, but they can be the most dynamic people when they are out in public. People act this way because they think they have to because that is the only time they can feel alive.

You need to like yourself before you can be truly happy. Other people will see this and appreciate you more for it, and then you can integrate it into every other aspect of your life.

There is no point being amazing at work but having absolutely no love life. It's redundant to push yourself to the physical limit, not because it's your passion but because you hate your body. These are not healthy goals. Happiness should be the ultimate goal, not success. We cannot look after ourselves purely from a self-preservation point of view. We need to look inward and observe ourselves from a psychological and emotional point of view.

If the inner psyche disintegrates, it will come across in the outward appearance. You can look absolutely beautiful but people can tell when there is something lacking. You can smile and laugh, but if you are not happy with yourself or your station in life, it shows—and people will pick up on that.

If there's no inner peace, people can't give it to you.
The husband can't give it to you. Your children
can't give it to you. You have to give it to you.
- Linda Evans

166. INSECURITY

No one can make you feel inferior without your consent.
- Eleanor Roosevelt

We may be insecure about being flat-chested or balding. We may be overly conscious of a mole on our face or something small like that. We can assume that this one little thing encapsulates all our depression, insecurities, and shortcomings of life.

These attributes are not the origin of our insecurity. Insecurity is an emotion, not a physical object. We don't like concepts that we can't see or quantify, so we tend to turn these insecurities into physical targets that we can project upon and lash out at.

We believe that if we got rid of these weaknesses, then all our sadness will vanish. We are empowering our insecurities because of this mentality. We are allowing it to control us.

I have seen many overweight people who are happy. Obesity is a problem, but being okay with the way you are is better than hating yourself so much that you can't face the day or starving yourself into a malnourished state.

It's only after people have had breast implants; hair regrowth, or laser surgery that they realize these insecurities weren't the source of all their problems.

What's even worse is they'll realize they are right back to where they started, except they are worse now—they had false hope, and they are probably financially strained.

My friend and I started to lose our hair. He got stressed and spent a lot of money trying to correct it. It failed. He became deeply depressed about it and said many times that if he had hair, he would be much more confident.

I just shaved my head. My mentality was, it's just hair at the end of the day, and a few ounces of fluff has no necessity. Why get hung up about it? Also, I save a lot on shampoo and combs.

Some get stuck in a permanent temporary job. Others waste time seeking approval from those who don't respect them. Some aren't satisfied until they make something of their lives.

But what does "make something of your life" mean? Wealth? Fame? Can you not "make something of yourself" simply by being happy? Or being a good father? Or getting the job you want? Or getting into a good college?

We shouldn't hold out for ambiguous catharses. We need to take charge of our own lives.

There is a statue inside every block of stone.
- George Orwell

167. INSOMNIA

*Insomnia is a gross feeder. It will nourish itself on any kind
of thinking, including thinking about not thinking.*
- Clifton Fadiman

A lot of people who claim to have insomnia sleep about six or seven hours a
day, just not necessarily during the night. A friend of mine called Keith had
this exact problem. He complained that he couldn't help it that he had insomnia.

I told him that he didn't have insomnia but a disorganized sleep pattern that
had to be reorganized. I knew this because I had the same problem years earlier.

He said it wasn't his fault, but as soon as he got home from work, he would
immediately go to bed. He would sleep for about four hours, until about 11:00 p.m..
After that, he was wide awake and unable to sleep for the rest of the night. He slept
from about 7:00 a.m. to 9:00. Then he would stumble into work, disoriented and
dazed. He was sleeping six or seven hours; it was just all over the place.

The fact that he said his problem wasn't his fault was his first mistake. He's acting
like his bad sleep pattern is involuntary, meaning he's not taking responsibility for
it. How could he expect to change for the better if he did not factor himself into his
own problem?

You choose when to sleep. If you're exhausted, what else are you going to do?
This sounds like you have no say in the matter, but you always do.

Unless you haven't slept in over a day, you can keep yourself up with simple
stimulation. Caffeine obviously is a big help, which you will find in tea, coffee, or
Coke. If you don't drink caffeine, try an energy drink. An apple is meant to be the
fastest thing for waking up the body, even more so than coffee!

This will be hard at first, but staying awake for another few hours is vital, so
when you do go to sleep at a more appropriate time, you can wake up the next day
refreshed.

No matter how tired you are, get up early! The earlier you get up, the earlier you
will go to sleep. This simple technique will make the "insomnia" disappear quickly.
It shouldn't last more than a few weeks.

Insomnia is often misdiagnosed. It is quite rare, but most people will claim
to have had it. Insomnia, by definition, is a severe lack of sleep (e.g., fewer than
three hours of sleep in one night, or going days without any sleep). This can cause
irreparable mental damage and normally leads to manic depression. If you have this
condition, make sure it is correctly diagnosed. You should get medication in the
form of a heavy sedative or sleeping pill.

The best cure for insomnia is to get a lot of sleep.
- W. C. Fields

168. INSPIRATION

Let every nation know, whether it wishes us well or ill, that we shall
pay any price, bear any burden, meet any hardship, support any friend,
oppose any foe to assure the survival and the success of liberty.
- John F. Kennedy

Michael Jordan was cut from his high school basketball team. Walt Disney was fired from a newspaper for "lacking imagination and having no original ideas." Oprah Winfrey was removed from her job as a news anchor for "not being fit for television." The Beatles were rejected by Decca Recording Studios, who said, "They have no future in show business." Steve Jobs was fired from his own company when he was thirty.

I doubt there is a single successful, inspiring person that hasn't been underestimated, discounted, humiliated, and rejected. I bet the examples above were rejected, not once but countless times. They all thought of giving up at one point or another. Some came closer than others. When Michael Jordan was cut from his team, he ran home, locked himself in his room, and cried. Steve Jobs sank into depression when he was fired.

It's not about whether or not we fail; it's about how we deal with it. There are so many inspiring people that had no self-belief. Many novelists, like C. S. Lewis, writer of the *Narnia Chronicles*; J. R. R. Tolkien, writer of *The Hobbit*; and J. K. Rowling, writer of *Harry Potter*, initialized their names, and many other successful authors gave pseudonyms for their work because they were ashamed and afraid that no one would read their books. We tend to see inspiring people as legends, but they do have self-doubts and insecurities.

Horrible things happen to us throughout our lives, and it can knock our confidence. One inspiring person or experience can destroy any built-up insecurity, any repressed anger, or any reserved fear you have.

I know for an undeniable fact that people, like those mentioned above, have dealt with and beaten far worse problems than any I have.

The more the odds are against us, the more likely it is that we will give up. We forget that it doesn't matter how unlikely something is; it is always possible. Not only does it force us to do incredible things, but also it allows us to inspire others.

All this will not be finished in the first 100 days. Nor will it be finished
in the first 1,000 days, nor in the life of this Administration, nor
even perhaps in the lifetime on this planet. But let us begin.
- John F. Kennedy

169. INSTINCT

Man differs from other animals in that he is the most
imitative of creatures, and he learns his earliest lessons
by imitation. Inborn in all of us is this instinct.
- Aristotle

There was a defining reason why we have evolved to the extent we have. It was human beings' spatial ability that made us the dominant species on the planet.

Millennia ago, we would have to hunt, gather, or escape from wild animals. Spatial ability—the ability to calculate 3D patterns—involved knowing how to hold a spear, how to throw it, how fast an animal was coming toward you, how much time it would take before it got to you, how you had to hold yourself to be on the offensive and the defensive.

Spatial ability affects everything—sports (how to catch a ball or throw one), invention (where does a wire go to make a mechanism work), or combat (where to hit an opponent to cause maximum damage and with what level of force). The spatial ability in a male is the largest part of the human brain.

Yet we have let our instincts slide—understandably, of course. You don't have to live in a cave or fight a wild animal every day nowadays.

If you genuinely get a funny feeling about a person or get a weird vibe while walking alone in the dark, consider it. You don't get those sensations randomly. That's millions of years of evolution doing what it does best: making you survive.

Malcolm Gladwell's book, *Blink*, advises us that relying on instinct is better than intellectualizing situations. If a person seems chatty, friendly, approachable, and seems to want to befriend you, but if there is a part of you that feels you cannot trust that person for some reason, Gladwell would advise you to listen to that instinct.

Throughout your life, you automatically can detect genuine impulses, sincerity, and red-flag attributes in people that may pose a threat. Although you may not pick up on this on a conscious level, your subconscious will do this to protect you. You are far more adaptive and observant than you may realize.

Don't base everything on instinct. Instinct can be based on fear and violence. Scuba divers have drowned because they got an obstruction in their breathing passages. Instinct compelled them to pull off their masks to clear the obstruction, killing them in the process.

But instinct is there to protect you, and if it is warning you, it might be because it's warning you because it knows you are in danger. The fact that it's built in is like having your own interlinked bodyguard. Whether or not you act on your instinct, you need to listen to it. That's what it's there for.

Trust your instinct to the end, though you can render no reason.
- Ralph Waldo Emerson

170. INTELLIGENCE

An intellectual is someone whose mind watches itself.
- Albert Camus

When we were young, we assumed there were intelligent people and stupid people. We believed that they were simply "like that,' like it was luck of the draw.

In a manner of speaking, it is. Some people may be more genetically equipped than others in academia, giving them an automatic advantage. In school, we see students who don't try as hard that seem to reap all the benefits, and we see other students who constantly study that barely scrape by.

This can warp our perceptions, simply because we began learning from an academic point of view when we started school. At such a young age, we assume this is the only kind of intelligence, and if we are not good at it, we might see ourselves as uneducated.

As we get older, we realize the truth—stupidity is not an accurate idea. We are all equally gifted, not in skills but in intelligence. We can be geniuses in different subjects—every one of us.

Les Dawson, Colin Farrell, Arnold Schwarzenegger, and Robin Williams were considered to be the least likely people to succeed while they were in school. They were all labeled idiots. However, they must have some intelligence to have succeeded to such an incredible level.

My schoolmate, Chalky's dyslexia was so pronounced, he was borderline illiterate. Yet he could talk so well and could get into someone's mind so effortlessly, it was like he was psychic.

I have a friend called Jackie who is so articulate that he is simply nicknamed "the Dictionary." He can quote Shakespeare, the Bible, and the Quran and make it instantly relevant to your current situation. But he has never had a girlfriend or even kissed a girl.

My mate Jone has an IQ of over 150, which technically makes him a genius. He has so many problems with alcohol and drugs, however, that no one would ever believe his potential.

What is commonly and usually inaccurately deemed "intelligence" tends to fall under the category of academia. We forgot about intelligence can be experiential, creative, practical, contextual, componential, analytical, interpersonal, verbal-linguistic, logical-mathematical, intrapersonal, musical, emotional, or social. Find out which kind of intelligence you are good at.

We learn an art or craft by doing the things that we
shall have to do when we have learnt it.
- Aristotle

171. INTERPRETATION

All meanings, we know, depend on the key of interpretation.
- George Eliot

Detectives see the aftermath of a crime and must decide the cause. Whatever they come up with is not fact but an interpretation. To draw conclusions based on opinion and interpretation instead of facts is called *eisegesis*. The opposite is called *exegesis*. This is when you draw conclusions based on solid facts. Too often, we distort the two.

Here is a simple example: a man was once accused of being a serial killer by two police officers. They claimed he looked exactly like a sketch that an eyewitness drew of the criminal. When the accused man saw a picture of what the killer looked like, he pointed out that they both had the same hairstyle, but their facial features were completely different.

The two cops really wanted to catch this criminal, so they accused the first person they saw that bore the tiniest resemblance to the perp. An interpretation can be relevant, justifiable, inspiring, and applicable, but that doesn't mean it's a fact.

The life I have had and my interpretation of that life has set me on a path where one of the many stops was to write this book. The life you have had and your interpretation of that life may have caused this book to tickle your fancy. You might have dismissed it, or it might change your life—for the better or for the worse—or it simply may cause no change at all.

A book, a story, or a movie can be amazing, but perhaps you didn't like it. That is your interpretation. That doesn't make you wrong or right. You perceived it a certain way. There is nothing wrong or uncommon with that.

Have you ever seen a movie that you heard was amazing, and when you saw it, you only thought it was good because everyone said it was? Maybe you didn't see it the way everyone else did. Maybe you interpreted something that everyone else saw. Or perhaps you saw something that everybody else missed.

Interpretation, in some ways, is more factual than fact. It doesn't matter what the common masses think as much as what you think. If you allow yourself to be honest and not be corrupted by a mob mentality, you can be more real to yourself.

If you feel tempted to dismiss an idea, get the facts before you reject it. Alternatively, before you follow an idea just because everyone says you should, reevaluate what is important to you to see if the idea makes sense to you.

All things are subject to interpretation; whichever interpretation
prevails at a given time is a function of power and not truth.
- Friedrich Nietzsche

172. IT

No more things should be presumed to exist than are absolutely necessary.
- William of Occam

In life, there's always an "*it*." *It* can be anything and take on any form. *It* can be a person, an event, a day, a time, an object, or a moment. Either your wife left you before *it*, or you got cancer after *it*. There is always a life before and after *it*. And we let ourselves be controlled by *it*.

You may have been in a period of happiness in your life. You may have been relatively happy for years without a problem in the world—and then something happened. *It* happened. Your parents got divorced. Your mother left. You got kicked out of school. You broke your leg. You got dumped. Your brother died. Your whole life hasn't been the same. Looking back, you can see a descending spiral. There is a specific incident where you can calculate precisely where *it* began to crumble.

Bad things always happen. You cannot avoid them, but you can avoid allowing something bad from taking control of your life. You can use *it* as an excuse forever so you will never push yourself as much, never take chances, and never try as hard as when things were good.

Wallowing gets boring and depressing almost instantly. Blaming others or random circumstances that no one has any control of is easy but extremely repetitive, and eventually your friends and family will get tired of your whining about *it*!

It is not real—at least it doesn't have to be. If you break a bone, bones heal. If you still think that it is the end of the world, you need to broaden your scope of what the world is actually made up of.

We have all gone through devastating times and have no idea how we coped. Some of us did cope; others gave in to the power of *it*, convinced that *it* was the end of their lives.

It is probably annoying how I have italicized *it* repeatedly, but I have to prove just how much we use *it* as an excuse. We act like *it* is a real, physical, touchable activity. We act like *it* is a real wall, a literal boundary, and behind *it* is the rest of our lives. *It* is something we invented. We can unmake *it*.

There are *its* that haven't happened yet. "Everything would be fine if I just lost a few pounds or if my soul mate would just notice me."

If you're not happy with yourself to start with, you won't be happy once you get what you wanted. What you want is not as important as how you feel right now. Once you are aware of that, then—and only then—can you make some real progress and move on.

"It" doesn't have to exist.
- Anon

173. JEALOUSY

When a pair of magpies fly together,
They do not envy the pair of phoenixes.
- Lady Ho

One of my housemates, Bob had an audition for a big musical. He was still in acting school at the time, and his teachers insisted that the audition was out of his league. Nevertheless, he auditioned and got the part. He was in a ten-week production, got an agent, and was paid more than he could spend.

Bob was the envy of everybody. The singers of his old college saw themselves as eternal understudies to Bob. People started being less and less happy for him and got more and more jealous. Bob didn't change, and he didn't get big-headed. The only thing that changed was people's perception of him. The way Bob saw it, it was easier to complain than to understand.

But I saw a different side of Bob since I lived with him. After the musical ended, so did the money. He had to borrow money and scrape up every bit of cash to buy the most basic necessities, yet people were still jealous of him because they only saw him in the spotlight.

But he was barely getting by for months after that. It took a year before he really landed on his feet. To this day, he is doing well for himself in the acting world, but the point stands: we hate those we cannot overshadow.

It's ironic because we never seem to be jealous of a person who is happy but over physical things. We are jealous of someone who has a beautiful girlfriend but perhaps not of the relationship.

How often do you hear someone say something like, "I wish I was happy"? It's usually, "I need an iPad" or "If I don't get a Starbucks, it'll ruin my day."

A good mentality to avoid jealousy is this philosophy: "You can't be jealous of one thing; you have to be jealous of everything." You might be jealous of your friend because he has no money worries, but he may have huge insecurities with confidence. Your friend might not have money problems because that is all she focuses on, which means she may neglect every other part of her life. We envy people by simplifying their lives. We want their money or power with no strings attached.

But there are always strings attached. If you looked at every person in your life that you are jealous of and ask yourself if you would trade your life for his or hers, you will most certainly say no.

The person of whom you are jealous may be no more satisfied in his or her position than you are in yours and is probably jealous of another ... and possibly you.

Don't waste time on jealousy. Sometimes you're
ahead, sometimes you're behind.
- Mary Schmich

174. JUDGMENT

One should look long and carefully at oneself before one considers judging others.
- Moliere

Most of what we judge others for, either individually, as a mass, or conceptually, is misunderstood. We know this for a fact because we have been judged ourselves in the same light.

Yet instead of giving others the benefit of the doubt, we choose the easier, more hypocritical road of judging others in the same way.

Anyone can play the judge in a debate, but it's not an official title. The judge is meant to give the final verdict in a courtroom but not before the lawyers, witnesses, defendants, and jury have their say. It's all too tempting to just skip to the final judgment.

If those with the highest authority can make the gravest mistakes, what chance do the rest of us have? We naturally simplify other people's personality types. The less we know them, the more inclined we are to do this. We always wonder why there are so many crazy people on the street, on the train, at the bus stop, or on a night out, but that's because we see people in a moment of anger, fear, or depression and make a snap judgment.

If you saw a guy go berserk in a train station because of the ticket price, you would see him as a guy with anger issues. This guy could be angry about a serious matter that happened earlier, and he is just acting passive-aggressively.

But you will never know that. You will just deduce the situation with minimal understanding and not give it a second thought.

You might see others as drunks, jocks, divas, and so forth, but you will not put yourself into a personality archetype, and so, will be astonished by how others perceive you.

If different people view you in different ways, you will unconsciously use this as an argument against them. You might think, "All my family think I'm quiet and shy, but you all think I'm loud and attention-seeking! You both can't be right!" That's true, but this mentality should not be justified to dismiss those judging us but to dismiss ourselves in judging others. Your judgment is your opinion. It's not set in stone.

But how do you stop other people from making snap judgments about you? You can't. People will judge you no matter what. But you should only care if you have truly done something wrong.

If they judge you because they misunderstand what you have done, inform them. If they don't accept it, that's their problem. Focus on yourself. You have no reason to lose sleep over it. Just don't judge them for it.

Good judgment comes from experience. Experience comes from bad judgment.
- Jim Horning

175. JUSTIFICATION

Those who lack the courage will always find a philosophy to justify it.
- Albert Camus

Our mess always seems smaller, our wounds deeper, our arguments uncounterable, our problems bigger, and our mistakes insignificant. We all vastly overestimate how justifiable we are.

A friend gets drunk and embarrasses himself at a party, but when you do the same, it's different because "it was the first time in ages." You hate when people get angry, but you think you're allowed to because you need to blow off some steam. You keep judging others, but you get defensive when people judge you.

When you get frustrated when someone tries to defend yourself, ask if you would do the same thing if the roles were reversed.

Justifying oneself is a self-defense mechanism. Protecting our ego is human nature. But when we know we are wrong, we need to accept it—for everyone's sake as well as our own.

In the long term, it's not healthy. We will just keep making the same mistakes. It's embarrassing when we have to keep justifying our shortcomings.

If you spend that much time validating yourself, you have to be doing something wrong. Justifying limitations prevents you going beyond them.

We cannot use setbacks and tragedies in our lives to rationalize our current station in life. In Dublin, I know a lot of drug addicts, most of whom will remain so for the rest of their lives. I try to encourage them to leave that kind of life behind, but they would say that I was born with a silver spoon in my mouth, so I can't understand.

One dangerous thing people do is to justify themselves with a tragedy. One drug addict, Wayne, said, "There's no point in living any other kind of life. I have no money, no food, no home, and all of my family is dead."

It is horrific that some people have to go through that, but I doubt Wayne's family would appreciate him using them as an excuse for throwing his life away.

Indulging in tragedies can be used as an excuse to never change. Some people don't just justify with tragedy, but they also try to justify the tragedy itself.

Natural disasters can be accused of being humanity's punishment or the wrath of God. Earthquakes, volcanic eruptions, and tsunamis are devastating, but they are natural occurrences. Mother Nature has no prejudice over her victims.

We don't need to justify everything. We can't. Some things just happen, and we deal with them as best we can. Once we try to justify the unjustifiable, we will inevitably start finding someone to blame.

It's more fun to arrive a conclusion than to justify it.
- Malcolm Forbes

176. KINDNESS

> Nature makes us human. Our actions decide whether we
> become monsters or maintain our claims to humanity.
>
> - Anon

In a terrorist attack in Egypt, twenty-one Christians were killed at the hands of terrorists. A few days later, several Christians went to church. Although they were terrified they might be killed, they felt like they had an obligation to attend mass because it was Christmas Eve. When they got to their church, there was a mob at the entrance… but they were all Muslims. The mob had a message for the Christians. Do you know what it was?

"If the terrorists want to kill you, they have to kill us too." They acted as human shields to protect the Christians, and no one was attacked.

When Jonas Salk found the cure for polio, he could have earned the equivalent in today's currency of seven billion dollars. However, he believed medicine should be free and gave his cure away without accepting a fee.

A delivery driver for Domino's Pizza named Susan Guy had a few customers who ordered the same pizza every week. One day, Susan noticed a weekly customer had stopped ordering. A reasonable person wouldn't think twice about this. Some people mightn't even notice. Or if they did, they could reasonably assume the customer was away, forgot to order, wasn't in the mood for pizza that day, or had gone on a diet.

But Susan felt in her gut that something was wrong and went to the lady's house anyway. She banged the door and the window, and there was no reply. Some people would assume she was out, but not Susan.

She rang the police and demanded they break down the door because she had a "feeling" this elderly woman, whom she barely knew, was in trouble.

Can you imagine how this sounded to a police officer? Susan had no evidence. She didn't even know the woman. All she had was a gut feeling.

But she was right. When the police broke down the door, they found the old woman had fallen and had been unable to get up for the last three days. Nobody else checked on her so she would have had no way of getting up without Susan's intervention. If Susan had been wrong and the woman was fine, this story would sound very different—Susan would sound insane—but Susan's mentality was that it was better to risk an embarrassing situation if it might save an old woman's life. As unlikely as that is, it completely paid off.

All of these stories show that kindness isn't just heartwarming, it's a necessity. There is nothing more hopeful in life than random acts of kindness.

> The superior man understands righteousness,
> the inferior man understands profit.
>
> - Anon

177. KNOCKS

The race is not to the swift or the battle to the strong nor
does food come to the wise or wealth to the brilliant or
favor to the learned but time and chance happen to us all.

- Anon

We get knocked down a lot in life. We might want something and an obstacle gets in the way and knocks us back. When this happens, we just need to get back up and reach our goal.

But there are times when the knock we received was more damaging than we realized. If a professional football player tears a hamstring to get a touchdown in the last five seconds of the Super Bowl, he will be hailed as a player that made the final difference and saved the game. He can easily be swept up in all of this, believing his own hype, and then become a part of a media circus.

He can get so swept up; he may not realize how much damage he did to his hamstring. He may never walk properly.

I used a football player as an example because it makes it easier to convey an actual physical knock, but I read last week about an NFL player who can barely remember playing professionally. He was one of the greatest players in the eighties, but he got so many head collisions, he only has jigsaw pieces of memory of his time on the football field.

Knocks remind me of Jenga; the game where you stack blocks on each other and then try to balance more and more under fewer and fewer pieces.

You can seem fine about the daily stresses and the overflowing amount of "stuff" to do that plops its way into your lap. You try your best to keep it together. You gradually go into a slump, but every once in a while in life, you collapse under the weight of it all.

You need to register knocks on a deeper level. If your broken leg has healed, has your psyche healed too? Do you feel vulnerable now that you have physically experienced fragility? Even a broken bone can register 40 percent physical and 60 percent psychological, depending on the circumstances.

For a football player, a broken leg can register far more psychologically than physically since they injured the body part responsible for paying the bills.

Do the physical knocks have mental consequences? Do the mental knocks have physical ones? Discover for yourself.

If you suffer a setback or disappointment,
put your head down and plow ahead.

- Les Brown

178. KNOWLEDGE

The scientific approach to the phenomenon of human nature enables us to be ignorant without being frightened and without therefore having to invent all sorts of weird theories to explain away all the gaps in knowledge.
- D. W. Winnicott

We are all knowledgeable about different subjects. We may consider ourselves experts in our own fields, no matter how insignificant they may be. No one may know as much as us about how many goals Pele scored or in which comic book did Superman die.

We can take pride in what we know, but it is a question of practical knowledge or if we know enough. We can always learn more. Our capability for knowledge knows no bounds.

Every day I learn as much new information as possible. I jot down anything I hear that I may deem relevant for future reference—historical events and figures, new psychological theories and concepts, for instance.

But the most important thing about all of this that a lot of this knowledge stays with me. We can grow as human beings through examination of others and ourselves, but we can broaden our scope with new ideas, people, and philosophies.

There is so much we don't know, but how much of what we don't know can we do something about? Most information is attainable now, thanks to the Internet being at our every beck and call.

What about unattainable knowledge, though? Why are we here? What is the meaning of life? There is no knowledge that validates such questions. If there was, there would be no quest for it because it would have been on the news and end all future debates on such matters.

Go out of your way, and read books by Nietzsche, Joyce, or Joseph Campbell; read *The Art of War* or *Crime and Punishment*; admire old art and sculptures; revisit history; see the world; explore outside your comfort zone; talk to new people to whom you wouldn't normally talk. There are endless ways to discover new knowledge.

This is how you decide what to believe, what you know, and what you think you know. You will never know all of the answers about life, but it's nice to explore.

You can see how much knowledge can change your morals, your beliefs, and your perceptions. Remember: knowledge doesn't create something in you; it harnesses what you already have. There is no shame in not knowing. There is shame in not finding out.

The reading of good books is like a conversation with the best men of past centuries – in fact like a prepared conversation, in which they reveal only the best of their thoughts.
- Rene Descartes

179. LABEL

> Giving a phenomenon a label does not explain it.
> - Taylor Caldwell

Have you been in a situation that was positive, and then your environment changed or moved—you got a new job, went to college, found a partner—and found people unreceptive and unfriendly? When this happens, it may not be because it's a bad place or a bad area.

It could be that in those first few days or even first few seconds of meeting new people, snap decisions were made about what to believe about you, and they solidified, channeled, and spread.

I have a friend called Caoimhe who is one of those people you simply can't dislike. I have known her for years and have never met a person that didn't fall in love with her instantly.

That's what everyone thought of her until her parents got divorced. Within a month, a lot of people hated her. You might think this is quite harsh, but the divorce happened in the same week that she started college. All her friends before college knew she took it pretty hard, but they thought she was dealing with it really well.

Her new classmates didn't know this since she intentionally didn't talk about it because she didn't want to be a burden. She was still pretty shaken up about the divorce but because she didn't speak about it, her classmates misread her reaction to it. They saw her as depressed, easily knocked, and a diva. That became her label.

We can have multiple labels simultaneously. Society thinks it is good at analyzing situations and people, but it tends to categorize and label with childish simplification.

You might believe that someone who's short can be an easy target and someone who's big is more prone to intimidation and authority. But it can work both ways. A person who is short in stature can be tougher because he or she has more to prove. Constantly being picked on as a kid may make him or her more antagonistic and confrontational.

Alternatively, big guys may not have been in many fights because people were too scared to fight them, so they have no fighting experience and could be easy to overpower.

We label all walks of life—race, tradition, people, and customs—but we should not put things into little boxes or categories for us to label.

We should just let things be. Let ourselves be. Just be an individual. Defy categorization.

> I'm just gonna try and dodge the label
> and keep doing what I am doing.
> - Matt Damon

180. LAZY

If you don't want to work, you have to work up
enough money until you don't have to work.
- Ogden Nash

Every day you do nothing is a whole day of wasted potential, knowledge, pleasantries, and experience thrown away. You can't complain that you're unhappy because you have nothing to do when you have so much free time to make a difference.

Some people just wait for salvation to land in their laps. It's even worse when it does land in their laps, and they just shrug it off. If procrastinators had a hundred different choices, they would find a hundred ways to throw them away.

Others may think that it's okay to do nothing, as long as they're not doing anything bad. If you stand still, you go backwards before you go forward. If you're doing nothing, you're undoing everything else. Don't wait for your ship to come in; swim to it. If you want dreams to be true, don't oversleep. Pray to God, but keep rowing to shore. We have to stop thinking of new ways to do nothing.

Here's the big question: why are some people lazy and other people motivated?

One word: dopamine. It's a chemical in your brain responsible for reward-motivated behavior. If you are near to achieving a goal, your brain will produce dopamine, which is responsible for giving you a little buzz to reward you and to let you know you will feel a more powerful sensation once you fully accomplish your goal. But if you are far from your goals, you get no buzz.

So how do you kick-start this feeling? With a constructive mentality. Say you need to finish a big project at work. If you look at it as one big job, you'll think, "I am nowhere near finished!"

But if you break it down into mini-jobs, you can say, "Great! I finished phase one!" You might have many phases to go, but you can see progress. Any progress will motivate you, giving you a bigger dopamine rush every time.

Some people are hard workers when they have to be, but they make excuses when they have free time. I know people who studied rigorously in school, but when they left, they did nothing with their lives. They only studied because of pressure from their parents, but when they became adults, they felt no motivation to do anything.

Remember, it's what you learn after you know everything that counts. You can have an education or talent, but it is useless if you lack the drive to enforce it. To do nothing is a decision.

Blame is just a lazy way for a person to make sense of chaos.
- Doug Coupland

181. LEARNING

The first problem for all of us, men and women is not to learn but to unlearn.
- Gloria Steinem

John Naisbitt famously said, "We are drowning in information but starved for knowledge."

The most fascinating aspect of human beings is that we are smart enough to know how the mechanics of the universe work—metal, electricity, fire or matter. We're the only ones who know what they are and how they work. It's not just the physical world but also things like ego, morality, and mortality. With a lack of knowledge based on our evolutionary intelligence, we will try to arrive at the best conclusion to all situations.

But we are nowhere near finished evolving. We're still learning, and there's still a lot more we have yet to uncover and understand. I don't just mean just lying around; I mean finding brand new concepts.

We can laugh at those flies that bang their heads on the window, not realizing the glass is there. It seems so simplistic and idiotic, but we can be just like that fly. We keep making the same mistake, and we don't even realize it. If we do realize it, we seem never to learn from it.

There are two kinds of people who want to learn: those who want to learn by reading or watching the Discovery Channel, and those who go out and find what they are passionate about. If you want to know more about a country, do you just read about it or do you go there? If you want to know more about a new culture, do you research it or experience it?

I don't believe "the only way to learn is the real deal." Don't throw a kid in a river before he can swim. He needs to start in the kiddy pool. It's nice to be adventurous, and you can "jump into something new" within reason, but be aware of what you're getting yourself into. Live and learn. If you don't do one, you can't do the other.

We hate it when we make mistakes, but we can't dwell on them. Each mistake is one more lesson learned and one less mistake to make. You can learn from mistakes only after you make them.

There is no absolute way to summarize life so it can be understood; you just have to go through the experience itself and pick up whatever you can for the rest of the journey. There is no instruction manual. Life is a foreign film without subtitles; you're forced to learn the language.

Even when you think you are in the middle of learning something valuable, remember that hindsight is a wonderful thing. Most people aren't learning what they think they are learning. It's usually something deeper. Most life experiences are not one-off lessons.

I don't think much of a man who is no wiser today than he was yesterday.
- Muhammed Ali

182. LEECH

It is easier to live through someone else than to become complete yourself.
- Betty Friedan

The friends we have are those who bring out the best in us. It's not just because they are a great laugh, or we have the same interests but because they make us feel funny, secure, and happy.

We could have more selfish reasons than that. Maybe we need friends to make us feel good. Or maybe they have access to money, drink, and drugs, and we have befriended them just to be a part of that. If that is your reason for befriending them, you could be perceived as a sycophant; a leech sucking the life out of someone else to thrive.

There is a Pascunese word called *tingo*. This is to borrow from someone over and over until they have nothing left. You may take and take, and when you have taken all they have, only then will you realize how one-dimensional your friendship was.

My old housemate, Bob suddenly got a lot of acting work after appearing in a massive musical. He was also getting a lot of people in his life who barely knew him. Those he used to know were suddenly back in his life. They wanted to congratulate him, say that they always knew he would make it, and that they so happy for him.

But then they would ask for a favor. They needed money or a place to stay. Since Bob could was successful, they thought he would be selfish to turn them away since, in their own minds, they always supported him.

It disheartens me that people would be so fake and so desperate to get a taste of what Bob had. The most ridiculous part was his ex-girlfriend, Andrea, who was trying to rekindle their "relationship" (all two days of it), now that she was "available." When he refused to get back with her, she was furious. I heard her say, "I should have stayed with him when he became an actor. That way, I would have been famous too!"

Knowing her, if she'd stayed with him, he would have never become a success, and she would've left him for someone who did.

A leech's life is barely a life. It's dependence. What happens when that person you are leeching off leaves or disappears? Do you curl up and die or find someone else? Or do you just grow up and find yourself?

It's great to have friends there for you, especially when you need them during hard times. But when you need them all the time, they stop becoming friends and turn into an addiction.

Mimicry is the most common form of flattery but it is not your own.
- Anon

183. LEGACY

Immortal mortals and mortal immortals, living
the others death and dying the other's life.
- Herodotus.

A legacy is something you are destined to inherit. In the *Denial of Death*, Ernest Becker discusses that we are always afraid of the unknown. Since death is one of those unknowns, we build up an "immortality project" that will outlast us. We hope we can do this through our children, our achievements, or our teachings.

How we initiate our legacy depends on how we perceive reality. If there is an afterlife or at least a belief in the afterlife, then maybe you look at your legacy from a moral point of view.

Or if you don't have a belief in a life beyond this one, maybe having children is your legacy, knowing that your bloodline doesn't end with you.

Or maybe you want your name in history books. Some may argue it's redundant and even hypocritical to argue the need for a legacy if you are not around to enjoy it.

Do you need a legacy? Would you rather be a legend than be happy? We all have a set idea of success in our minds, and we can work our entire lives to strive for it to ensure we will be talked about when we are gone.

But why? We won't be alive to appreciate it. It is the ultimate cliché, but we should do as much good as we can, not for vain reasons, like being immortalized or crystallized into history, but because it's the right thing to do, and it's what we are passionate about.

Norman Borlaug has saved more people than anyone in history with his research. He didn't do it so people would chant his name when he's gone. You probably have never heard of him, so he clearly was not trying to make himself famous. He was just trying to dedicate his life to the noblest cause.

Live your life, be happy, take nothing for granted, take as many offers as possible, and die with no regrets. Do we have to stretch the seventy-five or so years of a human life to the infinite?

Susan Ertz said, "Millions long for immortality who don't know what to do with themselves on a rainy Sunday afternoon."

Death is a part of life. One way or another, though, we will leave some sort of legacy. After all, a person's life is his statement. Most want to be remembered when they die. It's better to be remembered while you're alive.

The only thing more important than your first
impression is your lasting impression.
- Rob Liano

184. LIES

No one means all he says, and yet very few say all they
mean, for words are slippery and thought is viscous.
- Henry Brooks Adams

How to Get the Truth Out of Someone is a book that deciphers many differences
between liars and truth-tellers, such as:

- Truth-tellers usually don't know or don't remember when you ask them
  something that happened months ago. Liars cover their tracks and have
  answers ready.
- Don't listen to what the accused is saying. Listen to what he or she is not
  saying. He or she only focuses on certain details and is vague about others.
- The main difference between a liar and a truth-teller is that a liar hopes to
  be believed rather than expected.

It is commonly said that the most powerful weapon is the truth, but I think it can
be the twisting of truths. Some lies are more believable than truth. A lie is the
only substitute for the truth. It's not a great one, but it's the only one we have and
seems to be used just as often.

Lies always take more energy, yet we lie every chance we have. We almost never
say what we mean and never mean what we say.

We can be so good at lying that we don't even realize how often we do it. We lie
about lying. We lie to survive, for interviews, selling ourselves, breaking hearts, or
to avoid being ostracized, feared, hated, or laughed at.

We lie about what we think, believe, say, hear, dream, like, love, and hate. We
don't even have to say anything to lie sometimes. Knowing something that a friend
has a right to know but not telling can be considered lying because our silence forces
the friend to believe something we know isn't true.

When we don't want to lie but don't want to divulge all the details, we just give
people the broadest interpretation of the truth. Some would argue that is still lying
because it is misleading.

Do we need lies? Could you go a day without lying? Try it. I'm not saying you
should tell the truth all the time, but you should give it a shot for a day to see how
difficult it is. You can gauge how often you actually lie on a daily basis.

As shameful as it sounds, however, there are times when lies are necessary. I
am not promoting lying, but it's not as evil as it's made out to be. Lying all the time
is irresponsible, but the occasional white lie can relieve pain or stop someone being
seriously hurt—mentally, physically, spiritually, or intimately.

Three things cannot be long hidden: the sun, the moon, and the truth.
- Buddha

184 | JAMES EGAN

185. LIFE

The universe is not only queerer than we
suppose but queerer than we can suppose.
- J.B.S. Halone.

There are so many metaphors to describe life. Life is like swimming. You have to keep moving or you sink. Life is a play without a script, with us improvising as best we can while being criticized by everybody.

But here is my favorite: imagine there is a gigantic mathematics problem. It has never been solved, but you decide to have a crack at it. It's tough; some things are beyond you, but you know a thing here and there, so you might get it right. It takes ages, and there are some parts you are not sure of. Some of it is guesswork, and you might even cheat or skip a bit here and there. After a while, you have an answer. You don't know if it is the correct answer, but it looks okay.

Then you see other people have done it in a completely different way. Their answers are all different. Nobody can work it out and come up with the same result. Some aren't even close.

Now imagine this problem is life.

At times, we think we simply don't get life. But maybe you get it a little more today than you did yesterday and that counts for something.

We do stupid things in an attempt to enjoy life, but we shouldn't overdo it. Drink and drugs are not "grabbing life." Trying to enjoy life too much speeds up ending it.

You may have the opposite problem and are scared of living life. Not enjoying life because you're scared of new experiences is not a life truly lived. Which is better: live long or live? Life is more than just avoiding death. A house unkempt is not as bad as a house unlived.

You may not do crazy things because you are focusing on work or family. That's good because you're not neglecting important parts of your life. You may intend to do these crazy things when you have some free time.

What if that time never comes? If you want to see the world, bungee jump, or open a new business, it's better to do it in the prime of your life than when you are old and tired.

Imagine you are in a river, holding on to a rock so you don't get caught in the current. There's a time when you have to let go and accept the flow of the river and of life. You never know where the river will lead, but it will lead you nowhere if you stay in the same place, holding on, waiting for help that never comes.

As Henri Berguson said, "Any living thing that tries to stand still in the evolving flow of time becomes mechanical and thus comical in action."

If life doesn't have that little bit of danger about it, you'd better
create it. If life hands you that danger, accept it gratefully.
-Anthony Quayle

186. LIMITATION

Limitations are primarily in the software, not the hardware.
- Dr. Wilson van Dusen

Usually we believe we can't do something because someone told us that we can't. You can't play football, because you were told that you couldn't kick a ball to save your life. You can't dance, because some delinquent sniggered at the idea. You don't try, because if you fail, it proves them right.

Trying is more important than succeeding—that is what my school principal used to say. He was the only teacher who didn't tell us off when we answered a question with, "I don't know." He would simply retort, "How do you know you don't know? You haven't even tried to answer!" He was right. We probably know more often than we think we do, but we are too afraid to be proven wrong.

That is the source of limitations. Believing that the limits have already been set before we have a chance to get near them will ensure that we never perform to our full potential.

Imagine you had a speed limit of fifty miles per hour, and you have to get to your destination as soon as possible. You are so scared that you might go over the speed limit that you only go twenty miles an hour. The only way you can get there in time is if you go at forty, maybe forty-five miles per hour. But that's the problem. People get scared, not just of limitations, but of approaching them.

Failing once is not just common; it's inevitable. But you can decide how close you want to get to failing before you reach success.

All the most successful people have sat on the cusp of failure at some point. They balance on the wall of limitations, with one side holding success while the other held failure. They play a dangerous game, but playing it is the way to win.

We assume we reach our limits sooner than we actually do. Learning a new skill takes time to absorb. To quit at any point, assuming you have already reached your threshold, makes learning a waste of time.

Human beings tend to exaggerate for effect. The problem is that we start to believe it. When we say that we "cannot," we believe it is actually impossible to perform the desired task.

It may be time-consuming, rigorous, exhausting, painful and, in some cases, actually impossible to achieve a task. But you won't know if something can be achieved unless you try. If I knew for an undeniable fact that I couldn't succeed at something, I wouldn't waste my time doing it.

But when do we ever know that to be the case? How do we know where our limitations truly lie? Maybe there are no limitations. That idea should inspire us to never give up anything after a single attempt.

To go too far is the same as not to go far enough.
- William Congreve

187. LINGER

All that is buried is not dead.

- Olive Schreiner

For years, my friend, Moira couldn't go into her deceased husband's study for more than a few seconds. The idea of him sitting there as he did for decades, still doing his work, still building some contraption, and still muttering under his breath that he couldn't find the right tool, came flooding back to her mind anytime she entered that room.

She felt like he tainted the room. She could not perceive it as any other room but his. She decided to leave the room as it was, to help her grieve—like closing a scary book before its end.

But her son, Miles came back to the house after getting married. His wife was expecting a baby, and they didn't have a place to live. After much discussion, Miles decided to turn his deceased father's old study into a playpen for his son. Within a few weeks of the baby's being born, Moira started to see the room as her grandson's room, and her grief seemed to vanish.

She could have shut the door to her grief. It is easy to do, especially if you have lost a partner or someone you have known for decades. Some losses are understandable. But that doesn't mean you can't live your life.

Getting a horrible vibe from an unsettling memory can linger in homes, in possessions, or in people. A beautiful person may remind you of true love lost. A song you haven't heard in years may remind you of an ex with whom you never got closure.

Even the knowledge of something bad creates a lingering sensation. I stayed at a hotel in Munster years ago. I needed a room for the night because I had an interview the next morning. Since it was just for one night, I asked if I could have the cheapest room.

When I asked why the room wasn't expensive, I was told that a famous lord died on his first night in that room. The room had always been tainted since then, apparently.

I thought it was nonsense, but as soon as I went into the room, I felt an instant chill. I felt a cold feeling throughout my one and only day there.

After my stay, I reflected on that creepy room and asked myself, "Did I make it creepy? Would it have been creepy if I hadn't known of the lord?"

Probably not. It made me realize that although it's difficult to stop bad energies from lingering, we are in control. We create them through feelings and memories, but because we create them, we can also end them. By ending them, I don't mean dismissing or ignoring them. I mean changing or recreating them the same way Moira did. Use it as an excuse to create something beautiful.

You can't hold a man down without staying down with him.

- Booker T. Washington

188. LOGIC

A mind all logic is like a knife all blade. It makes the hand bleed that uses it.
- Rabindranath Tagore

There are those who consider emotion a weakness. At times, it can be. It can blind us with love, hatred, or the ability to tell the difference between right and wrong. Logic relies on facts, and people can find comfort in it. But logic can be as much of a crutch as emotion.

Although we are creatures of logic, we are also creatures of emotion, and emotion often overrules us. To use an observational, and analytical approach to dealing with someone being overly emotional can be ineffective because there is no empathy.

When I had panic attacks, I felt like I was about to die. But in the back of my mind, I knew I was in no danger. I assumed I could force the anxiety to stop through willpower.

But that mentality made it worse. Panic attacks happen because of an imbalance of emotions. If you try to keep a lid on them, that will imbalance them more, and they will fight more to get out.

We can't fight everything with intellectualization. We are allowed to feel. We weren't given emotions for nothing. In our darkest hour, emotion and empathy will always be more important than logic.

If someone close to you dies, you might keep strong to help other people who fall apart. That is commendable. You may come across as brave and strong, but you are reacting to the same tragedy a different way. You are not necessarily stronger because you bottle up your feelings. It just makes your inevitable reaction more unpredictable.

Forcing yourself to intellectualize can be difficult in social dynamics, arguments, work, or love interests. Stop thinking. Start feeling.

I remember when two friends of mine, Dunne and Fionn, were asked to retell a story of a great night out they'd had.

Dunne just told the facts. He explained what happened as if it was a chore, listing details like, "We went here. Then we did this. We met this guy." That gave no sense of character. That story gave no idea of what Dunne was like as a person.

But when Fionn recounted the tale, he gave a much better sense of what kind of night he had and what kind of person he was because he was emotionally invested in the story.

Occasionally, you have to let your heart rule your head. Logic can take you from point A to point B, but imagination will take you anywhere.

No mistake is more common and more fatuous than appealing
to logic in cases which are beyond her jurisdiction.
- Samuel Butler

189. LOVE

Affection is responsible for nine-tenths of whatever solid
and durable happiness there is in our lives.
- C. S. Lewis

Love is like heaven but can hurt like hell. The heart has its reason that reason cannot answer. Your perfect love is rarely convenient love. People's dreams are conflicted. They want prosperity, distinction, fame, and power. People always say they want love or to find their soul mate, but they never wish for happiness, not realizing the two go hand in hand. Better to have love and nothing else than to have everything but love. It's the biggest hole to fill.

What was your first experience with love? The first is the most important, no matter good or bad it goes, because you compare it to all forthcoming events.

If you are in a relationship now, how does it hold up, compared to your first? Is it better? Is it worse?

This isn't just with love but with everything. You need to observe patterns and differences with past and current relationships to see if you are learning from experience or are making the same mistakes.

Most first loves fall apart because you were young and naïve—or your partner was. There can be much impairment with love.

There are those who have never loved or worry that no one has loved them or no one ever will. Some people feel incapable of love or they keep hurting those they supposedly love.

Or maybe you have warped into a spiteful person because a former partner betrayed you. When this happens, it can make you lose faith in the whole concept of live.

I believe the hardest thing with love is not turning it into a dependency issue. Erich Froom says, "Immature love says I love you because I need you. Mature love says I need you because I love you."

My wife and I don't regard ourselves as soul mates; we are just lucky to have each other. To believe another person is the answer to all your problems makes it more likely that problems will ensue. That's not real love. That's addiction. If you had an argument with your other half, you would both deal with it as best as you could. If you believed your partner was the only thing worth living for and you couldn't bear being alone, you would act desperate and be far more erratic about the slightest problem. This behavior has good intentions but nearly always scares the other person away. Then you will find yourself alone.

When you are in love, people will mock you for being corny. Some people may not like your partner and may accuse you of being blinded by love. Love only seems blind because the heart is capable of seeing things the eye cannot see.

At the touch of love, everyone becomes a poet.
- Plato

190. LOYALTY

Without friends, no one would choose to live though he had all other goods.
- Aristotle

Loyalty is not limited to just friends. There is the obvious loyalty from a pet obeying its master, your obedience to your parents, your protection of a company, or your reliability in a team sport.

Loyalty is tested when we have to trust someone based on what we think we know of a person and how this outweighs their intentions, even when their intentions seem bizarre or wrong.

We should look out for each other. If circumstances put us in a tight situation that may look suspicious to an outsider, but our friends know we only have good intentions, we admire their loyalty to us.

But there is a trap to loyalty. If a person we care about is doing something immoral, and we choose to do nothing, does that loyalty become immoral? The sad truth is our friends can be wrong and our enemies can be right. We are all fallible beings. Our enemies are not necessarily wrong about everything.

An obvious example of when loyalty forced people to go too far is Nazi Germany. At first, it seemed to be about empowering Germany and Austria, so the natives were loyal to the cause. But the cause became more corrupt until it became absolutely evil.

The Nazi machine changed so gradually over the years. (Adolf Hitler was *Time* magazine's man of the year in 1937 for crying out loud!) Within a few years, the Nazi Party no longer represented its original intentions. To be disloyal to those original values could be considered dishonorable.

To walk away from a loyal friend, group, or collective after their intentions transmogrify into something evil isn't betraying the morals you held true. It's just common sense.

I fell out with a friend recently because he was not the person I once knew. When I cut him out of my life for being unreliable, nasty, and duplicitous, I didn't feel I was being disloyal to him.

He was not the reliable, considerate, and encouraging person I once knew. I know people change over time, but he didn't seem to have a single characteristic left that I originally befriended him for.

Trust your friends, but don't follow them blindly if their intentions seem suspicious. They say that love is blind, but friendship closes its eyes. We may need to peek through one eye just to check on our friends.

For we do not easily expect evil of those whom we love most.
- Peter Abelard

191. LUST

All socializing is to hide our lustful desires.
- Mystery

Neil Strauss's *The Game* is a book that describes how the author went from a geek to the best pick-up artist in the world. He explains that a group of pick-up artists taught him the art of seducing women, and he himself became a teacher of the art.

Neil Strauss is a journalist who has done many interviews with famous people, before and after he wrote this book. He's interviewed Tom Cruise, Britney Spears, the Rolling Stones, to name a few. Neil was intrigued that all these rock stars, actors, and singers were just as flawed, vulnerable, and insecure as any normal person.

This mentality helped Neil have a lot of relationships. In his book, he says, "A lot of guys are intimidated by an attractive woman, and they dehumanize her because our culture perceives beautiful women as commodities. But I think if you're able to walk up to a person and get to know them, and you see their flaws and their impurities, and realize that they're like you, then you can humanize them again."

Our perception of happiness is warped, thanks to modern media focusing on beauty. A so-called "ugly guy" could be with a supermodel. He could be the nicest person in the world, and she could be the most selfish, insecure, and manipulative woman, but society would dub him as "the lucky one."

Neil's books detail how many guys are unfulfilled, even after they get with the women they want. It's because they have fallen into the trap of lust. Most men will seek out a partner based on many things, but at the top of the list is often appearance. It's not right, but it is understandable because it is the most visible trait.

Even Neil and other pick-up artists have their own insecurities. Pick-up artists who have been with hundreds of women may not be able to maintain a single stable relationship.

I know people who have slept with countless women but never had a girlfriend. They have never been with a person longer than a month. People like this usually look amazing, as they rely on their appearance to get with others, instead of winning them over with their personality.

Giving in to this lifestyle makes you become part of a cycle, one that usually creates mind games to build status and ego, such as who can get with the best-looking person or who has slept with the most people. When you start thinking about that, it stops being about a relationship or harmless fun and becomes a game.

Life is made up of desires that seem big and vital one minute and little
and absurd the next. I guess we get what's best for us in the end.
- Alice Caldwell Rice

192. LUXURY

Even in a time of elephantine vanity and greed, one never
has to look far to see the campfires of gentle people.
- Garrison Keillor

We complain how everything is so expensive and yet, we make more money than ever. Back in the old days, a television was a luxury. Now we have three plasma-screen televisions with digital HD, broadband, and access to hundreds of films. Every technological gadget is connected to the other, and it still doesn't seem enough.

People are so intoxicated by luxury, but comfort makes us careless. There is such a focus in modern society on getting new things and having the latest technology that people want to buy a gadget or new dress or a piece of jewelry even if they can't afford the bare necessities.

We stress when we are financially strained. When we suddenly find ourselves in possession of a bit of cash, we reward ourselves, rather than use it on more urgent and immediate priorities like rent and bills.

This mentality is similar to a person trying to be healthy. You exercise to stay fit, but you become so exhausted that you reward yourself with a snack full of fat and sugar, which puts you farther from your goal.

What's scarier is that luxuries can become competitive. If one person buys an iPad, everyone buys one. If you don't have one, you feel left out, and you can even become ostracized. This can socially effect you because people can act like you are falling behind or not clued in to the most recent popular trends.

Some people use it as an excuse to be lazy. People like this have no motivation because they are too comfortable. When you have everything, you can't be motivated to do anything.

The most hypocritical attribute is when a person who struggles with money makes something out of his life and becomes financially secure, and people assume he was always like that; that he didn't have to work for it. This is called the prejudice of luxury.

Society can hate rich people like Bill Gates because he lives a life of luxury that we can never have. Luxury doesn't equate to happiness. Bill Gates didn't inherit his money. He earned it. And he gives more money to charity than anyone in the world.

We shouldn't rely on luxuries to confirm that we are happy. Surely it's better to be happy with what we have than to have everything and want more. We need to appreciate it and not become obsessed by it.

Every luxury must be paid for, and everything
is a luxury, starting with being in this world.
- Cesare Pavese

193. MAKEOVER

*I'm not going to change the way I look or the way I feel to
conform to anything. I've always been a freak. So I've been a freak
all my life and I have to live with that. I'm one of those people.*
- John Lennon

If you're unhappy, you may want a change. You may dye your hair pink. This may seem weird to some people, but if that's just who you are, you should go for it.

If you are going through a hard time, and you think that changing your hair color is the best way of dealing with it, you may have to consider that the issue hasn't been resolved. Makeovers are meant to show the new you, but they are usually used to hide the real you.

You can use the change as a substitute for dealing with your problems. You don't need to force a change. If you force it, it's not coming from a natural impulse. If you're trying too hard to change, it may be out of desperation or peer pressure.

Not all makeovers are bad. They can be helpful, even necessary. My friend, Chloe came out as a lesbian when she started college. People didn't believe her for months, so one day she snapped and transformed herself so she looked extremely butch. Before this, she looked like a typical skinny girl with blonde hair. With her makeover, she had spiked, dyed hair; leather; chains; and piercings everywhere. This look symbolized change as well as rebellion. This drastic makeover worked because people started taking her sexuality seriously.

That was a few years ago. Nowadays she looks quite similar to how I used to know her. That rebellious look wasn't her. She just had to do it to get people's attention.

People can become so accustomed to how they think you are that when you change, they don't notice or believe you, unless you declare it from the rooftops. A makeover can be good because it can help you make a difficult transition in your life. When you change, just remember what you once were.

*I mean there is something sort of insincere about changing your nose.
If that's all that makes or breaks you, the shape of a piece of cartilage?
I mean if you're going to go through life building everything on that.*
- Felice
(After The Fall)

194. MANIFESTATION

Expect everything and anything seems like nothing.
Expect nothing and everything seems like everything.
- Samuel Hazo

Lee Brower had a simple example of how to use manifestation techniques as a means to create a positive influence in your life.

Lee had a rock in his room. Any time he looked at the rock, he would have a positive thought, and he would feel grateful for everything he had, everyone who was there for him, and everything he had accomplished in his life. He kept this rock in his room, so it kept him positive. It was beside his bed, so it was the first thing he saw when he walked into his room. When he came in after having a bad day, or he lost his keys, or got stuck in traffic for an hour, he would storm to his room, see the rock, and instantly be put into a passive, tranquil mood.

Did Lee have a significant memory involving this rock? Did he have it since childhood, or did he see it on an important day in his life?

No.

So why use it? His answer was simple: why not? We manifest negative thoughts with things that don't matter all the time, so why can't we do the same with positive thoughts?

My former neighbor, Clara refused to drink out of green cups. She had a controlling boyfriend who had green cups at his house, and he went berserk if she used one without asking, or didn't wash one properly, or didn't put it away in the correct cabinet. After they broke up, Clara learned that she had manifested negativity with green cups. If she is at a house that has nothing but green cups, she will not drink. By comparison, using a rock to feel happy and peaceful doesn't seem crazy. Whatever works.

We usually use some sort of good luck charm or family heirloom, but you can use anything. You don't have to wait for an epiphany to happen. If you are going through a dry patch, you don't necessarily have to wait months or years for the perfect moment to turn it all around. You can choose to channel all the positive energy by simply choosing a totem to empower.

I know it sounds silly because there are no real connections to these objects. It may be silly to have such faith in such an insignificant item, but the brain loves stimulation.

Even if we don't believe in the paranormal, the mind craves superstitions, luck, and wacky stories. If the brain had a choice to be stimulated by something nonsensical or something negative, which one would it choose? You become whatever you think of.

If we give power to negative things, we could
do it for positive thoughts as well.
- Lee Brower

195. MASKS

The mask, if worn long enough, will be the face.
- Stephen Fry

Some professions require a uniform like a police officer, a fire fighter, or a nurse. The reason why is because the colors, symbols, and accessories represent and encapsulate what the job is about.

But why use a uniform as a symbol? We wear uniforms so when the job is done, we can take it off, so we don't bring the job home with us. If a police officer had a rough day, he can take his uniform off to relax. If he keeps wearing it, it can be a reminder of the difficult aspects of his job.

We need that uniform, that mask, that identity to preserve a way of thinking to get the job done. The mask can create an illusion that can work to our advantage. A police uniform will represent authority, even if the officer is unassertive. A fireman's outfit encapsulates bravery, even if he is terrified. We need to hide our true feelings from time to time to achieve certain goals.

Masks can represent hiding, pretense, and lies. Everyone wears masks, some bigger or more extravagant than others but masks all the same.

We know it's not healthy to hide our true feelings. It's deceptive, fake, and manipulative, and it can be detrimental to our health.

Studies have been done on criminals who wore masks to commit their crimes. They didn't just wear masks to conceal their identity; the criminals felt like they were looking through someone else's eyes. To them, their crimes felt like they were watching television, which desensitized them to the bloodshed. So, when masked criminals attacked or even killed people, they often said that they felt no empathy, and the experience didn't feel real.

When you hide your feelings, you look at everyone instead of connecting to how you feel. That's why analytical people tend to have problems with identity, connection, and empathy.

We wear masks because we don't want to be a burden, or we are going through a rough time and are trying to shake it off. In times like this, we put on the Party mask or the Overcompensating mask.

A mask looks like a face, but it's never going to fool someone into believing it's an actual face. The same applies to our true feelings. When we pretend everything is okay, people can usually see through it.

Ask yourself what masks you put on and how often you wear them. When do you take it off? In front of whom? How many people have seen your real face? Have you? Do you think you could spare more time for people to see the real you? Let them. They probably don't know what they are missing.

Behind every face, the mental emptiness deepens.
- T.S. Elliott

196. MATURITY

Age is a very high price to pay for maturity.
- Tom Stoppard

I believe there's a part of us that should always be a kid. To lose our most innocent side would be depressing. We need to grow up, but a part of us should stay forever young. Every child needs attention, even your inner child.

But at the same time, we all have to grow up, whether we like it or not. What age are you? What age do you feel like? What age do people think you are?

These answers can vary dramatically. People have thought I was ten years older (in a good way) or ten years younger (in an immature way.) What age group are your friends? Do you act more mature or more immature around them?

In certain circles, we can talk about politics, religion, our future, and so on. We might talk about general things to other friends, like sports, movies, travel, and so on. Then when we are in the presence of our other friends, the best topics that can be brought up are cartoons, video games, fights, and spreading rumors.

This might be because this is what we and our friends want to talk about.

Perhaps this is how people see us and judge our level of maturity.

When I was in Dublin, I was the youngest person in my class of fifty and was seen as a kid from a backward town in the middle of Ireland.

Four years later, I was one of six people in the final year, consisting of students mainly in their thirties. My friends had a newfound respect for me.

This is when people thought I was nearly ten years older than I was because I talked in a certain way, I looked a certain way, acted a certain way, and presented myself in a mature way.

However, when I went to England, it was as if I went down to the bottom of the totem pole again and had to drag my way back to the top. I was once again seen as a simple Irish kid.

It was patronizing because for a while, people would talk to me in a dumbed-down way, and then they were astonished when I used a polysyllabic word. "That's not like you!" they would say, but I had to remind them that they decided who I was very quickly when we first met.

If you are seen in an immature light, people will not talk to you on your level. They'll see you as a kid. Or they might think you're a boring old man or woman, but they don't know how much fun you can be.

Prove them wrong. Never let your inner child disappear, but allow yourself to grow on a mental level.

Age' is the acceptance of a term of years.
But maturity is the glory of years.
- Martha Graham

197. MEDIA

> What the mass media offers is not popular art, but entertainment which is intended to be consumed like food, forgotten, and replaced by a new dish.
> - W. H. Auden

Remember those thousand-word essays you'd write in school? Do you remember that feeling when you were two hundred words short, so you'd write a lot of filler to reach the word-count quote. That's media on a daily basis but with a lot more filler.

Most people in the media want to educate and inform society, but there are those who just want to make a name for themselves or a bit of easy cash. They do this by spreading gossip and misinformation.

We are bombarded by bad news daily. Why? Because it sells. Good news makes us feel all warm and fuzzy inside, but it doesn't make us want to buy a newspaper.

We have all seen astonishing stories that spread through Twitter and Facebook and countless other sites, but then it's uncovered as a hoax. I tend to give it a week or so before I take any allegations or life-altering discoveries in the news seriously. If it sounds too crazy to be true, it nearly always is.

We forget that imperfect human beings make the media. Nearly everything said is opinion, and any fact can be manipulated, even by accident.

Nowadays, information is so accessible due to the advances of the Internet and connectivity. You would think this accessibility would improve the efficiency of the media. It has, but it can also create more panic.

With millions of people online giving their opinions and supposed facts through statuses, YouTube videos, and vlogs, it's easy to understand how misinformation can spread. Most people think they are making a statement when they spread false facts, oblivious that they are causing damage. With the media in our ear the whole time, we don't know what's true or what to believe.

The media can also affect what we are supposed to like and what we are supposed to hate. What is cool now can be different tomorrow. At one time, redheads were considered demonic. Nowadays, they are deemed exotic because they are rare. In the past, voluptuous women represented power. Now the media perceives women like this as malnourishment. The media will change perceptions like this again and again in the future. Don't get sucked into the mob mentality. Media is only true until tomorrow. Media should resolve panic, not create it.

> Media exist to invest our lives with artificial
> perceptions and arbitrary values.
> - Marshall McLuhan

198. MEDITATION

Meditation is the soul's perspective glass.
- Owen Feltham

Meditation plays a big part in many belief systems. Buddhists desire to be at one with themselves. (This is where the word "atonement" comes from him since Buddhists seek to have "at-one-ment." Hindus believe in Brahman; a sacred power that sustains the inner meaning of all existing things. Christians follow kenosis—self-emptying or cleansing.

But if you are not religious, can you still meditate?

Of course. The two concepts never had to go together. Buddhism involves one of the most famous practices of meditations but does not hold the idea of a personal God. Meditation is about equanimity, which is a calmness of the mind. You don't have to pray. You should meditate to explore your mental and spiritual self.

"Spiritual" is a word that people are quick to dismiss. I used to believe that meditation was one of those concepts that you have to be "into," and it doesn't suit everybody.

A friend of mine was spiritual, so I tried it out for her sake. I thought it was silly and even if I wanted to like it, I was not the right guy for it because I have dyspraxia. Dyspraxia is a motor learning difficulty, so I have trouble putting something into practice, even though I understand it. It's also difficult to concentrate on any one thought.

But I stopped being dismissive and gave it a shot. Meditation has done more for my dyspraxia than anything. Meditation was more effective than diet, pills, or cognitive exercises designed for dyspraxia. I was using my impairment as an excuse that I couldn't meditate, yet the meditation helped it immensely.

I went through two years of daily meditating for at least half an hour. I don't do it as often as I used to, but when I get stressed or frustrated, I just listen to my music, and it makes me feel at peace.

I am not suggesting you have to meditate in the traditional way. This is not a guru book. I do suggest that you find your calmness of mind in your own way. Meditation doesn't have to be sitting in a Buddhist stance, humming and chanting. It can be listening to music, going for a walk, looking at clouds, walking through a forest, lying on a beach, or having a scented candle bath.

Meditation is not about thinking. It's about feeling. Allow yourself to feel and nothing more.

Meditation is the tongue of the soul and the language of our spirit.
- Jeremy Taylor

199. MEMORY

Yesterday is but today's memory, and tomorrow is today's dream.
- Khalil Gibran

People worry that when they're seventy, their memory is impaired. However, they have 97 percent of the brain cells at that age, compared to when they are twenty. Although your memory does get worse as you age, it's nowhere near as bad as you think.

Once a thought is in your brain, it stays there. You can't truly forget anything. If you still have trouble retaining information, don't worry.

If you find the right memory tool, you can retrieve memories more efficiently. This memory techniques are called mnemonics.

One such mnemonic is chunking. This is where you split what you need to remember into bullet points. Trying to remember a speech is tough, but if you pick out distinctive words or phrases, you will remember the words that come just before and just after. This is more effective than learning it linearly.

Sense memory is another technique. When you try to remember what somebody said, the sense memory you are relying on is hearing. If you rely on all your senses, it's more likely you will recall more details. What mood were you in? How did the person say it? What did you eat? What could you smell? This technique will help you paint a more accurate picture of the memory.

But the most effective technique is probably memory association. You remember details about your favorite movies or books because you can associate with them. Unfortunately, it's a little bit difficult to retain a sixteen-digit bank number.

Or is it? You can associate images with any number, no matter how large. If you had to memorize 437101163912, you can associate an image with each number. For example, a car has 4 wheels, a stool has 3 legs, the 7-10 split is a common term in bowling, 11 looks like goal posts, and so on.

This technique may sound silly, but it works because it stands out. All silly things are memorable. This is the key. When you need to remember something, make an image that's positive, inventive, colorful, and funny. No more dull dates or names. Don't stress about your memory. Have fun with it.

Life is all memory, except for the one present moment that
goes by you so quickly you hardly catch it going.
- Tennessee Williams

200. MENTAL HEALTH

Your body hears everything your mind says.
- Naomi Judd

When we picture someone who is powerful, dominant, and in control, we usually picture a person who is big, brawny, and well built. We act as if physique is how we should define who we are.

But no. The mental self should always come first.

Only in recent generations have we focused on the psychological side of humanity. Religion always had the intention of cleansing our inner being, but it was not until Sigmund Freud broke ground with his theory of psychoanalysis that we comprehended how much is going on in our minds and how much we can benefit from understanding it.

He made us aware that the human psyche or ego is made of two forces: the id, which is the repository of our subconscious desires; and the superego, which is responsible for controlling instinctive wishes.

His work also helped us understand why mental deficiency exists. Madness used to be seen as a disease—and a contagious one at that—so doctors did little to correct it, frightened they would catch it themselves.

In a manner of speaking, they can. Being surrounded by unstable people can fracture your inner psyche over time. Insanity is the inability to differentiate between right and wrong, but what is considered right and wrong changes with time, along with law, belief, ideas, and morals. As you can see, it's not that simple.

We're all closer to the brink of madness than we would ever care to admit, and that is not an exaggeration.

One in ten people will suffer some sort of mental illness. When you look at so-called crazy people gibbering to themselves, you may find it sad or even funny. You must realize that this can happen to you if you are not careful. Learn to address your problems openly with yourself and those you trust.

To stay physically fit, you need to be mentally fit. Florence Nightingale was the first medical nurse who tried to tie the knot between physical health and mental health. She looked after her patients not in a cold and calculated way. She chatted to them and made them feel like friends rather than patients because she believed mental health was as important as physical health, if not more important.

We have to be aware of this if we go through any trauma, whether a broken arm or a broken heart. No matter how much pain our bones or muscles are in, we need to ask ourselves, "How am I doing mentally?" If we don't, we may learn the hard way that not all scars are physical.

A healthy outside starts from the inside.
- Robert Urich

201. MISTAKES

If it has to choose who is to be crucified, the crowd will always save Barabbas.
- Jean Cocteau
(Le Rappel a l'ordre)

Life is like the children's game of Chutes and Ladders—except there are a lot more chutes and they drop you farther down.

There must be trial and error to achieve success. If we gave up after the first mistake, there would be only error. With trial and error, problems turn into mistakes. Mistakes turn into good attempts, which then turn into good work, which turns into great work.

We can be devastated when we screw up or when we don't get what we want. We keep being surprised when we make mistakes, as if they are not a part of life. How else could we learn?

Whatever goals you have, you will make mistakes from time to time. Instead of reacting to any screw-up or setback as if it is the end of the world, give yourself constructive criticism. "That didn't work. Why didn't that work? What will I do in the future to ensure that doesn't happen again?"

You can't start great. Alfred Hitchcock made many films at the start of his career that were universally panned. He made almost fifty movies before he directed *North by Northwest*, *Vertigo*, and *Psycho*. These three films are considered to be among the greatest movies in cinematic history. His work got better over time because he wasn't afraid of trying new things. Above all, he wasn't afraid of potential failure.

We shouldn't ignore mistakes, because that will condemn us to repeat them. We need to see our mistakes not as problems to dismiss or dwell on but to overcome. Watching others fail in life can stop us from making mistakes in the first place. Every time I was tempted to go back to gambling, my temptation would fade when one of my friends lost money in a casino. His tragedy prevented mine. People can be better mirrors than the one on the wall.

Anytime you're going through a problem, look at all the problems you got through in your life. Is your current problem the biggest one? Is it even that big of a deal? Overcome it like you did everything else.

There are three ways to learn from a mistake: hear of it, see it, or—the most effective way—do it.

A blunder – apparently the merest chance – reveals an unsuspected world, and the individual is drawn into a relationship with forces that are not rightly understood. Mistakes are the result of the suppressed desires and conflicts. They are ripples on the surface of life, produced by unsuspected springs. The blunder may amount to the opening of a destiny.
- Joseph Campbell

202. MODESTY

At least I have the modesty to admit that lack of modesty is one of my failings.
- Hector Berlioz

There is an old story about three kids in Africa who had to cross the desert to reach the other village. To ensure they didn't become dehydrated, they were each given half an ostrich egg filled with water. Since the ostrich is the largest bird and carries the biggest eggs, there should have been more than enough water for the children to reach the other side without utter exhaustion.

As they set out on their journey, one of the kids felt thirsty. The other two had not drunk yet, but he thought that if he had a little sip, it should be fine.

The water was so good that he couldn't stop himself from drinking more. Before he knew it, he'd drunk all his water. He was shocked, but the other two boys had not noticed, because he was lagging behind them. He didn't want to feel humiliated, so he said nothing and carried on his journey.

As they traveled, the other two boys took a sip of water every once in a while. Eventually, they noticed the third boy hadn't drunk at all. When they asked why, the boy simply said he wasn't thirsty. The two boys could not believe this.

By the time they made it to the village, the two boys told the villagers that the other boy had traveled the whole desert without drinking a sip of water and that he must be blessed. The men and women of the village were so astounded, they didn't even realize his ostrich egg was empty.

The boy did not say anything, because he didn't want to get caught. His shame was misinterpreted as modesty, which allowed his journey to become a bigger and bigger story in the village.

I am not condoning the child's actions. He lied, but we should focus on the aftermath.

If you don't brag, people tend to make your achievements greater than they are. You shouldn't deny it or boast about it, but accept it. Don't oversell yourself, but also don't undersell yourself. They say the best response to any compliment is a simple thank-you. Anything else can be considered arrogant or unappreciative. If you are complimented, embrace it.

Modesty is for the forgotten.
- Hector Berlioz

203. MONEY

A lack of money is the root of all evil.
- Mark Twain.

When we have a bit of money to spare, we treat ourselves. If we have a good bit to spare, we buy a new coat, game, or movie. If you find yourself in an abundance of sudden wealth, expect to go wild with it.

Unfortunately, we give in to this mentality even when we are in dire need of money. Imagine you need to pay the rent desperately. You suddenly get a bonus from your job, and it's just enough to cover the rent. You worked so hard for it, and it's been so long since you've had a chance to enjoy yourself that you decide to go on a spending spree, buying lots of unnecessary paraphernalia.

I have seen these exact circumstances time and time again. Sudden wealth blinds current circumstances. We naturally reward ourselves for a job well done.

But we do this even when it's not practical. We all fall victim to this self-defeating reward system when money is involved.

If money is the source of happiness, why are people always trying to get rid of it? The University of Michigan surveyed what countries are considered the happiest and put Nigeria as number one. The average Nigerian makes the equivalent of £250 per year. Americans make over one hundred times that, yet they were in sixteenth place.

We have to get out of this mentality that money automatically brings happiness. If anything, money brings pressure for the future. We need to learn to be responsible with money. We need to learn to save money. We call the practice of storing money "savings" because we are saving ourselves.

If you are reading this and thinking that it's not that simple, I apologize. I know many people who are in dire financial states. I have seen countless people, however, who claimed never to have had the right opportunity, but they waste any money they had on anything but necessities.

You may be in the worst financial state imaginable. You may be living in poverty and squalor, but if you have income, the only way to get by is to prioritize.

If you buy what you don't need, you steal from yourself. Money is an easy thing to fall in love with. You're not made rich by treasures but by how you use them. Use money. Don't let it use you.

Never spend your money before you have earned it.
- Thomas Jefferson

204. MONITOR

Don't think. Thinking is the enemy of creativity. It's self-conscious, and anything self-conscious is lousy. You can't try to do things. You simply must do things.
- Ray Bradbury

When I spoke about being on autopilot in a previous chapter, I talked about how we tune out and do the bare minimum, but we still carry out the necessary steps we need to perform in the day. We need to be aware of what we do.

The opposing problem is monitoring yourself. You do this when you are overly conscious about yourself. If you are insecure about your weight, you monitor everything you eat, how quickly you eat, if you gain or lose a pound, or if you feel bloated.

Monitoring can make us obsessive, paranoid, and even delusional. Self-awareness prevents us from ever living in the moment.

It's horrible to have our lives put under a microscope by others—every action scrutinized, every motion corrected, and every notion challenged. But what is worse is to be the one gazing through the microscope.

There can be good monitoring. When I shattered my toe, I naturally monitored my posture, how much weight I was putting on my leg, and what my surroundings were in case I knocked against something.

When it began to heal, I monitored the difference in my flexibility, durability, speed, and strength. Within a few weeks, it was second nature, and I didn't give it a second thought, to the point where I forgot at times which of my toes I broke! In times of injury or any radical change, of course, our monitoring sensors will be hypersensitive.

But we must allow ourselves to turn them off occasionally. My friend, Sheehan slipped a disc years ago. He said it's pure agony. But what's worse than the pain is how it affected him mentally. He constantly monitors every movement he makes. Ninety-nine percent of the time, his movements won't affect him, as long as he doesn't do anything drastic. Sadly, his paranoia has forced him to constantly monitor himself, impairing him from embracing life.

This may be an extreme example, but we all monitor in one way or another–for minutes, hours, days, weeks months, or years. We may stress about how we present ourselves to new company, be overly conscious of how we eat, become prone to anxiety attacks, and so forth. You can torture yourself by monitoring your whole life, but you need to monitor how often you monitor yourself.

I admire our ancestors, whoever they were. I think the first self-conscious person must have shaken in his boots. Because as he becomes self-conscious, he's no longer part of nature. He sees himself against nature. He looks at the vastness of the universe and it looks hostile.
- John Shelby Spong

205. MOOD

Comedy is tragedy that happens to other people.
- Angela Carter

Have you ever been to a celebration, such as your birthday or a party that you couldn't enjoy? It might have been an amazing day but you couldn't enjoy it because you were in a bad mood. Maybe something bad happened just before you got there that threw it all off. Maybe your sweater got ruined, you lost your phone, or you had an argument just before the big celebration.

It is unfortunate because, not only will you probably remember that day as a letdown, but whatever little thing ruined that night will probably escape your memory.

I remember I had tickets to go see a comedian. I couldn't wait. But then I had an argument with a friend. The reviews of the comedian were excellent and all my friends who saw the performance loved it. But I thought it was rubbish.

A year later, I saw it on DVD and thought it was hilarious. At first, I thought the comedian must have had a bad show when I saw him, but then I found out that the DVD was recorded the exact same night I was there.

I realized that the show was tainted because of the quarrel I had with my friend. I can't remember what the argument was about. The only thing I remember was that it was insignificant.

It can actually be bad to be in a good mood sometimes. My father won ten thousand euro the same day my classmate got kicked out of school. I was over the moon about my dad's winnings, so my friends thought I was acting self-absorbed and not being sympathetic.

I found out that I got into the college I dreamed of the same day my housemate broke up with his girlfriend of six years.

You may think that acting upbeat isn't selfish because you are simply focusing on the positive.

That's well intended, but others will probably perceive you as ignorant, naïve, and not acknowledging the gravity of a situation. In all these situations, I needed to let go of my ego and ground myself.

When things are going your way, it's easy to miss how everyone else feels. It's great to ride a buzz when you get a streak of good luck but you need to notice where other people are mentally. Don't lose sight of them.

Nothing helps a bad mood like spreading it around.
- Bill Watterson

206. MORALS

Cowardice asks the question, "Is it safe?"
Expediency asks the question, "Is it politic?"
Vanity asks the question, "Is it popular?"
But Conscience asks the question, "Is it right?"
- Martin Luther King

Human beings naturally want things to balance out. We prefer symmetry. We try to fix things before they get worse. This can be as simple as a slanted painting being turned correctly or as epic as seeking justice for a murder. This concept is built into us on a genetic level. It's why we see things as polar opposites, good and evil, black and white.

You might think your morals set you above the underachievers and delinquents and that you are better than they are. It's great to have a high moral code, but we need to avoid developing a superiority complex.

We can use our morals as an excuse to view others as lesser beings to us. Our morals can also prevent us from enjoying life.

My friend, Yvonne was a born-again Christian. She is a wonderful human being, but can be irritating when she goes out to socialize. She will judge my friends and will complain that they all smoke too much and drink too often. She believes she is above all of that.

She acts this way every single time she goes out, which has caused her to make a lot of enemies and not enough friends. You don't have to put down people just because they don't have the same ethics as you.

I haven't had a drink of alcohol since September 14, 2004. When I go out, I don't look down on my friends for drinking. Alcohol isn't automatically bad. It can be if you are not in control or have a lack of willpower. If you enjoy a drink, then go for it! It's not my thing. I don't enjoy the taste or the sensation, and I have saved a ton of money by giving it up.

No matter what we do, what we say, and how we react, we can nearly always tell whether what we are doing is right or wrong. We have a genetic imprint of what is right and what is not. Yet there are certain forms of cruelty, like teasing, bullying, beating, torture, psychologically breaking down, mind games, compulsive lying, revenge, vandalism, and violence that occur daily.

If I went around my life with a little rule book and said, "You can't do that! You can't do that!" I would lead a sad life.

This book is advisory. It is not gospel. Claiming your morals set you higher than others is hypocritical. Control your morals. Don't let them control you.

I know only that what is moral is what you feel good
after and what is immoral is what you feel bad after.
- Ernest Hemingway

207. MOTIVATION

A champion needs a motivation above and beyond winning.
- Pat Riley

I used to have a problem getting up in the morning. I got up with the bare minimum time I needed to get to college or work. This problem didn't give me much chance to wake up properly in the morning, so I was drowsy for the whole day.

I kept saying to myself, "I want to wake up early tomorrow," but it seemed ineffective. I realized that I was using the wrong words. I needed to say, "I am going to wake up tomorrow at 6:00 a.m."

The next morning, I jumped out of bed the instant my alarm went off. After a while, I didn't even need an alarm clock. I said to myself, "I don't need things to motivate me. I can motivate myself."

We say we want a pay raise or we would love to have a new car, but we need to use the right words. Don't say, "I want" or "I wish." Instead, say, "I am" or "I will." Make it sound like an inevitability, rather than a want.

If you want something, see it as a need more than a want. I found it hard to squeeze in time for the gym. I remember my friend, Stefan came to the gym to pick me up one day. When a gym instructor came up to Stefan and asked if he wanted to join, he said, "I'm not paying for something I can do at home."

That was a great point, but it was stated for the wrong reasons. Stefan didn't exercise at home because he had no motivation. But when you make the effort to go to the gym, you feel like you have to work out.

Days later, I bought barbells and dumbbells and worked out at home. That way, I could work out more with less time wasted and more money saved.

Stefan's comment motivated me more, but he didn't even realize that. He never did any exercise at home or try to get healthy, even though his health was such a massive concern that he worried about consistently.

Isaac Newton wrote his great work *Principia Mathematica* that forever changed the perception of the basic laws of physics. He only wrote it on a bet to prove a mathematical theorem.

Even though this isn't the most admirable stimulus, it shows how any motivation can change the world. Action is reaction but you don't have to wait for that action. The action can be in your mind.

If you look at the world as it is, it will be what it is. If you look at what it could be, you will be motivated to change it.

People often say that motivation doesn't last. Well, neither
does bathing - that's why we recommend it daily.
- Zig Ziglar

208. MYSTERY

A lot of the fun lies in trying to penetrate the mystery.
- Anthony Hecht

Legendary director and master of suspense, Alfred Hitchcock, famously said, "The greatest explanation to a mystery will never be as interesting as the mystery itself." The unknown always fascinates us. And we can use the unknown to our advantage.

There's a famous pick-up artist called Mystery who has a tactic to keep people fascinated in a conversation. If you are a successful and rich actor, the best thing to say is not, "I'm an actor." Although this statement could intrigue people, it might make you come across as arrogant.

The best thing to say is, "I work in acting." Leave it at that, and focus on the person you're speaking to. People will think, "What does he do? I want to know more." If you divulge all the facts, you leave nothing to talk about. If you hint at a juicy tidbit, it's more intriguing. It can turn into a little game, and you can have some fun. You can do this with your work, your name, your home, or your accent. If anyone asks where my accent is from, I usually say, "Guess." This can go on for twenty minutes, which is more fun than just telling them.

Think about someone you know who is confident and has a high social status. Now think of someone else who seems to have high status but his or her confidence is a charade. What is the difference between the two?

The facetious popular people always talk about when they met a famous celebrity, how much money they have, or how successful they are.

We put up with people like this because they are entertaining. But if they don't let us get a word in edgeways, except to trump us with their next tale, we won't hang around forever.

Most of us know people who pull off the high social status with true, effortless cool. They don't make much attempt to be more than who they are. They don't sell themselves. They don't declare themselves. Typically, they are more interested in talking to you than you are about talking to them.

My favorite conversations are when I talk to people like this. It tickles my interests in certain subjects, and I want to meet up with them again to find out all the other little stories that they implied.

Mystery adds to the fascination, intrigue, and desire. If you know how to make people curious, they will want more, crave more, and need more. That's why magic tricks are so effective. They give us a glimpse of the magic beneath, and it's up to us to discover what really makes it tick.

The eternal mystery of the world is its comprehensibility...
the fact that it is comprehensible is a miracle.
- Albert Einstein

209. MYSTICISM

The New Age? Ha! It's just the old age stuck
in a microwave oven for fifteen seconds.
- James Randi

Do you know why you are worrying and unfulfilled all the time? Because you're prone to too much self-examination. You appear social, even the life of the party, but in a way that only convinces others. You are all too aware of the facade. This means that you find yourself playing a part. You'll disengage yourself to the point where you will find yourself surveying everything going on and feeling incapable of connecting.

In the past you've learned to be disappointed by people. You instinctively keep people at arm's length, until you decide they are to be allowed over the magic line, into your group of close friends.

You may ask, "Why is so much of this making sense? How can you be reading me so accurately?"

Well, I can't. Psychological illusionist, Derren Brown used that reading to a group of strangers in his television show, *Tricks of the Mind*. The participants couldn't understand how he did it, until they realized that he gave them all the exact same reading. He just broadened the interpretation enough, so they heard what they wanted to hear.

We want people to "get us." We force things to make sense because we want them to. Relying on unexplainable logic can force us to do stupid, unhealthy, and even dangerous things. We all see different shapes in the fog, and we can see what we want to suit our needs. We can't rely on mysticism. If you have genuine problems, find a more reasonable outlet. Be careful what you see and be even more careful what you want to see.

If you show advanced technology to a person or group who have never seen it, it would be utterly unexplainable. It would be seen as a mechanism based on principles so alien that it would be akin to magic.

What we can't explain tends to have a mystical arc to it—until we can explain it. We should try to understand the unknown, not embrace it. Cut the superstitious cords and acknowledge the facts.

The mind loves the unknown. It loves images whose meaning is
unknown, since the meaning of the mind itself is unknown.
- Rene Magritte

210. MYTH

> It would not be too much to say that myth is the secret opening through which the inexhaustible energies of the cosmos pour into human cultural manifestation.
> - Joseph Campbell

Mythology is psychology misread as biography, history, and cosmology. "A myth is not a fairy story," says Gilbert Ryle. "It is the presentation of facts belonging to one category in the idioms appropriate to another. To explore a myth is accordingly not to deny the facts but to re-allocate them."

In myth, great stories become a depiction of multilevel events from various time periods, woven together into a symbolic event portrayed in stories. Throughout history and across the world, we have similar fables involving deities, divine prophecies, and epic battles, from Ancient Rome to Greece, from Odysseus and the Cyclops, to the antediluvian time of Adam and Eve. These are all wonderful stories. But they also all contain another similarity: skepticism.

We tend to go too far with these stories, one way or another, either seeing them as history or dismissing them entirely, forgetting that there's a message in there. We tell fables such as these to illustrate points. We jazz up these stories to make them stand out. As time goes by, legend becomes myth, and people don't take stories like this seriously anymore.

A totem is a good example of myth making. A totem is a force to recreate the truth, to do something ritualistic for a greater understanding of things. A totemic mysticism is spiritual but in its mysticism, it can be truer in the abstract than reality.

Another thing we don't acknowledge is modern mythology. Instead of searching for answers in mythology, we make our own mythology every day. Our myths don't have superpowers or Grecian godhood, but we immortalize our heroes, our sportsmen, our friends, and our family. We talk about them to others and pass down stories about these people that no one may ever know or meet.

"The funniest guy you will ever meet!"

"It was the best goal you will ever see!"

"I never saw a woman as beautiful as her!"

They exist in myth, but that doesn't mean they aren't real. All myths have a grain of truth in them. That is how they became a legend and stand the test of time. You leave out the ugly bits.

> All the great legends are Templates for human behavior.
> I would define a myth as a story that has survived.
> - John Boorman

211. NAIVETY

> The world is full of fools, and he who would see
> none should live alone and smash his mirror.
> - Claude Le Petit

Naivety is when we no longer blame our ignorance on innocence. Children are innocent because they are young and know no better. Who are we to burden them with what reality has in store for them? They can't comprehend it. We barely can as adults.

A time comes when they have to embrace the world they harbor, the good and the bad. But they may want a bit more time of ignoring reality and staying within their own self-built microcosm. That's naivety.

As a child, my friend, Johnny had a simple understanding of his parents. He loved them without question, obeying their every command, but the complexities and secrets of their lives were unknown to him. His father was a drug dealer, and his mother was beaten regularly. Johnny only saw what he wanted to see. Looking at them positively was an understandable coping mechanism as a child. But as an adult, he just came across as ignorant and blind to the truth.

I suppose it's naivety when the truth is right in your face, and no matter how much closer it gets, you can't see it because your eyes are closed. A fool sees not the same tree that a wise man sees.

James Dewar said, "Minds are like parachutes. They only function when they are open." So we have to open ourselves to everything, even bad things.

Why? Because it's there. To dismiss the dark side of reality will not make it go away. On the contrary, not allowing yourself to acknowledge the harshness of the world will leave you vulnerable to it.

Accepting the potential for bad things to happen may give us a little fear, but it can prepare us in the long term. If the fool would persist in his folly, he would become wise.

I don't mean you need to be aware of every tragic part of life. Negative people can be naïve to the joys of life. You can be naive in good and in bad ways. There are a lot of bad things going on in the world, some you don't know and never heard of. But the same goes for good. There is so much good in the world. You just need to find it.

> There are only two classes of pedestrians
> in these days of reckless motor traffic – the quick and the dead.
> - James Dewar

212. NARROW-MINDED

It is better to be high-spirited even though one makes more
mistakes, than to be narrow-minded and all too prudent.
- Vincent Van Gogh

Plato's Cave was the idea that if you were chained in a cave your entire life and
all you saw were shadows on the wall, that is all you would think there was to
the world. If you were unchained and explored outside the cave, you would see that
there is so much more.

We forget that our opinions and interpretations aren't fact. We forget that we
do not see more because we do not explore further.

We can rely on a never-ending routine. We need to venture out of our comfort
zones and safe havens. Some people can't see the wonders before them.

Some go through a forest without seeing firewood. The more we stick to our
ways, the more likely we will dismiss any new experience.

We are quick to shoot ideas down because "new" means "unknown," and
unknown means there's a chance of danger, fear, sadness, and pain.

That's true, but there are also chances for happiness, excitement, thrills, and
fun. The best way to open a mind is to do just that, open it. Let people in. Let
opportunities into your life.

There are so many incredible things going on in the world that you don't even
know about. There are some things we will never know about because the world is
so big to take it all in.

But we can know about them if we actually go out and open ourselves to
everything life has to offer. We won't get around to experiencing everything, but
we should experience as many wonderful opportunities as possible.

When we try to have new experiences, there will be bad ones as well, but good
and bad are better than playing it safe and experiencing neither.

Some people don't conform to change because they don't want to compromise
themselves, or they have a simple background or a simple set of ideals they live by.
Being from the Irish midlands and living in the middle of nowhere, I know firsthand
what it is like to be set in my ways.

It is good to a degree, but if you want to experience more and you are not fully
satisfied where you are, just remember that you have no scope of the world until
you have seen it.

Just look at David Attenborough's *Life* or *Planet Earth* or anything on the
History or Geography Channel, and see how much of a world there is to live out
there. If you see anything that tickles your fantasy, seize it.

The test of a first rate intelligence is the ability to hold two opposed ideas
in the mind at the same time, and still retain the ability to function.
- F. Scott Fitzgerald

213. NEEDS

> Just as treasures are uncovered from the earth, so virtue appears
> from good deeds, and wisdom appears from a pure and peaceful
> mind. To walk safely through the maze of human life,
> one needs the light of wisdom and the guidance of virtue.
> - Buddha

Needs and wants drive us. But we act like some of our wants are actually needs. We feel like we need a reputation, authority, and money. These are not needs, but we act like they are of life-or-death importance.

If you asked a hundred people what they need in their lives, almost no one will say the big one: happiness.

Is being happy more unlikely than being famous or rich or simply the desire for happiness? How many people are rich? Now how many people are happy? How many of the rich and famous are happy because of their money?

It's weird, considering that to find fame and fortune, you need ridiculous patience, blind optimism, insurmountable tolerance, unrealistic skill, godlike charisma, a million other things, and a ton of luck. You can do everything right and still miss out because luck is the biggest factor.

But there is no luck in happiness. You don't need anything to be happy. Usually, the less you have, the better. I've seen people with everything in the palm of their hands, yet they remain utterly miserable. I know others with little to nothing to their names who manage to remain satisfied and contented with their current station in life.

All you need is a positive attitude and good perception of life. It may sound too simple. And it is. Like all "too simple" things, we don't focus on being content with ourselves. We concentrate on the material world too often. We concentrate on the empty glamour of the world.

We see the things that can genuinely make us happy, like family and a relationship, as inconvenient chores.

To be rich, powerful, and famous are what I call un-needs. An un-need is a want disguised as a need. We assume they bring happiness. So we won't work on the happiness ourselves. Happiness doesn't come in a bundle. It's not a package deal with wealth or popularity.

It comes separately, and you have to find it in other places—not in big estates or fancy cars but in the little things that matter.

> Men take only their needs into consideration - never their abilities.
> - Napoleon Bonaparte

214. NEGATIVITY

If you are going through hell, keep going.
- Winston Churchill.

You have sixty thousand structured thoughts per day. Of all those thoughts you have on a daily basis, how many would you say are negative and utterly impractical?

Negative thoughts create a cycle. If you dwell on a bad thought, you start associating with other bad thought. They are what psychologist Bob Doyle would call "like thoughts."

If someone says, "Don't think of a black cat," you will think of it because the command, "Think of a black cat" is still apparent.

So if you keep worrying about depression, the word "depression, depression, depression" will keep swimming through your head.

Don't say, "How do I stop being depressed?"

Say, "What do I have to do to turn this around?"

If you're having a good day, the slightest thing can ruin it. It only takes one bad thing to start before it sets off a chain reaction of bad luck. Negative thoughts are contagious, but so are positive thoughts. They're just harder to catch.

But why do bad things happen to good people? As Michael Bernard Beckwith points out, "We live in a universe in which there are laws, just as there is a law of gravity. If you fall off a building it doesn't matter if you're a good person or a bad person, you're going to hit the ground."

A lot of people believe the world is always getting worse, when in reality, it is always getting better. We hear "terrorism" and "gang war" on the news but crime is constantly going down.

We believe that we are destroying rain forests, yet there are more trees in the world than in the last hundred years because unlike before, we replant them in massive quantities.

Despite unhealthy living and worry about viruses and superbugs, human beings live twice as long as they did a 150 years ago.

If reality bites, bite back. Make it a world you want to live in.

You will never find the answer until you stop asking why you
can't do something and start figuring out how you will.
- Mark Hooper

215. NEUTRALITY

*The hottest place in Hell is reserved for those
who remain neutral in times of great moral conflict.*
- Martin Luther King Jr

There are times where being impartial is the best course of action. We can be pressurized to have an opinion about every scandal, to spread the word on every conspiracy, and to take action on every corrupt politician. Having a say in every new development seems practical, but it can undo your good intentions.

In 2010, Philadelphia's Kensington Strangler stalked and killed three prostitutes. People were disgusted that the police couldn't locate the killer. They had to take action. They were out for blood, so when an anonymous page on Facebook said a person called Triz Jeffries may have been near the area at the time of the murders, that was enough to condemn him as the killer.

A lynch mob surrounded his house, ready to exact their revenge upon Triz. He narrowly escaped with his life after the police insisted the terrified youth wasn't a suspect.

When the Twin Towers were destroyed, a lot of people were petrified and confused. They wanted an enemy to blame, and they were so overwhelmed by hate, a lot of the wrong people had to suffer the consequences. Too many people were perceived as the enemies.

Even after all this time, many people still which nations were involved in that attack. It's okay to stay neutral until you have more of the facts.

When conflicts happen in the world, you may want to stay neutral for several reasons. You don't know what side you are on. You need to know more before you make a decision. The conflict doesn't interest or concern you.

But when you act neutral, people can bully you into a confrontation. People can even become hostile to you.

"You won't stand up for your country!"

"If you're not with us, you are against us!"

"If you do nothing, you are no better than the enemy!"

I am not saying you should always be neutral. It can be the worst thing you can do in certain situations. If it is an issue that resonates with you, then go for it.

But don't be rash. Educate yourself. Know both sides of the argument, and don't blindly follow someone else's passion. Only follow your own.

*If you are neutral in situations of injustice, you have chosen the side of
the oppressor. If an elephant has its foot on the tail of a mouse and you
say that you are neutral, the mouse will not appreciate the neutrality.*
- Desmond Tutu

216. NEW AGE

From the astrologer came the astronomer, from the alchemist
the chemist, from the mesmerist the experimental psychologist.
The quack of yesterday is the professor of tomorrow.
- Arthur Conan Doyle

Noumenic is something or someone whose existence is theoretically problematic. Such forces play a big role in mysticism.

There are mysterious and misunderstood arts: tantra, alchemy, hypnosis, and many other cryptic practices that have been tarnished by pretenders, misconception, and ignorance.

The concept of hypnosis is indisputable and completely legitimate, but I know plenty of people who have no belief in it whatsoever because they have seen too many fakes and scammers pretending to be hypnotists. Often misunderstood or misinterpreted, there are always little truths to even the most blasphemous taboos.

I love magic in its art and its philosophy, but it can be used to prey on the gullible. You may think it's just entertainment, but magic feeds that part of the brain that lets us fool ourselves in our beliefs. We can read about physics, chemistry, and biology, but if you find a source of tantalization for a human being, we can be quick to switch off our logic.

New Age mysticism can grab our attention with trinkets and intrigue us with vague concepts like crystals, auras, voodoo, and Wicca. These matters are often described with the vaguest explanations. Charlatans have preyed on the gullible with New Age nonsense for thousands of years. We may be telling the future with tea leaves instead of human blood, but in the end, it's the same tricks and the same rituals with the same intentions.

Have you ever heard the Magic Teapot argument? It is said that there is a teapot between Earth and Mars, randomly floating in space. A teapot is so small, and space is so vast that it would be impossible to find it or scan it to prove its existence or validity.

In a nutshell, there is no way to know if it is actually there. But at the same time, you can't prove it's not there! You could scan all of space, and it can be said that the teapot is too small to be recognized, or it moved out of the way, or you just didn't find it. This argument has been used to show how ridiculous it is to believe in something without any facts or logic.

We have to be careful and skeptical when dealing with concepts that contradict the basics of science and common sense. We can spend decades, centuries, and even millennia trying to discover the truth. So we need to stop wasting precious time and money on nonsensical and archaic concepts.

Apodictic – true and needs no proof. Logically certain. Incontestable.
(Oxford Dictionary)

217. NICE

Innocence always calls mutely for protection, when we
would be so much wiser to guard ourselves against it.
- Graham Greene

If being nice got you everything you wanted, we would all be nice. But bad things still happen. I don't mean bad things will happen, like losing your job, getting dumped, or personal tragedies. I mean people will literally take advantage of you for being a good person.

You may have a friend who is a considerate and amiable person and would do anything for you. You should feel lucky and grateful to have a friend like this.

But if your friend has a tendency to be this nice constantly, then it hints that they need to please you because of some insecurity of needing to be liked.

On their part, this may not be true. Your friend is probably acting nice because of the way they were brought up.

Nevertheless, the more habitually it happens, the less rewarding it feels, the less we value it, and the more we expect people to act this way in the future.

We should be kind when we can afford it, but we shouldn't try to prove anything by attempting to please everyone at every possible encounter. People will respect you more with the occasional nice gesture. We appreciate favors more when they are few and far between.

I'm not saying you have to be a jerk, but being nice doesn't have to be your main priority. Don't assume people will accept you based on kindness alone. Lots of kind and harmless people have problems with socializing, status, and self-assurance. It's like they have to be nice to overcompensate because they have nothing else to offer. It's a turn-off.

Bosses, producers, playwrights, company owners, artists, presidents, and leaders do not become who they are by being nice. They may be likeable, but it doesn't have to play a part in being successful. Whether or not they are arrogant, in the real world, people mainly care if they can get the job done and if they can be trustworthy.

If you ever get frustrated about not getting what you want or being taken advantage of because of your good nature, then change your priorities. You don't have to change who you are as a person. Nice guys only finish last if that is all they are.

Innocence is like a leper who has lost his bell,
wandering the world meaning no harm.
- Graham Greene

218. NOSTALGIA

Room don't change, ornaments stand where you place them, only the heart decays.
- Graham Greene

When I broke up with my first girlfriend, I found myself drifting down memory lane. I reflected on how we use to talk about our future, and we truly believed our time together would never end.

Then I noticed something funny. I remember her wearing a dress she never owned; the two of us dancing, even though I have two left feet; and how we would go home and talk about moving in together, even though we were probably arguing. The experience made me realize how much I embellished our memories together.

A false memory is often created either by telling a lie so many times that you actually think it's true or by fusing two half memories together.

Relying on nostalgia can be a fear of the future. You can try to recreate the old days by going back to your old hometown to live again. You might get back with an ex-partner because your more recent partner dumped you, and you don't want to be alone. You can become so obsessed with recapturing your childhood that you could be neglecting your family or friends. Nostalgia is a self-defense mechanism to cast our minds back to a more relaxing time that probably never existed.

We complain how computers are too complex, even though they are constantly improving. We are annoyed there's nothing on television when we have countless channels. Everything is more accessible, yet we say it was better in the past.

People may be nostalgic not just of their own lives but also throughout history. You can latch onto a past you weren't a part of.

People may see history as being far more interesting, but the future will appreciate today's wonders in hindsight. There are just as many glorious moments in today's world than in any era. It would be a pity to live through them and not notice or be a part of them.

People go on about "back in my day," but our days are today, and that's what's going to make a difference, more than anything in the past. Tomorrow's good old days are happening now.

Youth is vivid rather than happy, but memory
always remember the happy things.
- Bernard Lovell

219. NOW

There was a reviewer a while back who wrote that my pictures didn't have
any beginning or any end. He didn't mean it as a compliment, but it was.
- Jackson Pollack

Imagine your situation in life right now. How did you go about today? What did
you do to get to the point where you are reading this book? Maybe reading this
book was the first thing you did when you woke up, or maybe it was the last thing
you did before you went to bed.

Now think about your situation at this same time last year. This time. This day.
How close or far are you from your goals? Are you any nearer? Do you have new
goals on the horizon?

Thinking like this is more fascinating if you are in similar situations but there
are minor differences. If you are in your second year of college right now, how
different do you feel compared to when you were in your first year? Or maybe you
are in your second year in your new home or the second year at your job. How were
things this time last year with your partner? Better? Worse? Are you single now?
Have you moved on to someone else?

What about your relationships with friends and work colleagues, classmates,
neighbors, or housemates? Your mentality? Your insecurities? Your wants? Your
priorities? How does it compare to last year?

If you have the same partner, job, house, college, financial, and social situations
as you did last year, does that mean you are the same person now? Do you view
anything in your life differently? If so, is it for better or for worse? Do you have
different ideas, concepts, philosophies, problems, revelations, intentions, phobias,
and dreams?

You can latch on to the past or dwell on it. They can both be just as damaging
because you are not concentrating on your life at the moment. I've seen people in
a great position in life, but they don't realize it, because they dwell on the past or
dread the future.

I suppose the biggest question is, what was the path you took to get from the past
to the now? Almost every advertisement talks about the future. Most psychology
talks about what happened in the past. Both of them are equally significant, but
they are just behind the most important of the three: the present. History is the
prologue to now. If you do nothing now, then the past means nothing, and the future
is nonexistent. We become most powerful when we utilize the three of them—to
learn from the past now to create our future. The present is yours to shape. Life is
just about today.

The present is an age of talkers, and not of doers, and the reason is,
that the world is growing old. We are so far advanced in the Arts and
Sciences, that we live in retrospect, and dote on past achievement.
- William Hazlitt

220. NUMBERS

A good decision is based on knowledge and not on numbers.
- Plato

We are bombarded by numbers daily. Two dollars a gallon. Two for the price of one. Sixty-four kilos. Seven hundred gigabytes. Two thousand calories a day. Elections. Polls. Bar charts. Trigonometry. Only two days left. Fifty percent off. Tax increase. Rates are doubling and tripling. Twenty-four hours open. Square roots. Lottery unlikelihoods. Pie charts. Mobile numbers.

When the mind can't cope with the scale of human suffering, it turns to the cold comfort of numbers as a way to organize and categorize the unimaginable.

Numbers like millions, billions, and trillions are used too often nowadays when discussing people and money. It's easy to be dehumanized by it.

I'll show you. Imagine a human being. Now imagine two people. Now three. Five. Ten. Twenty.

When you get to picturing twenty, can you actually tell if there are twenty people there? At what point do you just simply round off and just picture the number? Now imagine this problem with trying to picture millions or billions.

Numbers can be unreliable, but we assume that a number is a golden nugget of fact. Dr. Joel Best wrote *Damned Lies and Statistics*, and he points out the problem with numbers. If a company made a profit of four billion dollars, can we suggest that somebody actually counted this? If you had to count one-dollar bills, one per second, it would take thirty-two years to count to a billion.

I understand that they have a superior method of calculating, but there will be a margin in error when dealing with such a tremendous number.

If unemployment is down by 42 percent, that's good. If crime is down by 12 percent compared to last year, we feel secure.

We tend to accept these numbers because we can't comprehend them, so we allow the masters to do it for us. But numbers change and people are flawed.

Robert McIntyre, director of Citizens for Tax Justice, and Stephen Slavinsky, director of budget studies at the Cato Institute, were asked to divide the national debt of America to the best of their ability. Not only did they have completely different numbers in the trillions, but they divided it into different percentages, trying to explain where all the taxpayers' money goes. In fact, if you got any number of experts to divide it, it would be rare to get two matching answers.

There are sure to be statistics littered in this book. It's impossible nowadays to deny, ignore, or be affected by them. I try to explain rather than prove my point with numbers, but the fact is, you have to draw your own conclusions.

You can come up with statistics to prove anything, 40% of all people know that.
- Homer Simpson
(The Simpsons)

221. OFFERS

Say, "yes" more.
- Danny Wallace
(Yes Man)

There is an old joke that talks about a great flood that swept through a town. Many people fled to avoid drowning, but one man stood on top of his rooftop and prayed. By the time the water was up to the second story of his house, a rescue boat came to help him, but he said, "No. God will save me," and he continued to pray.

By the time the water was up to his knees, a helicopter came from above, demanding that he get in, but he insisted that God would save him.

He drowned. In heaven, the man asked God, "Why wasn't I saved?"

God replied, "I sent a boat and a helicopter, didn't I?"

Although this is a joke, it does highlight a problem people have with accepting offers. In Danny Wallace's book, *Yes Man*, he creates an experiment in which he simply says yes to everything for six months. To say a universal yes to everything sounds silly because people can easily take advantage of him.

So to avoid falling into stupid or dangerous situations, he doesn't literally say yes to everything; he just accepts every opportunity he can.

Shortly after finishing Wallace's book, I was at an airport, and I had to find a table where I could sit to eat. The only place left was beside a guy I didn't know. Normally, I wouldn't pester a stranger with awkward small talk, but the book taught me to be open and accept any offer, so I chatted with him.

A week later, I befriended two people I met through chance encounter. A month after that, I met a guy called Ben in a pub, and we hit it off. Six years later, I am still good friends with all of them.

This mentality encouraged me to chat to a woman on a train years ago. She is now my wife. (So, I have to thank Danny Wallace for my marriage!)

By accepting more offers, you will find yourself doing activities you thought you would never do, talk to people you would have no chance of ever meeting, and open doors for yourself socially and financially.

It is impossible to change your situation if you don't change yourself. Something has to start the ball rolling, and it has to start with you because it is your life you are trying to change.

Waiting for calls or offers is not enough. Put yourself out there, and allow yourself to be in circumstances where you will get offers.

If you go for an audition, there will be hundreds of people who have more experience, who are better looking, more well connected, more suited to the part and more talented. So you're probably not going to get it.
But you are definitely not going to get it if you don't go.
- Robert De Niro

222. OPENNESS

The brain's calculations do not require our conscious effort, only our attention and our openness to let the information through.
- Marilyn Ferguson

I was talking about life-or-death situations to a bunch of friends, one of whom was a psychotherapist called Tom. We were discussing how would we react in all sorts of hypothetical scenarios, such as the classic situation - if someone came at you with a knife, what would you do? Even if you never hurt a fly or raised a hand, the self-preservation part of you would kick in. The animal within you in order to protect yourself. Tom pointed out that everyone has this side to them, even the seemingly most innocent and harmless people you could fathom.

I am not saying we should use that level of urgency all of the time. I am simply saying that there are parts of the human psyche buried deeply, and we only use them when we have to, not realizing that we can use them whenever we want.

Most of us are not open enough. A lot of factors can prevent us from opening up. We might worry what people think about us, our environment, our friends, how we were raised, what we believe, and so on. We have a lot of excuses not to fully express ourselves.

Do you wonder how accurately you present yourself? Only by being open can you do this. If you hide everything, no one will see that amazing person you are deep inside.

You know when you meet someone that says the weirdest things? You assume they talk like this for attention. But some people act this way because they are completely open. They can be too open to the extent that they are not even ashamed. People like this don't care what other people think of them, to a point where they refuse to repress who they are as a person.

This is admirable, but it can go too far. You can come across as weird, creepy, chauvinistic, or racist. If you were to voice every thought you had, it would be a lot to absorb. Too much. You have heard your friends say things while they were intoxicated that you never thought they would ever say while sober.

But it's there, deep down somewhere in the mind. We all have it. We need to control when we are open with ourselves and how much we choose to share. If we let it out in small bursts, it will come out more controlled.

It's better than to keep it in, as it may explode out of you when you are drunk or emotional, and then it can be misinterpreted.

If you have a problem, voice it. If you have an idea, let it be heard.

We need to give each other the space to grow,
to be ourselves, to exercise our diversity.
- Max de Pree

223. OPINION

> When two opposite points of view are expressed with equal force the
> truth does not necessarily lie midway between them. It is possible for one
> side to be simply wrong. And that justifies passion on the other side.
> - Richard Dawkins

There are no absolute truths. All claims are relative, even this one. What is funny for one person is insulting to someone else. When a small custom is considered harmless in one culture, it may be deemed sacrilegious in another.

Opinion is ambiguity. It's not how things are. It's how we feel things are. No matter how logical your opinions are or how calm you are when you express yourself, opinions will clash, and you will experience hostility.

What makes opinions tricky is that we are biologically designed to think that we are special. It's a means to stay alive. If you felt worthless, you would feel depressed and accomplish nothing. Feeling unique and having something important to say is a strong driving force.

However, it causes some problems when everybody needs their opinion heard, and everybody's opinion has to be right. We can't all be right, but that logic doesn't stop people from challenging each other. You may believe you deserve to be heard more than others. You might believe your views are true because "they feel right." Perhaps you see your own beliefs as solid, irrefutable facts, and any mild disagreement is perceived as an attack of the highest hostility.

When we get defensive, we say, "Am I not entitled to my opinion?" You are entitled to your opinion, if you allow other people to be entitled to theirs. What other people believe may mean nothing to you, but it could mean everything to them.

Research has shown that the more opinionated a person is, the more self-destructive they are. If you are naturally intelligent, it's easy to see others as idiots. If you are naturally well-built, it's tempting to perceive others as weak-minded and lacking in willpower.

These thoughts are there to elevate you, but they can force you to think you are better than everyone else, making you come across as arrogant, narcissistic, and defiant. In the end, you will push people away, or they will push you away as they tire of your egotism.

But opinions can't be dismissed. They may not be factual, but they have the potential to be factual. A theory can become a fact if it is given an opportunity to be viable. If we allow some opinions the chance to be excrescent in society and life, then perhaps we can validate them if they are accurate. Opinions can be more powerful than facts.

> If one were to order all mankind to choose the best set rules
> in the world, each group would, after due consideration,
> regard its own as being by far the best.
> - George Herbert

224. OPPORTUNITIES

Most of what matters in your life take place in your absence.
- Salman Rushdie

A movie agent spotted Natalie Portman at a pizza parlor when she was only a kid. She contended against hundreds of girls for the lead part of Mathilda in the movie *Leon*. Because she was the youngest person to audition, she was told she didn't have the maturity for the role.

She went to the audition anyway, won the role, and launched her acting career. She found fame because of a chance encounter, as did a handful of others, but millions of actors strive for this dream and so few achieve it.

She might have missed that opportunity if she hadn't been there that day, if she'd been sitting somewhere else, or if she'd come in a minute or two earlier or later.

The same could be said about the agent that accepted her. He could have walked into any other café or shop or bar and picked up some other potential actor.

But the fact is she said yes to an opportunity. That is the biggest factor to her success. Since opportunity can come at any time, we must seize it when we can.

Curiosities, drama, and trivialities can catch us off guard when we try to pursue our goals. These are not opportunities. These are distractions. Think of all the opportunities you lost by being too lazy or too tired or too scared.

Years ago, I had a long night out and got back to my friend's house at 7:00 a.m. I woke up with only a few hours sleep and remembered I'd promised I would go on a date with a girl.

The thought entered my head, "Should I bother? I'm too tired, and she probably won't even show up."

My friend said to me, "What do you have to lose?"

And guess what? That girl became my wife. My life would be completely different if I had been too tired to meet up with her. It would've been such a lame excuse to miss such an amazing opportunity.

It's better to regret things you did than things you didn't. Never miss an opportunity to miss an opportunity. Don't look a gift horse in the mouth. Just take advantage of a heaven-sent opportunity.

As the old saying goes, "God gives every bird a worm, but he doesn't throw it into the nest."

Difficulties mastered are opportunities won.
- Winston Churchill

225. ORGES

The mind will always rebel at a direct command – go to sleep, fall in love, stop crying, don't get angry, say you're sorry, take back what you said, you don't have the guts to do that, listen, stop talking, relax, be quiet, wake up.
- David Mamet

It's vital to learn from an early age the value of taking orders. It's difficult to teach a child to be obedient, but as we grow older, we understand that to accept orders willingly is necessary.

When we are young; from being a toddler all the way to be a teenager, our immaturity will want us to defy authority and rules and regulations. It's only when we need to get a job that we understand the importance of obedience.

But too much obedience is just as dangerous. Some incidents happen in everyone's life that no one ever forgets. One such incident is when you are given an order that you know is morally wrong. This can be at work, in school, or from your family, friends, or loved ones.

My friend, Blake was a teacher in college. In one staff meeting, the principal said that the teachers had to decide the fate of a student called Pol, who they believed wasn't putting in the effort. They decided to expel him.

Blake knew Pol personally. Blake knew Pol was a hard worker, but he was battling depression after his father died of stomach and lung cancer.

Blake brought up this issue in the staff meeting to the rest of the teachers. The principal believed that since Blake had a personal relationship with the student, he was protecting Pol and was too close to the issue to see it for what it really was. Blake didn't put up a fight and agreed to expel him.

He told me that he has never been more ashamed of himself. Blake believed he could have talked the rest of the staff around to his way of his thinking. He didn't, because he was scared of what could potentially happen to his career. So he followed the principal's orders, knowing that he was wrong.

I could've given a much more obvious example of how following orders is unethical, but that personal story of my friend really touched me.

We can't always defy those who give us orders, or we would never have a job. Talking back would do wonders for our ego but keep our wallets empty. No one likes taking orders, but we can look at them in a practical way.

Punishment may make us obey the orders we are given,
but at best it will only teach an obedience to authority, not
a self-control which enhances our self-respect.
- Bruno Bettelheim

226. ORIGIN

No one thing is the root to anything.
- Richard Dawkins

Richard Dawkins is obsessed with the origin of life. He is aware that there is no one single answer to everything. There are many key factors, some more important than others but not one answer that could potentially encapsulate everything.

We love encapsulation. We want to find the source of our depression, the key to our frustration, the origin of our anger, and the reason behind our eternal questioning. We ponder in a way as if there is only one answer, which once unlocked will create a chain reaction that will explain everything. But does knowing the origin truly make us understand life any better?

A lot of our insecurities are mysterious in origin. You are going to have to locate the answers yourself.

I emphasize the word "answers," not "answer." Don't con yourself into thinking that you will find an answer to your insecurities or queries or whatever it is that you want to get to the bottom of, and think that is it.

One of my friends, Terra had anxiety attacks and didn't know why. With counseling, Terra realized that she had abandonment issues due to her father's leaving her at a young age. With this revelation, Terra assumed she was cured. Sure enough, her anxiety seemed to vanish.

But within six months, Terra's anxiety came back worse than ever. She went back to her counselor and uncovered a repressed memory of her father taking advantage of her. After this, her attacks subsided. This time, Terra wasn't naive to think her anxiety is gone for good, as she was already proven wrong.

Terra wanted to know the origin of her insecurities and took the first explanation that made sense. Even understanding the origin of our insecurities doesn't undo years of psychological trauma, but it does help. It just doesn't make it go away overnight.

I cannot promise that the quest for these answers will relieve pain but they are worth uncovering.

Just don't be too satisfied when you find an answer. Don't be too quick to give up digging. You may dig the wrong way or hit a hard spot, but you'll get there eventually. You will keep finding things locked away. It may seem fruitless because there seems to be no end, but I believe you should keep going. You keep unlocking answers the further you go.

All difficult things have their origin in that which is
easy, and great things in that which is small.
- Lao Tzu

227. OVERCOMPENSATION

A wrong concept misleads the understanding; a wrong deed degrades the whole man, and may eventually demolish the structure of the human ego.
- Muhammed Iqbal

Have you even met someone who seems too nice, too funny, or too splashy with his or her money? All of these traits are considered positive attributes. We like when people are comical or charming, so how can that be considered wrong? Can too much of a good thing be a bad thing?

If you are naturally a funny guy but you're insecure, it is tempting to put the "funny side" of you on top of what you cannot deal with. We all have insecurities, and we try to limit them.

If we can't limit them, we try to ignore them or distract ourselves from them. Who wants to acknowledge their insecurities every waking moment? Why can't we just enjoy ourselves in the way we know we can?

Just because you are a funny guy doesn't mean that it will be perceived that way, especially if it's pushed. If you are overcompensating, even if you are not aware of it, others may notice it.

There was this guy called Langford in college with me. He tried to befriend everyone in the whole school and everyone in the area. It meant so much to him. He tried too hard. He needed to be liked because he was bullied at school in the past, and he wanted a fresh start.

But because he was forcing it, it came across as desperate. It was easy to see through that. He didn't want a friend. He needed one.

My friend, Jack befriended almost everyone but in a casual way. He wouldn't go out of his way to befriend everyone but over time, he became mates with the majority of the school. He didn't push it, even though he could have because he was funny. He talked to new people to see what they were like, unlike Langford who tried to make them like him by impressing them with wild stories, jokes, and undermining students. Jack was being a friend, not an entertainer.

Overcompensators are always the same—people with fragile self-belief so they puff up an idealized image of themselves. They would be more respectable if their supposed achievements were glimpsed rather than shoved in people's faces.

I would love to have a friend pick me up in his car, only to find out then that it was a Porsche. That would be more admirable than a friend who yammers about his brand-new car nonstop.

They say images are more powerful than words. Don't talk of your achievements; let people see them and say nothing—that is more humble. No one listens to a braggart more than the braggart. Don't toot your own horn. Let others do it for you.

He who rides a tiger is afraid to dismount.
- Chinese proverb

228. PAIN

Fear is pain arising from the anticipation of evil.
- Aristotle

Pain is considered universally bad, but there is good pain, and there is bad pain. In the rain, you can get soaked so badly, you reach a point where you can't feel the water. Getting hurt physically or mentally can work the same way. We might see this as good pain because we get used to it. As Friedrich Nietzsche said, "What doesn't kill you makes you stronger."

This is not always true. And even when you come back from intense injuries, are you mentally stronger? We may get such a painful physical injury that we forget that it affects our minds as well.

But there is also good pain. I saw a documentary about pain sensors in the human body. There was a story of a woman jogging, who took a wrong turn and fell off a cliff. She landed on her feet and shattered her kneecaps.

The fact that she survived was not the incredible part; it was that she felt no pain. It wasn't because she severed a nerve but because it was a self-defense mechanism.

We forget sometimes that pain has a purpose. We feel pain to warn the body that it is under attack. The sharp sting we feel is the body alerting itself to a danger; the compulsion to shout is for surrounding people to help us.

But this woman's pain was so severe that to experience it would have caused the woman to pass out and therefore make her unable to heal efficiently.

The part of her spine that sends the signal to the brain to make it aware of pain hardened so all warning signals bounced off it.

She crawled for days until she came across two people, and within seconds, the goo in her spine softened, and she felt an intense pain and passed out. It was one of the few times where pain wouldn't have helped.

Although this example shows that pain isn't always necessary, it helped me understand again why we need it. If you have a sudden pain in your back, you may have pulled something. If you have a weird tingle in your arm that won't go away, have it checked out.

Do you have rare but quite painful sensations in the back of your eye? You might think it doesn't happen that often, so it can't be anything severe.

Your body has to remind you only once to let you know that something is wrong. Your body doesn't alert you for fun. It alerts you to ensure that you take steps to stay alive by avoiding injury or danger. Expect pain in life; just be careful how you take it.

Your pain is the breaking of the shell that encloses your understanding.
- Khalil Gibran

229. PANIC

To him who is in fear everything rustles.
- Sophocles

I saw a documentary recently about a daredevil called Matt who lives his life doing crazy feats. He drove a jeep off a cliff, jumped off halfway, and then parachuted to safety. That's just a Tuesday afternoon to this guy.

One day, Matt went scuba diving with his friends. His buddies stayed on the ship while Matt dived to the bottom of the ocean. Suddenly, something went wrong. His apparatus malfunctioned, and instead of fifteen minutes of oxygen, he had thirty seconds. He couldn't resurface in time as he was at least five minutes deep. He would have to wait a minute just before he reached the surface to decompress, or he could die.

That means he had to stay under water for six minutes. The average human can only hold their breath for four minutes.

His friends picked up on Matt's malfunction on the ship's monitor and expected the worst. All they could do was wait for his lifeless body to resurface.

After six minutes passed, Matt re-emerged completely fine. In fact, he wasn't even out of breath. They asked, "How could you have possibly survived?"

Matt answered, "Well, as soon as I realized my oxygen tank was depleting, I swam up a hundred feet, took a breath for about a second with the oxygen I had left, and kept doing that until I got near the top."

"Why didn't you panic?" his friends demanded.

"Because I would have died," he answered.

Matt wasn't just being rational. In a dangerous time, we tend to automatically go into fight-or-flight mode. It is every organism's final fail-safe.

In many situations, including this one, Matt's fight-or-flight mode would have made him remove his mask, condemning him to a slow, painful death. It would happen by reflex, not with conscious thought. So why didn't it?

When Matt was checked at a nearby hospital, his doctor discovered something fascinating. The reason why Matt didn't panic was because the fear part of his brain was deactivated. He spent so many years doing crazy stunts that his brain literally turned off his panic sensors. Matt has since dedicated his life to finding people who have anxiety and urges them to face their fears.

If you're scared you might not get promoted, jump out of a plane! After falling thousands of feet, you will feel like nothing can scare you.

It's been shown that if you were to perform a scary activity, fear would register in your brain. If you did the activity again, your brain will only register 50 percent of that fear. It cuts in half every time. If it's cutting down to 25 percent, 12 percent, 6 percent, and so on, nothing will eventually scare you.

Fear is the thought of admitted inferiority.
- Elbert Hubbard

230. PARANOIA

You know you've got paranoia when you can't think of anything that's your fault.
- Robert M. Hutchins

The book *Cleaning Yourself to Death* talks about how we are more immune to dirt than we are to cleaning products. Although we worry about keeping things clean, how often do we get sick from dust? Now, I understand that some people may be overly sensitive to dust. However, we act like it is a universal problem; a pandemic that needs to be eradicated no matter what.

But we have had two million years to build up immunity to germs and grime.

How many years have we had to build up immunity to cleaning products? A few years, maybe? Actually, it's probably less since products are constantly modified with new chemicals. I am not suggesting you should keep an unclean house. But I am giving a general example of how paranoia works against us.

Nothing feeds paranoia more than itself. Paranoia is an overwhelming fear. It's not fear exactly but the idea of fear. It's the idea that something may happen, rather than it will.

Paranoia is usually vague, illogical, and often derived from misinterpretation. Meerkats in the wild are always in a state of alertness and panic. If you take the meerkats out of their natural habitat and put them in a zoo, guess what? They still panic. They are pointlessly stressing themselves, not understanding that they are in no danger.

But they have an excuse. Meerkats are biologically designed to have a heightened alertness to pick up on every alteration within the area. We aren't. We can choose to be scared of the world.

It's horrible to watch people who believe that someone is out to get them or that there is some immense conspiracy. They live in constant fear. It can work as a mass effect, which turns into a mob mentality of fear.

A few years ago, the banana market in China collapsed after an unfounded rumor suggested that the fruit might contain SARS. There was a 90 percent drop in banana prices, which bankrupted growers.

But an investigation proved this claim was untrue. This accusation is a perfect example of how gossip turned into paranoia on an epidemic scale.

We used to fear witches, ghosts, and demons. A few decades ago, we feared Communists and nuclear decimation. Now we fear viruses and terrorists. If we scare ourselves with the nonexistent, we stand no chance facing real danger.

The thing you fear most has no power. Your fear of it is what has the power.
- Oprah Winfrey

231. PARENTHOOD

The first half of our lives is ruined by our parents;
the second half by our children.

- Anon

*T*abula rasa means a blank slate. This is what our mind is considered to be as a baby, before we have experienced the world. What fills that slate to begin with is vital. It will shape us into becoming who we will be for the rest of our lives.

That is why parents have to be careful. One unconsidered parental move can spell insecurity in their child's life. It doesn't take a laboratory or a crazy scientist or a potion to make a monster. Bad neighborhood, bad family, or a bad upbringing is all it takes nowadays.

Tipping the table too far, one way or the other, can create warped perceptions of reality or psychological resentment. This is why parents have to be careful in being too harsh or too nice. Both ways can be equally damaging.

Bad parents can push children to be better than they are because the children want to prove that they are better than their family.

Parents can also dote on their children so much, they grow up believing they can always get what they want. Being spoiled early can make them take everything for granted and be incapable of appreciating anything.

Parents tend to blame themselves for most of their children's faults, but their children will choose how to live the way they deem most worthy. Parents may treat two children the same way, and one will grow up happy and the other become rebellious.

The reasons why they became like this can be a direct response to their upbringing, but everyone is different. Everyone sees life in his or her own way. Parents may blame themselves for their children's problems, but none of us should use our parents as an excuse for our shortcomings.

Yes, it does have a negative effect on us if we have suffered harsh times. Bad memories can hamper us. However, if we don't let it go, we can pass on that negativity to our children, and the cycle will continue.

It's almost like exacting revenge on your children because your parents weren't there for you, but there is no sense in this. Why punish them when they have only been brought into the world? This may give you some kind of warped therapy or semblance of redemption, but if children are punished for no reason, it will mess with their heads. They can become insecure and depressed because they don't see the point of doing anything in life if they will be knocked down for it.

Respect your parents. They play the biggest role of your life.

How true Daddy's words were when he said: all children must look after their
own upbringing. Parents can only give good advice or put them on the right
paths, but the final forming of a person's character lies in their own hands.

- Anne Frank

232. PASSION

It's not childish to devote oneself to a craft rather
than a career, to an idea rather than an institution.
- David Mamet

J. M. Barrie was a playwright during the early twentieth century. He wrote many
plays but could never reach that level of success that so many strive for.

Then he wrote *Peter Pan*, which immediately overshadowed all his previous
work. The question is, why? What made *Peter Pan* his best work? Why did it capture
our hearts? Why is it revered as one of the greatest childhood stories?

Well, let's break the play down. It's about a boy who never wants to grow up. J.
M. Barrie felt like this throughout his whole life. J. M. Barrie lost his brother as a
child. This traumatized his mother so badly, she neglected him. To make his mother
notice him, he dressed in his brother's clothes. Only then did his mother seem to
notice him. But as he got older, he outgrew his clothes, and his mother neglected
him again. He became obsessed with the idea of never growing up and never aging
to regain his mother's love.

If anyone else had written the same story, it would not have been as good,
because they wouldn't have had Barrie's passion for writing about innocence and
childhood. He wrote *Peter Pan* because he felt like he had to.

Following a passionate urge is a great driving force. Copies of Martin Luther
King Jr.'s speech were given to the audience, but he decided at the last minute to
improvise and created the "I Have a Dream" speech. This impromptu monologue is
one of the most famous speeches ever delivered. It has stood the test of time because
he wasn't just reiterating words on a page. He was unleashing his vision of a perfect
world from the depths of his soul.

Great performers sing great songs because they have a passion to not only sing
but sing the lyrics they wrote. It's why musicians tend to perform better when they
are singing songs they created.

You may think you are following your passion, but you're not. You might want
to be a lawyer but only because it runs in your family. Maybe you think you want
to be a doctor because your parents are forcing you to be. Maybe you want to be
a football player because all your friends are. Perhaps you want to go to Australia
because you're sick of living at home. Or do you want to be an actor abroad, just to
escape from your boring life?

Don't do anything brash unless it comes from a genuine impulse and a real
passion.

If a man hasn't discovered something he will die for, he isn't fit to live.
- Martin Luther King

233. PAST

The past is what provides us with the building blocks.
Our job today is to create new buildings out of them.
- Theodre Zeldin

Memory exists so we can learn from our mistakes. If you forget the past, you're condemned to repeat it. If you can't change the past, take responsibility for it.

There are some things that happened in the past that we can't make sense of like a tragedy or heart-breaking event.

If you can't make sense of the past, it can stay with you like a residue. Some people are controlled by the past. We can become traumatized by what's come before, and we continue to latch onto it to make sure it never happens again.

With that logic, you relive the past every day. It's only in the past if that's where it stays.

You may have the opposite problem. Instead of using the past as a defense or a justification, you may utterly dismiss it. Nonacceptance is never a good way to protect oneself. You can't forget the past if you are unwilling to change.

The mother of a girl in my class, Muire, died suddenly when Muire was only eleven. She was devastated, but after a rocky start, she eventually came through and is now a positive, wonderful human being.

My old classmates from primary school met up with me over a decade later, and we asked questions like, "What would you change about your life?"

Muire said, "Nothing."

One guy, who didn't mean to sound rude, couldn't help saying, "But your mother died when you were a kid."

She said very casually, "I know. But I got by it. Don't know how but I did. I know someone whose mother died when he was thirty. Never recovered. Maybe I wouldn't have recovered if that happened to me now. Whatever happens, you need to get on with your life."

It's amazing how she had the strength not to use the past as an excuse. If she had, it would be difficult to judge her. She was stronger than that. I know many others who use lame excuses to justify not moving on. Our past deeds do affect us but do not dictate who we are. If bad things happened to you, don't be overruled by them. If good things happened to you, let them play a part in your life as much as possible.

To have a new vision of the future, it has always first
been necessary to have a new vision of the past.
- Theodre Zeldin

234. PATIENCE

A stumble may prevent a fall. Sudden actions cause sudden reactions. When we are being patient, it's easy to become lazy. When you are waiting for lucky breaks, loans, good news, a phone call that may make or break you, the perfect job, a life-changing encounter, your other half appearing and ending all your problems, you need to be unreasonably optimistic in your patience.

Patience hurts, but impatience hurts more. Let's say you are waiting for your lucky break. The days, weeks, months, and years of waiting can tear your soul when you're not getting anywhere. You need to stay active. I know many people who put out CVs every day, always looking for new contacts, keeping fit, keeping the social life alive, and looking out for alternatives if things don't go their way.

We can't dwell too much on waiting. Once the ball is out of our court, once we are unable to affect the final outcome, we should put it out of our minds.

At times, we may look like we failed, but only time can show our successes. Khaled Hosseini's best-seller *The Kite Runner* was dubbed a "slow burner." It was published in 2003 and wasn't successful at first.

Over time and through word of mouth, it became the 2005 best-seller in the United States, won a South African Boake prize, and was adapted into a movie.

It took two years for this to happen. Just because you can't see the ball rolling in your favor, it doesn't mean it's not happening.

Fate rarely calls us at a time of our choosing. A minute of success can save years of failure. In most businesses, you have to be dangerously patient and illogically optimistic, and your one chance can be missed before you know it.

When we are met with potential failure, we try to control it. It's like trying to control a natural disaster. You have to let it pass through. It sounds like the most unhelpful advice in the world, but not everything has a solution.

Patience has the same problem as being polite. People mistake you for being a pushover because you can tolerate a lot. Beware the fury of a patient man. Take heed what people are capable of achieving with persistence on their side.

Give me six hours to chop down a tree and I will spend
the first four hours sharpening the axe.
- Abraham Lincoln

235. PEDESTALS

A lot of people put all that stuff on a pedestal, and they won't touch it.
But I don't think that's the reason they did that.
I think they played that stuff out of pure joy.
- Brian Setzer

If a person is of a higher status or wealthier position than you, it doesn't mean they are necessarily more inclined to be right, contented, or pleasant. It doesn't mean they have worked harder in their lives. Some people gain success through luck or chance more than skill, cleverness, or expertise.

Even those who do obtain success through hard work should not necessarily be put above others, as if they are suddenly infallible. They are the same people they were in the past. Just because they have grabbed everyone's attention doesn't mean they are above us or should be considered as such.

We can put anything on a pedestal and worship it as if it is superior to us. We can do this with objects, goals, ideals, and even people.

We do this with people we know or people we admire or find attractive, especially with celebrities. But we can turn against them when these extraordinary people do ordinary, mundane, or offensive things because it breaks our illusion. This can be dangerous if the person you put on a pedestal is someone close to you.

Imagine you put your father on a pedestal. What if you thought your father was perfect and could fix any problem, but then you discovered he was an alcoholic? It could destroy your perception of him.

What if you invested so much energy on falsely worshipping something or someone and feel like you got nothing back? That feeling can mess you up. But that's only if you fall victim to the pedestal trap.

It is merely an idea that those we put upon pedestals are above us. Let's not look at pedestals metaphorically. Let's look at them literally and physically. Imagine you are placing these people or beliefs on top of an actual pedestal.

But the pedestal was not simply there. People constructed it. It was placed where it stands. What we place on the pedestal is within our control. We put them there voluntarily. It's normal to have strong beliefs or to have enormous faith in somebody, but there is such a thing as overkill. Everyone can experience imperfection, falls from grace, and even downright failure. The longer people stay on a pedestal, the higher the drop if they fall.

If we listened only to those "above us," everyone below would be forgotten. Never set anyone or anything above you. Don't bring things down to your level. Rise to the level you wish to succeed to and eventually surpass it. Whatever lies on the pedestal, don't be afraid to reach out and take it.

A pedestal is as much a prison as any small, confined space.
- Gloria Steinem

236. PERCEPTION

> We tend to perfume and reinterpret; meanwhile
> imagining that all the flies in the ointment, all the hairs
> in the soup, are the faults of some unpleasant someone else.
> - Joseph Campbell

Ludwig Wittgenstein said that if a lion could speak perfect English, you would be unable to have a conversation with one. Its comprehension of the world is so alien from ours, it basically lives in a different world.

A dog can't understand some concepts and will never comprehend things like gravity or destiny, but it can understand things like behaving for a treat.

There are some tribes in the world that are so far from civilization that they do not understand concepts like politics, science, numbers, or stress.

When we think about finding our other halves, a simpler mind may think of procreation.

Although animals can never understand many concepts, a lot of people won't either, due to deprived childhoods, traumatic experiences, and indoctrinated beliefs. Our perceptions can be warped from an early age, which can make us miss out on many of life's wonderful opportunities.

Sometimes, we get stuck looking at the world with a negative perception, and we can't get out of it, because we can't change the past or our current problems. Although we can't change the way things are, we can change how we perceive them.

Have you seen that famous illusion of a candle that if you look at it a certain way, it's looks like two faces?

There's another famous image that looks like a nonsensical smudge at first. But if you look at it under a certain light, it becomes a face.

Some people see the two faces before they see the candle.

Some people see the face before they would call it a smudge.

Some people look at a couple fighting, and they see an argument, while others will see something worth fighting for. Some people might see someone who is friendly, while others may see someone as overly friendly.

If you were depressed and then you were suddenly happy because you had a good night, you must realize that feeling is momentary. You'll go back to your old self. You must change your perception of reality to truly change.

When you watch television, you are watching the world through various perspectives and ideologies, and this melds with your psyche. Everything alters your perception, and your mind will take it onboard as well as it can. Just make sure you are getting the most of all the worlds that you harbor.

> Who looks outside, dreams;
> Who looks inside, awakens.
> - Carl Jung

237. PERFECTION

We need the courage to be imperfect.
- Sofie Lazarsfeld

You don't need a perfect life to be happy. There was a time when we were just happy with what we had. Now we are bombarded from all directions with advertisements and catch phrases like:

- "This product is the best on the market."
- "Try the latest software addition."
- "It doesn't come any better than this."

But why does the up-to-date washing machine break down when your "over-the-hill" machine never broke one single time in over ten years?

Why is your new phone the best on the market when you can't get a signal for more than a couple of seconds, and the Internet keeps coming and going?

Why are you paying double or even triple for your Internet deal, when the salesman swore you would never have to pay as much in bills again?

Because we are constantly promised perfection, we become frustrated when we don't receive it. A lot of people get annoyed when they are not popular enough, and some people are happy just to have a friend.

Some people's standards in terms of dating are so high that they reject nice, genuine women to chase girls that don't exist.

Most of us dream of being those who are the best at what they do in sports or entertainment because we believe that is the only way to be happy.

But being the best doesn't mean you're infallible or content. When a person has never been beaten, every victory makes them believe they can't lose. When that happens, they've already lost. An inevitable defeat will be far more damaging.

Wanting to be the best is a great motivator, but we have to be careful not to allow it to warp our mentality. Perfection is not a practical dream because nothing lasts.

Let's say a tray in your hand represents your goals. The tray is perfection; it represents everything you want.

Now let's add some weight to the tray. Adding the smallest additional weight can tilt the tray. With enough weight, the whole tray can completely tip over.

We should not spend time wanting the best thing possible; we should take what we get and make the best out of every good and bad situation.

If you want everything, you are going to be bombarded by disappointment. Not being able to settle for second best will force you onto a very lonely road.

A perfection of means, and confusion of aims,
seems to be our main problem.
- Albert Einstein

238. PERSONAL

I've learned you can make a mistake and the whole world
doesn't end. I had to learn to allow myself to make a mistake
without becoming defensive and unforgiving.
- Lisa Kudrow

We are sensitive creatures. The heart has always been the core of human beings,
even though the brain is what really makes us *us*. We feel it in our hearts
when we get criticized, embarrassed, bullied, humiliated, or dumped.

If your boss said your work isn't up to scratch, you might take it personally.
Your boss is telling you this because his job relies on you doing yours. Your lack of
progress affects his, and he needs to remind you of that to make sure everything
keeps in check.

It's not uncommon for a person to believe that their boss is telling them off
because he hate them. If you have this mentality, this will cause your work to worsen.
The relationship between you and your boss will sour, all because you misinterpreted
constructive criticism as an insult.

This can happen because the person who is criticizing you has a certain way of
talking, phrasing, and gesticulating that seems strong and intense. Even if a person
gives us constructive criticism in the nicest manner possible, we can still see it as a
personal attack.

Usually when we feel like we are being personally criticized, it is just a
misunderstanding. For example, one of my bulimic friends voluntarily got sick
after most meals.

She got aggravated at people in the class because she believed her classmates
would gorge on food deliberately to rile her. She became resentful and hateful until
she couldn't take it any longer and confronted her class about their subtle bullying.

But they didn't know what she was talking about, because they didn't know she
was bulimic. She assumed it was obvious, but the students didn't have a clue. They
sat beside her during lunch break, eating our greasy food, oblivious to her problems,
but she assumed they were doing it to mock her. If they had known she had serious
issues with food, they would have never dreamed of upsetting her.

In situations like this, you might take things personally because you may have
unresolved issues. If what others say cut deep, maybe you need to look deep. Your
issues can all end if you address what's going on inside of you.

Forget your personal tragedy. We are all bitched from
the start and you especially have to be hurt like hell. But when
you get the damned hurt, use it. Don't cheat with it.
- Ernest Hemingway

239. PERSUASION

> In making a speech one must study three points: first, the
> means of producing persuasion; second, the language; third
> the proper arrangement of the various parts of the speech.
> - Aristotle

When we don't get our way in an argument, we may react as if the opposer is stubborn.

Let's say you are arguing about something on which you are unquestionably right e.g. someone is being racist and you're explaining to them why prejudice is fundamentally wrong. If this argument concluded without changing the other person's mind, at least you can acknowledge it's their fault and not yours, right?

Just because you are in the right doesn't mean you are going about it the right way. There are two factors to take into account with persuasion.

The first factor is energies. Everyone has different energies, and some agree and disagree with each other more than others.

This is not a vague concept. It is called the Laban Efforts. Rudolf Laban categorized that there are eight energies in terms of moving and speaking: float, glide, dab, slash, punch, press, flick, and wring. These are based on how your energy is in terms of speed, strength, and flexibility. If you are unpredictable and erratic (slash), it's not clever to argue with a person with that same erratic energy. Fighting fire with fire can be redundant. Sometimes, you should fight fire with water. Try a relaxing way like floating or gliding. This energy focuses on calm manners of speaking and moving so the opposer will not feel threatened.

If that fails, what about making your argument in a bullet-point form? Some ways are ineffectual, but there should always be one method that the opposer doesn't become defensive or offensive with.

Another method is actioning. If you say, "You should reconsider," in an argument, what action are you using? Are you soothing the person? Are you threatening them? Befriending? Humoring? When an argument isn't going your way, the biggest mistake you can make is use offensive actions. You might blast the other person with snide comments, bulldoze them with insults, and bludgeon them with threats. How is that going to persuade anybody? There is a small chance it might, but once you realize it's not working, change your tactics.

There is no specific method or energy that always works, but you won't know what works until you exhaust all options. There is no point just focusing on one way and then hammering it into the ground. It's like kicking a dead horse. No matter how hard you kick it, it stays dead. Persuasion is better than force.

> Some think people are great persuaders because they are
> born that way. None of us are born talking. Great
> persuaders are great listeners. Find the values of others.
> - Anon

240. PHOBIA

Fear is not a lasting teacher of duty.
- Marcus Tullius Cicero

P hobias are not natural fears. They're irrational. There is a convoluted logic to phobias, and it can be tricky to pin down the origin. Before you get defensive and say your fear is genuine, let me give you a few examples of phobias:
- Rhabdophobia—fear of being criticized and then beaten with a magic wand
- Barophobia—fear of gravity.
- Arachibutyrophobia—fear of peanut butter sticking to the top of your mouth
- Hippopotomonstrosesapplequippedaliophobia—fear of big words

Trust me when I say there is a fear of everything. There is literally a fear of everything—it's called panophobia. There is even a fear of fear called phobaphobia. I have friends afraid of wooden spoons, balloons, and infinity.

If a phobia sounds non-sensical, it can be easy for people to dismiss it. But just because the fear doesn't make sense doesn't mean the fear isn't real. However, these fears usually stem from something subconscious. Because of that, you need to solve the issue subconsciously.

The most common fear is spiders. The technique for getting rid of a physical fear (but not limited to it) is called flooding. This method requires you to be flooded with fear. If an arachnophobe was put into a room full of spiders, he would be terrified, but if he couldn't get out, he would build up a resistance.

I used to have claustrophobia, which is a fear of small spaces. I wandered into a friend's garage, and his father locked it, not knowing I was in there. I screamed for two hours until they realized I was trapped inside. I got so scared of being trapped, I ran out of the room for years if I was watching a movie scene where the walls started closing in.

When I discovered the flooding technique, I utilized it. I would watch scenes in movies like this over and over until it didn't bother me anymore. Then, I spent more time in confined spaces until I became desensitized to it.

If you feel like you are not up to that, there is a more gradual technique. If you are an arachnophobe, look at a picture of a spider. Although looking at it might freak you out, you have to realize it can't touch you.

Then move onto footage of an arachnid on TV. Their erratic movements are what get to most arachnophobes, but you know that it's not a real spider.

Now move onto a real spider! But if it's in a sealed jar, it can't touch you. Just look at it until that realization sinks in.

If you unseal the jar, don't worry. The spider still cannot get out. And with a few more steps, you will have the spider in your hand without even worrying. If you justify your fear, it will never go away.

As soon as the fear approaches near, attack and destroy it.
- Chanakya

241. PHYSICAL HEALTH

I would do anything to be muscular except exercise or eat right.
- Steve Martin

You have to dodge all the traps of food like salt, sugar, stimulants, additives, and chemically altered food, while having your regular mix of carbohydrates, protein, vitamins, good fats, a lot of water, and your five fruits and vegetables a day. You need to do this every single day. That's a task that's next to impossible to maintain.

On top of that, you are expected to do at least half an hour of exercise daily. Once or twice a week, you should do more intense exercise for at least an hour. That sounds impossible with your hectic ever-changing schedule in life. Sure, you can squeeze it in if you make a few changes, make sacrifices, decide on your priorities wisely, and so on, but the question is, how important is it to you?

Well, as Edward Stanley said, "Those who think they have no time for bodily exercise will sooner or later have to find time for illness."

Bodybuilder, Bill Philips said that people are under the impression that if they exercise, it doesn't matter what they eat. However, the reality is that if you exercise, it matters more what you eat!

If you worked out intensely, your body goes into repair mode; reknitting muscle fibers and reconnecting micro-fractures in your bones. But this takes a lot of energy. How do we receive energy? Food! But you can only get into shape if you put the right food in your body.

If you don't give your body the correct energy, it won't have the strength to break down complex foods that contain processed chemicals, additives, or MSG. This will make you lose muscle and put on fat. This will push you further away from your goal.

But let's look at the problem of having too much exercise. When your body is healing, it is repairing damaged tissue. It can take seven to ten days for a muscle to completely repair itself after it is under intense stress.

Because of this, going to the gym every day is going to be redundant. Your muscles might get smaller because they are being damaged under intense workouts, and you're not giving them a chance to heal, so they simply get weaker and smaller.

It's not a chore you can neglect. It's your body. You only get one. You owe it to yourself to look after your physical well-being. There are three rules: eat well, routinely exercise, and have a good sleep. You start compromising even one of these rules, and it will catch up with you before you know it.

The food you eat can be either the safest and most powerful
form of medicine or the slowest form of poison.
- Ann Wigmore

242. PILLS

One led to two, two led to four, four led to eight, until at the end it was about 85 a day - the doctors could not believe I was taking that much.
- Corey Haim

I know there are disorders that can only be regulated by pills. There are horrible stories of people who are encouraged to throw away their tablets, which results in their deaths. I am aware that there are people who are so beyond help and so far gone in terms of mental damage that steady medication is the only way to maintain a semblance of stability.

I don't want to offend anyone with this chapter so what I have to say is not for the people who need pills but are simply using them as a cheap solution.

A pill is the promise and indication that the answer to all your problems lies in one little tablet. There are countless different kinds. There are drugs like Speed and Ecstasy, or there are the seemingly more friendly pharmaceutical-type like antidepressants and Ritalin. They all have the same intent: to release, to relax, and to unwind.

There are those who look down on drugs but may become obsessed and reliant on "safe drugs." You don't have to be a druggie to have a drug problem. You may not even see what you take is a drug.

When I suffered panic attacks, I never felt more helpless in my life. It was a battle I could not see. I was fighting with my mind and felt like I would accept any solution. When I went to the doctor for advice, I was prescribed antidepressants.

Whe my friend, Eoin, saw the tablets I had, he told me he became addicted to him, which caused him to become a drug addict. After hearing that, I tossed the tablets in the bin and beat the panic attacks through willpower alone.

That made me realize that pills shouldn't be the first solution to a problem. In many cases, they should be a last resort.

Even if the pill seems to work, it's not that simple. There may be side effects. These side effects may not become apparent for some time. The effects might change. The pills might stop working. I might have lose my medication or forget to take them after becoming heavily reliant on them.

I could have been drugged so much, I couldn't feel my problems anymore, but that wouldn't stop them affecting me. After all, it takes more than a few chemicals in a tiny capsule to beat years of repression and mental disorders.

No matter how happy tablets make you feel, they won't keep you there. But it can take the edge off to help you find the solution yourself.

Medicine is not only a science; it is also an art.
It does not consist of compounding pills.
- Paracelsus

243. PLANS

A good plan violently executed now is better
than a perfect plan executed next week.
- George S. Patton

In Greek mythology, Theseus had to enter the labyrinth of Minos to slay the demigod, the Minotaur. The labyrinth was such a gargantuan maze, everyone who had entered had perished by the hands of the half-man/half-bull monster.

But Theseus managed to slay the monster and found his way out easily. He entered the maze with a ball of string and let it unravel as he made his way through the enormous dungeon. After he slew the beast, he followed the string back to the entrance.

Some things are impossible unless you plan them step for step. If you want to diet, you can't just say, "I'm going to be more healthy."

You need to plan how you are going to eat, how you intend to exercise, what you are allowed to eat, how you will control cravings, your ideal weight, what you will do if you injure yourself or fall behind, and so on. The more you plan, the more you can adapt to setbacks.

Don't just think of a plan. Write it down. You will be more compelled when you can physically see it. I look at my to-do list every day. Looking at my goals daily spurs me to actually fulfill them. If my to-do list was in the back of my head, I would make excuses and put it off.

Being constantly reminded makes me do many things I thought I would never do, such as volunteering, writing, stand-up comedy, catching up with friends I hadn't seen in over a decade, and so forth.

But there's one thing more important than plans: contingencies. When your plan completely collapses, how do you adapt?

My wife is the most organized person I know. She leaves nothing to chance. But life can catch the most organized people off guard. Years ago, we sat down and wrote out our five-year plan and our ten-year plan. We were as detailed as possible and talked about kids, money, jobs, holidays, savings, loans, etc.

But the following week, my wife was unexpectedly diagnosed with cancer. She said she felt sideswiped because there was no suspicion that she was ill.

She spent eight months recovering, and in that time, her original plan shifted. Some priorities took a backseat, and others were scrapped and replaced. Her new plan was to focus on getting better and to pick up her old plan afterward. Straight after the honeymoon, she was back to her original priorities, with a few tweaks and minor changes.

Plans can get set back, but your goals will only fall to pieces if you fall to pieces. You can avoid this. Don't just plan for success. Plan for failure.

If you fail to plan, you plan to fail.
- George S. Patton

244. PLATEAU

The dream begins with a teacher who believes in you, who pushes and leads you
to the next plateau, sometimes poking you with a sharp stick called "truth".
- Dan Rather

When we reach a plateau, it is at that point that we feel like we can't move any
further, or we don't know how. This can happen academically, socially, or
with dieting, work, and exercise.

Imagine you want to get into good shape, so you work out, go running, do push-
ups, lift weights, and eat right. Sure enough, you drop a few pounds and lose a bit of
belly fat. You feel the burn, and it makes you feel fantastic.

But then suddenly, it stops. No more results. No weight loss. No fat loss.

"Okay," you say. "I'll just exercise more or run longer or lift more weights."

But once again, there seem to be no results. Why?

Human beings are the most adaptable creatures in the world, but we can adapt
too well. If you suddenly lift tons of weight, it will shock your body because it's not
use to it. It will pile on the muscle to counter the weight-lifting to avoid injury.

If you lift more, you will not get the same shock value, because it's expecting
the extra weight. Even if you do the best workout ever, your body will get used to
which muscles you use for those specific exercises. Your muscles never get bigger
than they have to.

So what you need to do is shock your system again a different way. I might go
for a run on Monday, do skipping on Tuesday, lift weights on Wednesday, start my
morning with yoga on Thursday, and go for a swim on Friday. Be one step ahead of
your body. Apply this to everything.

If you keep doing the same thing, and you keep getting the same negative
results, then try a different method. And I'm not just talking about exercise but life.
My friend, Niamh kept meeting drunk guys in sleazy bars and had bad relationship
after bad relationship, so she swapped tactics and found a man online. They are
now engaged.

An actor friend of mine was sick of getting small parts in amateur plays, so he
set up his own theater company. He constantly gets great reviews.

We need to find more variety in what we do and how we approach things. You
can create the best combination to benefit your life. If one way stops working, you
can just create another way. The possibilities are endless.

With Positive Mental Attitude, failure is a learning
experience, a rung on the ladder, a plateau at which to get
your thoughts in order and prepare to try again.
- W. Clement Stone

245. PLAYING THE CARD

A manager has his cards dealt to him and he must play them.
- Miller Huggins

When tragedy strikes, we can decide if it will consume us by deciding how much we will let it get to us. We have seen wonderful people change for the worse because they got a knock in life. Two people close to me lost their fathers suddenly, and they got little chance for closure.

When my mate, Donie's father died, it took control of him, and he wallowed in self-pity. I couldn't judge him when he became erratic and antagonistic, because he would remind me of what he was going through. I couldn't argue because I couldn't comprehend the pain, the loss, and the grief at that time in my life. He lashed out, even when he was wrong in an argument, and say he was confused because his father's death made him irrational.

He was "playing the card." It sounds like an oversimplification, but at the end of the day, he was using that tragic loss to justify his unjustifiable behavior. You can play even the best move only so many times before it becomes stale.

My old housemate, Cassie had a tragic story that was even worse. Her father was diagnosed with prostate cancer. He had to go through chemotherapy, and the doctors were not sure if he would make it, but after many hard months, he beat it.

Two years later, he was diagnosed with liver disease. He had even less chance of survival, but after a lot of willpower, determination, and patience, and with Cassie by his side, he prevailed. The worst was behind him.

Or so it seemed.

After two years, he was diagnosed with lung cancer. It was terminal. He was given three months to live. He died in one. Cassie was the last person to ever talk to him on the phone, and he passed away shortly afterward.

She was crushed by this loss. To make matters worse, Cassie's house was burgled two months later. The thieves stole her television, consoles, DVDs, laptop, and her camera—the same camera that contained every picture Cassie had of her father over the last few months.

If Cassie had become a shell of the amazing person she was, no one would have blamed her or been surprised, or argued with her. She had gone through the worst thing she had ever gone through, and she will probably never go through anything as difficult as that again. She had the opportunity to wallow.

But she never "played that card." Watching people like her beat something so big gives me the hope that I can soldier anything.

Each player must accept the cards life deals him or her:
but once they are in hand, he or she alone must decide
how to play the cards in order to win the game.
- Voltaire

246. POINT OF VIEW

Everything we hear is an opinion, not a fact.
Everything we see is a perspective, not the truth.
- Marcus Aurelius

American philosopher, Thomas Nagel asked, "What's it like to be a bat?" He wasn't asking what would it be like for a human to be a bat. He was asking what's it like for a bat to be a bat. It doesn't know how our world works so it would perceive everything in a way we can't imagine.

When we judge others for their mistakes, we usually assess what they are doing is wrong, based on what we would do in those same circumstances. When we think like this, we are not taking into account the lives they have led, the area they grew up in, or the family they were raised in.

If you judge a person for being selfish, sexist, or dangerous, don't forget that they may only be like that because that is all they have ever known. It may not justify the behavior, but it might explain it.

If you think other people's point of view may be skewed, the same can be said about you. Nicholas Epley and Erin Whitchurch did a study in which they took photographs of a group of test subjects. They then altered the pictures through Photoshop and made eleven versions, one of which was unaltered. Some of them were heavily altered, where the subjects looked more attractive, and others made them look far less attractive.

When the test subjects were asked which of the photos was the original, what do you think their answer was? The majority insisted that the altered picture, in which they were more attractive, was the genuine photo.

This is why people hate pictures of themselves. Because we look different in real life than how we view ourselves in our mind's eye.

Everyone perceives you differently than how you perceive yourself. If they say you have a problem, they could be wrong. Or maybe they can see a part of you that you can't see. You can't look at a statue from the inside. You need to look at it externally to view all its tiny delicate details.

Walt Disney used to watch his movies from the audience's point of view to see if they wanted to watch the same things he did. If they didn't match, he would change aspects of the film, rather than stubbornly think his original vision was right. This attitude made him one of the most famous filmmakers in history.

We need to be aware that no matter how adamant we are in our point of view in any matter, other people's points of view exists.

Meditation is the soul's perspective glass.
- Owen Feltham

247. POPULAR

Great things are not accomplished by those who yield
to trends and fads and popular opinion.
- Jack Kerouac

Just because a book or movie suddenly becomes popular doesn't necessarily mean it's good. Terrible movies make tons of money every year. Rubbish books sell out all the time.

Oscar Wilde said nothing could come from something deemed popular. Although I don't completely agree, we can't help but associate popularity with negative connotations.

From my experience, whether a person is genuinely nice or horrible, the ability to keep up with new trends, such as clothes, music, and gossip, seems to be the biggest factor that decides a person's popularity. This is not a bad thing. I have plenty of popular friends who are the loveliest people that everyone likes.

But that doesn't mean popularity can't be a bad thing. If you are up-to-date with recent trends, there is always somebody else who isn't. You can make people like this feel self-conscious by bullying and humiliating them. The more you undermine other people's status, the more it elevates yours. Unsurprisingly, doing this can become intoxicatingly addictive.

We spend so much of our youth trying to dive into the world of popularity. When we are finally in, we fight so hard to scramble back out to carve out our own identity.

Popularity is one of those fictional goals that promises total relief from the feeling of inferiority. You can be tempted to be popular and be one of the "cool gang." You will be pressured to give up on your principles or face the likelihood of constant ridicule. That's the oxymoron with popularity. By definition, "popular" should be "well liked."

But popularity tends to turn into a manipulative and controlling game. Popularity isn't about being well liked. It's the illusion of being liked by everybody. Surely, if you are universally liked and admired, you wouldn't have enemies. But most "cool circles" dedicate a lot of time to bitching and gossiping about other people. Forcing a divide between people and creating a "them versus us" rift is the complete opposite of being popular. You shouldn't try to be a part of something that is a sham.

Why exert so much energy to be a part of something so meaningless? Use that energy for something else more practical. The popularity game is just that; a game. Nothing more. If you give into it, you will ignore and neglect the important things.

Fame is a vapor, popularity an accident, and riches take
wings. Only one thing endures and that is character.
- Horace Greeley

248. POSITIVITY

Your smile will give you a positive countenance that
will make people feel comfortable around you.
- Les Brown

There are two kinds of people: those who will bring you up and those who will bring you down. The second type are those who say you are naive to think positively because we live in a horrible and corrupt world and to see it as anything else is delusional.

But here's the reality. If you were blind, deaf, mute, or autistic a few decades ago, you would have to be cared for by your family for the rest of your life. Now, there are centers for understanding and correcting these problems, and these unfortunate souls can lead very fulfilled lives, get jobs, have families, and be a part of society.

We have animal centers, technology getting more advanced, and vaccines eradicating more and more diseases.

Hundreds of years ago, slavery, burnings, and barbarism were common. Today, the charities of the world get more and more donations every passing day to make the world a better place.

Every day, there is a little less of the Third World on the planet. In the last twenty years, over a billion people have been lifted out of poverty. That's a ten-digit number! One billion people are free from starvation.

Every aspect of life is improving daily, be it technological, historical, geographical, anatomical, or psychological.

But some people think that's not enough. Cynics will always focus on the flaws to any new invention, concept, or idea. Why destroy an idea? Even if it is wrong, new ideas need to be given a chance.

But this isn't enough for some people, because everything needs to be perfect. Everything needs to be better.

But everything is getting better! People insist on comparing the problems and limitations of the world with a world that only exists in their heads. At least, for now. This ideal world may very well exist soon in the future.

There was a time when it seemed humanity was at its ebb wherever you looked in the world; there were massacres through bastardized beliefs, rampant plagues, humanity living in savagery, dedicating their lives to the death of others.

But wait. These things still happen—nowhere near as often, but that's the point. It's diminishing. As more time goes by, there will be less and less of this in the world. Positivity is growing, whether you are a part of it or not. Since it is here to stay, you might as well be a part of it and speed up the whole process.

The world is ALWAYS getting better but we always think it's getting worse.
- Penn Jilette

249. POSTURE

A good stance and posture reflect a proper state of mind.
- Morihei Ueshiba

Anytime I went to a masseur or an osteopath, I would hear the usual, "Wow, you have so many knots in your back."

"If you keep walking like that, you will get arthritis."

"I've never seen anything like this before!"

F. Mathias Alexander dedicated his life to the Alexander technique, a technique to correct bad posture and revert your body to its original form.

We are born with almost perfect posture. Alexander always said that kids show exactly how we are meant to stand, sit, bend, and turn because they haven't had a chance to develop bad habits yet. Everything is still new to them. When kids learn to walk, they can't wait to experiment with moving around. As we get older, we take it for granted.

However, as soon as we go to school, we get trapped in this awkward hunched posture as we are told to be quiet by teachers and work for hours on end. This starts in school and continues into college and even into adulthood, if we get an office job.

Alexander was an actor and found himself abruptly losing his voice when he performed theatre. Desperate to find the cause of his vocal problems, he looked in the mirror while performing his lines. He realized that when he acted passionately, he instinctively pushed his neck forward in an uncomfortable stance, and thus closed off any sound coming out of his throat, which was impairing his voice.

So, he practiced lines in front of the mirror for months while maintain his posture and eventually, cured himself of his obstructing habit.

But then he became fascinated by posture. He pondered, "If I had these habits and didn't know about it, then surely everyone has similar habits as well!" This is how the Alexander technique was created.

People can be skeptical about the Alexander technique, believing their problems are too far gone to be helped. Alexander said no one is too far gone. His methods can be used for people with arthritis, osteoporosis, scoliosis, growths, painful pregnancies, and hunches. Alexander's greatest student had polio in her legs and was bound to a wheelchair. But with his techniques, she was able to walk again.

Even if you think your posture isn't a big deal, the sooner you correct it, the better.

Unless some misfortune has made it impossible,
everyone can have good posture.
- Loretta Young

250. POTENTIAL

Continuous effort - not strength or intelligence –
is the key to unlocking our potential.
- Winston Churchill

A friend of mine who performs marathons spoke about how his coach motivated him, not just with running but with everyday life. When I was going through hard times, my friend would give me some of his coach's wisdom. He used to always focus on potential. This is what he used to say:

"Stamina is how long you can go. Potential is how long you let yourself go. To me, it doesn't matter how high your stamina is. If you're potential isn't there, if you can run more, do more, be more, but you're not giving it your all, that's wasted talent. I don't care if you come first. I have more respect for the guy who came last if he tried harder. If he tried as hard as possible, I don't care where he comes; he's a winner to me. I don't care if you're a gold medalist. You don't deserve what you have. You got what you have because you were born right. That stops you from pushing your limits because you don't have any. You don't know what it's like to get to the top by the skin of your teeth, tearing muscles, sweating blood, pulling a hamstring—that's the only victory I want you to strive for."

The point that the coach was trying to make was all the potential in the world means nothing if you don't try to follow it. You may not know you're the best writer in the world until you pick up a pen. You could be the best athlete in the world, but you will never know until you push yourself.

I am not suggesting you attempt everything. If you try a new activity or sport and your heart is not into it, there's no reason to continue. But if you enjoy it, it doesn't matter if you are good or bad. You can get better. Nobody starts perfect.

My friend, Miller loved rugby and wanted to be a professional player. But in one game, he got tackled badly and injured his knee. This incident ruined his dream.

The practical thing that Miller could've done was convert that passion into something else. But he didn't. He just wallowed. All the potential became wasted.

If you don't replace a passion, it becomes a void, an emptiness of potential.

My friend saw a girl selling jewelry was meant to resemble food. She thought they looked tacky, and she assumed she could do better.

Many people make exclamations like this, but the difference was she actually did it. She makes a lot of money now by making this jewelry. It may not seem like the most obvious or the most impressive talent to possess, but you can't argue with lucrative results. Whatever you are good at, invest everything you have in it.

Everyone has, inside of him, a piece of good news.
- Anne Frank

251. POVERTY

What is the matter with the poor is Poverty;
what is the matter with the rich is Uselessness.
- George Bernard Shaw

Some people believe there is no point in giving money to the poor if we haven't yet solved our own problems in modern society. But we need to remind ourselves that we do not have to deal with some of the horrific problems that the less fortunate have to deal with on a daily basis. We should appreciate it if we were not born on the edge of a tectonic plate or an area prone to natural disasters. We have to give the rest of the world a chance. Why rebuild so often in modern society when there are so many places where they haven't started building in the first place?

We can get trapped in our own lives so often, it can become so easy to switch off any empathy for the poverty-stricken. Doing so helps us justify our petty insecurities.

People can feebly justify this behavior by thinking these poor countries are populated by racist zealots and mad terrorists. However, poverty is the mother of crime. These people do not deserve to suffer just because they had the inconvenience of being born on the wrong continent.

But what about personal poverty? What if you were born in squalor? Are you stuck in that lifestyle forever? No. Anyone can escape if they have drive.

James Dyson couldn't sell his invention, the Dyson vacuum cleaner, even after five thousand prototypes, and so had to forge his own company. He is a billionaire now.

John Caudwell bought twenty-six brick-sized phones called mobiles to sell in 1978. Now he is worth two billion pounds.

No one knew of Richard Branson's potential because his dyslexia was so bad, he was considered illiterate. He is now one of the richest people in Britain.

Twelve publishing houses rejected J. K. Rowling before Bloomsbury published *Harry Potter and the Philosopher's Stone*. She was only accepted because Rowling's friend knew the publisher and accepted her work as a favor. Rowling's friend told her to get another job because nobody makes a living from children's books. She is the first self-made billionaire author in history.

There are countless other "rags to riches" stories. You can do more than just listen to them. You can aspire to be one of them if you are stuck in a slump in your life. If you are financially stable, that doesn't excuse you. Take care of the rest of the world. You are a part of it. Live a bit more for others in need.

If all of us acted in unison as I act individually there would be no
wars and no poverty. I have made myself personally responsible
for the fate of every human being who has come my way.
- Anais Nin

252. POWER

Nearly all men can stand adversity, but if you
want to test a man's character, give him power.
- Abraham Lincoln

The easiest way to see a person's true self is to place that person in authority. Some people might find themselves in a position of power for once, and their ego goes wild. They say, "Finally! After all the toil and trouble I had to put up with, my talents and skills have been ultimately recognized. I am going to take a break." But you can't take a break from life, although that doesn't stop most of us trying.

The most common quote about power is, "Absolute power corrupts absolutely." I believe that real power could be absolute power without imposing it.

The greatest example of this ide is Lucius Quinctius Cincinnatus. Cincinnatus was one of the counsels for the Roman Republic. In 460 BC, he retired to his farm. When some of the nearby tribes became trapped and besieged by invaders, he was appointed dictator out of desperation, simply because he knew the area where the invasion took place.

This decision was extreme since Cincinnatus was a peasant at this point and he was suddenly given full authority over the army and the city of Rome.

However, in just over two weeks, he defeated the enemy.

Amazingly, he relinquished his power and gave up his office, returning contently to his farm. He was meant to serve at least six months as the nation's leader, but he felt he had done all he had to in sixteen days.

He is a true example of how absolute power does not consume us, and we can walk away from it. This has inspired people throughout history, including George Washington, who refused to become the dictator or king of the United States after the Revolutionary War.

Despite the great power that we can wield, we are still but men and women. With all this power, the thing you need to control the most is yourself.

If you have a power surge taken away from you, and you're back to being a nobody, you realize two things: you're no longer a god, and you never really were. All power has a moment of god-fall. John Steinbeck believed that power doesn't corrupt but fear of a loss of power does.

Power can be displayed without ego, without arrogance, and without corruption. Power-tripping is about control. Make sure you are in control of yourself before taking the trip.

I hope our wisdom will grow with our power, and teach us,
that the less we use our power the greater it will be.
- Thomas Jefferson

253. PRACTICAL

The study and knowledge of the universe would somehow be
lame and defective were no practical results to follow.
- Marcus Tullius Cicero

For centuries, gold has been the standard-bearer for value. It was built upon its rareness, as well as its intrinsic beauty. Diamonds, while not considered a form of conventional currency, have always been considered a source of riches with an air of status.

But these materials have absolutely no point or use, save what we give them. We only make them what they are because they are uncommon. Their uselessness adds to their mystique as much as their scarcity.

When you look at it like that, it's crazy that society obsesses about something so unnecessary. But how much of what you do is necessary? Look around your room. How much stuff do you need? How much stuff do you use? How much stuff doesn't have a use?

Everyone has impractical ornaments, clothes out of fashion, shoes you don't wear, items taking up space, and objects in the cupboard gathering dust.

It's not harmful as long as it doesn't get obsessive or financially straining. But it all adds up. It is quite common for us to have a look around and realize the pointlessness of our own paraphernalia, and so we have an epic clear-out.

But we tend to do this only when things get extreme. It takes years before we realize how much of what we have is unnecessary. We need to be constantly aware of how much practicality plays a role in our lives. Or more importantly, we need to ask how often does procrastination creep into our daily routine?

It's not just about material. Your behavior can be impractical. Partying all night and bragging about who you slept with all of the time makes you feel great, but it doesn't pay the bills. Is going out, having a good time a bigger priority than having a permanent home?

You should fill your life with practical people. They can be helpful because they are reliable and supportive. Or maybe they are extremely successful at work, which spurs you on to be the same.

Some friends in your life will distract yourself from your goals, and you need to be careful how often you associate with them. When you focus on anything except them, they will make you feel like you are letting them down, but you need to know what's more important.

We all need our fun time, but we need to prioritize how much time we can spare in order to do what needs to be done. As Ralph Emerson suggested, "Make yourself useful to something and to someone."

Life is too short to stuff a mushroom.
- Shirely Conran

254. PRAYER

> Prayer indeed is good, but while calling on the gods
> a man should himself lend a hand.
> - Hippocrates

We always pray that our dreams will come true or that our personal tragedies will end.

But we have to make things happen ourselves. Praying is a good beginning—an understandable and common driving force to commit to any goal. Unfortunately, it is pointless unless you commit to fulfilling that prayer. We have to get it out of our heads that praying is enough.

Prayer should not be a substitute for action. As Gandhi said, "An ounce of practice is worth more than tons of preaching." And that is coming from a man who did a lot of both.

If a catastrophe on a pandemic scale occurs, what do we do? We pray.

Then, we go about our lives. If we see someone who is in need, choosing to pray for them can be the same as doing nothing. We need to go out of our way to make changes to people's lives and the state of the world on an individual or collective scale.

If you were in need, and you thrust out a helping hand, would the response "I'll pray for you" be sufficient? Of course not. We don't need prayer. We need help! Hope is a good breakfast, but it is a bad supper.

A prayer that I find quite practical is when people say, "Give me strength." If you say this mantra, you're admitting you want to be stronger to get through a difficult time. This mentality can actually help, whether we are religious or not, because we can be strong through pure willpower.

Here is an impractical example: a friend of mine was forced into an arranged marriage. She prayed every night that her husband would stop neglecting and beating her. Every time this happened, she asked God why He abandoned her. Unfortunately, she took no steps to change her circumstances. She was waiting for God to save her.

I do not wish to disrespect those who find prayer a key factor in their lives. But we shouldn't feel like it is the only way to make a difference. Praying can be admitting defeat because we do not know how else to make a difference.

We also tend to pray for physical things, as if they equate happiness. We all want something in life, but it's the journey that makes it worthwhile, not just the end results. We should work on our achievements, not wish for them.

> The gods can only laugh when one prays for money.
> - Japanese Proverb

255. PREJUDICE

When Hitler attacked the Jews I was not a Jew, therefore I was not concerned.
And when Hitler attacked Catholics, I was not a Catholic, and therefore, I was
not concerned. And when Hitler attacked the unions and the industrialists, I
was not a member of the unions and I was not concerned. Then, Hitler attacked
me and the Protestant church – and there was nobody left to be concerned.
- Martin Niemoller

We look back on history and see how backward and stupid people seemed to
be; how women were repressed until the Suffragettes made a stand, and how
black people were segregated until Martin Luther King Jr. intervened. We look back
and think, "What was the big deal? We are all the same. Thank goodness we are an
integrated community now."

But in the absence of racism, we find other ways to discriminate. The prejudice
may not necessarily be against a color or sex but over any minor difference, such as
your accent, your clothes, or your Zodiac sign. People will always find something
about you to hate and judge.

I know racists who think their prejudice is more justified than their ancestors,
but they give the same vague, ignorant explanations to defend their hatred.

It's difficult to keep a clear, objective view of life today. We cannot see that, in
some ways, we are still as backward as our ancestors were and have some serious
growing up to do about how to respect each other. We have to start looking at others
as a resource, not a roadblock.

My homeland, Ireland, had few foreigners until the millennium. During the
2000s, hundreds of thousands of foreigners came into the country, mostly from
Nigeria, Lithuania, Romania, and Poland.

Crime started to rise—not from the foreigner but from frustrated Irish people
who felt like foreigners came to steal their jobs. Ironically, I know many Irish people
who complained there were no jobs or money, so they had to move to England and
therefore, they became the "job-stealing foreigners." They didn't even understand
the hypocrisy in that decision.

I saw an article last week by someone online (who insisted he wasn't remotely
racist) which read: "If we got rid of all the foreigners, we would not have all of this
crime." By that logic, we should get rid of all men, since they cause 97 percent of
crime, rape, and murder. You can't just ask to get rid of a mass of people and assume
all problems will just dissolve.

Every country is getting more and more integrated over time, with more races,
religions, and cultures. They are here to stay. The only difference between us is we're
different.

Intolerance of groups is often, strangely enough, exhibited more
strongly against small differences than against fundamental ones.
- Sigmund Freud

256. PREPARATION

I feel that luck is preparation meeting opportunity.
- Oprah Winfrey

In the Battle of Thermopylae, seven thousand Greek soldiers waged war against the army of the Persian king, Xerxes. Of those seven thousand Greeks, there were three hundred Spartans, led by King Leonidas.

When Leonidas saw his soldiers were being slaughtered, he realized he needed to develop a strategy that would make the Persian army's numbers count for nothing.

When only fifteen hundred soldiers Greeks remained, Leonidas ordered his men to line up at the front of a narrow road in between two cliffs. When the Persians attacked, their numbers counted against them. If Leonidas's men held their ground, their enemies couldn't pass without them getting in each other's way or tripping over each other.

The Spartans held them off for three days but then lost, only because one of the soldiers betrayed them and told the opposing army of a secret passageway to get to the other side. Nevertheless, it is an amazing story that shows the necessity of preparation. A well-crafted plan can make the impossible possible.

If you had a week to study for a test, how long would it take for you to prepare for it? Would you be lazy and wait until the last day? What if you had a month? A year?

What if there was a sudden change of plan, and the test was tomorrow? That's what life does. You need to be constantly prepared to survive. You never know what opportunity will present itself or when.

Isn't that a good enough incentive to start preparing for any possibility? Or probability? You can prepare in a certain way for a test because you know when it is. You can coordinate. You can have time to break it down, have separate time for leisure, and cram in the last remaining hours. There is no day marked on your calendar that says, "This is the day I become successful."

There are times when we can go months without a regular income, but we have to keep ourselves fresh with exercise, typing, and retyping CVs. Once we miss an opportunity, we have to start over. There is no point in going down a hard road without preparation. We need a clear path to awe before we raise a finger.

We all want to aim for success, so we need to be prepared, socially, financially, mentally, and physically.

The only thing worse than being out while opportunity comes to your door is to be in and not bother to answer. Don't wait for what comes next; prepare for it. Hope for the best; prepare for the worst.

The best preparation for good work tomorrow is to do good work today.
- Elbert Hubbard

257. PRESENTATION

Be the best You you can be.
- Anon

We like to present ourselves in a certain way. How we present ourselves depends on the people, location, or circumstance.

People have an objective idea of who you are, based on your presentation of yourself in their company. The real question is, how much of that is actually you, and what stops you from becoming that? A lot of people who come across as confident and desirable are insecure and self-loathing.

We all have our problems, and we like to forget them. If everybody thinks you are the party animal, even if you believe you are not, their belief can flush out your insecurities, at least for a while.

Then the insecurities come back because you may not like the idea that your friends love this persona you have created that is not really you. But can it be?

If your friends think you are funny, and you don't, why is that? I am sure there is a deep psychological reason why you are like this.

If you want to come across as confident, you are already halfway there if your friends believe you are. What is meant to happen is:

- you don't feel confident;
- you recreate yourself to be more confident;
- your friends see this new you and overtime accept you as being confident; and
- you gradually become more and more confident.

If you manage to bypass step two, that's great!

But if your friends already view you as being confident, even if you are not, you skip straight to step three.

The most beautiful people can feel like they are the ugliest. The most envied person may be the loneliest. The richest may be the most depressed.

You can become anything. If your friends already believe you are that thing that you want to be, then prove them right by becoming it.

Offer the best version of you to the world.
- Anon

258. PRESSURE

You can't run with the hare and hunt with the hounds.
- Anon

Probably the first time any of us feels pressure is when we start school. When I was five, my classmates wanted to see if I could climb a tree. I had to do it, or I would suffer the greatest punishment that can be bestowed upon a child—being called a chicken. I couldn't live with the shame.

Five minutes later, I fell and had scratches all over the left side of my body. I was lucky I didn't break anything.

Peer pressure is the idea that you will be less than you are if you don't abide by the majority and compromise what you want to do, in accordance with what everyone expects you to do.

But there are pressures that are a lot harder to escape than by simply saying no to something stupid—like being expected to do well in school every day, for every test, from the ages of five to eighteen. A single disappointing grade can be met with arguments, ridicule, and other punishments that weaken your soul.

It doesn't stop there. You can be expected to replicate your parents' success or take over your family business. Expecting approbation for choosing another path can be hard and can be seen as a sign of betrayal, even though you have no control over the situation into which you were born.

You're expected to get a job, then get a good job, then get the highest rank in your job, and then to keep yourself there, maintaining all other employees, while simultaneously being pressured to maintain a family, buy fancy things, wear nice clothes, pay for pricy holidays, and do bits and bobs or catch up with friends everywhere in between.

We can't even feel the pressure anymore. Occasionally, we forget that what we are doing is not what we want to do. We are just too scared to disappoint anybody.

We do need to be aware of what others think, but it is not as important as what we think. We all have wants and dreams. Spend life with someone who makes you happy, not someone you have to impress.

Let's take the idea of pressure literally. Imagine you are told to push a button. You don't want to. So your hand is grabbed, and you are forced to push the button against your will. If you are forced to do something or pushed on an intimidating or threatening level, there is no natural impulse there.

That type of pressure is misguided. Why fulfill someone else's dream? Why act out another's desire? We can share a dream. We can carry the torch of another torchbearer. But we cannot compromise our dreams or squash them by setting someone else's dreams on top of ours.

Courage is grace under pressure.
- Ernest Hemingway

259. PRIORITY

The Good of man is the active exercise of his soul's faculties in conformity with
excellence or virtue...Moreover this activity must occupy a complete lifetime.
- Aristotle

Ecotone is the area between two types of landscapes that are beside each other
(e.g., forest and city). At times, one may overlap or take over the other, such as
tearing down trees in the forest to broaden the city.

The same thing can happen with our priorities. One priority may seem harmless,
but it may collide with another priority. They can get in the way of each other or
cancel each other out, and we end up getting nothing done. Goals shouldn't be mixed
with "things to do."

A hobby shouldn't be considered a goal. It's something that will give you
momentary release. Accomplishing a goal can be everlasting. A goal redefines you
and forces you to achieve bigger and better goals.

Some have "goals" that are vague and can be used as an excuse to be lazy.

Some people want to have it all. I was writing this book while auditioning and
rehearsing for a play, doing stand-up comedy, and shooting an independent film,
which I had to prioritize around my shifts at work. And I was doing all of this at the
same time I was getting married!

I thought I was being practical because I was keeping myself busy, but I was
spreading myself too thin. I was doing a lot of things at once but never getting one
thing done. I was being a jack-of-all-trades but a master of none.

We may have talents that we throw away because we don't know where our
priorities lie. My friend always got depressed because he was too shy to approach
a woman. He said he preferred to be popular than smart. He is arguably the most
intelligent man I know, but he would chuck it all away for a girl.

It's impossible to prioritize everything logically. We are a society that will be
more impressed by an explosion in a movie than an Olympic gold medal.

We spend trillions of dollars on dead worlds when half the planet can't grow
their own crops.

Some people have hobbies, like sports, reading, and exercise. And some people
like getting drunk or getting into fights. That's not a life. That's a lack of one—a lack
of control and direction. We need to know where our priorities lie.

> The very best thing for a person is health
> Second good looks and third honest wealth,
> The fourth to be in the prime of your life
> With people around you who cause you no strife.
> - Plato Gorgias

260. PROCRASTINATION

> We know what happens to people who stay in the
> middle of the road. They get run down.
> - Aneurin Bevan

We act according to our needs; to be more precise, we act according to what we think we need. There are few needs to the common man, but they are vital—so vital that it would be wise to focus on them and not on petty pursuits.

If you had to do a task in a month or a day, you might be more likely to achieve it in the day because you don't see the time limit as a luxury. That stops you from getting complacent and lazy.

I always like that story about that tightrope walker who balanced a pint of milk on a spoon in his mouth without spilling a drop, while walking from building to building on a tightrope. When asked how he did not fall off, he simply said he didn't think about it. When he was asked about being distracted by noise, or the people below, or spectators with their flashing cameras, he said he didn't think about it. So when he was asked what he was thinking about, he said, "Don't drop the milk."

The first movie I ever saw was *The Wizard of Oz*. Throughout the whole movie, Dorothy is trying to get home assuming that, once she sees the wizard, he will solve her problem.

However, the great and all-powerful wizard is not as great and all-powerful as she assumed, and it turns out that she could have gone home whenever she wanted by simply clicking her ruby slippers together and wishing her way home.

When this movie was released, it was torn apart by critics for being nonsensical and idiotic. The ending sounded like a lazy cop-out.

But it's not. The movie was saying that the person who will have the greatest effect on your own life is you. People will inspire you, and you will strive to achieve a standard of those you respect, but it is you who will decide how far you go.

Bricolage is a term used to describe the ability to create, simply by using the tools currently at your disposal. Some people can be flung into any situation, and they will adapt to their surroundings and use what they find to get to where they want.

Other people will use it as an excuse. Being aware of what is practical and what is inadequate can stop you from fueling your idle hobbies and fixate that potential energy and effort into sensible aspects of your life.

> Work is only noticed when it's not done.
> - Anon

261. PROMISE

A guy will promise you the world and give you nothin', and that's the blues.
- Otis Rush

My old housemate, Richard was really bad with girlfriends. He could get with any girl, but he always cheated on her. He claimed his latest girlfriend was "the one," and then he would find anyone to replace her with soon after.

One day, he grew up and started going out with a girl called Niki. Niki knew of Richard's reputation, but he promised he was a changed man. He seemed to be. He convinced everyone.

Then came a day when Niki accidentally picked up his phone and started talking to his other girlfriend. She dumped him instantly. He desperately tried to make her understand why he did it. He said it was in his nature, and he promised to do something that went against what he always did and how he always acted.

I heard him say to her, "Do you have any idea how hard that promise is to keep?"

She retorted with, "But you made the promise."

There is no point trying to justify a broken promise if you are the one who made it. There's a difference between the pitch and the reality.

Some things you can't promise or shouldn't. There is wiggle room within reason, but even the word "promise" is thrown around too often, like so many things nowadays. A broken promise, even a lie, was considered a source of endless shame and ridicule once. Now it's a daily routine.

"I can't make it. Something came up."

"I would go, but I have that other thing to do."

"I can't do it. I have stuff to do."

You should notice how vague the examples above are. Isn't it sad that people make such lazy excuses to justify a broken promise? A promise was originally a vow, meaing it was supposed to be unbreakable.

Now it is just a word we use to comfort and reassure. That may sound nice and understandable, but you can do the exact same thing with a lie. A lie and a broken promise go hand in hand.

If you are ready to make a promise, think about it thoroughly. A promise that is intended to be kept or upheld deserves a lot of thought.

If broken, the shattered trust is one of the few things that may never recover. Whether the promise is to a friend, worker, partner, or family member, once it's gone, it may never return.

Alternatively, keeping promises is the best way to maintain or raise trust. Make every promise you make precious.

He is poor indeed that can promise nothing.
- Thomas Fuller

262. PROTEIN

We're so conditioned to believe that we need enormous amounts of protein
or we'll wither away. Look around, we're not withering - we're fat.
- Kris Carr

Most people believe protein is the most important food group. Its purpose is
to build muscle, so society always holds protein in the highest regard and
usually considers carbs and fats as the bad food groups.

In reality, they are all equally important. Yes, if you want to put on muscle, you
need a plentiful portion of protein in your diet. But if you just eat protein, it will
count against you.

Protein doesn't magically enhance your muscle tissue. It can only work with
a balanced amount of fats, vitamins, and carbohydrates. To eat one food group
and dismiss the others is like doing a mathematics equations but leaving out a few
numbers. The whole thing falls apart without certain factors.

Forty-five grams per day is considered the recommended amount of protein
for a human being to function. If you exercise intensely for the purpose of muscle
building, you will need to eat approximately twice as much.

It's not common knowledge that there is actually a limit to how much protein
you can eat. If you eat protein excessively, it will have the same effect as eating too
many carbs—it will turn to fat!

There's an easy way to figure out how much is too much. You just need to
double your weight in kilograms and turn that number into grams. I'm 70kg. So the
maximum amount of protein I should eat per day is 140g.

I asked my bodybuilding friend, Mark, "What is the biggest mistake people
make when they try to understand how protein works?"

Mark said many people believe that if they eat huge amounts of protein, they
will get results. The reason why we need so little protein per day compared to the
other food groups is because it's the most difficult one to break down. It needs time
to be absorbed into our bodies. The amount you eat needs to be spread throughout
the day evenly. The body has the work hard to process protein but has to do very
little to turn it into subcutaneous fat.

An average build person's daily diet should consist of 60 percent carbohydrates
and 20 percent protein. And guess what? Bodybuilders eat the exact same proportions.

So if you think bodybuilders are doing nothing but eating protein and neglecting
the other food groups, you are mistaken.

I need protein from food rather than supplements.
- Travis Barker

263. PSYCHOSOMATIC

The mind and body are linked. The mind affects the body
and the body affects the mind. No way around that.
- Anon

There is a stigma to psychosomatic problems. It's easy to perceive the word "psychosomatic" to mean "an illness that is not real."

That's not what it means. "Psychosomatic" is when the mind has made an illness real. It's when you have mentally created a physical ailment.

When my father and my wife were in the hospital, I was constantly ill. I rarely get sick, so I couldn't understand why I was getting stomach bugs and migraines when my family and wife needed me most.

Before that, it was easy for me to look down on people who would take days off college or work because of stress-related illnesses.

Only in recent years have I realized how vital a role the brain plays in keeping us physically fit. It's not uncommon to disassociate the mental and the physical. Often, we will focus on one while neglecting the other.

But the brain is in the body, so of course one affects the other. Your antibodies are constantly trying to ward off any germs and bacteria. It needs to be permanently attentive. How can your body perform to the best of its ability if you are constantly tired, stressed, and not getting enough sleep?

The world can make us paranoid and overly concerned about our health, which, ironically, can make us ill.

Did you hear about the new Asiatic flu or South African bug? Do you remember how panicked society was about Mad Cow disease? Or swine flu? Everyone thought they had some illness or disease, so people started making themselves sick. We wouldn't necessarily get the illness we were afraid of getting, but it's a self-defense mechanism. Let me explain.

A vaccine is an injection of a virus that is so small that our antibodies will effortlessly be able to combat against it. Your body will know how to attack it and be prepared for an actual attack from a virus, so you never get sick from it.

Your immune system is a battle station. If it thinks there is an enemy on the horizon, it will ready itself for attack. But much like an overeager army, it may fire off a shot before there is any attack.

If you keep thinking about a cough, your body will over-prepare for one, and you will develop it unnecessarily. It takes effort for your body to fend off any illness. It can take days, sometimes weeks, to rid ourselves of sickness. That's a lot of energy wasted that could be used for something far more practical.

The wish for healing has always been half of the battle.
- Lucius Annaeus Seneca

264. PUNISHMENT

If people are good only because they fear punishment,
and hope for reward, then we are a sorry lot indeed.
- Albert Einstein

My friend, Gabriella had a bad break-up with her boyfriend of four years. This break-up hurt her so bad, she decided to give in to asceticism, meaning that she would avoid all sexual relationships. Not only that, she avoided most human contact. She avoided holding hands with the opposite sex and shot down every compliment because she was terrified of being hurt again.

My friend, Kris was abused by his father and eventually kicked out of the house. He went from a charming, sweet, handsome guy to a trash-talking, self-loathing vagabond who dismissed any genuine offer that could further his life. His upbringing forced him to believe that he deserved a bad life.

My friend, Conroy got bottled over the head while he was out in town. He became so paranoid of being attacked again, he refused to leave his house for years.

Locking yourself away is all well and good for protection, but we have a right to live our lives the way we envision.

Being constantly punished can warp us into a twisted version of our former self. But what's worse is when we punish ourselves. It's far too straightforward to see masochists or self-harmers as weird, sick, and disturbed, but we can fall into this trap one way or another. There are far subtler ways to give into self-punishment.

Being overprotective can be another way to punish yourself. It's difficult to tell if we are punishing ourselves or if we just have high standards, ideas, ambitions, or morals.

For example, if you want to look skinny, do you eat healthy or starve yourself? The latter is a sign of self-punishment. Punishing oneself, at times, is simply misinterpreted self-protection.

In the story above, Conroy refused to go out in case there was a similar incident to when he got hit with the bottle. Staying in prevented him from enduring any harm.

However, it only protects him from external physical harm. Staying indoors caused emotional problems and psychological harm. Overprotection is like wearing a lot of padding; it can stop you from getting hurt but you can't move, you can't breathe, you can't feel, and you can't live.

We cannot allow break-ups and bullies to force us to hate ourselves. If we do, they will win. We have to do the opposite and get on with our lives. That is the ultimate way to show the oppressors that they failed. That is their punishment.

Nobody can hurt me without my permission.
- Mahatma Gandhi

265. PUPPET

> I've got no strings to hold me down.
> - Pinocchio

You can't expect to be the dominant one in every situation. Yes-men, employees, minimum-wage workers, flunkies, lackeys, drones, underlings, goons, subordinates, subjects, pawns, flunkies, cogs in a machine, instruments, or tools—the puppet master's puppets have many names.

Pinocchio was a wooden boy who wanted to be a real boy. He wanted to be his own person. We can be puppets of an overprotective partner, a controlling parent, or an employer addicted to dominating subordinates.

We allow ourselves to be puppets because we believe, in some way, that it will help us. We believe we are worming our way to the big time. But nobody likes a worm.

Whether or not a puppet realizes it, it's hard to respect someone who allows himself to be used. The only way to stop being a puppet is to cut the strings.

My old school principal made his students clean the bathrooms and empty the trashcans because he couldn't bother to hire a janitor to do it. Nobody questioned him because he was in charge, and they wanted to be in his good books. He knew this and regularly took advantage of it.

You assume that your act is commendable, even gratifying in the master's eyes, but you might be too small to notice how you are perceived from his point of view. If you want more responsibility, you can't get it unless you ask. If you are not happy with your designation, you need to decide what to do, rather than accept it unwillingly.

Most people start at the bottom rung, intending to climb to the top. But it's not a fair climb. It's every man, woman, and child for themselves. You will have people climbing above you or at the top kicking you back to the bottom, to reaffirm that they are at the peak. The lower you are, the easier it is to keep you there.

What you have to do to succeed is to make massive leaps upward. You may fall farther than where you were originally, but that is the risk you take to get to the top. It's worth it. There is no other way to climb so high unless you take a risk once in a while.

> Stone walls don't make a prison nor iron bars a cage.
> - Anon

266. QUESTIONS

> We can't solve problems by using the same kind of
> thinking we used when we created them.
> - Albert Einstein

*I*nside the Actor's Studio is an interview program where actor and writer, James Lipton, asked questions to famous actors about their lives

He ends by asking questions made famous by Bernard Pivot, such as, "What are your favorite and least favorite words?" The most interesting and memorable for me was Johnny Depp. His favorite word is *why*? His least favorite word is *no*.

He said that as a kid, he questioned everything. He questioned parents, friends, and mentors about rules, laws, and life.

He never saw it as defiance but as a way to gain knowledge. He said that there is too much of our going along with what we are told.

Bill Bryson, author of *A Short History of Nearly Everything*, explains in the introduction of his book how he reached a point in his childhood where he wanted to know absolutely everything. This happened when he saw a book with a front cover that showed the inside of the earth. He couldn't wait to read it and discover how the world really worked!

He read the book in a matter of days, discovering how the core works, how hot it is, and how old the earth is.

When he finished, he simply thought, "How do they know there is a core? "How do they know the earth is 4.6 million years old?"

His book explains how we know all these little facts that we just take at face value. He even corrects some information that we commonly believe that is actually wrong. You shouldn't take information at face value. It's not stubborn to question. It's not unnatural to ask why.

It's not about finding answers to questions but exploring them. Sometimes questions can be answers. The universe needs someone to question it.

The paradigm shift is the concept conceived by Thomas Kuhn; as we ask questions about concepts, our discipline will move forward and will broaden our ability to understand such concepts. The more we challenge ideas, the more we strengthen them, and the more we grow.

Questioning is a part of life. You need to doubt yourself, ask the hard questions, get upset, and come back from it all stronger to find yourself.

> To raise new questions, new possibilities, to regard old problems from a new
> angle, requires creative imagination and marks real advance in science.
> - Albert Einstein

267. QUITTING

Age wrinkles the body.
Quitting wrinkles the soul.
- Douglas MacArthur

When a goal is too hard to reach, too time-consuming, or too tiring, we feel like quitting. Quitting can happen after seconds or decades. You can quit over an activity, like going to the gym, or you can quit a dream, like becoming a superstar.

The more time you give to something, the more disappointing it is when you throw in the towel and give up on what you are passionate about.

If your passion changes, that's okay. But if the fire still burns within you, it's there to be stirred.

Obviously, there is quitting in a good context, like giving up on smoking or drinking. But it's ironic because quitting something we love sounds much harder than something we hate, yet it is more common! How many dreams have you quit? How many bad habits do you still possess? Quitting a passion is like giving up a good addiction. It's like we chose the wrong addiction to give up.

Sorites paradox can be used to explain quitting. Sorites paradox says that continuous smoking can kill you, but no individual cigarette will, and that is the exact mentality people have when they don't want to quit a craving, even when they should.

But you can use this mentality to stop quitting good things. I wanted to take my running exercise seriously. When I ran, I applied the logic of Sorites paradox constructively. No matter how much my legs were screaming for me to stop, I kept saying to myself, "I will eventually not be able to take another step ... but it will not be the next step ... so I should keep going."

With this mentality, I tripled the distance I could cover in a matter of days with no extra training. All I did was just change my way of thinking.

Look at quitting as the road of no return. When you are on the road to success, a point will be reached when you will be exhausted. Every fiber in your being will tell you to turn back.

But a point can be reached that can change that mentality. It is not the goal. It is beyond the halfway point. This is where the journey is longer to go back and walk away from the goal than to just keep dragging yourself to the finish. If you gave yourself ten years to be successful at what you are passionate about, and you feel like quitting, do you really want to lose those ten years?

You are allowed to quit. But if you quit a passion, you quit on yourself.
Many of life's failures are people who did not realize how
close they were to success when they gave up.
- Thomas Edison

268. RACISM

Someone steals your handbag so you kill their
second cousin on the grounds they live close?
- David Hare
(Stuff Happens)

The only two animals on earth that are racist are humans and dolphins. It has been known that dolphins kill porpoises (which is a cousin of the dolphin) for no reason regarding survival, food, or self-defense. They can gang up on one, kill it, and leave. But why would the dolphin share this trait with human beings?

The dolphin is the most intelligent animal, apart from us. This makes the dolphin a highly evolved creature.

However, racism is part of evolution. As we progressively get more intelligent, racism kicks in as a self-defense mechanism. We are wary of things that do not resemble the norm. It is a simplified mechanism that assumes anything new is bad, but it is engrained in us. We need to look at different people with reason rather than let biology overwhelm us.

Racism can be based on the ill-conceived "logic" that since the foreigners in a country are a minority, anything bad that they are alleged to have done must account for a much larger percentage than the normal. They only look bad because they are a majority of a minority.

You may have had a bad experience with a foreigner, which can impair your judgment with other races. Don't you think your opinion of a race of millions that's based on a taxi driver you encountered while you were abroad or the foreigner who mixed up your order at a cafe is nothing more than an oversimplification?

Of course, racism can stem from war and fear. During 9/11, many people hated Afghanistan, Pakistan, Iran, Iraq, and Saudi Arabia (even if they didn't know which country was responsible for the atrocity).

If you don't know where Iraq is on a map, you shouldn't have an opinion on it. You can act like other countries are full of terrorists, but most people only love their country because they were born in it. It's crazy that the lines that divide our nations divide us from each other. These lines don't actually exist. We chose where to put them. We could have decided to put the line of any country ten feet to the east or a hundred miles to the west. People kill for an extra few yards of mud. Why trust an imaginary line?

Issues aren't black and white, but they're the only colors some people can see. Racism is a problem, not a war. The tragedy of racism is we are all human.

It doesn't matter if a cat is black or white, as long as it catches mice.
- Deng Xiaoping

269. RATIONALITY

Rationality is ineffective against the irrational. The only thing that works is fear.
- Jack Donaghy
(30 Rock)

Many people are under the impression that the Neanderthal was the imbecile of our ancestors.

But these archaic humans were superior to our ancestors. In some ways, they are superior to the modern man.

But how is this possible? If that is true, why are they extinct? Compared to our direct descendants, Neanderthals were greater in height, durability, strength, and intelligence, and they were superior in building and using tools.

But most importantly, they reached full maturity at sixteen years of age. Unfortunately, this supposed advantage is the actual reason they died out.

They learned to settle down and live in peaceful villages, while homo sapiens (which is us,) were still savages with a "survival of the fittest" instinct. As the homo sapiens grew desperate, tired, and starved, they invaded the Neanderthals' homes, stole their food, and killed them.

Although the Neanderthals were physically superior, they were too civilized to partake in a fight. Their instinct was to run, hide, and protect their loved ones. This mentality had nothing but good intentions, but it led to their demise.

Here's a modern example: If a knife-wielding teenager burst into your house in the middle of the night, he might be able to overpower you, even if you're stronger, bigger, and more mentally stable.

Theoretically, you should have the physical advantage, but your civilized mind would want the teen to leave the house without engaging in physical confrontation.

If this happened to me, I genuinely wouldn't know what to do. In hostile situations in the past, I tried to be calm and use rationality and reason. But why would logic work on the illogical?

A different tactic is needed. Everyone is different, so you can never predict how people are going to react, but you need to try different things. See what works and what doesn't. Maybe you need to show a bit of anger or do something unpredictable to show the person is not in control. If someone is trying to scare you, prove to him that you are not afraid. Or do something to scare them. Rationality is a necessary tool in life, but there are times where it simply doesn't work.

Never argue with an idiot. They will drag you
down to their level and beat you with experience.
- Anon

270. REACTION

Any reaction is better than none.
- Gavin Rossdale

The most famous quote about "reactions" is the law of thermodynamics: every action creates an opposing and equal reaction.

This applies to daily life. If we are given an opportunity, we should take it. If we get a blip, we should deal with it and react to it in a way that will not hinder our goals, our wants, or our needs.

Another important law is the law of inertia: an object in motion remains in motion until acted upon by an outside force.

This is that feeling when you have a string of good luck. If several positive things happen to you, it's like they create and open more and more doors. If this happens, accept them. If the ball is rolling in your court, keep it rolling. Don't let it sit still, and don't let anyone else take it. Because once it's gone, it takes a while and a lot of effort to get it back.

But let's not neglect another rule: "The object at rest tends to remain at rest."

Imagine one day taken out of your life like it never happened. It could be yesterday, two months ago, or a day where you think you did nothing. Now imagine how different things would be now. More importantly, how different could this make you as a person?

Our deeds determine us as much as we determine them. If there is something you need to do, do it. If there is something that you have time to squeeze in, and otherwise you won't have another chance, drop whatever you are doing, and do it. I procrastinated for months about four things I needed to do. They were:

1.   Cancel my phone subscription.
2.   Book my hotel and flight for the summer.
3.   Update my travel insurance.
4.   Get my deposit back from my old apartment.

For months, I decided I was too busy to perform these annoyances, as there would be a lot of "please hold" on the phone, forms to sign, letters to send, and claims to write.

When I had some time off, I decided to take care of these four nuisances. Do you know how long they took? Fifteen minutes. Not each one. Altogether. I wasted so much money giving my cash to companies, even though I wasn't using their services.

Now if I have something to do, I don't wait. I just do it. People need to act more and wait less.

The meeting of two personalities is like the contact of two chemical substances; if there is any reaction, both are transformed.
- Carl Jung

271. READY

> When I am getting ready to reason with a man, I spend one-
> third of my time thinking about myself and what I am going to
> say and two-thirds about him and what he is going to say.
> - Abraham Lincoln

My friend, Cantwell had a small part in a movie years ago. On the first day of shooting, everyone had to arrive at 6:00 a.m., when there would be no traffic or busy streets, so they could do a scene in front of a fountain.

But the pipes in the fountain had frozen, causing the shot to be delayed by two hours. By the time the fountain was working, there were too many people and too much noise in the background. They had to give up and try again the next day. They couldn't shoot the next day because the female lead was unavailable. They couldn't film the day after that because the director already hired out a mall to shoot another shot.

What would the director do? Would he cancel? Cut his losses? Cantwell remembers hearing the panicking director say, "It all falls apart on the first day."

This example illustrates how you may feel ready, but circumstances beyond your control force you to compromise. But what about when you're not mentally ready?

A year later, Cantwell had the lead in a movie. A limo pulled up to his house at 4:00 a.m. on his first day. He thought, "I am so ready for this!" The limo took him to the set. His assistant took him to his room. He was told he would be needed at 7:00 a.m. He read for a while, watched TV, and went through his lines. The assistant returned at 7:00 a.m. and said one of the lights was faulty, so Cantwell would be needed at 8:00 a.m.

He watched television and thought, "I'm not as good as these actors! What if they fire me?" He flicked through a few film magazines and read about actors being criticized in their latest movie. He feared he would suffer the same fate.

He tried to take his mind off it by going through his lines, but couldn't remember them. His assistant called him back, and he went on set. While on set, he looked at the faulty equipment, a drunk cameraman, light operators not paying attention to their work, and a director didn't want to be there. As Cantwell sat down for his scene, he said to himself, "I am not ready."

The film was never completed, probably because a lot of people involved in the movie thought they were a lot more ready than they were. We can learn from Cantwell's failings. It wasn't his fault. Just because we feel we are ready for something, we won't know for certain until we are close to obtaining it. When it's up close, we see the ugly side of it, the real side of it. That's when we will know if we truly want it.

> I'm always ready to learn, although I do not always like being taught.
> - Winston Churchill

272. REALITY

Our intention creates our reality.
- Wayne Dyer

There is a concept called *mimesis*, which literally translates to "holding up a mirror to nature." The word "mimic" is derived from this term. It is used to explain a concept of when an author replicates his views and opinions in a story. His thoughts and beliefs are usually fused together in the main character of a narrative. This technique is used to make us empathize with characters in stories, books, and television. However, we can invest so much empathy in a fictitious story or character that we start detaching ourselves from reality.

My friends use to watch *The X-Files*. They said that all the conspiracies in the show were real, and everyone was oblivious to the existence of the real world. They, however, had their eyes open.

But when something actually happened in the real world—a monumental shift in politics or a momentous discovery—my friends didn't bat an eyelid.

Saying "the real world" isn't useful terminology. When people say, "the real world," what world do they mean? Political, religious, family, biological, luxury, propaganda, spiritual, cosmic, universal, conceptual, or historic?

You can't live in them all, so you try to juggle the best ones. Whichever of the "realities" I dominantly lived in, people around me said that I needed to get back into the "real" reality.

But reality is opinion. You can't ever tell the truth about the world because nobody knows what's really going on. People don't know how the world works because they watch too much television—or not enough.

We are all ignorant on different subjects. I know things go on in the world that I have never read in a newspaper or seen on television. You know things occurring in the world of which I am completely oblivious.

The world is so big, and we can only process so much. If we tried to acknowledge every aspect of reality, we would go mad or get depressed. As the old saying goes, "The less people know about how sausages and laws are made, the better they sleep."

We can't take life too seriously, but we also can't abandon it. People don't want to hear or talk about terrorism. Their interpretation of the world is temporarily broken because they just bought new shoes or got a raise at work.

Unfortunately, tragedy can bring us back to reality and give us some perspective on our problems and priorities. The world makes you grow up faster than you want to.

Find the balance. Don't live in terror, and don't live in naivety.
You can design and create, and build the most wonderful place in
the world. But it takes people to make the dream a reality.
- Walt Disney

273. REBELLION

It is human nature to instinctively rebel at obscurity or ordinariness.
- Taylor Caldwell

If you leave some things alone, they won't cause trouble. Even if they are potentially hazardous or dangerous, to get involved can exacerbate a situation a hundredfold.

Look at prohibition as an example. Alcohol was banned in 1920 for thirteen years in the United States. The intended result was diminishing crime and violence caused by alcohol.

Instead, prohibition accidentally ushered in the age of organized crime. Al Capone bootlegged and smuggled alcohol, turning himself into the most powerful man in Chicago. His actions created gang wars and turned law-abiding citizens into criminals overnight.

While people were dying or going to jail, Capone was making $60 million annually. And this all happened because of a law that had nothing but good intentions. We all want order, but when we force order, it will always be met with rebellion.

We have experienced this sort of defiance from a young age. Becoming a youth, the hormones are like a power surge. It can be too much for the body to handle. That's why we lash out. We're not kids anymore. All that stuff about eating right, doing our homework, and keeping our mouth shut goes out the window. We just say, "Make me!"

This behavior is understandable. It can be argued that it is justified. Parents start parenthood by giving kids everything and then taking things away, piece by piece. It messes with their values. When you are a kid, what your parents say is fact. They can never be wrong. You base your life and morals on what they say and do, and what they bring you up to believe.

That is why it is so shattering the first time you see them make a mistake. Either you feel like you've been lied to or the world just got a lot more uncertain.

We all, at some point, probably have acted like a bit of a rebel and let a bit of darkness in. But darkness is not an actual force. It's just a lack of light, like coldness is simply a lack of heat. We need to rekindle that warmth. We need to find that light once more.

Being a rebel in the darkness may make you seem cool and mysterious, but when you are in the dark, you can't see what you are doing. You can't tell what's going on or what's around you. When things start to not go the way you hoped or planned, you may realize that you are not as tough as you thought. You can't fool the darkness by trying to be darker.

I'm not afraid of the darkness outside but the darkness inside.
- Shelagh Delaney

274. REJECTION

If you don't play the game, you can't win.
- Neil Strauss

Jerry Seinfeld has a famous sketch about fear and failure. He says, "According to most studies, people are more afraid of public speaking than death. … So if you go to a funeral, you're telling me you would rather be the guy in the casket than the guy giving the eulogy?"

As ridiculous as this sketch is, Seinfeld makes a point. Most people are terrified of public speaking. But why? If you screw up and make people laugh at you, what's the big deal?

Because people take it personally. If we are afraid of spiders, we know that the spider doesn't disdain us specifically. When we deal with rejection, however, we think it does.

If you asked someone out on a date and they said no, it feels like they rejected you as a person. That is a horrible feeling. This is why we get so hurt by rejection when we ask people out.

But there are endless reasons why a person can turn us down. Maybe you were rejected because you were unassertive, not their type, you came across as creepy, smug, arrogant, they are already in a relationship, or you caught them at a bad time.

When you are rejected, it's not because people don't like you. How can they? They only just met you. It's because you didn't present yourself the right way. You can be a great person but come across as unconfident, inconsiderate, or simply nervous. It's not the real you, but the person who rejected you doesn't know that.

Being rejected for a job can be offensive as well because it's like someone is saying you are not good enough. The employer tends to make vague, dubious statements like, "We decided to go another way," rather than "You're not good enough for the job." That very well might be what the employer thinks, but you never know. Maybe the company really did want to go in another direction.

If you are bad at dealing with rejection, it might be because of parts of yourself that you are hiding. When you are rejected, you get offended and think, "How can they think that way about me when I am genuine, honest, and funny?" They mightn't know you are like that so show those qualities.

One of the most powerful fears humanity has is rejection. We are so afraid that we don't put ourselves out there with regard to relationships, jobs, and socializing. By doing this, we are rejecting ourselves.

You miss 100% of the chances not taken.
- Wayne Gretzky

275. RELATIONSHIPS

It's not what's said that decides a relationship but what's unsaid.
- Anon

It's not a relationship without a fight. At the start, skeletons pop out of the closet. The more time that goes by, the fewer skeletons pop out, but they start hurting more—they were hidden so far back that you never knew something like that could exist.

Some people can get with any man or woman but are incapable of keeping one. They know the mechanics of getting to the sexual stage but don't know how to take it further. A lot of people fool around, but when they are ready to settle down, their real side has been seen. Now they can't be considered relationship material.

A relationship is not judged by the amount of time spent together but how you act in the relationship itself. Just because you are in a relationship for years, or engaged, or married, or have children doesn't mean things are working.

One of my friends, Lynn, was with a guy, Emerson, for three years. Emerson said he loved her, even though he already had a girlfriend, Lliana, who was in the hospital. Not a good start. It was a clear warning that it would never work, but Emerson and Lynn gave it a shot.

It only went downhill, but he made so much effort in dumping Lliana to get with Lynn, and she was lonely. Neither of them wanted to admit it was a big mistake. They continued to go out for a year, even though they always argued. Eventually, it ended. A year wasted! Easily avoided. The signs were clear, but she ignored them. This is not uncommon. You may already be in a dead relationship. Don't feel like you are being cruel to get out now. If it's going nowhere or you are not happy, then you need to reconsider what you want.

You might crave being with someone, but when you are, you toy with him or her. People play games in relationships to make it more interesting, but that's the main reason they don't work; they don't know where they stand.

In my first relationship, my partner and I did not have a single fight for almost a year. When we did inevitably start arguing, we never stopped. It's not how you react during the good times that define a relationship but how you react during the bad. When couples fight, it can bring them closer together because they get a touch of what it's like to be alone.

They say the hardest part of a relationship is ending it. Well, that's what most people tend to believe. I personally believe that's the easiest part. All you have to do is stop trying. That's why nearly all of them end. The hardest part of a relationship is keeping it.

Truth is everybody is going to hurt you, you've
just gotta find the ones worth suffering for.
- Bob Marley

276. RELIABILITY

Simplicity is prerequisite for reliability.
- Edsger Dijkstra

Trust is how much faith you have in someone. You can trust someone, and that person will do everything in his or her power to not let you down in terms of protecting you, safeguarding secrets, and being there when you're upset.

Reliability is how often people are actually there for you when they said they would be. Guarantee is not a delivery.

Let's say you have to get up early to drive a friend to the airport. You know you have to get up at 6:00 a.m. to get there in time. Your friend has put his or her trust in your hands. You accept that trust by preparing everything, prioritizing things, and going to bed early. You have consciously taken steps to ensure you will be there for your friend.

But there's a problem. Your alarm doesn't go off. Did it not work? Did you forget to set it? It doesn't matter. Your friend missed the flight. He or she trusted you, and you blew it.

It wasn't because you were selfish. It's not like you tried to sabotage your friend's journey. It's because you made a mistake.

Here's the big question: was that a one-time problem, or do mistakes like this regularly occur? You can be untrustworthy with your friends, family, lover, siblings, classmates, and work by spilling secrets, lying, or doing the complete opposite of what your trust represents.

A trust is broken when you consciously do the opposite of what you previously pledged when declaring your trust in the first place.

Reliability doesn't necessarily need conscious thought. It's usually the opposite problem. You can be unreliable because you weren't conscious of what you were doing or what you were meant to do. You just weren't thinking. You simply weren't considering every protocol. Or you didn't acknowledge the steps you needed to take to be reliable.

When you let people down, it might be tempting to make excuses. Justifying your mistakes is understandable from time to time. If you keep finding yourself being unreliable, you really have to reconsider prioritizing your life.

You need to be mindful and aware. You need to be there for your friends, your workers, and your family. When reliability goes, trust goes soon after.

One should always have one's boots on, and be ready to leave.
- Montaigne

277. RELIGION

Give a man a fish and you will feed him for a day.
Give him religion and he will starve to death praying for a fish.
- George Carlin

Religion was thought to fill four gaps in our lives: explanation, exhortation, consolation, and inspiration. Can that be argued?

You bet! No theory is safe in religion. If you say to a believer that you don't believe in his religion, he might react as if you are attacking him.

It is in our right to criticize religion because we have the freedom to criticize ideas, even if these ideas are sincerely held beliefs. This is one of the fundamental freedoms of society.

Most people naturally act out their lives in accordance with their beliefs, so you can understand why they get so defensive. Religion isn't just faith; it's perception.

Blaise Pascal said that human beings have a God-shaped hole, which they feel they must fill with religion. We are compelled to believe in it.

Pascal's Wager suggests that it cannot be logical to disbelieve in God. If he doesn't exist, whether you believe in him or not, you gain or lose nothing in death. But if you believe in him and he exists, you gain total bliss. If you disbelieve in him, you are destined to spend eternity in hell, so why not play safe and believe in a Creator?

There are several contradictions with this concept. Surely with this logic, you could convince yourself to believe in anything after death. What if you believe in the wrong heaven, the wrong God, or the wrong version of the Holy Book? Does that make you more damnable than if you believe in nothing?

If you are a believer, you may accuse me of insulting your own religion. Religion, if it was purely theoretical, was important for teaching us moral standards. Believers have a stigma for being gullible, but it's just as bad to have a belief without proof as it is to disbelieve without proof.

Only when religion goes too far does it become nasty. When we start warping ideas to try to understand vague concepts, it's counterintuitive. One example would be the classic "God works in mysterious ways" quote. It's so vague; you can justify anything without proof. Have faith but within reason.

There's an invisible man living in the sky who watches
everything you do. And the invisible man has a special list of ten
things he does not want you to do. And if you do any of these ten things,
he has a special place, full of fire and smoke and burning and torture
and anguish, where he will send you to live and suffer and burn and
choke and scream and cry forever and ever 'til the end of time!.....
But he loves you!
- George Carlin

278. REMEDY

A desperate disease requires a dangerous remedy.
- Guy Fawkes

I cured my panic attacks with cognitive therapy and self-hypnosis. Cognitive therapy rewires your routine of thinking so your chain of thoughts that tend to become negative will become positive. If I were to ever go through a renascence of panic, I would call upon my therapy and hypnosis again. So far, regular checks have kept it at bay.

But what surprises me is that modern civilization has become skeptical of these remedies and many others. My brother has been permanently cured from migraines by having two acupuncture sessions. Acupuncture is often sneered at for being an archaic pseudoscience, but my brother shows that acupuncture is a genuine healing routine.

We laugh at kung fu movies when a warrior performs a magical tap that can knock someone out, or someone miraculously heals a person using the nonexistent power of "chi."

Yet I cannot explain how my friend Leon, a martial artist of over twenty years, can use his Wing Chen to immobilize someone double his size, using two fingers with little force, in a seemingly insignificant body part.

I've seen a documentary of a youth who had his ear cut off. There was nothing doctors could medically do … conventionally. Thanks to the rarely used treatment of leeches, they were able to salvage his ear.

So what's the problem? The tricky part with such solutions or cures is they are not backed up 100 percent by biology or chemistry. When we hear of people looking at problems and explaining delicate issues with uninterpretable philosophy, vague energy, and archaic wisdom, skepticism is a natural reaction.

Over the last century, our superstitions have dwindled more and more. Unless solid truths are abundant from every possible solution, we are too quick to put lesser-known remedies in the same box as the Tooth Fairy and the Easter Bunny.

I am not suggesting throwing away pills and medicinal needles for whatever ailment you may have and replacing it with some ancient mystical remedy. That's a dangerous dogmatic way of thinking I have seen too many times.

Some sicknesses can only be cured through medication. There are some problems that can't be cured through conventional terms, but they can be cured unconventionally.

I have seen the incurable be cured. I don't mean through faith or miracles or prayer. I mean through not giving up after conventional treatments have failed them. When all else fails, why not try something different?

Everyone suffers wrongs for which there is no remedy.
- Edgar Watson Howe

279. REPRESSION

It is impossible for a man to organize his life with repressions.
- Arthur Miller

Sigmund Freud developed the backbone of how we perceive therapy. We can understand the long-term repercussions of our "issues" and our lack of dealing with them.

Before Freud's teachings became common knowledge, society didn't even understand the concept of repression. Repression can cause mental disorders. Up until the late nineteenth century, such disorders were considered to be signs of the devil.

Although it is a relief that we can address repression, it is a matter of how aware we are of our own. Everyone suffers repression of some kind. It's human nature. When you are four or five years old, you start to develop attributes that will solidify in our mind. These can be fears, beliefs, morals, and even sexuality. Any number of things can happen in this time that can affect you in the long term. You can move house, be viciously bullied, have a new sibling in the family, suffer an assault, or endure a divorce, injury, or death. These can all potentially happen while your mind is still building itself.

It's like brain surgery. It requires absolute concentration, and the slightest distraction can result in cataclysmic results that can affect the individual for a long time.

But repressed issues don't just occur from incidents in our childhood Traumas occurring at any time can create repression. A death will always have an effect in our lives, but it can alter the development in our minds in unexpected, invisible ways if it happens during infancy or puberty.

Denial is unhealthy because you are denying yourself. To not understand where you are coming from is damaging because you are the one who has to live with yourself.

If you do not know why you are angry, sad, or scared, then that's worse than the actual problem. It can transmogrify into something dangerous.

You may need help from a counselor or an empathetic friend. Maybe you just need to ask yourself some hard questions. I went to see a counselor for a year after my panic attacks. It helped tremendously, but nothing helped more than questioning how I felt every day and why I felt that way.

For someone to understand you is a relief, but for you to understand yourself is even greater.

Hateful to me as the gates of Hades is the man who
hides one thing in his heart and says another.
- Homer
(The Iliad)

280. REPUTATION

A reputation for a thousand years may depend
upon the conduct of a single moment.
- Ernest Bramah

Reputations can be good or bad, but there can be bad connotations to both. You might have a reputation as a drunk or a sleaze-bag, which is a horrible title to be burdened with, no matter how true or false it is. You may be known as the nicest guy or the most clever and have the burden to live up to it forever.

Politicians and presidents have this worry, as every incriminating detail will come back to haunt them. Even if you never did anything incriminating, what about the people with whom you associate? Or what if you did something that could be misinterpreted?

But if your good deeds can be twisted into something negative, then surely you can do the opposite. You can embrace your reputation, even if it's perceived in a negative context. When the public sees a celebrity as a loving family man and then it is discovered that he is having an affair, it can ruin his career and life.

You have to be careful, though. If you are constantly labeled, you might get stuck living as that label because it's so hard to change people's minds. That mentality is forcing you to never change.

When I had my panic attacks, my ex-housemates saw me as weak. I corrected my problems four months later and haven't had one since. My housemates were so used to seeing me as a fragile weakling that they insisted that my newfound confidence was a pretense. They even said my future wife was a charade and the relationship was a sham.

This devastated me, as I saw it as a breach of trust. They saw how upset I was and said that it validated that I was pretending to be confident even more. I came close to undoing all the progress I had made because of their utter lack of support.

They kept seeing me as I was and not who I'd become. It's easy to judge people for their past deeds long after they have changed for the better. It's not healthy, because you are condemning somebody that doesn't exist anymore.

Don't get locked into a reputation. Don't be defined by what people think or say about you. Define yourself by who you are and what you do.

Let it be harder for people to pin you down with a label.

Your character is what you are, your reputation is what others think you are.
- John Wooden

281. RESOLUTION

Divide each and every difficulty into as many
parts as is feasible and necessary to resolve it.
- Rene Descartes

When you can't resolve a problem, an argument, or a misunderstanding with a friend, partner, or family member, you might say to yourself, "Why bother?" Most arguments end with a slammed door or a smart comment. By the time you have calmed down, it's too late to resolve the issue.

I thought about this when I had a falling out with a friend. He betrayed my trust worse than anyone has in my entire life. Enraged, I said that he was dead to me. When I calmed down a few weeks later, I didn't know if I could resolve it. But I would never know unless I tried.

I imagined there was a graph that measured my resolution with my friend. Zero percent is "I forget he ever existed," and 100 percent is "he is completely forgiven." Let's say at the moment I stormed off, we were at 25 percent.

We may never get to 100 percent, but if we try to talk about what happened and what went wrong, maturely without anger, spite, or denial, we can bring it up to 40 percent, 50 percent, 60, 70 percent. As long as it's higher than 25 percent, at least we can end it better than it was.

We met and talked like adults. Although we are not as close as we were, it's as good as it's going to be. It would not have reached that point if I hadn't tried.

Resolution is necessary, especially in death. My housemate, Edgar despised his father with a vehement passion. Edgar wrote him letters explaining in graphic detail how much he hated him and explained why every bad thing that happened to him was his father's fault.

His father got sick and died, and my friend thought, "Thank God." But all the unresolved issues started to well up, and he sank into depression. He hated himself for not clearing the air when he had the chance.

There's a bond between all people and energy beyond physical form. That energy never grows or shrinks. It's always constant. We feel empty when someone dies because we feel like a whole chunk of that energy is gone.

But it isn't. It's spread around to the ones the deceased knew and loved. That's why a death always has the power to bring people closer together. It has the power to resolve family matters.

You may not get another chance—until the next death. Or not at all if the one who dies is the one you are trying to resolve with.

If you have the chance, take it. To resolve is exerting, but nowhere near as exerting as any number of ramifications from a lack of resolution.

Fortunately analysis is not the only way to resolve inner conflicts.
Life itself still remains a very effective therapist.
- Karen Horney

282. RESPONSIBILITY

I have never accepted what many people have kindly said – namely, that I inspired the nation... It was the nation and the race dwelling all round the globe that had the lion's heart. I had the luck to be called upon to give the roar. I also hope that I sometimes suggested to the lion the right place to use his claws.
- Winston Churchill

We always need to be aware of our responsibilities, whether they are at work, in the household, or life in general. We cannot neglect our responsibilities as a son or daughter, a parent, a partner, a worker, or a boss.

Responsibility does not necessarily mean taking charge but knowing what you are in charge of. It's tough to know where you stand or how much you can shoulder. It's difficult to know whether to be a sheep or a shepherd. There are times where you will be a cog in a machine. There are times where playing a small role for a much greater cause is necessary. But at some point in your life, you should play the biggest role.

You can always achieve more, do more, and be more. To do that, there are times when you need to take on mantles, shoulder great weights in life, put your trust in others, and be trusted by your peers in getting things done and being responsible for any mistakes you have made.

Ignoring your failures or shirking responsibility will not ensure you will get to your goals faster. You can't cheat or shortcut your duties in life. It just guarantees you will make the same mistakes over and over.

Some people go the other way and play Atlas, trying to carry the heavens on their shoulders. Some people feel like they have a lot to prove, so they will take charge, not knowing how much they are capable of. It's just like starting in the gym and trying to lift the heaviest weight. It's great to have that self-belief and motivation, but it's just not possible. We can't burden ourselves with all of the responsibility, because it would mean we would have to bear all the stress.

If we share certain duties with others, everyone can focus on their individual jobs more efficiently than if we try to juggle everything alone. No manager could run his or her business alone, just like no number of workers could run a business without a manager. Every great accomplishment throughout history was not achieved alone. Many started alone but their mission or message gathered followers. One person can spur on countless more. That's when you see results.

We are not just people. We are all ideas, ideals, symbols, and inspirations. Responsibility will not fit in our hands. It must be shouldered. We can't be expected to do every job. But we expect every job to be done. Know what your responsibilities are and never neglect them.

Never in the field of human conflict was so much owed by so many to so few
A medal glitters, but it also casts a shadow.
- Winston Churchill

283. REVENGE

It is a revenge the devil sometimes takes upon the virtuous,
that he entraps them by the force of the very passion they
have suppressed and think themselves superior to.
- George Santayana

Love is supposed to be the biggest driver of all emotions, but tests on the human psyche show that there is a more powerful driving force—revenge. Vengeance in our hearts will make us indistractable. We can neglect all other aspects of our lives to fulfill some petty vendetta.

Don't believe me? Imagine if your soul mate was in front of you but was about to leave. You have to convince them to stay. If you don't, you will never see them again. How quickly would you react?

Now imagine your soul mate was murdered. The murderer is in front of you and is about to walk away. Once he does, you will never see him again, and he will get away with killing your one true love. Which one of these situations would get a bigger reaction?

When you are overwhelmed by the desire to seek revenge, you may not be able to be bought, bullied, negotiated, compromised, or reasoned. You can convince yourself that revenge is the only closure.

We give into revenge because we believe people have wronged us. Or maybe it's because we can't make sense of our own insecurities, and we to take it out on somebody. If that is the case, we need to ask how much responsibility we bear for our own wrongdoing?

Revenge feels like it has to be fed. When you start having negative thoughts, you can't dwell on them. It will create a cycle of self-destructive energy that can get you into trouble, danger, or jail.

Is that worth it for an act of revenge that will accomplish nothing except saying, "I told you so" or "I showed you"?

Human beings are evolving, so we rely on solving and creating, not breaking and destroying. Both reactions involve control and power, but the vengeful kind is dying out in our genes, much like bloodlust and violence.

You can't help being angry every now and again, but you can choose what do with it. Revenge is just not practical. Vendettas don't do much for your bank account or child support.

An eye for an eye leaves everyone blind. Vengeance is, at best, a hollow reward. Usually the best vengeance to those who have wronged you or doubted you is to prove them wrong or live a fulfilled life.

He that studieth revenge keepeth his own wounds
green, which otherwise would heal and do well.
- John Milton

284. REVERSE PSYCHOLOGY

Don't read this chapter.

"**F**ine, don't do the washing up."
"If you want to go out instead of stay in with me, that's okay."
"Go on, do it. I dare you."

We feel so smart and sneaky when we get what we want using reverse psychology.

But there's a problem. Everyone knows about this psychological ploy. We think we are crafty when we use it, but we forget that it's not a phenomenon; it's a standard reaction to human beings.

We are attracted to opposites; we like balancing things out. We look for the equilibrium. If we are pushed, we pull, and if we are pulled, we push. So when you know people are using reverse psychology on you, you may choose to defy them on purpose. Otherwise, you would feel like you were being manipulated.

But not everyone uses this form of psychology to be sly. We normally do it to avoid hurting each other's feelings. Telling a friend or family member that they should make the right choice is nicer than demanding that they just "do it!" So, you may not be using psychological tactic to be devious.

It is good to look out for reverse psychology when you are being manipulated. It's necessary to recognize it if you are in the presence of someone who is looking for a quick buck or has an agenda.

The opposite problem will occur when you may not even realize that reverse psychology is being used. This can be good or bad, depending on the situation. There are circumstances where the person using reverse psychology wants the other person to pick up on it, at least slightly, even if it's on an unconscious level.

Here's a basic scenario: Michelle wants to go out but Sammy wants to watch the football game. He says he will join her after he is finished watching the game. Michelle doesn't want to come across as needy or forceful so she says, "You can watch your game if you want, but I wish you would come with me."

Sammy stays in and watches his game, since he wasn't forbidden to.

Afterwards, he comes to join Michelle, but finds her furious for reasons Sammy can't understand. He didn't disobey her. He was given a choice. So what did he do wrong?

The sentence reads more on the lines of "You'll be sorry if you watch the game because I wish you'd come with me."

We can rarely encapsulate precisely what we mean in a sentence. We need to read between the lines. Don't listen to what people say. Listen to what they mean.

I try to lie as much as I can when I'm interviewed. It's reverse
psychology. I figure if you lie, they'll print the truth.
- River Phoenix

285. RIGHT TIME

Life is about timing.
- Carl Lewis

Is there something you promised yourself you would do a long time ago but you still haven't fulfilled it?

The reason we tell ourselves is that it's not the "right time," as if there is a "right time," and this "right time" lurks in the future. When it comes, it will be obvious and apparent.

Then we perceive the future as a set thing also. The future is an eventuality, but it is notoriously vague. We can prepare for it, we can even predict it, but we will never be able to anticipate every variable that the future holds.

It's never the right time to do anything important. You just have to do it anyway. Priorities will switch around. There will be confusion with what's more important. There will be rushing and a lack of preparation. There will be the temptation to quit and constant frustration.

Look at all the important decisions in your life such as starting a relationship, getting a new job, taking up a new skill, or dropping an old habit. Did any one of those things happen at an appropriate time?

You can't dance around a "right time." We just have to jump in. You may notice, on reflection, that some of the biggest decisions you have made happened at the completely wrong time.

I met my future wife three days after the worst day of my life. I hit rock bottom, but what could I do? Have a pity parade? Focusing on her was the only thing that could bring me back up. And it did.

So, look around your house, your room, your diary, your half-completed projects, and ideas that you wrote down that you never began.

Reflect on the chats you had with your friends about doing so-and-so. Was it all hot air, or did you ever intend for these things to be actualized? Is the "right time" just an excuse? Is it just the broadest way of shirking progressing ourselves? Do you assume that you are not yet ready to pick up the slack of life now but assume your future self will be? We get busier as we age and have less time for leisure. There will be less time for there to be a "right time," if such a thing exists.

Just get on with your life. It's not a question of if it is the right time. It is a question of if you can make time. It's never the right time, but if you don't do it, you never will. There is no empty slot in the future. You must juggle your life to get everything done.

The right time is any time that one is still so lucky as to have.
- Henry James

286. RIGHTS

All human beings are born free and equal in dignity and rights.
- Universal Declaration of Human Rights

Hammurabi set up his code in ancient Babylon in 1760 BC. The Hammurabi Code was made up of 282 laws. It was the first law system that endured. Many people don't know this. Then again, many people don't know a lot of things about their rights.

When someone is arrested, it's not common for the person to say something under the lines of, "I know my rights! I'm innocent!"

It's true that everyone should be aware of their rights. Not being educated about the law can cause you to be harassed, attacked, scammed, robbed, arrested, or locked up.

But we also need to know what is and what is not legal. If you broke the law without realizing it, that's not going to stop you getting arrested. Ignorance isn't an excuse. It's like the old saying goes, "Just because a kid doesn't know an electric fence is on, doesn't stop him getting shocked."

What many of us believe we know about the law is based on television and clichés. You know how people are allowed one phone call after they get arrested? That's not true. If that surprises you, you need to get a lot more acquainted with your rights.

Even if you are a law-abiding citizen, you can be killed if you don't know your rights. Do you know the protocol for being stopped by a police officer? Even if you are innocent of all crimes, making one wrong move while being questioned by a cop can cost you your life. In situations like this, you need to arm yourself with education.

When I had my rights violated at work, I took my boss to court to have him sued. The case couldn't have gone smoother, and I was awarded a settlement.

But I have seen so many defendants in court have their cases dismissed because they weren't prepared.

Legal matters are among the biggest confrontations we will ever have in our lives. It is wise to know exactly where we stand. Don't just renounce guilt and believe people will accept you based on that. You need to be ready, prepared, organized, and strategic. If you aren't sure about a law or a protocol, research it. Go online, consult a lawyer, police officer, or other authority figure, or inquire at your local police station.

We hold these truths to be self-evident, that all men are created equal,
that they are endowed by their Creator with certain unalienable rights,
which among these are life, liberty and the pursuit of happiness.
- Thomas Jefferson

287. ROLES

Daughter am I in my mother's house but mistress in my own.
- Rupert Kipling

There are four kinds of roles we fit into:
- individual—for yourself (e.g., secure yourself mentally, physically, spiritually, psychologically)
- work—financially secure yourself
- personal—socially (e.g., friends, family, partner, son, father, brother)
- citizen—yourself in a larger community (e.g., activist, charity)

The question is, which of these roles mean the most to you? Is work your biggest role? Is one of these roles nonexistent for you? If so, why?

Psychologists say you can grade these roles (e.g., "B" for work, "C" for personal). Or you can go deeper by saying "my relationship x is a C but my relationship with y is a D." Some may not find this practical, although it is interesting to see how you grade yourself, in how big or small a role you play in someone's life or they to you.

What is your role in people's lives, and what is their role in yours? The best way to get the most out of your role is to define how people relate to what you wish to accomplish. What are your friend's roles in your life? Why are you friends with them? It shouldn't be just because they are nice, or you have a common interest. You should ask what they make you feel every time you meet them.

I'm friends with Mikey because he will always make me laugh.

I'm friends with Zelina because I have nothing to hide from her.

I'm friends with Elvina because she will defend me more than anyone.

Those are my friends' roles in my life. We need to surround ourselves with positive roles. If certain people don't provide a positive role in your life, leave them out.

It's also worth mentioning that some roles can blend together. Martin Luther King Jr. blended his role as a minister with his citizen role as a social activist. It was effective because some people may be interested in what a minister has to say but not a social activist, and some might be the opposite. He doubled his audience by syncretizing these two roles, and it made him the charismatic visionary that we knew.

Think of what we could accomplish if we unified our roles.

Never doubt that a small group of committed people can change
the world, indeed it's the only thing that ever has.
- Margaret Mead

288. ROUTINE

Habit and routine have an unbelievable power to waste and destroy.
- Henri de Lubac

Y ou can easily fall into a bad routine. Getting up late, staying up, and playing video games too much are routines that can cost you jobs, partners, and many other amazing opportunities.

You need to find good routines, but there is a trap to good routines as well. I had a housemate called Antoine who suffered from obsessive compulsive disorder. OCD sufferers tend to be freakishly clean and need to have everything done a specific way.

He was meticulous and methodical to the point where he thought there was something wrong with everything without his intervention. At first everybody admired how organized he was. But OCD becomes debilitating if it is untreated. As time went by, his need for cleanliness got more obsessive.

If his housemates left anything around the house, he threw it out. If his friends didn't put their brand new coats on a clothes peg, he chucked it into the trash. He used to measure his food because he started thinking his housemates were stealing it. They had to move out because his illness got so much worse. To him, his house had to be spotless.

Dirt accumulates, so his tasks could never end. It was unavoidable. So this compulsion that he saw as a necessity was redundant because the problem would always come back. I am not suggesting you should keep a filthy house, but I am suggesting that there are a lot more fun and practical things he could've done with his time that wouldn't have alienated him as much as it did.

We all have tasks. We all have to go to the launderette, do chores, and buy food for the week. But we need to ask ourselves, "How much time a day do we spend performing tasks, and how much of this time is genuinely beneficial?"

Most of us fight boredom with routine. It's easier to fall into routine than you would imagine. If you can tell where your friends are going to be on any given day, it's because they are stuck in a routine.

Good routines can be practical. They keep us in check. As tedious as they are, we all have to find an order for cleaning, mowing the lawn, shaving, etc.

Then there are luxurious routines. Friday night is the pub. Saturday is Movie Night. Sunday is Game Night. Routines keep us busy, stimulated, and organized.

At least they can. Bad routines are traps we fall into. Sitting around watching television for six hours on a Saturday sounds bad, but it sounds even worse if it becomes a routine. Too many bad routines make you lazy, and too many "good routines" make you obsessive. Do what has to be done, and set the right amount of time for yourself for leisure.

I hate having my life disrupted by routine.
- Caskie Stinnett

289. SAFE HAVENS

In every aspect of life, there is a security blanket, a thumb to suck, a skirt to hold.
- Isaac Asimov

Just because something is comfortable doesn't mean it is right, safe, healthy, or real. When we suffer grief or tragedy, people find outlets like religion, addiction, or repression. These safe havens may seem positive but they don't solve the problem.

The problem is still there fighting, and it could win any day. We need to get rid of the problem, not hide it. It's like an alcoholic getting drink taken away from him. That's a good start, but the obsession is still there. The dependency hasn't left yet.

A friend of mine was riddled with addiction to drink and drugs. He went to a preacher who claimed to be a healer who alleged to have the touch of God.

After this apparent divine intervention, my friend claimed his addiction had disappeared, and he did indeed stop drinking and doing drugs.

But I could still see him fighting the addiction. He believed it was gone, but we forget that a sudden absence of chemicals after so much time has biological consequences. Like any drug, it works on a cellular level. He believed that he was a changed man, but anyone could see him shaking, trying desperately to keep himself together.

Safe havens have nothing but good intentions, but it can leave people on the edge, always fighting to not give in to the addiction. Only a wall stops the addiction from breaking through. A wall is not indestructible. It can be broken.

Even if that wall is never broken down, that doesn't necessarily mean the person "won." If they spent a lot of time in his life terrified that he might cave in to temptation, that does not sound like a life worth living. Or you can leave that place and leave everything behind you forever.

I fell into this trap when I told myself that I wouldn't get angry anymore. I used music and denial as my safe haven rather than deal with the issues that made me angry. I thought I was being strong, not giving into my rage. I thought I was being mature and reasonable.

But I wasn't. I was just putting a wild animal into a corner, poking it until it did what all cornered animals do and went berserk. That's why I had my panic attacks. I kept holding back every negative emotion as a means to protect myself, and I ended up damaging myself. I realized that a safe haven is good, but to rely on one is not living in the real world. We need to venture out there. How else can we grow?

A fool is a man who never tried an experiment in his life.
- Erasmus Darwin

290. SCIENCE

A new scientific truth does not triumph by convincing its opponents and
making them see the light, but rather because its opponents eventually
die, and a new generation grows up that is familiar with it.
- Max Planck

Science is organized knowledge. Science has helped us understand who we are
and where we came from. It has advanced us as a species and a civilization. It
has advanced our ideas, our scope, our vision, our medicines, and our travel.

In the last hundred years, it has advanced us more than in the last two thousand
years. Invention and discovery speed up a lot of things and open our eyes. Only
through curiosity, experimenting, trial and error, discoveries, and revelations does
anything come to be.

For millennia, religion was the natural way to explain things. We couldn't
comprehend the mechanics of the universe, so we had no choice but to fill the gaps
whatever way we could. Science finds, industry applies, man conforms.

If you told society centuries ago that our planet was round, and the only reason
we didn't tumble off was because of an invisible force field called gravity, it would
have sounded ludicrous.

Nowadays, we can embrace science, since it is here to stay. We can let simple
beliefs go.

But some are not ready to let go. It is hard to hold beliefs for so long and then
be expected to just throw them away. We can't accept humility, so we give into
stubbornness.

Science may not always have the answer. From time to time, we should embrace
our gut instincts over analysis. Feelings can be followed over statistics. We don't have
to put everything into a test tube. You can find answers without turning everything
into an equation.

Henri Poincare said, "Science is built up of facts, as a house is built of stones;
but an accumulation of facts is no more a science than a heap of stones is a house."

Science is not trying to be the ultimate wet blanket. Its purpose is the same as
religion: to uncover the truth. We shouldn't look down on those who just wish to
know more. One Galileo is enough.

Bertolt Brecht said, "Science is not to open the door to infinite wisdom, but to
set a limit to infinite error." So, science is not meant to be the savior of mankind but
a tool to allow us to have an understanding of the universe, so we can learn from
our mistakes. Truth exists; only lies are invented. People only fear science because
they fear the truth.

Probable impossibilities are to be preferred to improbable possibilities.
- Aristotle

291. SECRETS

A man's true secrets are more secret to himself than they are to others.
- Paul Valery

The Streisand effect is where an attempt to censor or remove a piece of information backfires, causing the information to be widely publicized. This occurs because anything secretive looks more interesting than it is.

Secrets are nearly always found out. The reality behind them is too alluring and enticing. We just can't keep secrets. We need to keep secret the fact that we have secrets.

You might get lucky, and your own personal secrets never get exposed. But you might wish they did get discovered to kill your guilt. Keeping secrets is lying at the end of the day. We can be torn, and it can eat at us easier than a regular lie because we don't have to say anything to be lying to people and ourselves. Not knowing secrets heightens them. The truth is never as interesting.

That's why it's best to avoid secrets because when we admit the truth, people don't believe us anyway. They prefer the jazzed-up version.

And why not? It's entertaining. Surely, we human beings would not go through so much effort to hide something so uninteresting and plain. There has to be more. That's the logic of turning a secret into a believable lie.

It's best to be as honest as possible. It might be embarrassing but anything you hide can be heightened, invented, and scandalized a thousandfold. Nobody really cares about the truth. They just want to hear the most extravagant gossip. Whether it is true or not is irrelevant for most people.

One of my friends came out about being a lesbian. She suffered from depression because of the stress of lying to everybody. She was worried she was going to lose friends, but when she came to terms with it, one of her friends said to her, "You're gay? It's the twenty-first century. It's not a big deal anymore!"

She was astonished (and a little offended) that people didn't make a bigger deal about it. Her friends knew she was hiding something. We could tell by her manner that there was something brewing deep inside of her.

As soon as she told the truth, it was like a weight had been lifted off of her. She was far more relaxed, happy, and unburdened. The truth never lives up to the hype. So it's best to just let it out as soon as possible. If you live with a secret, you live inside a secret.

When we keep a secret, we start to convince ourselves we have to maintain the secret or we will lose something. But a secret is only the end of the world in our own minds.

Three can keep a secret, if two of them are dead.
- Benjamin Franklin

292. SETTLE

If you look at life like rolling a dice, then my situation now, as it stands – yeah,
it may only be a 3. If I jack that in now, go for something bigger and better,
yeah, I could easily roll a 6 – no problem, I could roll a 6... I could also roll a 1.

- Tim

(The Office)

My father was a solicitor for accident claims. My father did all sorts of work, but the money was in accidents, taking up to 50 percent of court cases in Ireland.

Settlement claims changed after one case where a girder became loose from the ceiling and fell on a factory worker. This caused irrevocable damage to the worker's stomach. He was looking at a payment of up to 500,000 euro.

During this case, the laws were changed so court cases could be diverted because of a choice offered by the government. The government offered an immediate sum of money to the client, saying it would be better than a larger sum of money years later that wasn't fully assured.

Which would you take— a potential 500,000 euro in the future or a guaranteed 80,000 euro tomorrow?

Almost everyone will pick the quicker solution. Why? Because when you are in critical condition in the hospital, you need money immediately. If you want something done as soon as possible, you tend to take any half-baked version of it.

This is called hyperbolic discounting—accepting a guaranteed settlement now, rather than a grander prize in the future.

In the long run, settling is totally acceptable. We all want to settle down, have kids, and live in a big fancy house, for instance

But there is a bad type of settling. What if you have the same job in the same position, on the same floor and same hours for ten years? Is that what you want, or did you settle for it?

Did you meet a beautiful man or woman while you were with somebody else, and you never pursued it because you were afraid of hurting your partner's feelings?

I am not advocating cheating, but when we don't follow our hearts, it stays there, and we ask "what if?" Is your current situation equivalent to whatever standard you should be reaching in money, social circles, or relationships?

If there is an inner fire burning in you, no matter how faint, maybe it's not waiting to burn out but for you to throw another log on it.

The reason why we settle is because we run the risk of failure. Why risk it all for a little bit more when we are okay now? You need to ask yourself, "Is all right enough?" Do you want to be all right or happy?

Some do not choose, they settle. They go where they are pushed or pulled.

- Anon

293. SEX

It has been found that in early childhood there are signs of bodily activity
to what only an ancient prejudice could deny the name of sexual.
- Sigmund Freud

I f sex is so meaningless, why does everything we do revolve around it? Sex has been
taboo in our culture for a long time. Before that, it was beyond taboo; it was simply
never talked about or discussed. Every aspect of sex revolved around the bedroom.

But in the early twentieth century, American biologist, Dr. Alfred Kinsey was
the first person in modern times to study human sexuality in such immense detail.
To catalogue his work, he interviewed eighteen thousand people. Since then, sex has
been catapulted into discussion and is now one of the hottest topics.

However, one extreme is as bad as another and usually one extreme turns into
another extreme when push comes to shove. Sex wasn't talked about because sex for
pleasure was considered a sin. The act was originally deemed only for recreation.
Taking advantage of sex was sacrilegious.

But sex is the trigger to life, the catalyst of birth, which can be considered the
most wonderful thing in all the cosmos. So why would that be considered a sin?

Nowadays we are more open-minded about exploring our desires and fantasies.
You can discover things about yourself through sex. There are times when partners
or lovers fight, and sex can help bring people closer where words fail.

However, some people go the other way. They turn it into a game and are
manipulative, forceful, threatening, demanding, selfish, and even violent. The worst
damage is when we choose to be irresponsible about the consequences of sex, when
we play with the essence of life.

Sex plays a vital part in relationships and symbolizes a unique unity. A sexual
relationship with another person is considered the worst violation of this unity.

There are some overly concerned people who do not appreciate change and
do not want sex to be taught in schools, believing it is filling children's minds with
filth. It's not filth; it's biology. To deny biology is unhealthier than reading about
how your body and its impulses and desires work. Teaching it will help people
understand changes and hormones, dispelling myths, and showing what to do in
certain scenarios.

In a way, it would be silly not to teach it. It's necessary information to prevent
us from doing something incredibly stupid because of nonsensical superstition,
dogma, and simple ignorance.

Don't be ashamed of it, but take control and be aware of it.

Sex is emotion in motion.
- Mae West

294. SEXISM

Because I am a woman, I must make unusual efforts to succeed.
If I fail, no one will say, "She doesn't have what it takes."
They will say, "Women don't have what it takes.
- Clare Boothe Luce

Allan and Barbara Pease wrote many books about the relationships and differences between men and women including *Why Men Don't Have a Clue and Women Always Need More Shoes* and *Why Men Don't Listen and Women Can't Read Maps*.

The titles may be sexist but they illustrate a point. The books explain that who is superior of the two sexes is not up for debate. Men's and women's brains are hardwired so differently that there are not enough similarities to put them in the same category!

We like to regard men and women as the same. We are not the same. We are equal. Our wants, desires, approaches, programming, skills, preferences, and mannerisms are as different as our anatomy and design.

A man's number-one survival instinct is to procreate. A woman's is to look after her young. There lies the problem. This means that as soon as the man has had sex, he tends to lose his drive and may leave for someone else.

A woman's instinct doesn't end. She has to carry on, looking after her young.

Biology doesn't necessarily involve logic. If a man was extremely attracted to a woman and found out that she was infertile, this would probably not deter him. Sadly, this may be a bonus to some men because they will feel no responsibility for any potential consequences.

It is engrained in our DNA for sex to be a massive drive to continue mankind's existence. The worst thing is that's only one example. What we look for in a partner is very different. What we think the other looks for in a partner is awfully dissimilar to the reality, and a lack of understanding of that fact creates a lot of clichés about what men and women really want.

We have to accept the fact that we are worlds apart in some ways. Even our basic wants and needs can be drastically different. To have a set idea in your head of how the opposite sex works is the first step to bad relationships, unreliable partners, and failed marriages.

The Bible teaches us that woman brought sin and death
into the world, which she precipitated the fall of the race...marriage
for her was to be a condition of bondage, maternity a period of suffering
and anguish, and in silence and subjection, she was to play the role
of a dependent on man's bounty for all her material wants.
– Elizabeth Cady Stanton

295. SEXUALITY

What freedom men and women could have, were they not constantly tricked and
trapped and enslaved and tortured by their sexuality! The only drawback in that
freedom is that without it one would not be a human. One would be a monster.
- John Steinbeck
(East of Eden)

The template of a human fetus starts as a female structure. Six to eight weeks after
conception, the fetus receives a dose of male hormones called androgens, which
decides if the fetus will alter to a male or female configuration.

A second dosage afterwards will affect the child's sexual orientation. The second
dosage should be more than the first amount. If not, that can affect the sexuality of
the boy or girl. The first dose of androgens can make a fetus male, but if the second
dosage isn't enough, he can develop with a feminine brain structure and is likely to
be effeminate, gay, or trans.

The first dosage could be small; turning the fetus into a girl, and the second
amount received could be large to make the girl masculine, a lesbian, or trans.

It's rare for the first dose to be less than the second because complications tend
to happen as the pregnancy progresses, which is why there are statistically fewer
lesbians than gay men.

It's not the devil's work; it's biology that causes different sexualities.

If you have a problem accepting a person's sexuality, you need to ask why. There
are numerous reasons that are utterly illogical.

You might feel disgusted by a person's sexual preference because of religion,
a bad upbringing, or some sort of sexual trauma that has twisted your mind. The
only form of hostility I can understand (although it is unjustified) is the idea that
a person who has come out about his or her sexuality has been lying to you and
keeping secrets.

People delay being open about their sexuality because they are afraid of this
exact reaction. This worry delays the inevitable coming out for years, making every
passing year feel like they are building the lie even more. It's a dangerous cycle that
never ends until they stop living the lie. They have to come out one day, and they
might as well get it over with.

There are some parts of ourselves that are built in, and sexuality is one of
them. It is a part of our society and us. The one thing that is more important
than accepting sexuality is accepting your own sexuality. There are clichés like
"You're just confused," or "You are going through a phase." There is no question that
whatever preference we have ingrained into our DNA is staying there.

When we touch the place in our lives where sexuality and spirituality
come together, we touch our wholeness and the fullness of our power, and
at the same time our connection with a power larger than ourselves.
- Judith Plaskow

296. SHEEP

I cannot and will not cut my conscience to fit this year's fashions.
- Lillian Hellman

Do you know how stem cells work? When a cell is dead, it becomes a blank slate, but if you put it beside another cell, it replicates it. Put it in the bloodstream, and it becomes a blood cell. Put it in a bone, it becomes a marrow cell, and so on. There is no thought involved. It's an automatic decision.

What's most interesting is people are the same. Nobody's the same in different company. We can be empty shells, imitating our surroundings. We're only cool in the nightclub, successful in front of friends, and affectionate only with lovers. If we are taken out of these situations; our personalities become as blank as those dead cells.

When I was about fourteen, there was a teachers strike in my school. A few days later, the students started to strike as well. I didn't have my homework done, so I saw it as an opportunity to get out of trouble. What kid wouldn't?

The students said they had the strike because it was ridiculous that the teachers' strike prevented them from having a full education.

The truth is we just wanted to get off school, including me, because I didn't know any better. We didn't understand the politics behind the teachers' decision. Less school—that's all it boiled down to.

Some of my friends still went into class, saying they would not just follow the crowd. One of my friends called me a sheep because I was just going with the majority, having no mind of my own.

That annoyed me at the time, but it came as a revelation years later. Over the years, I accepted less and less of what the majority said, liked, and hated and just listened to my heart.

There have been countless times on websites like Twitter and Facebook where a dubious source of information spreads throughout the Internet before it turns out to be fake. This can be a fake picture or quote or news story, but it can get people riled all over the web, and they work themselves into a frenzy. Don't go along with everyone else. When in doubt of an Internet story, just research the source.

People will laugh at you for having a different voice, but that's exactly why you need to be heard. It is tempting to give into the collective voice of our surroundings, but do not allow that compromise you.

If you are going to be a sheep, make sure you know who your shepherd is. Be in charge of all of your own decisions, and let no one compromise you. If we lead ourselves, we do not need leaders.

I am not afraid of the lions led by the sheep.
I am afraid of the sheep lead by the lions.
- Alexander the Great

297. SHYNESS

Many a man is praised for his reserve and so-called shyness when
he is simply to proud to risk making a fool of himself.
- J.B. Priestly

Most of us have a problem with shyness at some point; either in certain circles, awkward circumstances, being dissected by a disapproving parent, a phase where we are trying to find out who we are, at a new school, growing up, or moving. Maybe you have battled shyness throughout your entire life.

Shyness has a lot of negative connotations that vary tremendously. At first, being quiet seems harmless. After all, you can't pose much of a threat if you're timid, right?

If only people weren't so cruel. If you are timid, it can mean that anything can be said about you, and you will be too quiet to defend yourself. This problem can start off by your peers saying that you are antisocial and awkward, but it can quickly turn into your peers saying you are creepy or disturbed. At a certain point, any vicious rumor can be spread about you.

Bullies usually get bored if they don't get a reaction, but if you are an easy target, then they will take notice. If you are reserved, you will become their own personal punching bag, either physically or verbally.

Being shy can affect you throughout your life. You can get picked on in school, you will come across as insecure to potential friends and partners, and you will seem spineless at work.

Shy people seem as if they have less to say than anyone else. I think this couldn't be further from the truth. How many attention-seekers do you know who just blab about the same rubbish 24/7? The louder people tend to be and the more they talk, the less they seem to have to talk about. If you talk all the time, you run out of material and just spew out the same old garbage.

From my experience, shy people are quiet because they feel different. There is something about them that distinguishes them from everyone else.

Of course, while we grow up, anything different is considered wrong, so they keep these traits that distinguish them locked away from everyone. All the shy people I know usually have the most incredible personalities just dying to get out. If you want to take control of your life, you can't be quiet about it. There is no such thing as a quiet leader.

If you are not a shy person, make the effort and befriend those who are. It can only take a little nudge to let their true selves burst out.

Do not underestimate the determination of a quiet man.
- Iain Duncan Smith

298. SIGNATURE

A signature is your own unique marking so make it stand out.
- Anon

George Best could score a goal as long as he had the ball. He could score with his left leg or his right leg. It didn't matter. He could headbutt the ball into the net as easily as someone could kick it in.

Leonardo da Vinci was not simply a good painter; he was a creator of new art. He perfected the technique of *sfumato*, a blending of the edges of objects to allow them to gradually blur into each other with a beautiful fluidity.

Many fighters have come and gone, but no one shone as bright as the Wing Chen master, Bruce Lee. We have all seen him perform a devastating strike with impossible speed while belting out his signature yell.

We all have a signature in our sports ability, our humor, our writing, or dancing. We can all do something that no one else can do. I don't mean you are necessarily the best at something, but you may have a distinctive trait that brings a quality of your own personality to whatever you do.

We often make the mistake of attempting to replicate our hero's technique. When Colin Farrell became a Hollywood star, many of my acting friends copied his look, his attitude, his clothes, his jewelry, and his tattoos. They even got their hair cut the same way as the Dublin-born actor.

But that doesn't work. If an agent wants to hire a Colin Farrell-like actor, he will get Colin Farrell! He acts that way because that's who he is. His characters will always have a part of his own identity grafted to them, so it would be illogical to copy his characteristics.

If you want to stand out, copying someone else is the worst idea. A certain style may work for one person, but that doesn't automatically prove it will work for you.

If you asked a thousand professional footballers what their weekly regime is, you will get a thousand different answers. You are guaranteed to get a lot of similarities, but you will get a lot of dramatic differences too.

My friend, Bryan hated his written signature. Then he realized something. He thought, "Why don't I just change it?" And so, he did. Now he likes how it looks.

Over time, he reflected about it more and more and deliberated, "What else do I not like about myself and the only reason I haven't changed it is because I never thought I could? What other limitations am I forcing myself to keep?"

Our signature in life should be more than just a scribble on a check or a doodle at the bottom of a piece of paper.
- Anon

299. SIGNS

Some protect the here and now. Others protect the
long-term invisible, unlikely, or non-existent.
- Anon

I once had a dream where I was drowning. When I woke up, I realized that there was a leak in my ceiling that was dripping on me, which I obviously incorporated into my dream subconsciously. This is common in dreams. We hear a noise or song, and it can find itself playing a part in our sleeping mind.

But we don't just do this with dreams. We incorporate random aspects of life simply because they are there. If you were going through a hard time and wanted to walk it off, and during your walk, you saw a wolf, you could make this wolf relate to your current state of affairs. Maybe it's there to show you that it could kill you, and life is so delicate that you should cherish every moment.

Maybe you don't care, and you are not scared. That proves you don't have to live in a world contaminated with fear.

It could be with its cubs, and she shows that even a ferocious creature can have a loving side.

It could be wounded and shows that even the greatest of us can be toppled.

This could have been a rabbit, a deer, or a penguin, and you would have a completely different kind of epiphany. Or you could have walked in a different direction and seen something else—or nothing at all.

But the point is that you only saw what you wanted to see. We don't need to wait for a signal. People wait for signs because they are too lazy to go out and do what they have to do themselves. You don't have to go by an invisible, intangible cosmic timer that, when the time is right, will tell you that you can now move on.

I'm not suggesting dismissing all signs. There is intuition, and then there is paranoia. We should try to see good signs within reason.

It is not uncommon to see bad signs that end up limiting us. One of my old friends, Stephanie, was on the way to the airport and saw a car speeding. Seeing it as a sign that her plane was going to crash, she turned the car around and went home. Naturally, there was no such disaster. The car and the plane have nothing in common. But she tried to connect them in a negative way and missed a flight.

When I was about to move to England, my friend just moved away from there, saying he had a horrible time. He begged me not to go. My friend had a history of bad behavior, which seemed to be the reason why he had to leave.

I did not see it as a bad sign. I saw it as a sign that I could prove him wrong.

The truth is, we don't need external attachments to grant us epiphanies. We can do it all by ourselves.

Foolish people do not understand that what is seen is merely their own mind.
- Mahayana Buddhist texts

300. SKEPTICISM

We need pessimists as much as we need optimists. An optimist
invented the airplane. A pessimist invented the parachute.
- Anon

Skeptics have a stigma of being dismissive. This is understandable, but it's a
tad extreme. A skeptic is not one who shoots down a new theory or idea. By
definition, a skeptic is a person who demands to see the facts before they consider
changing their mind.

Acting that way isn't dismissive; it's being careful. Skepticism is often mixed up
with cynicism. Cynics have a dismissive outlook on life.

In this world, there have always been charlatans, scammers, and con artists
with a too-good-to-be-true pyramid scheme, or they need your credit details just to
get their idea in the door. Skeptics will reject ideas like this and be accused of being
negative, but skeptics are the least likely people to get scammed.

Skeptics are not turning down new ideas and hopes because they enjoy it. They
are doubtful and prone to pessimism because their hopes have been too often dashed
by lies, hoaxes, and agendas. We live in a world where we are promised too much by
too many, where only one future can come, and it is rarely the one we envisioned or
hoped for. Friends backstab us, and family or partners can betray us. We counter
this by becoming harder.

We behave this way to protect ourselves. But we have to be careful not to reject
everything. This is tempting when we are utterly screwed over or have a massive
break in trust or faith.

You just say to yourself, "If I dismiss everything, I can't be hurt again." By
having this mentality, you end up hurting yourself. You will cause collateral damage,
losing the trust of your friends and family.

You don't have to become distrustful. You just need to be more aware and
considerate of whom you place your trust.

It's nice to argue with a skeptic. You can't argue with someone who's stubborn,
immature, dogmatic, ignorant, or xenophobic. But to argue with a person whose
mind can change by just looking at the facts is healthy.

Most people will never admit to being wrong. They are too proud for that. But
I have never met someone who lost respect for another person who simply admitted
that he or she wasn't right. It's one of the hardest things to do, but people will always
respect when you admit to your own mistakes.

Nothing fortifies skepticism more than the fact that there are some
who are not skeptics; if all were so, they would be wrong.
- Blaise Pascal

301. SKILLS

Skilled or unskilled, we all scribble poems.
- Horace

In the story "The Fox and the Stork," the fox invited the stork to eat at his house. The fox mischievously decided he would eat from a flat bowl, knowing the stork would be incapable of eating due to his large bill. He looked foolish, since he couldn't perform this simple task. The fox apologized for his trick and as an act of good will, he decided they should eat at the stork's house next time.

When they did, the stork prepared soup in a long-necked pitcher. The stork could easily access the soup within due to his bill, while the fox was unable to drink a drop.

Just because you are bad at something doesn't mean you are not good at something else. You are measured by your gifts, not your possessions. Everyone is equal but in different ways. Nobody is truly better than anyone else, overall. You can excel at a skill to the point of fame, but you may not be good at simple things, like stability in a relationship, moral matters, or staying out of trouble. The only thing that determines how good you are is what you choose to do and how much you put into it.

Dr. K. Anders Ericsson is a professor of psychology who is widely recognized as one of the world's leading theoretical and experimental researchers on expertise. He studies the cognitive structure of expert performance in domains such as music, chess, and sports and how expert performers acquire their superior performance by extended deliberate practice. He published a book called *Toward a General Theory of Expertise*.

He is most famous, however, for his talks about the "Ten Thousand Hour Rule." This is the idea that it takes approximately ten thousand hours of deliberate practice to master a skill. It would take approximately five years of full-time employment to become proficient in your field. It would take ten years of practicing three hours a day to become a master in any subject. If you want to master a skill, work out how many hours you have already achieved and calculate how far you need to go. You should be aiming for ten thousand hours. That's nearly 417 days straight!

Who would dedicate so much grueling time to any one thing? What can you be that passionate about?

Find it. Find something that you love so much, you can develop it to your dying day. If you think there is something that you are not good enough to try and dedicate that much time to, remember that everyone has gifts. Some just open the gift sooner.

There is nothing to it. You only have to hit the right notes
at the right time and the instrument plays itself.
- Johann Sebastian Bach

302. SLEEP

If you can't sleep, then get up and do something instead of lying there
worrying. It's the worry that gets you, not the lack of sleep.
- Dale Carnegie

Depending on your lifestyle, you may not be getting the right amount of sleep.
On busy days, you may get so stressed that you can't sleep.

When you have a day or two to unwind, you have a lie-in. When you wake up
eventually, you will be too de-energized to do anything for the rest of the day. That's
a whole day wasted! All the potential activity gone!

You deserve a well-earned rest, but if you sleep too much, you can't enjoy it,
because you feel lethargic and drowsy.

The human body needs at least six or seven hours of sleep a day to function.
Any more sleep than that, and you are wasting energy, which is hard to get back.

But a lot of people have the opposite problem of not sleeping enough. You might
think it's impossible to avoid.

"But what if I'm always busy?" you may ask. "My hectic schedule does not give
me the chance to sleep that much."

If you have a proper sleep, you will be able to do more because your body will
be much more alert. This means you can get more done faster, so you should have
enough time to have a proper sleep. It's a positive cycle.

Even if you think there are simply not enough hours in the day to have a full
sleep, try taking a nap when you have a break. It lets you unwind all that drained
energy for the first half of the day. After you awaken, you are ready for the rest of
the day.

Naps are extremely healthy. They slow down your heart rate, which relieves
stress and calms down the heart, which can add years to your life.

You might think you can't have your whole break turn into a snooze. What
if you need to get food or have other priorities, like meeting somebody or have a
business arrangement? What can you do then?

Well, power naps are all the rage nowadays, even though it's been around for
centuries. (Leonardo da Vinci slept for fifteen minutes every three hours.) A few
minutes here and there can make a massive difference. Don't torture yourself with
forcing yourself to stay awake. If you are tired, rest for a few minutes, and you will
feel more ready for the rest of the day.

Whatever you do, don't underrate sleep. Give your body a chance to recharge.
A ruffled mind makes a restless pillow.
- Charlotte Brontë

303. SMOKING

Course we're all gonna die some day. But do we have to pay for it? Do
we have to actually throw hard-earned dollars down on the counter
and say, "Please Mr. Merchant-of-Death, please, sell me something
that'll stink up my breath and my clothes and fry my lungs.
- Chewies Gum Rep
(Clerks)

It's impossible to say something about smoking that has not been heard a hundred times. Despite the amount of negativity against cigarettes, smokers seem unfazed.

Even with graphic advertisements against cigarettes, campaigns, bans, common knowledge of the damage it causes, and the fact it's the leading cause of death in the world; smokers are apparently unaffected by it.

If you smoke, why? Is it because you are stressed? If smoking actually stops you from feeling stressed, then why do you have to continue smoking? Have you ever met someone who smokes who's not trying to quit?

Cigarettes don't make you feel free. They give what they say—momentary release. If you put a prisoner outside his jail for five minutes and then drag him back in, he's not free.

There are tons of books you can read if you are seriously thinking about quitting. Or maybe you did quit, but the craving is still there after years of abstinence. You may feel like it is only a matter of time before you give in to it once more.

This is the biggest mistake about quitting smoking. You just don't quit and the craving is gone forever. Smoking is one of the most powerful addiction in the world.

But why is it so powerful? Because it's a chemical addiction. Your body will always crave it once it is in your body. You can take all of the nicotine patches in the world, and you can bite your lip every time someone whips out a cigarette, but you will still want it because the cigarette's chemicals are still in your body.

You may strongly disagree with what I am about to say, but more and more research proves it: smoking and the craving for smoking is cured through therapy. Hypnosis. Cognitive therapy. Relaxation exercises. This will kill the craving. Your body craves unconsciously, so there is no point trying to fight it consciously. You need to fight it unconsciously.

Giving up smoking is the easiest thing in the world.
I know because I've done it thousands of times.
- Mark Twain

304. SOCIALIZING

*If we reduce social life to the smallest possible unit we will
find that there is no social life in the company of one.*
- Jerzy Kosinski

How many close friends do you have who are not people you were forced to befriend? How many friends do you regularly see that are outside the circle of work and school? Some people have zero.

Many of my friends are from random encounters. On planes. Airports. Buses. Trains. We have this idea that we should shut people out and only converse at allotted times and designated social gatherings.

All of my friends that I just happen to meet in the moment usually started with harmless intentions, like asking for directions. You can tell quickly if someone is nice or not, or if that person is in the mood to speak with a stranger.

But why bother? What if you feel settled with your friends? Won't it be weird to meet someone who isn't from the same kind of life as you?

Over a hundred of my friends are in the acting world. What do they talk about the most? Acting. But what if I don't want to talk about acting?

Do you have friends you have known for years, but you wouldn't like them if you met them for the first time now? The only reason you may still be friends with them is some kind of warped loyalty. You may not share the same interests anymore, or you feel like you have outgrown whatever made you friends in the first place, but you tend to stick to people you always knew just because you are used to them.

Why settle for your circle of friends? Why can't you add a few more to the mix? What's really stopping you? You can never have too many friends, and everyone has something to offer, especially if they are from a different walk of life to which you are usually unaccustomed.

We must not forget to look at it from the other point of view. If a person approaches you, don't dismiss him or her as a "local crazy" or a "con artist." Who knows? You might make another friend.

A few years ago, I asked a woman on the train if London was the third stop or the fourth. She answered, and we could have left it at that. But I could gauge that she was a friendly person, so we kept talking. One thing led to another, we swapped numbers. All these years later, we are enjoying married life.

How different would my life have been if I acted more introverted, or if I was more socially awkward? Don't be afraid. Show everyone what you have to offer, and they will offer much in return.

*People have really gotten comfortable not only sharing more information
and different kinds, but more openly and with more people - and
that social norm is just something that has evolved over time.*
- Mark Zuckerberg

305. SOUL MATES

> You want to believe that there's one relationship in life that's beyond betrayal.
> A relationship that's beyond that kind of hurt. And there isn't.
> - Caleb Carr

Writer of *Speed Seduction*, Ross Jeffries, coined the word "oneitis." Oneitis is the feeling we have when we think we have met "the one." Oneitis is the idea that we will meet someone and convince ourselves that this person will make us feel complete. But then it falls apart, and we are meant to learn the lesson, "Once bitten, twice shy."

But we don't, because oneitis rarely happens once. We meet more than one of these supposed "ones." My friend, Stav said that he knew he'd met "the one" because he could "feel it." It's irrelevant if you can feel it. You felt it the last time. You'll feel it the next time.

But is it wrong to romanticize the idea of a perfect partner? Yes! If you genuinely believe you've met your soul mate, what will you do when he or she is no longer a part of your life? It would destroy you. Any other partner after that would feel like second best.

We invent stories to make it sound like destiny. We distort facts and tweak details to give an encounter with a stranger that fairy-tale vibe. "I only met my girlfriend because I missed the train. I was meant to miss that train!"

This may seem like I'm trying to ruin any romance you felt or feel over previous partners or current partners. I met my wife on a train. It was not destiny. It was chance. It's like bumping into an old friend in a large city. It seems so unlikely, so the encounter must have cosmic significance.

But we rarely take into account the amount of "almost encounters." You could have been in front of your old friend, classmate, neighbor, potential boyfriend, future wife, or future divorced wife, but you didn't see that person.

We want to jazz up our lives, but it can warp our minds. I was devastated when I broke up with my first partner. Then I heard about oneitis. Just from a little change of perception, I got instant closure.

If you simply go out of your way to meet people instead of inventing romanticized delusions, you are more inclined to have healthier relationships.

(Husband No.1)There's no doubt Nicky is the one I want to spend my life with.
(Husband No.2) Michael is the beginning of a happy end.
(Husband No.3) This marriage will last forever. It will be third time lucky.
(Husband No.4) I've never been happier.
(Husband No.5) I love him enough to stand by him no matter what.
(Husband No.6) There will be no more marriages or divorces.
(Husband No.7) John is not Husband No. 7. He's No. 1 all the way.
(Husband No.8) With God's blessing, this is it, forever.
- Elizabeth Taylor

306. SPECIAL

Particles, chaos, inertia, entropy. The universe doesn't give a damn.
- Anon

The Copernicus Principle is the idea that we're not special or unique. We used to believe that the earth was the center of the universe. We discovered that our position in the universe is only important because we are at a reasonable distance from the sun to sustain life.

Beyond that, there is no divinity concerning Earth's location in the cosmos. Our world is simply of countless orbs, spinning in the eternal black.

We want to be special, but we can't deny our place in the universe and the inevitability of our time on Earth. Mankind hasn't been around long in the grand scheme of things. If life on Earth was condensed into a year, human life wouldn't fill a single day.

Being special is embedded into every one of us as a biological and evolutionary tool to justify our existence. We are all individuals and believe we are not parts of the trivial attributes of the majority. But maybe we only become trivial on a collective scale. We pretend our problems are unique to justify our inability to correct them.

Understanding biology helps us learn from our mistakes and our intentions. It also helps us break primitive programming such as "feeling special."

Am I suggesting that we are not as special as we have always been led to believe? No. All people of Earth can create great change in a positive way. Some will motivate others through their accomplishments and failings, and a few here and there will accomplish their goals. If you think you can perform great change and intend to mold the world in some way, then go for it.

However, if you turn this on its head and are stuck in a rut, or you have had a sudden run of bad luck, or bad things just seem to keep happening to you, you might think, "It will all turn out fine in the end because God has a plan. Because it's meant to be. Because everything happens for a reason."

If you choose to do nothing because you believe there is a higher purpose for you, you may be disappointed. If you honestly believe that you are special, and there is something grand waiting for you just behind the corner, then shouldn't you seek that out and delay no longer? What is this idea people have of thinking everything will turn out fine and dandy because they want it to?

If you want things to work out for you, see to it that it does. No one is in charge of your life except you. Not the universe. Not anyone else. Only you can decide how special you really are.

The significance of man is that he is insignificant and is aware of it.
- Carl Becker

307. SPECULATION

> Eyes and ears are bad witnesses to men if they
> have souls that understand not their language.
> - Anon

McCarthyism is the scariest kind of speculation. It is accusing a person without evidence, but the accusation is enough to sway others.

The termed was coined during the 1940s and '50s when Senator John McCarthy accused people of being Communists and had innocent people arrested for treason.

Over time, it created wild speculation, as people were blinded by narrow interpretation. It's like gossip on overdrive. Mob mentality on steroids.

It's easier to persecute than to understand. If you were in a group of twenty or so, and you went up to someone and made a wild accusation, it will cause everyone to speculate, even if it was untrue. Just hearing the accusation, having no knowledge of the facts, will nevertheless plant seeds of inquisition, curiosity, and suggestibility in people's minds.

The longer we live, the more we experience and the more we learn. But the more we live, the bigger our presumptions can be. We should look at a much longer timeline than experience: history.

There is perhaps no greater example of McCarthyism than the Salem witch trials in Massachusetts in 1692. During this period, anyone could be accused to being a witch. The only way to stop being accused was for a person to say she was bewitched and therefore accuse another person.

Only by confessing to witchcraft were the women of Salem acquitted and saved from being hanged. It condemned their names, however, and the reputation of their family and loved ones.

Many people couldn't risk harming their family name and chose death to spare others. They couldn't win. Every way out led to a trap. Even reading about it now is terrifying because speculation like that still exists.

When others spread gossip or rumors, you might stay out of it. But you don't have to do or say anything to become a part of speculation. People can see something—see you talking to someone else; catch the last ten seconds of a conversation—and they can jump to their own conclusions.

But why? Everyone will, from time to time, be the object of speculation, some more than others. You can't avoid it, but you can to choose to be as little a part of it as you can.

> Nostalgia often leads to idle speculation.
> - Paul Getty

308. SPITE

A hero is an ordinary individual who finds the strength to
persevere and endure in spite of overwhelming obstacles.
- Christopher Reeve

Human beings see things in symmetry.
"One good turn deserves another."
"You scratch my back; I'll scratch yours."
"An eye for an eye."

When someone bestows good upon us, we tend to repay the favor, but if we are wronged, we seek judgment. We desire rectitude.

You can be spiteful of anything. You can be spiteful to the whole world because it didn't deliver all the things you wanted in life. You can't pick a specific person to blame at times, so you just take it out on everybody. Or you pick a person who reminds you of yourself and project your insecurities onto him. If you can't get what you want, then no one can.

You can invent any logic to be spiteful. We all draw lines in life that we won't cross. Like a game. Like children.

If we start losing, we scribble out the lines and draw new ones. Like children.

You have to work to live, but if you hate your crummy job, you can take it out on everyone. You can refuse to turn up to work because you got told off the last time, which forces your coworkers to work harder in your absence.

You can refuse to hold a door for someone you don't know on a train, so he or she misses it, just because you are fuming at the price of your ticket. You don't know the person, but this can be a warped way to balance out your frustration.

Spite originates in insecurity. We all suffer pangs of it from time to time, but there are those who carry it like luggage. They are ready to dole it out at any time.

To be spiteful to the world or even at a specific person for sophistic reasons implies a much deeper insecurity.

You need to ask yourself, "Am I being spiteful? Where is it stemming from? Why do I get angry with certain people who don't deserve it? What is it about them that riles me? And why? What can I do to stop this?"

Spite is never an answer. It gives us fake satisfaction. We may feel momentarily empowered, but it is a hollow feeling. Learn the origin of any animosity you may have and expel it or transform it into a practical force.

If you want to balance out a snide remark, or you are sick of being bullied, prove the world wrong instead of taking it out on the world. Use that negativity to force you to become better than you are.

Determination gives you the resolve to keep going
in spite of the roadblocks that lay before you.
- Denis Waitley

309. STAGES

I am a part of all that I have met.
- F. Scott Fitzgerald

Isn't it frustrating when people don't understand you? What's even more frustrating is when you cast your mind back to a time when people did get you. You tend to drive yourself mad, trying to figure out why it isn't working now.

A few years ago, you may have had bulletproof confidence. Even the biggest hurdles that life threw at you couldn't knock you down. But now you cave when even the smallest thing is chucked at you. You may find yourself angrier, scared, or depressed. You are easy to irritate, and you can't understand why.

When you feel like this, you say to yourself, "This isn't me! I'm not like this! I'm always happy! What happened to me?"

When you feel like this, it doesn't change the fact that you are who you are. Maybe in the past, you felt more content. You feel like that's who you really are.

But no. That's who you were. You cannot say you are not yourself, no matter how tempting that is. If you feel horrible, scared, or angry, you are still you.

That may sound depressing, but you need to look at it constructively. You never stay constant in one set emotion or emotions. Life happens to you, and circumstances change your perceptions, mood, and emotions. In five years' time, you will change again, compared to now. You can promise yourself you won't, but you can't stop life coming at you.

And that is okay. Although you cannot stay constantly happy, you also cannot stay constantly angry or scared. These are just stages you go through in life.

Some of your friends might see you as the Nice Guy or the Funny Guy. There are others, perhaps in another time in your life, who think you are the Loser, the Dork, or the Idiot. And maybe it's because of how they met you, where they met you, or what you were going through at the time.

So when you feel like you are going through the worst time of your life, the most ineffective advice tends to be, "It will pass." Whether a bad time in your life is full of hours of pain, days of self-evaluation, months of a mid-life crisis, or years of grief, you must remind yourself: it will pass.

It's not about taking advice. It's more about understanding that bad times move along, and you can decide how quickly they move on with a positive perception and deciding when to get back into gear.

There is no set version of you. If you see someone being a jerk, or pathetic, or aggressive, don't label him. He may not be the Angry Guy. He might just be going through that stage of his life because of a recent event. Give people the same common courtesy you would expect if people were in a position to judge you.

No journey travelled stays on the same plain. There will be the odd bump.
- Anon

310. STALE

Better to wear out than to rust out.
- Richard Cumberland

I cycled for the first time in years a few months ago. I was so out of practice that I was a bit wobbly at first. But within a few minutes, it was like I never stopped cycling.

A tutor of Tae Kwon Do can instantly call upon his knowledge of the martial arts in a dangerous situation if he commits regular practice.

If a classroom full of students is asked a question about a subject they looked at months ago, the one who studied regularly will remember the answer.

Notice how I said the word "regularly."

That's the trick. You can study all you want. You can dedicate years to developing your skills, body, memory, stamina, and your potential.

Muscle memory is great but only if you constantly work at it. You may get lucky from time to time, but you can't rely on knowledge or a skill you picked up years ago.

You may have dedicated a large portion of your life to an activity, but you may be rusty. Only when your former skills are needed do you realize that you may have been neglecting them. It's almost like starting from scratch, or it feels like a waste of time to have learned it in the first place if you are not going to keep new skills or knowledge for practical use.

The weakest reason for diminution in practical abilities is laziness. I may sound harsh, but let me explain: my friend, McDonaugh studied CPR when he was a lifeguard. A time came when a woman collapsed at a swimming pool, and he had to resuscitate her. He'd learned first aid so long ago that he couldn't remember how long he had to do compressions in CPR. Another lifeguard stepped in, and the woman was fine.

This shows the danger of not keeping ourselves up-to-date with our skill set. Don't allow your skills to fall into obscurity. Fuse your knowledge and experience with practice and exercise. I don't mean constantly rehearse or train, but check it now and again just to see if it's still at the same level.

My buddy Leon studied Wing Chen, the same combat technique as Bruce Lee. Every few weeks, he does a roundhouse kick. It takes five seconds, but he does it, just to make sure he can still do it.

We can spend so much time dedicating ourselves to our passions. It would be horrible if someone or something extinguished that passion, especially if we did it to ourselves. The only thing worse than not changing is regressing.

There's nothing worse than having everybody thinking alike, talking alike and having the same direction in mind. It gets stale that way.
- Alex Van Halen

311. STANDARDS

People mistake their limitations for high standards.
- Jean Toomer

When I got into an acting school in Dublin years ago, there were two guys who stuck out. One of them was called Noonan. He was simply the best actor I knew at the time.

The other guy, Wayne, was the most untalented actor I have ever had the misfortune to witness and be associated with.

But why was Noonan so good and Wayne so bad? Because no matter how good Noonan was, he always had the same motivation: "It could be better." This guy couldn't settle for second best. It's wonderful to see a perfectionist at work.

As you can guess, Wayne had the opposite mentality. He believed he was the most gifted actor in the school and would become a household name in the country. Unsurprisingly, he was kicked out of the school. No matter how much we tried to bring him back down to reality, his self-belief was narcissistically unrealistic. Since he believed he was the best, he felt like he didn't have anything else to prove, so he wouldn't try as hard. Wayne thought he had already achieved his goal, and therefore he had nothing to strive for, so he didn't try to be better.

But Noonan was never satisfied. He had standards. They were extremely high. It was like a wall that seemed impossible to climb and with enough practice, he eventually would reach the top, only to find the wall growing further. It forced him to keep pushing himself.

His standards were unrealistic, but that is what you need to really throw yourself in at the deep end. He didn't seem capable of being satisfied. If he did, then he would stop succeeding, breaking barriers, making discoveries about himself, and finding new goals and dreams.

To set yourself easy tasks will never make you reach anything but the ordinary. When standards are raised, so is the challenge, the chase, the effort, and the reaping of the benefit.

This can be unhealthy in certain circumstances because it is like you are punching over your weight. But why settle for anything less? Go for more than you can handle because with enough practice and experience, eventually you will be able to handle it. Then boost your standards once again.

Your standards can be high in anything: goals, the future, partners, food, books, education, experience, travel, friends, and life in general.

It's tough to setting your standards to a realistic level while making them high enough to make you strive for better. Your standards should be unlikely but attainable.

Keep up the old standards, and day by day raise them higher.
- John Wanamaker

312. STARVATION

Food can become such a point of anxiety - not because it's food, but just because you have anxiety. That's how eating disorders develop.
- Vanessa Carlton

President William Taft allegedly got stuck in his bathtub during his term in office. He decided that his increasing girth was posing a problem and so, went on a diet.

Many patriots used their president as a symbol of the "way to live," and so many people started doing the same. After all, it was 1911, businesses were booming, people were making more money, food was more accessible, and people were simply eating more.

But they were eating too much. Luckily, the president opened their eyes. This is when the obsession of dieting began.

Because of the pressures of looking perfect, I can understand the existence of eating disorders. I can talk about inner beauty, but if you feel like you want to be a certain size, then you should take the right steps to be happy.

You can't, however, just stop eating. Anorexia, bulimia, purging, and rumination are easily misunderstood, but the fact is this: your body has few absolute needs, but food is one of them.

If you starve your body, you will get ill. There is no beauty in deprivation. Most people starve to lose fat. When you starve, you lose a little fat, but you lose a lot of muscle, so you will actually be farther away from your goal.

It's ironic because there is such a heavy emphasis on "fat" being the prime example of unhealthy living.

I weigh 70kg. I can gain a lot more, even double that size, before it becomes extremely dangerous to my health. But I only have to lose 20kg before I am pushing irreparable damage to my body.

Don't be lulled by surveys of what "healthy" is. I don't believe in the Body Mass Index, which was devised by Adolphe Quetelet. He wasn't a dietician. He was a mathematician. He made this equation in a social physics class. It was a theory. I have seen a bodybuilder and an overweight person with identical BMIs.

It's an archaic method, and believing it makes people fall into a false sense of security. If you think your BMI says you are perfectly healthy, you may take those numbers at face value and not understand that your weight and your diet are two different things.

A lot of skinny people are terrified that being big means they will be depressed, yet they are depressed already. Happiness never ends with the desired physical image but with the right perception of life. Even if you achieve your perfect body, you can drive yourself mad trying to maintain it.

When I was anorexic it just seemed like I literally wanted to disappear. And now I would like to reappear.
- Portia de Rossi

313. STATEMENT

It's not that life gives us purpose but that we choose to give life purpose.

- Anon

In AD 72, the Romans led a siege against Masada, an impenetrable fortress on a mountaintop that could see armies coming for miles. Due to this incredible advantage, it had avoided being successfully invaded—for a time. After a year of attempted entry, the Roman governor, Silva, and his army breached the walls of Masada.

As they entered, they saw a very different sight than they'd expected. Everyone had been killed by their own hands. Only one person survived to deliver a message to Silva. The messenger stated, "Our children will not see slavery, our women will not suffer violation, and our men will not experience murder."

The people of Masada were going to die one way or another, but they chose to die by their own hands as a statement. Their only victory was to deprive the Romans of theirs.

All walks of life make statements in different ways. The point of a declaration is to perform an action that speaks on a larger scale. Animals urinate to mark their territory. A book is never just a story. A movie is more than two hours of scrolling images.

Human beings are more reactive to visuals than words. Even when someone gives us cathartic advice, we may not remember what he or she said exactly.

It can take years to get certain images out of our heads. Have you ever seen a painting that just stopped you in your tracks because it pulled you in?

Artists paint to convey a message. Their life is to make statements. Even if they were to paint a beautiful meadow, and it was just a meadow to them, and they didn't try to make it more than it was, we may still see something else in it. We might look at it and invent its statement. It's like we are making statements to ourselves to spur us on.

We all want to get things done. Or we want to undo bad things, be it the way someone treats us, or the way we are looked down on and treated differently.

You cannot just say "enough is enough" with most people. You need to make a statement that symbolizes "enough is enough."

Human beings naturally empower physical objects and events. If your partner gave you a key to his or her home, the key states that you are together, more than saying "I love you." Maybe getting that key back states, "I'm breaking up with you," more than the words themselves. Ask yourself what statements move you and why.

The afternoon of human life must also have a significance of its own
and cannot be merely a pitiful appendage to life's morning.

- Carl Jung

314. STATUS

You can get what you want with a kind word
and a gun than with a kind word alone.
- Al Capone

A l Capone infamously yelled at screen while in the movie theatre when he saw actors portraying armed criminals shouting and screaming. Capone would cry out, "Why yell? You have a gun!"

You have the means to be taken seriously with a lethal weapon. Why overcompensate by pushing authority? Why undersell yourself by forcing status?

My teacher pointed out that nobody has top status all the time; it changes with time, people, and environment. When he was in the room, he had the highest status, which is status 10, because he was the teacher. When he entered the room, class started because he said so.

But the second the bell rings and its lunch break, if he was to enter the coffee bar where our group met for lunch, he would have the lowest status—status 1. This is because break was a time for our class to socialize. He was not a part of that.

If I met him on a street, we would have similar statues because we were just two guys on our own time, not within the restraints or barriers of school.

Trying to be the big man is not the right way to go about "getting status." A person who tries to look important looks like a person trying to look important. Some people are only winners in their own domain because they're nothing else in the real world.

Even if you have a high status of 8 or 9, you may feel the need to stay on top and shred anyone who steals your spotlight or gets some attention. People like this assume their status is at the maximum. If your established status within the public eye was status 10, you wouldn't need to give into something so petty, just to glorify your image.

Those who have status 10 don't have to mock others to reassert themselves because they should feel no genuine insecurity.

When I say, "naturally high status," I mean those who give off an air of calmness, approval, or capability, without exerting much effort. They are not forcing it through their wealth, occupation, title, or looks but from a hidden inner power.

As the rich consume more and more, they are clearly not
going to want to downgrade their own status.
- Susan George

315. STIGMA

Within psychology and neuroscience, some new and rigorous experimental
paradigms for studying consciousness have helped it begin to overcome
the stigma that has been attached to the topic for most of this century.
- David Chalmers

There was an up-and-coming bodybuilder called Hooton who suddenly died while he was out partying. He wasn't even thirty. What do you think a bodybuilder would die of at such a young age? To help you narrow it down, I can tell you he died from consuming an illegal drug that made him lash out, get aggressive, and panic before his body overloaded, and he collapsed. Do you know what killed the bodybuilder? Cocaine.

Steroids would have been the obvious answer, and I am sorry if I led you to think that by repeatedly identifying him as a bodybuilder, but that's what we do.

Stigmas like this can make us extremely misinformed, which can lead to unnecessary crusades for causes we don't understand.

Professional WWE wrestler, Chris Benoit murdered his son and wife and then committed suicide in 2007. To date, the circumstances of their deaths are still a mystery, but there is evidence of trauma and dementia in Chris's autopsy.

However, most news outlets stated that Benoit killed because of "roid rage." Roid rage is a sudden, aggressive, violent streak with no warning. This incident lasted three days, and it was planned and thought through. It wasn't spontaneous. But because it was so horrible and tragic, people demanded something to blame. Steroids became the culprit.

I keep using steroids as an example because it has such a defined stigma, but we all fall victims to such stigmatism.

If you are overweight and you fall ill, people assume it's because you are overweight. A drunk becomes ill because he or she is a drunk; a smoker has a cough because he smokes; and a pill popper is depressed because she pops pills.

But we don't know that! We just look for the easy answer by finding the easiest way to identify people.

Chris Benoit did take steroids, but there was no hint that it had any part in his death. He was also on a number of antidepressants at the time. Many bodybuilders have never taken steroids, yet they are always asked, "What are they taking to be in such good shape?"—as if they cannot do it alone.

We may get stigmatized indirectly, through no fault of our own or from an outcome we could not prepare for. We may have to carry around many labels. But we choose to have prejudices on others. We need to be careful that we do not sink to that level of simplification.

Today, certain people file for bankruptcy, and
it no longer has the stigma it once had. Now it's almost
considered wise, a way to regroup and come back again.
- David Dinkins

316. STORIES

> All stories, if continued far enough, end in death, and he
> is no true-story teller who would keep that from you.
> - Ernest Hemingway

In 1928, theorist, Vladimir Propp analyzed over one hundred fairy tales and identified a series of recurring functions that schematized into an overreaching storytelling formula and the morphology of the folktale. His analysis has become a vital text in examining narratives in films, television, books, novels, comics, and oral narrative. No matter what kind of story we hear, see, tell, or invent, it will nearly always be one of eight core storylines:

- Achilles—the Fatal Flaw
- Candide—the Indomitable Hero
- Cinderella—the Dream Come True
- Faust—the Deal with the Devil
- Orpheus—the Taken Away
- Romeo and Juliet—the Love Interests
- Circe—the Spider and the Fly
- Tristan—the Trinity

It's impossible to think of a story that doesn't fall under those categories. It shows what attracts us in a story and a character and what they have to offer. Who our heroes are and what stories we use to dictate our drive and goals say a lot about us. When we were kids, we looked up to Superman because he was an uncompromising ideal. It looks silly now, but when we were kids, a character like that was crucial. It can help form that perfect idolized being we crave to be.

I have seen many people use wondrous stories, amazingly three-dimensional characters, intricate relationships, and tons of research to tell stories that are, at the end of the day, about one thing—people. But do we learn from these stories?

My school principal could quote almost any Shakespeare play and would talk with an unrivaled passion of the characters, their journeys, emotions, and goals. Yet he had absolutely no sympathy for anyone in real life who was suffering.

I've seen people cry at *Schindler's List*, but they are simplistically racist and notoriously xenophobic.

I've seen people talk about their heroes who died hundreds of years ago or fictional characters they love, yet they condemn the heroes of today.

One of my friends saw a movie about a man who neglected his family during his entire life. Immediately after, he rang his mother and told her he loved her. He'd never done that before. We let stories affect us, but we need to let them linger and incorporate their messages in our lives. Stories are not just a part of reality; they are a reality in themselves.

> Some stories are true that never happened.
> - Elie Wiesel

317. STRESS

I've chosen to treat my life more like a party than something to stress about.
- Martin Short

In the 1930s, endocrinologist, Hans Selye performed tests on mice, in which he played loud music at them constantly. Over time, the mice developed stomach boils from stress.

This experiment proves that stress is not just a mental problem; it will take its toll on our body. It can kill you more subtly than you think, with high blood pressure, strokes, and heart attacks. You may think these problems as unlikely and years away, but stress affects our posture, mood, energy levels, and health. It can kill you, with enough time.

My father was a solicitor. He had a lot of stress in his life. My father did incredibly well with his work, but because it is such a high-up job, he stressed with many clients, tons of paperwork, workers not doing their jobs, quotas to reach, and duties falling out of his control. So my father became irritable easily, even over minor things at home because the stress had drilled that into him for years.

When we are stressed, we tend to work louder and more aggressively but not necessarily any better. But as my father got older, he was aware that he was becoming stressed. He would just focus on different things.

If his train ticket expired, his mentality was, "I can easily afford another £12. Whether or not I have a tantrum, I still have to buy another ticket. But if I remain calm, at least I look less childish."

People freak out if they miss the bus, even if they know another one is going to come in fifteen minutes. We are in a bad mood all day if our phone goes dead or our iPad doesn't work. We've all seen a group of people going through the same problems, but they will all have different levels of stress. Some are always stressed.

It requires a lot of energy to create stress, so why not convert that power into a happy or funny feeling? To react positively like this is not denying your problems. You can have a laugh for a second and then get down to business, or you can get angry and stressed and then do a job erratically. It's your choice.

Stress affects everybody. It gets to you no matter how bad or how good your life is. It's a universal emotion. Nothing can stress you out more than yourself.

It's not stress that kills us, it is our reaction to it.
- Hans Selye

318. STUBBORN

Refusal to believe until proof is given is a rational position;
denial of all outside of our own limited experience is absurd.
- Annie Besant

Millennia ago, the South Pole started to freeze to the point where it was becoming uninhabitable. Over time, every animal migrated except the penguin. Many zoologists ponder why penguins were the only animals to survive on the surface of the South Pole. Why would any animal voluntarily stay in a habitat that can get down to -87 degrees Celsius? No one knows, but it is suggested that the penguins' ancestors were simply too stubborn to leave.

Sadly, stubbornness is an age-old problem with humanity. My old classmate, Donovan was a massive anti-Semite and homophobe. My friends gave up trying to reason with him years ago. I asked him to explain his hatred as graphically as possible. He did, and I explained for about twenty minutes the inconsistencies in his argument. Then he did something I never expected. He said, "I have been completely wrong this entire time."

This is the dream! How often do we hear one admit his folly? To completely change someone's opinion on something that has been built up for years is rarely changed in an instant. It's not impossible, as my example above proved. Maybe we don't force ourselves to have a good, mature, sit-down debate, as we are afraid it may turn into a heated argument. But if we don't, we do not know where we stand with other people on certain beliefs and opinions or why. It's better to at least try to change our friend's mind when his beliefs are inaccurate, wrong, or—in this case—dangerous.

More often than not, we act stubborn because we don't want to be humiliated. When we hear a counter argument, we don't even want to consider the possibility that we are wrong. We want to prove that we are right. It's self-preservation, but looking out for our best interests doesn't mean that we are right.

What do you get defensive about? Maybe you are so protective about an aspect of your life because you are afraid you might be wrong. Denying it will just make it worse. The nail that sticks out the most gets hammered down the hardest.

Stubbornness can be offensive or defensive. Don't be too forceful with your views, or you may be the one who's being stubborn.

Every trait becomes a negative characteristic when it becomes exaggerated. Stubbornness is the extreme of being principled. When you get overly defensive about your principles, you won't be able to see the difference between honoring what you are passionate about and being childish. Egomania and vanity are not worn well by anyone.

Many are stubborn in pursuit of the path they
have chosen, few in pursuit of the goal.
- Friedrich Nietzsche

319. SUBCONSCIOUS

> If you fail to plant desires in your subconscious mind, it will feed
> upon the thoughts which reach it as the result of your neglect.
> - Napoleon Hill

The subconscious mind is permanently alert to protect us from danger. Ironically, it can be the source of our own destruction. We are too intellectually smug to admit the human psyche is a great unknown, and we are too frightened to approach any issue relating to the mind.

Who we are is derived from the mechanics of the subconscious mind at an early age. Our experiences and parents' wisdom fuel our brain. Being taught one way makes it difficult for us to change, to learn, and to unlearn. When we become accustomed to certain circumstances, circumstances we are unfamiliar with seem scary or wrong.

This is not based on logic. It is simply our minds best understanding of how to protect the body it harbors. However, this is entirely based on the individual and his or her life.

At times, there doesn't seem to be a right or wrong in life, only interpretations. Never a set path. All our ideas, philosophies, concepts, wisdom, and distortions are based on our lives, yet it could be drastically altered if we lived life any other way, no matter how seemingly infinitesimal.

Can we really trust how we think? Whatever our vision is of existence—no matter how solid, definitive, convincing, or inexorable—it is nothing but a version of what we know. It'd be very different if there were any alteration in our lives.

So to say we are who we are because of what life threw at us can help us understand ourselves, but it can prevent us attaining our goals. Our subconscious may feed off past insecurities, former traumas, and buried grief. A tragedy or trauma may have happened at an early age. It is in the past now and cannot change, but our subconscious mind often tortures us by trying to make sense of the nonsensical.

Our subconscious makes no dissimilarity between constructive and destructive thoughts. It takes what it is given.

If you feed it anger, it will translate that into reality. If you nurture it with fear, it will produce phobias. If you sustain it with depression, it will construct walls and barriers. If you channel it with positivity, that will become your life.

> To be ambitious for wealth, and yet always expecting to be poor;
> to be always doubting your ability to get what you long for, is like
> trying to reach east by travelling west. There is no philosophy
> which will help man to succeed when he is always doubting
> his ability to do so, and thus attracting failure.
> - Charles Baudouin

320. SUBSTITUTION

If you have abandoned one faith, do not abandon all faith. There is
always an alternative. Or is the same faith under another mask?
- Graham Greene

Giving up smoking is tough. It's almost impossible. But do you know what's harder than quitting? The obvious answer is, not going back to the habit.

But there is something harder than that. It's not just quitting the smoking addiction but quitting the addiction, period. Quitting can leave such a colossal emptiness inside of you that you may feel like filling it with another obsession of equivalent proportion. It's not particularly effective if you're going to quit smoking and then eat loads of junk food instead. An addiction replacing another addiction isn't effective. Why swap one poison for another?

Substituting bad habits is a good idea, but you need to substitute them well. It's tricky because you may find yourself in uncompromisable situations.

What if you are on a diet, but your friends spontaneously want to get some fast food? You compromise and say, "Well, just this once," or "I'll just have a little kebab or a small bag of chips. That's not too unhealthy, is it?"

You are trying to make wise substitutions, but you need to be more prepared and adaptable. I always have little bags of nuts, seeds, olives, and other healthy snacks in my bag, so I am never in this situation. Unhealthy food is so accessible nowadays, but so is healthy food. You just need to know where to look.

You can find substitutions for your problems. You say you are only unhappy because of where you live. Then when you move, you blame your unhappiness on the people in the neighborhood. This is substituting the source of your insecurity. When you keep switching the source of your misery, the real source is you.

Some people will substitute throughout life—blame, action, commitment. We need to understand that replacing a bad habit leaves a big void, but it doesn't have to be filled with something bad. It just needs to be filled.

If whatever was occupying that void was negative, you can transfer that negative energy into a positive one. If you stopped playing video games, how about replacing it with a new hobby or activity? Take up the guitar. Explore. Try new places.

You can fill the empty space inside of you, and if you know what you're doing with your priorities, you will find that space overflowing. You will look back and laugh. You will be incapable of comprehending how such silly, impractical habits had such a tremendous hold on your life once.

But not anymore because you're just too busy having a good time.

If you criticize something then you have to have an
alternative, but we do have to try and improve things.
- Linford Christie

321. SUCCESS

The victory is in preparation.
- Winston Churchill

Although Simon Cowell had success with several hit records in the '80s, his label, Fanfare, went under in 1989, and he lost everything. He owed £300,000 in loans that took four years to pay off. But he bounced back a decade later and is now a multimillionaire.

Will Smith was an up-and-coming rapper and entertainer before the Internal Revenue Service assessed a $2.8 million tax debt against him and took many of his possessions. He was about to go bankrupt before he starred in *The Fresh Prince of Bel-Air*, showcasing his potential. He is now one of the highest paid actors in the world.

Before we look at what spurs success, let's see what spurs the downfalls. The seven deadly sins are gluttony, greed, sloth, lust, pride, envy, and wrath. Most people tend to forget about the seven virtues: courage, kindness, hope, faith, humility, patience, and love.

Benjamin Franklin, however, lived by thirteen virtues: temperance, silence, order, resolution, frugality, industry, sincerity, justice, moderation, cleanliness, tranquility, chastity, and humility.

With these ideals, he became an author, printer, satirist, politician, theorist, scientist, civic activist, statesman, soldier, and diplomat. He is mainly remembered as an inventor, creating the lightning rod, stove, bifocals, the lending library, the fire department, and countless others. If that wasn't enough, he made major contributions to the developing of American nationhood to unite colonies under one general government.

He had morals to keep him in check. We all need to find our own. We need to look into ourselves, see what makes us tick, and use that to accomplish all of our goals. No one starts as a success. Some of us will find success in flamboyantly expressive and visible ways, like Franklin's inventions. Others will find success in the small things, the little victories.

In ancient times, a man would have to pay his way to the top through war and bloodshed. Men were recognized by their strength.

Today, nothing could be further from that. It's all in the mind, either mental or psychological. People are immortalized by their intellect, status, ideas, and morals. So you can't blame your lack of success on your being short, unconfident, or that you got dealt a bad hand in life. Anybody can achieve the impossible if they have the drive.

What is our aim?.... I can answer that in one word. Victory, victory at
all costs, victory in spite of all terror, victory, however long and hard
the road may be; for without victory, there can be no survival.
- Winston Churchill

322. SUGARCOATING

As we unweave a rainbow, it becomes less wonderful.
- Richard Dawkins

Archaic religions were brutal. The ancient Greek titan, Kronos, devoured his own son to avoid his ever replacing his father.

The twilight of the gods, known as Ragnarök, was a cosmic god war in Norse mythology—a war at its most epic, bloody, and cannibalistic.

Even the Old Testament is utterly ruthless, recounting stories about plagues, torture, and genocide.

You couldn't imagine how graphic and even horrid so many primordial religions seem because they have been glossed over throughout time.

The Old Testament may be considered too terrifying for a child. That's why over time, Christianity and Catholicism has focused less and less on scaring us with an angry God perception and talks more about a loving God.

Even the most cherished fairy tales' origins were filled with bloodshed. Classic tales like *Rumpelstiltskin*, *Cinderella*, and *Little Red Riding Hood* were originally much darker than you would ever suspect. These stories stand the test of time because they teach valuable lessons to kids. But we want to teach children with stories and religion; we don't want to scar them for life.

When we need to sugarcoat tragedy or grief, how far do we go? When a person dies, consoling the family is difficult because sugarcoat the situation might make them feel worse. "At least she is out of pain" or "He's gone to a better place" might be considered patronizing and insulting.

When you have to tell someone a hard truth, try not to tone it down, but don't be blunt. Just tell the person in the most practical way possible.

I cannot stand a doctor who talks to a patient with medical jargon for five minutes, and the patient has no idea what the doctor is saying. The only thing the patient wants to know is, "Am I okay?"

We need to be straight with people. We need to tell people the truth as often as we can, especially when we are dealing with delicate subjects.

We should be careful how we deliver bad news to others, so they understand the circumstances, but we don't want to not knock them off their feet. We need to phrase it positively and effectively.

Constructive criticism is about finding something good and positive
to soften the blow to the real critique of what really went on.
- Paula Abdul

323. SUICIDE

A suicide kills two people.
- Arthur Miller

Never leave a depressed person too long with his or her thoughts. It can lead to the worst tragedy. Suicide is one of the most terrible, tragic, and unpredictable things in life. It is made all the more bizarre by the fact that in the entire animal kingdom, human beings are the most inclined to take their own lives. By far. So the big question is, why do we do it?

Statistically, people tend to commit suicide either on the first attempt or the eleventh. The people that fall into the "eleventh attempt" category can be misinterpreted as the "attention-seekers." That's a bad name to use, but what I mean is that these victims are those who wanted to be "found," so they could get help. They don't know how else to cry out for help. When they actually commit suicide, it is either an accident, or they just gave up trying.

Those who commit suicide the first time are those who are ready to accept their fate. They are prepared, organized, and know exactly what they are doing. These people are the scariest ones because they can be the last people anyone would expect to take their lives, and they have it planned months in advance.

The human condition is to strive, to improve, and to have purpose. Suicide is caused by an overwhelming sensation and apparent realization that your life is unbearable, and it will never improve. If this feeling outweighs your will to live, then your mind will choose suicide, rather than continuing an unfulfilled life.

We can't tell who will commit it until they try; who is attempting it as a cry for help; and who truly wants their lives to end? If they do want to end their lives, how can we stop them? Or make sure that they don't try again?

If you have felt like this at some point, the question is, "What is taking your own life meant to accomplish? Is it just to end your suffering, or is it to leave a message?"

We need to see why someone believes this is the right thing to do. People commit suicide for all sorts of reasons. Understanding the reasons will help us put their problems in perspective.

People commit suicide because they lost someone. I know they are trying to honor that death by joining the person, but it's better to honor a person's life by living your own.

To end your pain actually causes more pain. There is always someone left behind who has to suffer the grief. People commit suicide because they think no one cares, but we underestimate how much we hold each other to our hearts.

Hope is a necessity for normal life and the
major weapon against the suicide impulse.
- Karl A. Menninger

324. SUPERIORITY

All animals are equal but some are more equal than others.
- George Orwell
(Animal Farm)

Aristotle said, 'We should behave to our friends as we would them to behave to us.' Confucius said, 'Never impose on others what you would not choose for yourself.' Jesus Christ said, 'Never do to others what you wouldn't want them to do to you.'

This philosophy, which is known as the Golden Rule dates to 600 BC, showing that the concept of treating all wakes of life equally has been around since human civilization.

Some disagree with this philosophy. There are those who believe that not all men are equal. They believe that some are born "better" or were entitled to more.

This mentality is known as a superiority complex. It can create itself because of religion, wealth, skill, strength, snobbery, or intelligence.

Whether we utilize this imagined superiority through violence, snide comebacks, or silent judgments, we are all one and the same. We all fall into this trap. The funny thing is, you may gain a superiority complex because you think you don't fall into the traps that other people do. Even when I talk about how people fall into addictions and do stupid things, I can come across as snobbish, so even I have to be careful about my thinking.

I went through a massive superiority stage in my life. Most people go through it in their teens as part of their rebel stage, but I had it when I was about eighteen. While I was in college, I started to have more confidence, and I thought I had a grasp on how life works and how people think. But I was naive.

When I decided to stop drinking, I was met with a lot of confusion. I had less impulse to drink, watching those around me fall apart from alcoholism. I looked at others, thinking to myself, "Why sabotage yourself?" It was easy to silently judge everyone, but it only made me feel better superficially.

It wasn't just about drinking. I hated students who teased me for studying so much. Then I felt no shred of sympathy when they got kicked out of college.

I thought I was stronger than everyone else. But when I started suffering panic attacks, I felt like the weakest. I said to myself that I would never be that overconfident again. In hindsight, it was a necessary wake-up call.

I believe a lot more people fall into this trap than they believe or would like to admit. Just because you don't fall into some traps doesn't mean you don't fall into others.

Put others first.
- Confucius

325. SUPERSTITION

Ah, yes, superstition: it would appear to be
cowardice in face of the supernatural.
- Theophrastus

Superstitions originate from a lack of understanding. It is a way to fill in the
gaps. We invented stories and imposed ideas to understand any phenomena we
couldn't comprehend. It could be a red sky, an inhuman wail heard in the middle of
the night, or a rainbow. Nowadays we are blessed with science to explain all these
marvels, but stories and fantasies can be drilled into our heads, and it is difficult to
shake them off.

There is nothing in science that suggests why a black cat is bad. Why is it bad
only when it crosses your path? What if it half crosses and then turns around? Do
you just get half bad luck? Why does it have to be black? Have they tested different
colored cats? Who discovered this? When? How did they discover it?

Believing archaic beliefs such as this cannot be healthy because you will become
more accustomed to believing everything and developing into a very gullible human
being, prone to be taken advantage of.

Let me explain how superstition outstays its welcome in spite of facts. There is
a notion that a rabbit's foot is naturally lucky. Fertility has always been considered
important in our society, so people have considered the rabbit the luckiest animal
because it seemed to be the most fertile.

But it's not luck. It's just how rabbits are genetically wired. But people didn't
know that at the time, so they had to make sense of it whatever way they could.

When we have a half-baked theory of a concept, and then we find a better
explanation to understand the concept, it's tempting to latch onto the original
theory, simply because we have grown accustomed to it.

But you might have an example where a superstition was right. People can get
passionate and justify their beliefs by saying they broke their leg the same day they
walked under a ladder or shattered a mirror.

If you believe something bad is going to happen, it probably will. If you become
conscious of your foot, you will twist your ankle. If you are convinced you are going
to have an accident, you are probably not concentrating on your surroundings,
which means you might trip or bump into something. You may not notice if nothing
happens, but if it does, you may say things like, "Told you so," as if you wanted it to
happen just to justify silly beliefs.

We create our own luck. We can choose to create our own luck, good or bad,
without having to rely on a logic that doesn't exist. Don't be superstitious. It will
bring bad luck.

Superstition is rooted in the brain more deeply than skepticism.
–Johann Wolfgang von Goethe

326. SUPPLEMENTS

People think that supplements give you like a 200% boost in muscles or recovery or strength or energy or whatever but it's more like 10%. Are supplements going to make the final difference to ensure you will get a perfect body? No.
- Anon

To help boost fitness and exercises, it's not uncommon to take supplements, be it pills, powders, dissolving tablets, or protein shakes. Not only are people misinformed by the effectiveness of supplements, but many people misunderstand what they do.

I saw a documentary in which people who work with supplements in health stores were secretly filmed to see how much they knew of their product. When they were asked about the products they sell, many employees said scripted sentences like, "It makes you bigger," or "That one makes you strong," or "This one here builds the upper body," but rarely did they go into detail.

All supplements work on different things—hair, nails, cartilage, joints, marrow, muscle—but you need to be extremely qualified to understand all the complex chemicals in each of these supplements.

A lot of supplements create a placebo effect. After you take supplements, you will assume any change in your body or abilities is connected to the supplements.

Creatine is a common enhancement among weightlifters, and almost everyone who tries it will swear their bodies get dramatically bigger shortly after taking it. This surely proves it's enhancing your muscles, right?

Wrong. Creatine does make you bigger, but it does nothing to your muscles. That extra bulk you gain is water. Creatine is designed to help you retain more water, which your body requires when doing intense exercise. But when you want to look buff, and you see yourself getting bigger, you think it's your muscles because it's what you desire.

So what about the people who swear they can lift four times the amount they originally could?

It's psychological. You don't need enhancements. You have that ability in you from the start. You just believe it more when you think there are wonder drugs that can make you lift more, run longer, and be better.

Supplements do help but within reason. You need to have realistic goals. Many bodybuilders swear you can get a perfect body without relying on powders if you just train hard, sleep well, and eat right. Although supplements can give you a little nudge in the right direction, they are never as important as you think.

The only way to keep your health is to eat what you don't want, drink what you don't like, and do what you'd rather not.
- Mark Twain

327. SUPPORT

'Tis not enough to help the feeble up, but to support them after.
- William Shakespeare

If you are mending a broken shelf, your job doesn't finish when it is repaired. You need to stay to make sure it doesn't fall down again, especially if it looks a bit wobbly. You can usually tell if something is going to come down again, be it a shelf, a loose doorknob, or even a person.

One of my best friends, Sean, was ridiculed for being a mommy's boy. His mother was ill and battled cancer for years, so he was always there for her and spent more time with her than with his friends. He was all she had, and the feeling was mutual. In the final months, his mother was his only priority.

Were people sympathetic? Surprisingly not. A lot of people saw him using his mother as an excuse not to be social.

Inevitably, she passed away. Sean was devastated. His friends were there for him as shoulders to cry on, someone to talk to, and someone to unload on.

Sean thought his friends weren't going to be reliable during his grieving process. He was happy that his friends were there for him at his darkest hour. Or were they?

About three months passed, and it was like nothing happened. Sean's friends had done their part, so they reverted to their selfish selves. They ridiculed Sean, and even teased him about his mother. Although Sean's mother was buried, he still had to pick up the pieces since he had to deal with the will, her house, and unpaid bills.

But who was there to pick up the pieces for Sean? No one. Or maybe his friends did pick them up and let them drop again.

It took about two or three years for Sean to get out of the shock of his mother's death. He's fine now, although he does have moments of depression. The point is that the whole grieving process could have been so much easier and faster if his friends had been more consistently there for him.

There is no point just being there when friends have a fall. You need to be there for them to cushion the fall and to help them get back on their feet. What kind of friend are you to let them fall and then shove them back down every time they try to get back on their feet?

You don't pick and choose when to be there for someone. If you are not there, you are not much of a friend, and you have let them down.

You are not necessarily a moral person just because you are there for those close to you when things are at their worst. You're supposed to be there. You're expected to be there. People take time to recover, to heal, and to pick up the pieces. That's when you know who your real friends are.

Truth stands, even if there be no public support. It is self-sustained.
- Mahatma Gandhi

328. SURROUNDINGS

A constant struggle, a ceaseless battle to bring success from
inhospitable surroundings, is the price of all great achievements.
- Orison Swett Marden

Milieu is the French word for environment, although it roughly translates to "socio-literary context." It is used to describe how an age, a time, or a habitat can shape a person, which can inspire them to create poems, literature, and music. But our environment doesn't always shape us for the better.

We don't have to follow the pattern of our surroundings. If you listen to depressing music, it's because you relate to it, or it reminds you why you should be depressed. We adapt to the likeness of our surroundings, good and bad.

If you moved from a good neighborhood to a bad neighborhood, it could affect you in many ways: speech, jargon, conduct, posture, and attire. Even if you don't try to, it can happen as a self-defense reflex to connect and relate to others.

In your hometown, you have set ways and rules of how you behave that have gradually developed throughout your life, though they have mildly changed here and there. If you move somewhere else and get new friends, a new job, or go to college, that can change you. You may pick up some good traits and some bad ones.

If a positive person were in a bad environment, it would take its toll on the person's psyche. But you can use that to make a bad thing into a good thing. I moved from Laois to Dublin when I was seventeen. In Dublin, there was a lot more crime, violence, poverty, and people.

But some people who lived in the country got suckered into the drugs and drink because it was never accessible before. I thought, "I can decide what elements of Dublin I like and reject elements I don't like."

Your surroundings can be very small or very large. They can be your family, close friends, street, town, country, or neighboring nations.

When you think of your area, do you think beyond the street or beyond the town? Some who want to "get out of here" may be talking about their house or the country. They equate this with solving all of their problems. It's not just the place itself that affects you but the people. Being around negative people will wear you down.

Luckily, it works both ways. If a so-called "bad person" is put in a good environment, it can bring that person around. You can argue that it won't work because "that's not you." Is being depressed really you either? No one wants to be depressed, so give happiness a shot before you dismiss it. If you dwell in trouble, change your address.

It was only from an inner calm that man was
able to discover and shape calm surroundings.
- Stephen Gardiner

329. SUSPENSE

> How do you keep someone in suspense for twenty-four hours?
> I'll tell you tomorrow.
> - Anonymous Comedian

You may have a problem with holding conversation, talking to a stranger, starting a chat, or keeping a talk interesting. I'll talk about the techniques to make a conversation, starting with the most famous method: the cliffhanger.

In the Middle Eastern stories, *1001 Arabian Nights*, there is an overviewing story in between all of the tales about a Persian king called Shahryar.

His wife was unfaithful to him, so he had her beheaded. Believing all women to be untrustworthy, Shahryar took it out on everybody. Every day he got his vizier to find a young virgin for him to marry. As soon as they went to bed, he had his way with her and beheaded her before she got a chance to cheat on him.

He kept doing this until the vizier couldn't find any other virgins. The vizier's daughter, Scheherazade, said she would marry the king. When she did, they went to bed, and as the king prepared to have his way with her, she started telling an incredible story. The story had magic, djinns, wizards, sea journeys, monsters, and adventures. She was about to finish, but dawn broke, and so she said she would tell the rest of the story the following evening. The king reluctantly agreed, intrigued by the conclusion of the story.

The following night, Scheherazade finished her story but then began another one. Before she ended it, dawn broke, and the impatient king had to wait again.

After 1001 stories and nights, the queen said to the king, "My beloved, I have borne three children for you these past three years. Is that enough evidence to show that I would never hurt you?" The king forgave all women, and they lived happily ever after.

Most television programs, like *24*, *Heroes*, and *Lost*, use cliffhangers like this. The reason why people keep coming back to these shows year after year is because they are given a "to be continued" ending. Soap operas and comic books have been ongoing for over half a century, thanks to relying on this method of storytelling. The same principle applies in conversation.

There is another technique called "hooks." You may start talking about a certain subject, and then go off on a tangent and talk about something else, but you never have a chance to backtrack to the original topic. While telling a story, you may hint or imply another story and then carry on. The implication is the hook. The hook is so-called because it's left there, waiting to be pulled up again.

Making a note of this means that not only will there be always something to talk about, but your friends will want to meet up with you to find out the conclusion to your stories.

> There is no terror in the bang, only in the anticipation of it.
> - Alfred Hitchcock

330. SYMBOLISM

People need dramatic examples to shake them out of apathy and I
can't do that as a man, I'm flesh and blood, I can be ignored, I can be
destroyed but as a symbol I can be incorruptible, I can be everlasting.
- Bruce Wayne
(Batman Begins)

When the Castilian military leader, El Cid was battling the Almoravids during
a siege in Valencia, he was wounded in his second-to-last battle and killed.

If he died in his second-to-last battle, am I suggesting that he fought in his last
battle while he was dead?

Yes. El Cid was fighting a losing battle, and Cid's wife, Jimena, realized that the
troops were losing hope, since their leader had perished.

Or so they thought. Jimena had her late husband propped on his horse and sent
out to battle. His men continued to fight believing their king, although wounded,
carried on in battle. This idea helped the troops win because El Cid was not perceived
as a dead body; he was a symbol of hope.

Symbols can represent anything. The yin/yang symbol known as the mandala
represents good and evil. It is a symbol of philosophy.

Although symbols have certainly changed, from human sacrifices to the Nike
logo, they are still important. We once saw human sacrifices as a symbol of reward
and loyalty to the gods. We look at such ideas now with ridicule, and we discard the
idea that symbolism can produce some benefit.

But we allow symbols into our lives without realizing it. An acorn falling from
a tree is a symbol of rebirth. Darkness is a representation of fear and the unknown.

The Nazis saw the swastika as a sign of power, but it is more often seen as a mark
of corruption. Yet if this symbol is tilted and facing the other way, it is a figure of
peace. Those are three extremely different meanings, all lurking within one simple
emblem.

A star burning its light in the sky, even though the star died eons ago, can be a
symbol that your actions will affect those around you long after you are gone.

We need to embrace symbols. We can empower symbols to empower ourselves.
It may not have to make sense, as long as it makes sense to you. Not only can
you use symbols, but you also can become one. A momentary sign of bravery can
symbolize that anyone can be a hero. A defiant stance after one has been knocked
down repeatedly symbolizes that no obstacle can deter you. You may not intend it
or notice it, but if it happens, use it.

Symbols are not manufactured; they cannot be ordered, invented or
permanently suppressed. They are spontaneous productions of the psyche,
and each bears within it, undamaged, the germ power of its source.
- Joseph Campbell

331. SYSTEM

No written law has ever been more binding than
unwritten custom supported by popular opinion.
- Carrie Chapman Catt.

Do you believe that governments keep promising peace, but they only seem to deliver deeper wounds?

If the world were as corrupt as people believe it is, politicians wouldn't allow protestors to march and chant with signs and give out about figureheads and presidents who gave these people the very freedom they demand.

I understand the passion that fuels protests. A lot of protests have benefitted and changed the world. But protestors should spread awareness, not rob, burn buildings, and attack citizens. People like this cause more damage than the people they accuse.

We are freer now than ever before. We are free, mostly because of the sacrifice of our ancestors, rather than our own doing.

Some people say the government is a sham for taking our money away on policies or constructions that don't benefit society. But the fact is, it's a process to find new ways for us to better our lives, and every process has a trial and error.

It's sad to dub the billions of our hard-earned cash as "better luck next time," but the fact is, there's no better way to do it, at least for now.

We theorize about efficient ways to benefit our nations and pick the best one. It might work; it might not. If it doesn't, we act like the government conned us. If it does benefit us, people will complain and believe there is an underlying motive.

The government is not an evil force. It's like any mass assemblage—a group of the willing, chosen from the fit, to do the necessary. There are flaws in every system because flawed people made the system.

The sad thing is that the public just does not listen anymore. Our heroes have changed. Politicians can make their claims for decades about what the world needs, and people don't bat an eyelid.

If there is some part of the government which you have a problem with, sometimes you have to become a part of the system to stop it. Doing nothing, living off the grid and not giving anything back to society doesn't help anyone, including you. If you start acting above the system, everyone will do the same. No one can have society upon his or her own terms. If they seek it, they must serve it too. Those who expect to reap the blessings of freedom must undergo the fatigue of supporting it.

Labor without joy is base. Labor without
sorrow is base. Sorrow without labor is base.
- Anon

332. TEAM PLAYING

Always trust your teammates. No matter what. Or you have nothing.
- Eric Cantona

If a herd of twenty buffalo was attacked by a lion, the buffalo would flee. Naturally, the lion would give chase and would catch the slowest buffalo. Now that the lion has eliminated the weakest link, that group of nineteen buffalo remaining is collectively stronger, since the only one removed was the weakest.

A team will always be as strong as its weakest player. The more weak links that are eliminated, the tighter and more competent any group is.

If you find yourself in a team, you must be wary of this. If people are not pulling their weight, they need to be removed before they drag you down. If that weak link is you, you need to find a way to elevate yourself to the standard of your teammates.

Team playing has so many advantages. You work off each other, bounce ideas around, and give each other constructive criticism. Two heads are better than one. Your teammates can see your role as distinct from their roles, so you can have a more rounded understanding of each other's objectives.

Unfortunately, the more people there are in a group, the more likely that there will be arguments.

Team playing is difficult because we like being exceptional. It's hard to know which role you are going to play. Are you just another cog in the machine, or can you lead? Does nobody want to lead, or does everybody want to? Are there too many people or not enough? Whether you are in a group of three, fifty, two hundred, or a million, these problems hover.

Bill Gates and Richard Branson made their fortunes, not because of their subordinates but because of their partners and teammates. They all say that the key is communication, be it for a new idea or to address a problem. In a group, you may feel like your voice is not being heard, or you are given too much responsibility or not enough. If you feel that way, that can affect a group.

The ironic thing about teams is that they are formed to unite us, but this can separate others, who formulate other teams. This happens in sports, companies, and war. If you have one or a hundred competitors, they will grind you into the ground if you can't play along with them, not to mention your own team.

Imagine you are a footballer who hogs the ball so no one can score except you. When the opposition gets the ball off you, no one will pass it to you again because they know you're not a team player. Even if you do score—even if you do achieve your goal in life—it is usually a hollow reward if you stopped everyone in your life from achieving theirs.

Talent wins games, teamwork wins championships.
- Michael Jordan

333. TECHNIQUE

> By concentrating on precision, one arrives at technique, but by
> concentrating on technique, one does not arrive at precision.
> - Bruno Walter

If you are a psychologist, you may fall under the teachings of Jung or Adler. A
magician may be into escape art, sleight of hand, or misdirection. A novelist may
find the approach of stream of consciousness appealing or perhaps prefer a novella.

Techniques help us learn from the best and shape our craft to fit a more defined
and balanced approach.

If we rely on the technique, however, we can become drones. Performers can
walk into performance schools, wow the judicators with their talent, and receive
a place in the school. They can spend years in the school, learning the teachings,
methods, and techniques to fine-tune their talent.

When the students present themselves at the showcase at the end of the course,
the audience may watch an entire class of students performing with the exact same
style that, no matter how good it may seem, lacks the original ability of the actors
that got them a place in the school in the first place.

We should never lose whatever makes us special. It's easy to forget about our
original techniques when we find new knowledge, but we should never underestimate
what we can naturally do.

Elvis was iconic for popping his hips. You'll never read a book that tells you to
do that to improve your singing. But that was what Elvis did.

I'm not suggesting we should dismiss techniques. I'm saying that there are
people that don't need to be taught. They naturally have abilities without training,
books, teachers, workshops, or even an understanding of the concept they are good
at. This concept is called the Hieronymus theory. Some people don't need to know
how they do what they do. They just do it. They can do it better than any normal
person could with a lot of training, reading, and coaching. Some people are just
better equipped from the get-go. We need to find things our way. Techniques can
help hone our own abilities, but we can't rely on them.

Some people spend so much time investing in techniques that they may be
incapable of recognizing raw talent. A movie director auditioned Fred Astaire and
infamously said, "Can't act. Can't sing. Can dance a little."

Just because a so-called expert cannot recognize your potential because it
doesn't follow how they were taught doesn't mean they are right.

Greatness is indefinable. No matter how many books are written about it, no
matter how qualified someone is, and no matter how certain an expert seems to be,
you can't just follow a technique and expect success.

> You can be better than your technique.
> - Dave Brubeck

334. TEMPTATION

Tempt not a desperate man.
- Romeo
(Romeo and Juliet)

Temptation can gnaw at us for hours, days, weeks, months, years, or a lifetime before it sticks its claws into us, and we embrace it.

You may be one of those few who can celebrate the fact that you have avoided all of life's addictions. Just because you don't succumb to an addiction, however, does not mean you have eliminated all potential cravings.

A temptation is simply anything you want to do but shouldn't. You want to give in to temptation for any number of reasons: freedom, lust, money, spontaneity, empowerment, or redemption. You don't want to give in to the temptation because it might compromise your morals, or there could be dire consequences.

My old classmate, Aislinn was religious but questioned the existence of God during hard times. Before Aislinn found God, she associated with a rough crowd, which rubbed off her, compelling her to drugs. Then she found religion, and it ended her addiction.

But she didn't kill the temptation. She didn't deal with it. She just put religion on top of it, like putting a rug over a stain. There is nothing wrong with using religion to become a better person, but you can't ignore your past digressions. Her drug addiction didnt subside until she psychologically dealt with it years later. When she did, the craving vanished.

She had to come to terms with that fact that she turned to God to redeem herself rather than out of the goodness of her heart.

I stopped myself from gambling, but the temptation to go back to it took much longer to go away. Willpower didn't work, but when I asked myself why winning meant so much to me, the impulse to gamble dissipated.

Willpower against temptation is admirable, but it will only get you so far. Temptation can only disappear by dealing with it and asking yourself tough questions.

You may feel like you don't suffer from temptation, but you probably do. You may not give in to it, but you must be aware of temptation, or it can catch you off guard. You can be tempted to break someone's heart, to steal something, to quit your job, to run out on your family, or to leave everything behind you. It's just like every other problem. You can't just acknowledge temptation to you solve it. You need to know why you feel tempted.

Opportunities may knock only once but temptation leans on the doorbell.
- Anon

335. TENSION

One way to break up any kind of tension is good deep breathing.
- Byron Nelson

My friend, Leon is a professional bodybuilder. When he trains with weights, he can lift far more than people twice his size. A lot of muscle-bound people are stiff and inflexible. Leon is lightning quick. So how can he be so big and strong and yet so fast?

Because he lacks tension. When we have to perform a pressurizing or enduring physical task, what is the first thing we do?

We clench. We tense up. It's natural when we are scared or stressed, but it counts against us. It is one of our natural instincts that rarely works in our favor.

When Leon lifts weights, he doesn't clench or tense up. He takes his time. He deduces the exact point of holding a dumbbell or lifting a barbell and pushes his body to the limit without damaging any muscles. He might take a bit longer than most people, but it's better to be ready than to rush and hurt yourself.

Everybody holds tension somewhere. I have it in my shoulders. My shoulders are well developed, which I thought was good, but strong muscles usually beget tension.

Muscles under pressure—intense exercise regimes and painstaking workouts— will make you stronger and more muscular, if that is what you are after, but it will stiffen you up until you lose almost all your flexibility.

Not all tension is physical. If you got bullied a lot in school, you would hold your body in permanent anxiety and strain, like an animal who's about to be hurt. It's like your muscle memory's preparing for a beating that never comes.

You may have this sort of feeling for years. This can build in your body and develop tremendous tension, which can affect your vocal range, posture, and physical ailments in your later life.

It's not an uncommon belief that tension is derived from bad posture or other physical ailments, but it is actually psychological too.

Everyone has self-created apprehension and pressure in his or her body. An easy way to understand where your tension may lie is to ask yourself where your core is.

Where do you feel your center is or the part of your body that you lead with? When you stand still and then start to move, where do you feel your power draw from? It can be from anywhere—feet, arms, fingertips, nose, neck, or chest.

You may not even be aware of where your tension lies. You may need someone to look at you. It's obvious where it lies while observing another person, but it is hard to be aware of one's own tension.

Laughter can help relieve tension in even the heaviest of matters.
- Allen Klein

336. THEORY

It is a capital mistake to theorize before one has data. Insensibly one begins to twist facts to suit theories, instead of theories to suit facts.
- Sherlock Holmes
(A Scandal in Bohemia)

The great detective in literature, Sherlock Holmes, was obsessed with discovering the truth, no matter how easy it was to settle for a more supernatural explanation. Only with theory can we draw what it is real.

New theories come daily. There are new surveys, studies, statistics, techniques, medicines, and philosophies all the time.

People in the scientific world are generating new ideas in the mainstream about cosmetics, war, oil, politics, sex, people, atoms, the universe, religion, God, the mind, relationships, logic, and emotion.

But every idea, no matter how real or unreal it is, always starts as a theory. When a new concept is concocted, any new data can only work within the confines of that theory. Any information that seems to contradict that theory must be dismissed to avoid confusion, even though its intention is to prevent it.

It's only when these contradictions come in abundance, to the point where they overturn the original theory, that they are taken seriously, and they can start a new theory.

Theory becomes fact by trying to disprove it, not by trying to prove it. If you can't disprove it, it becomes fact. There's a modicum of truth in all theories.

There may be a combination of theories amalgamating into one big premise, and they discard elements of the hypotheses that are redundant.

Most people assume Charles Darwin created the evolution theory from scratch, but he was working off another theory. He used examples of Robert Chambers's book, *Vestiges of the Natural History of Creation*, as well as the transmutation theory, to help create his concept.

Most theories must go through a few changes before they become definite—or as definite as they can be for the time being.

Conjectures like evolution or the Big Bang may have gaps or holes in the suppositions as a whole, but that does not mean they're untrue. We must be patient with theories and give them a chance, especially when tackling such a notion as the birth of the universe or the beginning of life.

We need to acknowledge this because society freaks out about new theories. Give theory a chance, but don't label it as a fact until it is.

In theory, there is no difference between
theory and practice, but in practice, there is.
- Anon

337. THERAPY

I think everyone should sit down and write a book.
It's a lot like therapy but a lot less expensive.
- Norma McCorvey

Some people hate therapists because they are not "real doctors." But maybe some people hate therapists because they're more real than any doctor. The body's just a shell. The mind harbors who we really are.

If a client of a therapist gets depressed, people think the therapist is not doing his job. That's like putting a bandage on a kid and suddenly, he's indestructible.

There are some things we believe we cannot trust a friend to know. We need a third party. We need a professional.

But something therapeutic isn't necessarily therapy. Therapy doesn't have to be a counselor. It can be anything that makes you feel peaceful. What's therapy for you? Is it music? Someone listening to you? A pint at the end of a hard day?

You may not know something about yourself until you say it or write it down. It could be there in your mind for a while, even for your whole life, but it doesn't really exist until you give it a voice. When it is acknowledged, it's recognized.

There can be bad therapies as well, such as video games, drink, or even violence. We need to avoid these.

We are so polite as a society that we will not burden others with our problems. We don't want to be a load to someone, or we don't want to be labeled as an attention-seeker or moaner.

A counselor once said to me, "How do you feel when you wake up? What is the first thought that goes through your mind? How does it affect the rest of your day?"

It's like a dream. You probably won't remember your first thoughts, just like you don't remember your dreams. You have no recollection of them even though it just happened, even though it happens daily, and even though it may have a significant effect on you for the rest of the day, if not longer. We get so into a routine that we don't even realize the automatic thinking of the human mind.

Jot down what comes to you, and see what you write down. Or say it aloud. It's okay to ask yourself, "How do I feel?" It's okay for the answer to be, "Not good." If that's the answer, at least you know it. That's half the battle. You will never solve a problem until you acknowledge it.

That's what therapy is—acknowledgement. That's why therapists are so good at unlocking sections of who we are and making us aware of ourselves. But again, this isn't limited to therapists. Lyrics from a song, a line from a movie, meditation—these can force us to acknowledge a great truth within ourselves.

A person is not a vase to be filled, but a fire to be lit.
- Anon

338. TOLERANCE

Acceptance of what has happened is the first step to
overcoming the consequences of any misfortune.
- William James

The first person I knew who openly admitted he was gay was my friend Bobby. He came out of the closet to everyone, and we were all stunned. There was never any hint. He never acted camp, and he had a girlfriend for a year. He'd been flirty with girls since he was in primary school.

Bobby was admired, exceptionally intelligent, amiable, witty, and popular. Most people accepted his homosexuality because it didn't change all of the things we loved about him.

His family, however, were less than pleased. They had narrow-minded opinions of their son and sibling.

But they put up with it. He was their child, after all. They didn't kick him out of the house or anything. He still chats with all of them, still makes jokes, and plays football with his brothers and sisters. But he can't mention to them that he's gay. He can't bring his partners to the house. So what the family did was accept Bobby on their terms, not his. That's not acceptance; that's tolerance.

They were tolerating Bobby's sexuality as if it is a hindrance. They would refer to him as the "black sheep" of the family and would shun his achievements, even though he has accomplished more than any of them.

They refuse to see reason. Bobby was apprehensive that his friends wouldn't accept him. But if that happened, at least his family wouldn't betray him.

It was his friends, however, who gave him support, while his mother and father turned their backs on him and turned their backs on their role as parents.

It's tough to believe people still hold such narrow-minded perceptions on something so harmless. You may disagree with my calling it harmless because many have suffered due to bigotry.

What I mean is that coming out like Bobby did should be harmless. It would be, if people's understanding would broaden a little.

Bobby's fine now, but others aren't so lucky. We can't give in to snobbish ways and think we are being "good people" because we endure those we deem contemptible.

There is nothing special about tolerating the gay community while worrying you might catch something; chatting to foreigners while a parade of racist jokes dances inside of you; being polite to a disabled person while trying not to snigger under your breath; or thinking less of anyone different.

Tolerance isn't enough. Don't aim for anything less than complete acceptance.

Happiness can exist only in acceptance.
- George Orwell

339. TONE

> Wit is the salt of conversation, not the food.
>
> - Anon

Have you ever looked at an old text message and forgotten the tonality? Texting can be confusing because the receiver may misinterpret the message. The words are there, but the intention and intonation behind them may be missed. A joke may come across as an insult. A funny comment may come across as a blunt threat.

Misinterpreting tone is a common misunderstanding. We might give friends some advice, and they might get offended, and you might be confused as to why.

Eighty-five percent of how we communicate is nonverbal. The remaining fifteen percent is not just words but how we say them.

At some point, you've probably offended one of your friends with a joke, simply because of how it sounded. We need to be aware of this because we can be oblivious to how our words are interpreted.

One of my teachers in college had an atrocious way of making his points. Ironically, writing down his teachings on paper sounded like gospel, but when he spoke, he had a monotonous, unsympathetic, snide tone. He just wasn't a people person. Although he always meant well and never truly meant to insult anyone, that is all he did.

If you know how to control your tonality, you can use it to your advantage. Think of all those bad memories of people bullying you with verbal abuse, snide comments, and snappy comebacks.

You can change the psychological trauma of those events by simply altering the tone of the bad memories. Remember a time when you were trying your best at an activity like playing the guitar. Maybe it went badly and the next thing you remember is a bully interrupting with a sarcastic comment like, "Wow, that was absolutely brilliant!" It's not healthy to just dismiss the memory because if it hurt you, that hurt is still there.

What you need to do is say that comment in a dynamic, supportive, and encouraging way. Say it again, "Wow, that was absolutely brilliant!"

"You are so funny!"

"You are amazing!"

Are the comments above genuine or sarcastic? You decide! If they were said with malice, remember them again as spoken with humor. Reverse your negative thinking. Put a funny spin on any inconvenience or insecurity in your past.

> You can say the cleverest, wittiest, passionate, or
> most incredible things. And it counts for nought if you
> don't have the voice behind it to drive the point through.
>
> - Anon

340. TRADITION

I'm just saying that between Jesus dying on the cross and a giant
bunny hiding eggs, there seems to be a gap of information.
- Stan Marsh
(South Park)

Why does tradition exist? Is it to commemorate and remind ourselves of the importance of our beliefs, history, and ancestry? Or do we celebrate it out of convenience?

Is Christmas celebrated to ceremonialize the birth of Christ? Or is it to get presents and get time off school and work?

Some people aren't celebrating the holiday's original purpose. They just go through the motions because it's easier.

Halloween was celebrated by the Celts because they believed it was the day when the dead returned to the world of the living. The Celts would try to appear dead so spirits and ghosts would not attack them. Over generations, this concept turned into wearing scary costumes and trick-or-treating. There is nothing wrong with that. But it is remarkable how we celebrate so much, not knowing how it originated.

New customs and inventions are always being brought in. The 1920s were known as the Roaring Twenties because this was the time when technology moved so fast that tradition started to discontinue. People shed old-fashioned ways to settle for practicality as radio, cinema, and automobiles became plentiful.

A forced loyalty to tradition can hinder. There are some things more important than outdated tradition. People can hide behind tradition. In some countries or cultures, tradition is based on prejudice, sexism, or simply a lack of understanding.

For this reason, you may want to ignore or dismiss traditional values.

If you're an atheist, you may not see the point of Christmas. Or maybe you are a Christian, but you hate the way the holiday has been commercialized to focus more on presents.

You can choose how to celebrate any holiday, or you can choose to not celebrate it, but surely it would be best if you focused on the positive aspects.

Christmas encourages us to be nicer. It brings family and friends closer together. Focusing on aspects like that is better than rejecting it entirely.

Tradition is not a necessity. It is nice to pay your respect to your ancestors' ways, but it is not compulsory. It is a great tool to keep things in check, to remind us what is important, but we shouldn't give in to tradition for the sake of tradition.

Tradition, long conditioned thinking, can bring about a fixation, a concept
that one readily accepts, perhaps not with a great deal of thought.
- Jiddu Krishnamurti

341. TRAGEDY

A tragedy is a representation of an action that is whole and complete and of a certain magnitude. A whole is what has a beginning and middle and end.

- Aristotle

Y ou can build a powerful impression of yourself. You can believe you have made the best of yourself, and you are uncompromisable.

This mentality just leaves us unprepared when the unexpected happens. One day, the whole world seems to be going your way. The next day, a sudden reversal of circumstances can smash every positive thought and perception you ever had.

You and those around you can be struck with illness, disability, mental or physical impairments, depression, or death. It's like being a passenger on a plane going down. You have no control over what's happening. You just sit and watch, and feel completely helpless.

One universal trait of becoming a victim of tragedy is thinking it's not fair because it's not your fault. Tragedy can be completely out of your control, but you have a habit of seeking blame. You choose someone close to you or blame yourself. You become negative, depressed, angry, and hateful; demarcate yourself from reality; and live a warped perception of life or worse.

It is as if you are punishing yourself. Why else would this tragedy happen to you? You may feel like it happened because you deserved it.

But is our capacity for tragedy any greater than anyone else's? Tragedy strikes indiscriminately. It is you who choose how to react to it. The laws of nature have no say in the matter. Nature has no favorites.

Our reaction to tragedy can make or break us. But if we use it for good, not only can we remove all the negativity from our minds, but it also proves that tragedy can be the greatest fuel.

We can become stronger in our darker times, far more than ever in our good times. World War II is considered the darkest time in modern history. What many people don't know is that the United Nations was created as a direct result of the war, to ensure World War III never happens.

The Black Death forced society to improve sanitation immensely. Chernobyl was so devastating that it helped end the Cold War.

Peace can come out of tragedy. Even when you know you're going to get knocked down, you have to stand tall more than ever.

What you choose to do with your next volition, your next move, or your next act will define you.

> Heaven knows we need never be ashamed of our tears for they are
> pain upon the blinding dust of Earth overlaying our hard hearts.
> - Pip
> (Great Expectations)

342. TRAVEL

What an odd thing tourism is. You fly off to a strange land, eagerly
abandoning all the comforts of home, and then expend vast quantities
of time and money in a largely futile attempt to recapture the comforts
that you wouldn't have lost if you hadn't left home in the first place.
- Bill Bryson
(Neither Here Nor There)

Travel helps you develop a broader scope of the world. But how you travel can be just as important.

Will you travel to the neighboring nation, across the seas, to one of those tiny little islands near Fiji, or through a dozen countries in one season? Will you semi-retire abroad or travel around your own country to understand your own heritage?

Des Bishop is a London-born Irish comedian who spent most of his youth in New York. That sentence alone is hard to comprehend in terms of his home.

Although Des Bishop is an Irish comedian, his American accent makes him a target for ridicule. Even in Ireland, he can't escape mockery, even though he is more Irish in blood than anything else.

He has become successful by turning this bigotry into a practical force of entertainment. He has converted his life into comedy material, as well as into a personal drive to learn the Gaelic language, customs, and history. He traveled throughout Ireland to embrace his Gaelic heritage and has learned a lot about the Irish people.

Hundreds of countries, thousands of customs, endless beliefs, countless cultures, umpteen laws, and most important, billions of people are ready to meet you, embrace you, philosophize with you, and debate, challenge, appreciate, and fulfill you. But that can only happen if you pursue them.

The world is so big. You couldn't spend a hundred lifetimes seeing and appreciating every single detail the world has to offer.

It's not just about where you go. It's how you feel when you come back. If you had a good experience abroad, you should take a part of that culture home with you and inaugurate it into your life.

If you had a bad time in your travels, this can help you realize that you don't need to go abroad to fix your problems.

You might go away to get away from the stresses in your life, but you may see people abroad with much more difficult lives, and you will realize that you are actually pretty lucky.

Travel the world to see the world, not to run from it. There's nowhere you can travel where you can't learn something about yourself and the world.

A man travels the world in search of what
he needs and returns home to find it.
- George Moore

343. TRYING

Do or do not. There is no try.
- Yoda
(The Empire Strikes Back)

Usually there are two ways to do something. The first way is to break it down with theory, strategy, structure, and understanding. The alternative way is to just go into the deep end and jump right into it. Depending on the circumstances, both methods are sufficient.

Trying over and over and failing repeatedly calls our methods into question. When we keep failing, we need to sit down and reflect on our methods.

But we can use our analyses as a shield, an excuse to give the impression that we are doing work yet never fulfilling the experience.

We stop trying when our methods don't give us the results we want, but that's only if the method is primitive. There is a difference between a simple solution and a primitive one.

When we start a new activity, we may get frustrated if we don't find it easy. We tend to defend ourselves by saying, "I'm trying!"

That's good because trying means we are making an effort. But that may not be enough. It's like when you see a comedian who tries to be funny; it's never as funny as someone who is natural and effortless with his humor.

The harder we try, the less we seem to achieve. If we try over and over to accomplish our goals, we assume we will eventually accomplish them.

If you do the same thing repeatedly with the same results, reconsider your approach rather than succumbing to unhelpful repetition and unnecessary overexertion. You need to analyze your progress and keep trying, but never rely too heavily on either tactic.

Some even get sick of trying and try to cheat or shortcut their way to the top. Shortcuts are always longer. If a shortcut was shorter, it would be the real path.

If you cheat, you lose anyway. But if you lose properly, you can accept it and become better enough to win another day.

Arnold Schwarzenegger promised he would become Mr. Universe and Mr. Olympia in bodybuilding, a Hollywood movie star, and the governor of California. He had a simple philosophy during his bodybuilding days, which was a philosophy he carried in all his professions. He believed that doing one rep once with concentration was worth more than doing ten reps while distracted. There is no point in trying unless you are going to try to your full potential.

"Trying" has the potential to fail written into its definition. When you start a new activity, you are not expected to succeed. You are only expected to try. But with time, you will stop "trying" and start "doing."

Give us the tools and we will get the job done.
- Winston Churchill

344. UNCONSCIOUS

A life lived of choice is a life of conscious action.
A life lived of chance is a life of unconscious creation.
- Neale Donald Walsch

"**F**orget mind over matter. A better phrase is mind and matter in unity."
Professional hypnotherapist, Tom Ryan said that to me at one of his seminars.
He taught me the power of the conscious, unconscious, and subconscious mind.

The conscious mind has four tasks:
1. Analyze—finding pros and cons to all scenarios and figuring them out.
2. Rational—give reasons to action.
3. Will Power—force yourself to start/complete tasks.
4. Short-Term Memory—learn from past mistakes and successes.

The unconscious mind also has four tasks.
1. Self-Preservation—Your unconscious mind's top priority is to protect you from danger. It can be real (physical threat, mockery, failure) or unreal (irrational fear, paranoia, future problem).
2. Habits—biting nails when nervous, pulling hair when scared, biting lip when bored; addictions.
3. Emotion—unresolved anger, hate, or fear.
4. Long-Term Memory

What causes so much misunderstanding with our own mind is this: we deal with unconscious problems through conscious means. We don't understand that they are completely different sections of the brain. It's like trying to understand how a car works by using mathematics.

To stop smoking is almost impossible through conscious means. If you use unconscious means, it can be done. Simply saying to yourself, "Don't smoke don't smoke" won't work, because your unconscious mind just picks up the word, "smoke smoke smoke."

We love doing things we are told not to do. Think of absolutely anything in the whole world except an elephant in a top hat. Can you do that? Thought not!

Hypnotism is the best window into your unconscious mind and discovering the source of your unconscious insecurities and limitations.

Behavior therapy statistically has a 72 percent success rate after twenty-two sessions (That's six months).

Hypnotherapy has up to a 93 percent success rate in only six sessions, especially for addictions and phobias.

You may feel skeptical about these kinds of therapies, but if the conventional methods didn't work, why not try an unconventional method?

All forms of self-defeating behavior are unseen and
unconscious, which is why their existence is denied.
- Vernon Howard

345. UNDERESTIMATE

> A common mistake that people make when trying to design something
> completely foolproof is to underestimate the ingenuity of complete fools.
> - Douglas Adams

In chess, players need to protect the king. However, the queen is the most powerful chess piece and will do what she can to ensure her survival, as well as the survival of the king. Then the rooks, bishops, and knights come after that in terms of importance.

New players don't realize how important the pawn is. This piece can be forgotten and miscounted, so players concentrate on the big guns. They don't realize that the pawn is still in the game, gradually making its way toward the end. If you keep it for long enough, it'll get to the top and become the most powerful piece in the game.

The Wright brothers took flight on December 17, 1903. They flew ten feet above the ground, travelling 853 feet for fifty-nine seconds. Some would have seen it as a failure because the flight couldn't be maintained. But they just saw it as the first attempt and tried again.

When Howard Hughes broke the flight-speed record, the first thing he said was, "It can still go faster."

These examples are overused and obvious because we have seen their success. Let's use a current example of underestimation: the Large Hadron Collider, the biggest machine ever built. The day this sixteen-mile mechanism was turned on in 2008, countless people complained that it was a useless machine that never accomplished anything—a waste of money, and a danger to the planet. When the first test malfunctioned, it proved society's grumblings and pessimism.

What people don't realize is that the Hadron Collider has already accomplished something: fighting cancer.

For this machine to work, it has advanced particle physics more than any medical equipment in history. This has advanced every medical scanning machine—MRI scans, X-rays, CT scans, positron radioactive tomography, etc. The ability to detect cancer; figure out where it's going, how long it's been there, and how detrimental it is; and predict the cancer's next action and how to counter it is all owed to the Collider.

The reason the Collider is underestimated is the same reason anything or anyone is underestimated: it is misunderstood. You can be underestimated for being short, old, foreign—don't let it get to you. It's unfair to be underestimated, but you should never underestimate yourself, or you will prove everyone right.

> Never underestimate the power of a simple tool.
> - Craig Bruce

346. UNDERSTANDING

The crown of life is neither happiness nor annihilation, it is understanding.
- Winifred Holtby

In school, we have to cram information for tests and to improve our intellect. It's incorrect to force anyone to be drilled with information. Students only know their schoolwork because it's been shoved in. They don't "learn it" per se, any more than a computer learns a song just because a CD is put in its hard drive.

Of course you retain information when it's crammed. You may still know silly rhymes to help you memorize mathematics or all the states in America.

But there is clearly something automatic about it. It isn't fun. It is even less fun when you don't understand the concepts you have been forced to memorize throughout your life.

Just because you don't understand how something works as a mechanism, a symbol, or as an idea doesn't mean you can't be affected or benefit by it.

Most of us cannot comprehend the process that is carried out to create a computer, the clothes we wear, or how a matchstick works to ignite. But we can use them anyway.

If you wanted to know how a computer worked and you asked a programmer, a manufacturer, a seller, a user, and a hacker; you would get totally different answers.

The answers you get will not be necessarily wrong or contradictory. The people you asked would just have a different perception of understanding. We all have different levels of understanding, with religion, the future, goals, ideas, and everything else.

Does a businessman in a corporation know all the ins and outs of every facet that makes a company? Does he know the personal life of every worker in the building? Does he know how the building he works in was made?

No. He doesn't have to. He knows what he needs to know.

That doesn't mean we should discard things we don't understand. Trying to understand it can have the greatest effect imaginable. Edward Jenner was a country doctor in 1796. He didn't understand why an individual who contracted the harmless disease, cowpox, never contracted the lethal disease, smallpox.

No one understood this, but Jenner was the only person who tried to understand. His observation led to the creation of the first, vaccination and the eventual eradication of smallpox.

Just because you don't understand something doesn't mean it's wrong. There have been many concepts that were cast aside for centuries before they were accepted. Some are still misunderstood. And there are many more to come.

The dust of exploded beliefs may make a fine sunset.
- Geoffrey Madan

347. THE UNIVERSE

To make an apple pie from scratch, you must first invent the universe.
- Albert Einstein

There is a famous picture titled *The Pale Blue Dot*. You may have seen this image and not understood its significance. (If you haven't seen it, please look it up online right now!)

It is an image of black space with a tiny blue dot in the middle. It is said to be one of the most significant photographs ever, and I couldn't understand why.

Then I read what Carl Sagan, astronomer and winner of twenty-eight scientific awards, said about it. You will never read a better encapsulation of the human race or Earth or life than this single summary below:

"We succeeded in taking that picture, and, if you look at it, you see a dot. That's here. That's home. That's us. On it, everyone you ever heard of, every human being who ever lived, lived out their lives. The aggregate of all our joys and sufferings, thousands of confident religions, ideologies and economic doctrines, every hunter and forager, every hero and coward, every creator and destroyer of civilizations, every king and peasant, every young couple in love, every hopeful child, every mother and father, every inventor and explorer, every teacher of morals, every corrupt politician, every superstar, every supreme leader, every saint and sinner in the history of our species, lived there on a mote of dust, suspended in a sunbeam.

The earth is a very small stage in a vast cosmic arena. Think of the rivers of blood spilled by all those generals and emperors so that in glory and in triumph they could become the momentary masters of a fraction of a dot.

Think of the endless cruelties visited by the inhabitants of one corner of the dot on scarcely distinguishable inhabitants of some other corner of the dot.

How frequent their misunderstandings, how eager they are to kill one another. Our posturing, our imagined self-importance, the delusion that we have some privileged position in the universe, are challenged by this point of light.

Our planet is a speck in the great enveloping cosmic dark. In our obscurity, there is no hint that help will come from elsewhere to save us from ourselves. It is up to us. It's been said that astronomy is a humbling, and I might add, a character-building experience. To my mind, there is perhaps no better demonstration of the folly of human conceits than this distant image of our tiny world.

To me, it underscores our responsibility to deal more kindly with one another and to preserve and cherish that pale blue dot, the only home we've ever known."

The fact that we live at the bottom of a deep gravity well,
on the surface of a gas covered planet going around a nuclear
fireball ninety million miles away and think this is normal is
some indication of how skewed our perspective tends to be.
- Douglas Adams

348. USELESS

Nature abhors a vacuum.
- Francois Rabelais

If you look at a group—your family, your friends, your classmates, your work colleagues—you can see them as being the Group Who Does _____.

When a group has a common goal, we tend to break the team down so each person is in charge of certain things, which will help them collectively achieve their objective. We can see each other with some distinctive duty that makes them stick out.

It's hard to look at yourself from a third point of view and see what your role is. As a result, you may assume that you don't have anything to contribute to the group. You may appear useless.

Isn't it frustrating when one of your friends makes a reference that everyone understands except you? Or if everyone has a moment to shine, and you are left out to dry? Or when everyone has been to a place you have never heard of?

You may feel like you cannot compare to anyone else because they may be stronger, faster, or more successful than you.

A time will come when you will be the exact right person for the exact right time. My friend, Ben learned first aid while the rest of his friends went off partying in the Ibiza. He didn't have the money to go on the trip, and he felt left out.

Two weeks after he finished the first-aid course, a man walked by Ben and had a heart attack. He fell and smacked his head on a concrete corner of the pavement. Nobody else was around who knew CPR so Ben had no choice but to perform chest compressions until an ambulance arrived. The paramedics said it was a close call, and the man might not have made it if it hadn't been for Ben.

First aid is one of those things that you may never have to use in a desperate situation, but if the scenario presented itself, it can decide whether a person lives or dies.

I have seen amazing artists, actors, dancers, and singers give such incredible performances, but they feel like they are worthless because they don't have a real job.

They may use this feeling to fuel their work, especially in a play or telling a story that has themes of hopelessness. So they make their uselessness useful!

You are never useless. You may feel it. You may have blips. You may become misdirected, lazy, or go backwards. But you have just as much ability as anyone else to be amazing.

Man is the only creature that consumes without producing.
- George Orwell

349. VIOLENCE

Abel started it.
- Cain

Every generation has made us more civilized. Centuries ago, violence was widespread. Nowadays, it has diminished and seen as a last resort. Many of us rarely experience violence, either delivering it or receiving it.

Even in law, in the direst life-or-death situations, police forces are leaning to using nonlethal force, like rubber bullets and batons.

Violence has the same origin as anger—losing control. We can use it rationally to defend ourselves or use it irrationally out of frustration or desperation. Whether we use violence for rational or irrational reasons, we use it because we believe we are retaining control and order. But violence nearly always creates disorder.

You may feel that it's unavoidable at times, but we always have a choice. *Ferdinand the Bull* tells the story of a bull that chose to smell roses over fighting. Matadors would challenge him in the ring and entice him with taunts, but he refused to take part. A childish example, it may seem, but Munro Leaf wrote his story during the Spanish Civil War to show that we can choose to fight. Just because we are surrounded by violence doesn't justify our being a part of it.

If you speak English, and you are talking to a Korean, you are not simply going to adapt to Korean. You'll try speaking English, knowing the other person can't understand you, no matter how loudly you shout. You do it because it's the only language you speak. Violence is a language you force others to learn because you don't know how to communicate any other way.

Just because violence is a part of us doesn't mean it's necessary or practical. It is one of many parts of our biology and instincts that is dying out.

Through evolution, we are finding ways to replace these primal instincts that are no longer effective in today's modern society. Instead of violence, we are generating knowledge, debate, compromise, and common ground as a wiser alternative.

Some people claim to fight so we don't have to fight. Fighting for peace or respect or honor puts us at the opposing side of our intentions. We need to live in a world with nothing else to conquer. Only the weak succumb to brutality. Fights start over ideas, then morals, then people, then ownership, and then countries, but we are always fighting over the same thing—nothing.

Meet with open arms, not thrashing fists. Force is never a remedy.

The supreme act of war is to subdue the enemy without fighting.
- Sun Tzu
(The Art of War)

350. VOICE

Be silent unless your speech is better than silence.
- Salvator Rosa

When I was a kid, I was curious about the voice changing when someone hit puberty. The idea of speaking differently forever fascinated me.

However, I never realized, until I reached adulthood, that the voice never stops changing. I don't mean the accent; I mean we change how we use our voice. Some people speak from the backs of their throats or right behind their teeth, but we all change where the sound comes from throughout our lives. Why?

You may have a strong voice, but you may suffer a bad break-up. This knocks your confidence. Depending on how badly you take it, this might not be temporary. Knocks like this can affect your confidence, your posture, and even your voice. People will think you're shy. Eventually, you will be.

Others may have the completely opposite problem. One of my friends, Sobchak, has a loud, aggressive voice. He is not aggressive at all, but he sounds scary, even if he asks you the most innocent question. Your voice may come across as snide, smug, or sarcastic, even if you are being genuine.

What if people just don't listen to you? What can you do to gather their attention? Talk louder? No. That's shouting. Effortless articulation, enunciation, and projection are what you should be striving for.

Have you ever heard someone whose voice can effortlessly be heard from the other side of the room? That's not luck. Anyone can do that. You just need to be aware of your habits. You need to distinguish between your vocal habits and your accent.

One of my friends had to sing an extremely emotional song for a play. He wasn't a natural singer and had severe articulation problems. He especially didn't want to sing the song because it was too close to home.

But I had the great honor of witnessing my good friend belt out this song to a full audience, making them burst into floods of tears. He didn't have any experience in singing whatsoever.

So how did he do it? Because what he was singing about meant everything to him. What he sang about resembled his life. That connection, that shared experience, that level of passion came out of him like a thunderbolt when he sang.

After that song, he always had a higher level of confidence when he spoke. He just needed to find something worth speaking about.

If you care what you are talking about, so will people around you. If you don't have any belief in what you say, neither will anyone else.

The human voice can never reach the distance that is
covered by the still small voice of conscience.
- Mahatma Gandhi

351. WAITING

Waiting is still an occupation. It's having nothing to wait for that is terrible.
- Cesare Pavese

Imagine you are waiting for a train at a station, eager to get home. There are dozens of trains coming and going all the time on every platform. There is no monitor that tells you which platform you need to be at or what time your train is coming. You may need to ask a few people and hazard a guess as to which is your train. You make your decision and finally get to the stop where your train will arrive. Then you wait. You wait, and you wait, and eventually, the train at your stop comes in.

Now there is just one more thing you need to do to ensure you get home. You have to get on.

It's all well and good when the right opportunity comes along, but it's pointless if you're too lazy to get on board. A real opportunity isn't like a big train. It's not as obvious.

All the platforms and trains are allegorical to the confusion we feel when we are offered an opportunity. We don't even know if it is the right one! If you get on the wrong train, you can get further away from home. If you choose the wrong opportunity, you can waste time and money.

If you are waiting for the right opportunity, how can you guarantee that you will know when it comes along? An offer may appear like a great opportunity, but it may be a scam. Or you might get offered a small opportunity that leads to greater and better things, but this can never come to be if you don't try.

One of my favorite phrases of all time is this: Trying to be successful without putting yourself out there is like winking at somebody in the dark; you know what you're doing but nobody else does.

You need to get out there to be seen. Goals start with wishing, but wishing itself never gets to the final goal. You must take the first step yourself. Think of all your intended goals and dreams. How many have you acted on? We get so busy that we hope that a handful of opportunities just fall into place. But this is never the case. I know those who turn down offer after offer because they are holding out for something bigger.

They don't realize that there are times when you must take what you get. We can't start at the top. Refusing to do a bit of grunt work can be a form of snobbery. There are some jobs you won't want to do. But you will have to do them to get to the jobs you do want. If you expect things to happen, you will never make them happen. A reliance on random events never has a good chance of success.

All men commend patience, although few are willing to practice it.
- Thomas Kempis

352. WALLOW

There is no greater pain than to remember a happy time when one is in misery.
- Dante Alighieri

The biggest trap that actors can fall into is "playing the state." This means that if you're an angry character in a play, you play angry. If you are evil, you play evil, rather than playing a flesh-and-blood character with wants, needs, relationships, goals, and dreams, just like everybody else.

The reason why this doesn't help an actor is because no one ever thinks, "I am going to be evil now" or "I have to be angry here." I'm not just talking about acting but in real life.

One big exception where we do think like this is self-pity. In acting, we call it "Poor Me." My tutors would tell us off if we played a character as a Poor Me because it's overindulgent and not real, and so, it's not considered good acting. People do think like, however, when they wallow:

"My life is horrible!"

"I can't go on!"

"I hate my life!"

Trust me—I've been there. When my father became terminally and my wife got ill just before our wedding, I had moments like this. Like a kid who won't come out of his room, I would have a tantrum to make a point that no one understood, including me.

We wallow when we don't get enough empathy or understanding for our problems. Wallowing has one characteristic in common with anger; we cannot burn it out. We cannot build up immunity by using it. Wallowing doesn't weaken; it feeds itself. Wallowing begets more wallowing. It's not like nurturing; it's more like giving a parasite or a virus the sustenance it needs to survive.

A parasite needs a host to suck life off. If you allow it, it will grow bigger and bigger. Over time, it will take control over you and become harder and harder to remove because it's too powerful, and its appetite will become insatiable.

The only way to get rid of it is to starve it. If you don't give into it, it will dry up. So if you feel like wallowing, even for a second, get yourself out of the rut.

Jump into the deep end of reality. If you are afraid of failing again, getting hurt, or being used, that's life!

Go outside and explore the world. Remind yourself why there is so much good in it. When you're miserable, you will get sympathy. But if you keep at it, you will reach a point where no one cares, so you might as well be happy. Don't become a part of what can destroy you.

There is an eagle in me that wants to soar, and there is a
hippopotamus in me that wants to wallow in the mud.
- Carl Sandburg

353. WALLS

A lunatic cannot put out the sun by scribbling the
word, 'darkness' on the walls of his cell.
- C. S. Lewis

We build walls throughout our lives. Walls have many purposes; some of them are premeditated and some unintended. They sanction a solid foundation, they're strong, and they're hard to knock down.

We put up walls when we meet new people, when we're nervous on a first date, when we are being secretive, or when we are pretending we are unhurt by heartbreak. Walls can be there for protection but more often than not, they have a different purpose: they hide.

If you ask a troubled friend if she is okay, she'll probably say, "Yeah. Fine." That's a wall. Not going to a party because you "don't feel like it" can be a wall. Your partner dumps you with no notice, and you just shrug it off. Maybe you are just taking the break-up well, but it's much more likely you are screaming inside. Just because we can't see what's behind the wall doesn't mean it's not there.

I'm not suggesting smashing the walls down in your life. Some walls have been built up for so long that all the gunk in your life will come out too fast, and that's hard to control. When I had my first panic attack, I assumed it was a one-time event because I just needed to get it out of my system.

But my body had other plans (as did my mind, for that matter). Since I knocked down a massive wall in my life, all the bad residue and junk that stuck with me in my life came out all at once. I was bashed with attack after attack, boring deeper and deeper into my mind and memory. Every bad thought, emotion, and memory had built up for over a decade, and they came out in one burst, leaving me shell-shocked.

It was like my wall exploded, and it was taking time for my mind to build another one. That's what I wanted to do—build another wall. It would be stronger, but at the end of the day, it's just another wall. That's not therapeutic. The higher you build a wall, the more likely it will come crashing down on top of you and everyone else.

What I needed was to build a door in that wall, so I could open it to let people in, let myself go out, and show the real inner me to the world. If I needed time to myself, I would close the door. Having it closed all the time is not healthy. You don't have to stay behind the wall with your inner demons. You can get out into the big, scary world, and see what it has to offer.

In the end, it all comes to choices to turn
stumbling blocks into stepping stones.
- Amber Frey

354. WANTS

Fantasies have to be unrealistic. Because the second that you get
what you want, you don't- you can't- want it anymore.
- David Gale
(The Life Of David Gale)

Life is not about what you want but what you have. It does not matter what you
want, you will always grow tired of it, but you cannot grow tired of a need.

My housemate, Neil always complained that he couldn't chat to women. This
was one of the many reasons he claimed to be depressed. After a lot of trial and
error, he eventually got much better at talking to women and ended up getting with
a random girl every night.

But this wasn't enough. He wanted more. He wanted to have the intimacy of
a woman, and he was ready for a relationship. Again, there were a few misses, but
there was one girl he really wanted. Eventually, he won her heart.

His dream had come true, or at least it would have if he had accepted it. He said
he didn't want to be tied down, and so he cheated on her. As the months passed, he
kept moaning that he didn't have a girlfriend.

Wants are not needs. They are not as fulfilling as you might think. Often when
you get what you want, you immediately want something else.

We've seen it in toddlers when they want to play with a something because they
are not allowed to. Once they are allowed, they throw it away.

There are things that you want now that you may think you absolutely cannot
do without—an iPhone. A better job. A new house. A new life.

It is the oldest trick in the book. When you get what you want, you will get a
buzz. This buzz will last from a couple of seconds to a few weeks—maybe even a
month or two, if you're lucky—and then it's gone. You need to fill that hole with
something else.

American writer, Joan Didion said, "When we start deceiving ourselves into
thinking not that we want something or need something, not that it is a pragmatic
necessity for us to have it, but that it is a moral imperative that we have it, then is
when we join the fashionable madmen, and then is when the thin whine of hysteria
is heard in the land, and then we are in trouble."

When you cherish what you have, you see the true value of things, not just
lustful desires, or flashy technology but good friends, loving partners, loyal family,
and reliable people in your life.

Everything you need isn't everything you want.

The Rum Tum Tugger is a Curious Cat:
If you set him on a mouse then he only wants a rat,
If you set him on a rat then he'd rather chase a mouse.
-T.S. Eliot
(Old Possum's Book of Practical Cats)

355. WAR

It's easier to make war than to make peace.
- Georges Clemenceau
(Discours de Paix)

Sun Tzu said, "Victorious warriors win first and then go to war. Defeated warriors go to war first and then seek to win."

The worst thing about war is that it's so big but the idea behind it is so small. Wars aren't against armies but ideas. We need to find a middle ground rather than bombard each other with bombs, dogma, and forced propaganda.

Although you may think that now is the worst time in the world for war, it is gradually getting better. Mankind has always been covered in bloodshed. In the past two millennia there have been approximately 250 years of relative peace. That's eight percent of two thousand years.

You may think the world has gone to hell with constant wars. As soon as one ends, another seems to begin. But remember that at no point in history has war not been a part of civilization. But there is less war in society every day.

War is all that is offered in a world in desperate need of healing. We only go to war because we don't think there is any other way of making a difference.

But we do know how to make a difference, and we have. It's not the obvious ideas we have had hammered into us for years. It's a nice thought to end all war with peace and love, but we need something more practical and physical.

One of many examples would be England and France, who battled for eight hundred years but have stopped in the last century.

Why? Compromise. Or a more understandable word: money. Instead of killing each other for something they are not sure they want or not certain they will get, they just trade their imports and exports in the European Union.

This "answer" may seem a little anticlimactic, but as England and France proved, among dozens of other rivalries, you can't argue with the results.

If you want something from someone, rather than bully or fight, come to a reasonable deal. There is a lot less bloodshed, and it's more likely that both of you will get what you want.

There are those who are unfazed by war or don't comprehend its magnitude. You see it on television, but it's never real until you're knee-deep in it.

Don't fight wars; prevent them. The opposite of war isn't peace; it's creation. You can't end lives to save them. If you declare war on others, you declare war on yourself. As Omar Bradley said, "The way to win a war is to make certain it never starts."

Alexander the Great....when he had conquered what was called
the Eastern World...wept of more Worlds to conquer.
- Isaac Watts

356. WARP

But if thought corrupts language, language can also corrupt thought.
- George Orwell

You think you have met the best guy in the world, and he promised you the world. Then he left without telling you. Why? Because all men are pigs.

You work harder than anyone at work, and you are barely making ends meet. That new lazy delinquent has gotten a promotion because his father is a friend of the manager. Of course, they didn't think of you. After all, life is cruel.

If something bad happens to us—if an event occurs that conflicts with how we think, how we were raised, how we perceive life—we can get a "Does Not Compute" message in our mind, and we may try to make sense of the absurd.

We try to analyze bad luck, tragedy, and death, not understanding that we do not have control of every factor of life. But we might force it to make sense and drive ourselves mad in the process.

This can work a lot more subtly than you would think. I have friends that do not believe in homosexuality. I know someone who doesn't believe in heterosexuality! Those misunderstandings don't stem from tragedy or indoctrination. They come from misunderstanding or misinterpretation. You can't look at biology in a general way and then dismiss it. Dismissing concepts stems from a lack of understanding them.

If you try to understand them, there is a lot less conflict. If not, time will be your enemy. If you are prone to being dismissive, naïve, or hostile, time tends to distort these negative aspects even further.

It's a lot easier to warp a person's perception of life than you might think. There are so many aspects of history that were acceptable at the time, like slavery. The idea of an alternative way of living was illogical.

Maybe there is a way we are living right now that will be considered unacceptable in the future, but we haven't realized it yet, because we haven't reached that level of mental maturity as a generation.

Over time, a warped perception can be dangerous. That individual may see this warped perception of reality as the real reality and convince others that we can't see the big picture. In times of great difficulty, thoughts like this seep in. If you catch them quickly enough, you can avoid long-term damage. If not, you can get ideas that, once you think them, are difficult to unthink.

"Everyone is against me."

"It's everybody's fault but mine."

"Trust no one."

You can always trust yourself, but only if you allow yourself to do so and if you don't give in to insecurity and weakness.

All things can corrupt when minds are prone to evil.
- Ovid

357. WASTING TIME

What's not destroyed by Time's devouring hand? Where's Troy?"
- James Bramstom

We hate wasting time. Be it a few seconds on rewriting a text or waiting for a bus in the rain. We wait years for our partners to change before we give up on them, or we wait for a sign that there is more to life than the here and now.

I got on the wrong train yesterday. Wasted an hour. I was fuming. It put me in a foul mood for most of the day.

But just today, I met up with my friend, Zara. She was born into a cult. When she was twenty-five, she realized how false and dogmatic it was, and she left.

She believed she'd wasted her entire life believing what she was forced to believe. She had a difficult time for months after she left, but she recovered over time.

While chatting with her, I realized how levelheaded she was, and I couldn't believe I was in a mood because I'd wasted one hour the day before. She wasted twenty-five years, and she reacted more maturely.

One of my best friends broke up with her boyfriend recently. She felt like she had wasted two years of her life.

The reality is that most relationships don't end well. When they end, you will feel like the time you spent together counted for nothing.

When she speaks like this, she acts like she has literally lost two whole years of her life, rather than just the time spent with her partner. Her relationship didn't end well, but it can't have been a complete waste of time.

If you have found yourself in a similar situation, you need to recognize that you will change a lot in two years. You need to ask questions. How have you changed for the better? In what ways have you changed for the worse? What have you learned from this bad experience? Are you going allow it to affect you?

Delays with trains or being late for work are just minor inconveniences. They are pet peeves. They're part of life, and they are unavoidable.

The big time-wasters—the years, the decades wasted on the wrong guy or girl—amount to experience. That may sound like sugarcoating, but why get in a huff about something that has already happened?

You can't undo it, but you can make sure you never do it again. You wasted two years with a partner. Learn from it. Make sure whatever didn't work doesn't happen again. If you don't learn from it, then it's a waste of time.

It's like missing a lesson in school and then having to catch up. But these aren't ordinary lessons. They are life lessons. If you don't learn, then you pay. How long do you have to be in a bad situation before you leave?

Time has no divisions to mark its passage; there is never a thunderstorm or blare of trumpets to announce the beginning of a new month. Even when a new century begins it is only we mortals who ring bells and fire off pistols.
- Thomas Mann

358. WEAKNESS

When weak, pretend to be strong. When strong, pretend to be weak.
- Sun Tzu

The strongest thing people can do is admit they are weak. You can do this by accepting you have an addiction, coming to grips with your sexuality, or unveiling a self-inflicted scar.

You may feel like the whole world will laugh at you. But we are usually welcomed with open arms. We are not laughed at but commended. Vulnerability is not weakness but strength.

Who knows? You may have more people that understand you than you think. I didn't even know what a panic attack was before I had one. It turns out that one in three people have had at least one panic attack in their lives, and I had dozens of friends who empathized with me.

You might think you are strong by holding back your problems. That is denying a problem. That's running away. That's real weakness. Why would anyone act that way except because they feel the opposite?

To admit you're vulnerable means you have accepted you can be hurt, and you have been hurt. It's embarrassing at first, but it gets easier every time.

But what if people see you as weak because you are short, fat, or stupid?

You can turn any aspect of yourself against people by making them underestimate you. Let me explain.

Each fighting style represents a different philosophy, but most of them revolve around turning your opponent's strength into a weakness. If he's big, use speed. If he's heavy, use his weight against him.

One of the most interesting styles is Drunken Fist. This fighting style gives the impression that the fighter is drunk, uncoordinated, off balance, and weak.

That is the intention. The fighter lulls the opponent into a false sense of security, so he will be easier to defeat. Defenselessness is a hidden offense. Hands, which seem to swing aimlessly, are ready to grab an opponent. Fighters look off balance when they are prepared to strike.

It works similarly to the Rope a Dope technique, which allows the opponent to become overconfident and overexerted, while you conserve energy and wait for the opponent to tire.

That's when you pounce. I've seen people win tons of money in poker because they pretended they'd never played, so everyone went easy on them.

I've seen actors pretend to be underprepared in auditions, and then they blew everyone away in their performance.

Weakness is opinion. We can turn it into our greatest strength.

Although men are accused of not knowing their own weakness,
yet perhaps few know their own strength.
- Jonathan Swift

359. WEIGHT

The first wealth is health.
- Ralph Waldo Emerson

There are three body size templates:
1. Ectomorphic—a person who is skinny and doesn't put on muscle or fat easily
2. Endomorphic—a person who is naturally big and puts on fat easily
3. Mesomorphic—a person who is naturally muscular and puts on muscle easily

O f all the sizes to be, being overweight has the worst stigma.
Big people may eat excessively, but that means that, although they are having an excess of carbohydrates, proteins, fats, and vitamins; they are still getting their bodies' requirements.

Although excess is not ideal, it's better than depriving yourself of a natural source of sustenance. Too much water makes you bloated. No water makes you die!

If you are skinny but have a bad diet, you may convince yourself you are healthier than an overweight person. But an overweight person who regularly exercises is proven to be healthier than a skinny person who doesn't exercise.

If you want to be healthy, organize yourself, and develop a system before you start. This is vital. Most people who blindly start dieting or exercising without any preparation don't last more than a couple of weeks.

Some people are so big, they don't think it's physically possible to lose weight without surgery. I don't see how sticking metal prongs and having fat sucked out of your body is going to do wonders for your self-confidence.

My friend, Dave weighed 336 pounds. He wanted the main role in a musical, but the director said he was too heavy. So Dave gave it his all.

But is willpower enough? He couldn't run. His knees couldn't take the pressure. So do you know what he did?

He went dancing! He went clubbing six nights a week for six hours and lost 110 pounds in eight months.

By this time, the show had come and gone, but there was an even juicier role waiting for Dave in another musical. He auditioned and got the part, and he's been doing well since in his acting career and his well-being.

For those who believe they are too busy to exercise, check out Bill Phillips's *Body for Life*. It's a diet and exercise regime created for those who don't have the time to stay healthy. You never have to work out more than fifty minutes a day. With this diet and workout, I lost 42 pounds in three months and reduced my body fat from 21 percent to 10 percent. Give it a look. What's stopping you? If you procrastinate, you can't shed the weight.

The first law of dietetics seems to be if it tastes good, it's bad for you.
- Isaac Asimov

360. WILLPOWER

The greatest revolution of our generation is the discovery
that human beings, by changing the inner attitudes of their
minds, can change the outer aspects of their lives.
- William James

Abulia is to experience an absolute loss of willpower. It's horrible when you feel like you are incapable of doing anything right. We all experience it at some point in our lives, even those who succeed. Even Fred Smith.

Frederick Smith wrote a paper in economics class discussing an idea that overnight deliveries would become the norm in the future. He was given a C grade because his idea, although well-conceived, was infeasible.

Fred received quite a knock to his confidence, but he refused to give up. His idea was infeasible, but only at the time. He willed his idea into existence by founding FedEx. His idea changed the world.

Willpower works both physically and mentally. Mike Tyson was always a fighter, but he started off as a thug, getting into scraps that put him in juvenile prison for half of his youth. Yet, he was the champion of the World Boxing Council, World Boxing Association, and International Boxing Federation simultaneously, and reigned as world heavyweight champion at the age of nineteen.

He accomplished this thanks to his trainer, Constantin "Cus" D'Amato. Tyson knew how to fight, so what could Cus possibly have taught him? In the first week, he just talked to Tyson. Cus didn't train him physically until the week after. When he did, every time Tyson got tired or wanted to quit, Cus repeatedly shout to him, "Your mind is not in your way."

It wasn't just a lifetime of brutal brawls or big muscles that made Tyson a champion. What made the difference in the end was a constructive mentality and a few pounds of gray matter. That's the only muscle that matters. A correct mentality can be a better tool for success than anything else.

We all want to believe in ourselves, and it is difficult to juggle having self-belief and not being delusional and arrogant with unrealistic goals.

I think the difference is actually taking steps to make your dream become a reality. Rather than just wishing it, you need to ask, "What am I going to do to achieve this goal? What is the first step? What is the hardest step? What's the contingency? Is there an alternative? What are my hindrances?" These may be questions you don't want to ask yourself, but those who achieve always ask tough questions.

The whole is more than the sum of the parts.
- Aristotle

361. WISDOM

I rather like those books where chapters begin with a quotation.
- Ramsey Dukes

There are two kinds of wisdom. There is the wisdom we see in phrases, quotes, and famous anecdotes from heroes, actors, militants, celebrities, inventors, politicians, fighters, warriors, and comedians.

Then there is the wisdom we receive from those in our own lives. It can be from a friend, the dying words of an old relative, even a stranger passing by in a fleeting moment. I find this kind of wisdom more significant, for it is within our own lives.

We all have messages we live by—quotes from Aristotle, Socrates, Shakespeare, and many others—which are a great driving force in our trials in life.

When the going gets tough, and we are in dire need of help, often one close to us will impart to us some moving and astute words, and those words can make all the difference.

There is an automatic respect for the elderly, as they are meant to be the ones to display wisdom to the younger generations, be it a sage or a grandparent. We go through all these problems at twenty, thirty, or forty and act as though our whole world has collapsed on us, and we cannot pull through.

But then we see the older groups who had all the same limitations, bad luck, and grief. They got by. Maybe they have a few words that can help us.

When going through tragedies in my life, I heard a lot of great quotes about fear, anger, and depression that made me understand different facets about myself or gave me momentary relief because I had a glimpse of empathy.

But nothing is more powerful than someone who knows who you are and how you live, who knows of your passions and fears—a person who can look into your eyes and say, "I know how you feel."

Quotes are good, but they're only words, not people. People can know you and understand you. It's tough not to come out with trite phrases, but wisdom can exist without just spewing out universal answers.

That's cheating, and it's too easy to be nothing more than a quick fix. It's hard to say anything real anymore. We reiterate everything we hear. We forget how many things we say, how many real thoughts are untouched by reality, how many unaltered ideas we can call our own. That is our own wisdom. That is wisdom that we should spread and share.

Being given advice involves good intent, but to discover something ourselves is infinitely more powerful than being told the same thing. The price of wisdom is beyond rubies.

Where there is no perception, appellation, conception, or
conventional expression; there one speaks of "perfect wisdom."
- Mahayana Buddhist texts

362. WISHES

Live in contact with dreams and you will get something of their charm. Live in contact with facts and you will get something of their brutality. I wish I could find a country to live where the facts were not so brutal and the dreams not unreal.
- George Bernard Shaw
(John Bulls Other Island)

If you could work for free, what would you do? This is Cameron Johnson's philosophy for life. When he was a kid, he saw *Home Alone 2*, in which Kevin visits New York and stays at a skyscraper run by Donald Trump. In the movie, he also visits FAO Schwartz. At the time, it was the biggest toy store in the world.

Cameron was only a child, so he actually believed he could stay at the same hotel as Kevin because he wanted to. Most kids would. The difference was that Cameron acted on that dream and wrote a letter to Donald Trump, asking if he could stay in the room from the movie. His parents were traveling to New York soon, and he thought it was meant to be.

Trump was so won over by the heartfelt letter, he granted Cameron his wish and gave him an allowance of $1,000 to spend in the toy store. His parents were shocked by the drive their child had to commit so much to his dream.

But it didn't stop there. Cameron had his own business at the age of nine. At twelve, he was worth $50,000, selling his sister's Beanie Babies over the Internet, making more than his parents' salaries combined! He was making $15,000 a day in revenue when he was fifteen. He made his first million before finishing high school. To date, he is one of the world's youngest billionaires.

When he was asked how he views life, he said, "Do more of what you love and less of everything else."

His vision sounded ridiculous, but he didn't know it would work until he tried! Don't listen to others who say your dream is not going to happen. People too weak to follow their dreams will always find ways to discourage you from yours. It has to happen for somebody, and it can be you.

Focus on that aspiration and don't get distracted by other petty things. If you chase two hares at once, you will catch neither of them.

Some people think things will happen because they want them to. It's like putting fuel into a car without driving it.

When you try to fulfill your goals, expect failure, but react by not giving up. You know what they say, "Who's more foolish—the dreamer who dreams his life away, or the one so afraid to dream that he never even tries?"

You see things and say why but I dream of things
that never were and say why not?
- George Bernard Shaw

363. WORDS

Better than a thousand hollow words, is one word that brings peace.
- Buddha

Joseph Conrad was a Polish-born novelist who is most famous for writing *Heart of Darkness*, which was the basis for the movie, *Apocalypse Now*.

Interestingly, English is not Conrad's first language or his second but his third! Yet he wrote this book in English, believing that it was the only language that could convey the words with the relish that the Polish language couldn't.

I find it incredible that he could think of words on that level. He had to write in a more visceral language to make his story more grueling. He believed that words are the accent for action.

Some people use complex, formal language. You may feel comfortable with an extensive vocabulary, but it can actually hinder you more.

Take the word "pleonasmic" as an example. Do you know what it means? It means "unnecessarily complicated language." If you didn't know that, that's because pleonasmic is a pleonasmic word! Why use a word when no one knows what it means?

One of the best examples of how to use words effectively is Abraham Lincoln's Gettysburg's Address, which famous starts with "Four score and seven years ago."

Interestingly, Lincoln made this speech after Edward Everett gave a 13,000-worded monologue, which lasted two hours. But anyone in attendance only remembered Lincoln talking, even though his speech only consisted of 272 words and took two minutes to say.

Lincoln's speech is far more memorable because its succinct and straightforward. Unlike Everett's prattle, Lincoln spoke with no convoluted language and made his point clear despite how concise it was.

Human sounds started with grunts. They evolved into words, sentences, subordinate clauses, and finally into language. In our ancestors' time, we had to convey as much as possible with such limited language.

Before Shakespeare's time there were approximately five thousand words in the English language. By the time of his death, there were over eight hundred thousand. Shakespeare invented words all the time.

It's not just about finding the coolest words but the right words. Jobs depend on it. Relationships depend on it. Lives depend on it.

I hope the words you read in this chapter and this book are more than just noise. I hope you find some sense in them.

Whatever words we utter should be chosen with care for people
will hear them and be influenced by them for good or ill.
- Buddha

364. WORKING OUT

> If you've got a big gut and you start working out, you are going to get
> bigger because you build up the muscle. You've got to get rid of that fat!
> - Jack LaLanne

Picture this: you do lots of running, sit-ups, push-ups, and sports. You don't eat
perfectly, but it's not like you eat fast food every day, so you consider yourself
reasonably healthy.

But there's always another guy who seems to be doing not as much exercise who
is in terrific shape. How? This is the dilemma that my bodybuilder friend, Albert
faced. He exercised all the time but stayed fat until he discovered the secret.

I am about to tell you the single biggest mistake people make when they exercise.
Sit-ups, push-ups, and running burn calories when you do them.

But when you stop exercising, you stop burning calories. It doesn't matter how
hard you push yourself. You can only burn so many calories in a short time.

Isn't there a way to burn calories when you're not exercising? Absolutely. It's
called the "afterburn effect." Normally, when you use weights in a series of intense
exercises, you will get the "burn" we hear so much about.

But if you work several muscle groups simultaneously, they'll need a lot more
time to heal. The afterburn effect can last up to forty-eight hours after you've
exercised. How many calories do you think you can burn in two days straight?

Even if you are busy the next day at work, you will literally be sitting at your desk
burning calories. It feels like cheating, but it's the most effective tactic.

This is necessary for long-term fat loss because you need to burn 3,500 calories
to lose one pound of fat.

Even crunches are ineffective. They make your abs stronger, but they don't
help you lose belly fat. You would need to do 22,000 crunches to lose one pound of
belly fat.

You burn off less than a hundred calories being on a treadmill for half an hour,
and you will put it back on by having something as innocent as orange juice.

The afterburn effect is the only realistic way to go around this. This way, you
don't have to spend tons of time in a gym, because the work continues after you
leave, and you need time to heal.

Eating right makes a lot of difference. There are some people who are more
genetically equipped, and some people naturally put on muscle, but a lot of people
who are well-built are nutritionally savvy and understand how many grams of fat,
saturated fat, vitamins, carbohydrates, and protein is in the food they eat.

> Some people think I was born like this but
> it's a lot of work to be in this condition.
> - Lou Ferrigno

365. WORRY

There will always be a lost dog somewhere that will prevent me from being happy.
- La Sauvage
(The Restless Heart)

We all want to forget our troubles and relax, but sometimes we will not allow ourselves to be satisfied because we have lingering thoughts.

I was on holiday with my wife after we had only been going out for a year. Usually, we only saw each other every weekend or so. This was going to be the first time in ages that we could spend time together. We had two weeks together, so we had to make them count.

But she kept worrying because she knew there would be a work overload when she got back. For nearly two weeks, there was a never-ending thought racking her brain, and it wouldn't let her enjoy the holiday.

I said to her, "You are on holiday because you worked so hard. You deserve it. You are not at work now. You have no means of contacting them so they are on their own. I know you have a lot of work to do when you get back, but you can't affect or prepare for it when we are on the other side of the world. Worrying about it will not change the amount of work you will have. So until you can get to it, enjoy yourself, and let go."

We always find reasons to worry. They don't have to make sense. We create scenarios that we play out in our minds that will never come to be. We worry about age, health, money, jobs, family, crime, the past, the present, and the future.

The last three are, in a way, kind of funny. To worry about something that already happened is to worry about something that is irrevocable.

To worry about the future is to worry about something that hasn't even happened. Many of the scenarios we create of the future will never come to pass.

If you're worrying about something that's happening now, then change it. Let it become a future you will like.

I'm not going to pretend I don't worry. It's just that I try to catch myself worrying. We can waste so much time and energy worrying. Surely we can do something more practical with all of that energy.

What kind of worry do you have? Is it the type of worry that will motivate you to mold your future to your liking?

Or is it the worry that will turn you into a moaner and will never allow yourself to a have a day without stress because of circumstances you can't change? You need to find a practicality to your worry. If you can't, don't worry about it.

If a man will begin with certainties, he shall end in doubts; but if he
will be content to begin with doubts, he shall end in certainties.
- Francis Bacon

—

Lightning Source UK Ltd.
Milton Keynes UK
UKHW011243061021
391760UK00001B/162

9 781956 373387